2⁹⁹

IMAGES OF HISTORY

IMAGES
OF HISTORY
Twentieth Century British Columbia Through the Front Pages

WILLIAM RAYNER

ORCA BOOK PUBLISHERS

Canadian Cataloguing in Publication Data
Rayner, William, 1929–
Images of history

Includes bibliographical references and index.
ISBN 1-55143-089-4

1. British Columbia—History—20th century. 2. Canadian newspapers—British
Columbia—History. I. Title.
FC3811.R38 1997 971.1'03 C97-910422-X F1088.R38 1997

Library of Congress Catalog Card Number: 97-68866

Orca Book Publishers gratefully acknowledges the support of our publishing
programs provided by the following agencies: the Department of Canadian Heritage,
The Canada Council for the Arts, and the British Columbia Ministry of Small Business,
Tourism and Culture.

Cover design by Jim Brennan
Printed and bound in Canada

Orca Book Publishers   Orca Book Publishers
PO Box 5626, Station B   PO Box 468
Victoria, BC   V8R 6S4   Custer, WA   98240-0468
Canada   USA

97 98 99   5 4 3 2 1

To my mother and the memory of my father

But words are Things, and a small drop
of ink,
Falling like dew upon a thought, produces
that which makes thousands, perhaps
millions, think
> — *Byron:* Don Juan, *Canto III*

Read, that you may receive not only facts, but the significance of those facts
> — The Vancouver Sun, *Page 6 masthead, 1930s*

The past is all around us
> — *Lynn Margulis, biologist and author*

A Note on Newspaper Names

During their lifetimes, most newspapers tinker with their mastheads.
The Colonist and *The Columbian*, for instance, both added and dropped
"British" at various times. Likewise, the appellation "Daily" came and went
on many front pages. In the interests of brevity and uniformity, I have
avoided most variations in titles, even though the actual name on the
masthead may differ on the date in question.

Acknowledgments

The author acknowledges the assistance provided by *The Province*, *The Vancouver Sun* and the *Victoria Times Colonist* in granting permission to use newspage reproductions and certain photographs in this book. The copyrights in question are held by these newspapers. I also wish to acknowledge that many of the historic photos are reproduced courtesy of the Vancouver Public Library and the Provincial Archives of BC. Appropriate credit for all reproductions is given in the List of Illustrations. Finally, many thanks to my former colleagues and to various research personnel for helping to plug a few of the gaps. Also, to Tammy Francis and Commonwealth Microfilm Products in Calgary for providing the newspaper images.

(Because of deadlines and publishing cycles, newspapers often reported on historical events the next day—or later. The dates in the headline chronologies for each chapter are when the events occurred, not the day of publication.)

TABLE OF
CONTENTS

ODE TO THE
FRONT PAGE

"It was in the paper…"

Indeed it was. For one hundred years and more, residents of British Columbia have taken their history live from the pages of their newspapers. In 1900, as the twentieth century dawned, the press carried news of foreign wars, local disasters and provincial politics. Today, there is not much that is different.

But, as the province has ripened during this century, so has the press. BC's once-hectic growth has slowed and stabilized. The outer boundaries of this frontier chunk of Canada have been tamed with time. Our increase in population has become muted, despite immigration from all quarters. It is somewhat the same with BC's newspapers. Once raucous and undisciplined, willing to tilt at any establishment windmill, they have for the most part become members of that very establishment. Except in the remotest of locales, with the tiniest of circulations, the corporate bottom line has replaced the crusading editor. Like it or not, the press—along with British Columbia—has grown up.

This is not to say that things are done all that differently. The newspapers that still survive in the closing years of the century are direct descendants of those which existed (or were waiting to be born) in 1900. The newspapers of the nineties still collected the news, printed it and offered it to the populace in a tangible form. And it is still tomorrow's history text. Incisive and immediate (and sometimes wrong), the newspa-per is still the province's best window into the past as well as the present. On a regular basis over the years, our triumphs, our sins, our joys and our tragedies have been chronicled and interpreted in neat columns of type.

Some of this instant history—the grand, the compelling, the world-altering events—make it into the textbooks and are frozen for all time. But each event, whether it is the gunshot that started the Great War or the day the BC Lions won their first Grey Cup, entered our ken as news. Before it became history, it was printed as news. Everybody read it in the paper. Newspapers are our memories, before these memories are manipulated, polished and shaped into a palatable product that, weeks or months or years later, is often only a slick facsimile of what really happened.

True, the news is raw, often incomplete or confusing, occasionally written in haste and usually blunt in its presentation. But it is this daily knowledge, sometimes barely digestible and sometimes merely frivolous, that becomes the building block of history. Before we remember (and history is nothing but remembrance), we must experience. Newspapers offer that experience. More than that, they chronicle history, day after day.

All history, of course, is not Page One news at the moment it is written. Space, time and manpower, as well as editorial judgment, sometimes contribute to a significant story being placed inside. (The *Daily World* in Vancouver, for instance, reported on Page 2 of its

February 21, 1900, edition the first news of major Canadian casualties in the Boer War. Although several British Columbians were among those killed or wounded during fighting on the Modder River, *The World*'s extensive coverage did not warrant Page One play.)

To history buffs scrolling through the past, a specific, identifiable event, even if it is only mildly historic, should engender a sharply focused headline nailing down the issue. Not so, in many cases. When Premier Mike Harcourt announced a major shuffle of his bumbling New Democratic Party cabinet in 1993 after less than two years in government, one would expect the head on the story to acknowledge this salient fact. Instead, the headline across the top of the *Vancouver Sun*'s Page One read, "Harcourt Vows to Get a Grip." This is known as the "follow" or "second-day" angle and is quite common, even among morning newspapers. It is designed to disguise old news—i.e., something that happened the day before and which everyone should know about. So, even if the facts are indeed earth shaking, the follow head is supposed to tell the next-day reader that there is something fresh in the story.

Editors, publishers and newsroom decision-makers are not necessarily prescient. Putting out a paper requires equal portions of intuition, panic and accessibility. The story has to be recognized as such, a minimum of facts must be available, and enough time left to bring all the elements into a reasonably coherent whole. Page One decisions can be dictated by whim, prejudice, policy or simple fallibility. On the better papers, however, the Page One conference is strictly concerned with the merits of the news. What has happened in the past several hours that our readers should know about immediately, as soon as they pick up their paper? In other words, what is the best news available, be it dramatic, shocking, tragic, significant, pleasing or just plain funny?

There are exceptions—some of them there simply because a newspaper is a product and must be sold. In the days of head-to-head competition and multiple editions, the street edition available through newsies or vending boxes would shout a doomsday headline at passers-by one or more times each day. In other editions, destined for home delivery and thus pre-sold, that particular story would be in a less conspicuous spot on Page One, or even moved inside. And tabloids, with their limited display space, usually devote the front to one big, intriguing headline, a picture and some "teasers" to inside stories.

None of these decisions, however, are concerned with history. The city editor (or the foreign or national editor, because the news comes from all over) doesn't jump up and exclaim, "This is history!" They may argue that the event is unique, timely or simply of overriding interest and thus deserves a major display, but not that it is a historical biggie. There are stories that automatically become part of the texture of history, if the newsdesk warriors engaged in their constant battle with time and space ever stopped to think about them. The onset of wars. Natural and man-made disasters. Particularly heinous crimes. The death of someone famous.

Politics make history, too, but the nature of the craft is so transitory (here today, voted out tomorrow) that most newspapers approach political news with ingrained cynicism. Happenings at the legislature, or municipal council or the school board are just that—happenings. Apart from reporting the impact on the voter, the taxpayer or the businessman, newspapers usually don't dwell overly long on historical perspective. The long-term ramifications are consequently left for others to ponder.

History, like news, knows no father. It owes no allegiance. Arriving deaf, blind and mute, it remains stillborn until life is breathed into it. That life comes from the newspaper. By first defining history as news, the typographical midwife that is the press begins the process that defines the past. Today is a barely discernible ripple in the river of time. A murky frame from a cheap instant camera. The future, as Mort Sahl once said, lies ahead. Only yesterday counts, because that is where our memories dwell. Of all the species, only the human animal codifies the remembrance of things past. It's called news. The newspaper delivers our past to us each day.

Before we go any further, let's dismiss television news as part of the historical equation. TV news is entertainment, so it doesn't count. In newspapers, entertainment is part of the total package; on the picture tube, "the news" is just another form of enter- tainment. To even approximate the amount of information available in a metropolitan daily newspaper, a television news program would have to run for hours. And, of course, you can't turn the page if you find the station's selection of news boring. There's no way to go straight to the sports section, or the comics.

Even when it is at its strongest—capturing events live—the TV image is so transitory and fleeting that the network boffins had to invent their own kind of history. It's called instant replay. Every time television reruns the winning goal or the moment of disaster, it is depicting the past. And to make sure the viewer can really comprehend what happened, it repeats it in slow motion. Just like the newspaper. When a reporter writes a story, he or she is giving the reader a slow-motion replay of what occurred. By using background, placing the event in context and organizing the facts, the lowly, often anonymous scribbler is writing daily history.

We are talking modern newspapers here. In the early years of the century some papers were born expressly to support a political party. The news columns as well as the editorial pages reflected this bias. Today, the press is quite adept at separating news and opinion. Despite the alarums of ill-informed critics, the daily mix of news in any newspaper (small or large) is subject to the leavening factors mentioned earlier. There is no agenda, hidden or otherwise, to slant news or suppress it. And even with the advocacy journalism of the eighties and nineties, there is much more of a balance to this raw, ongoing history than naysayers suppose.

So elections, which are the most historic events of politics, are considered only in the context of the immediate present, with no attempt to extrapolate a particular party's victory at the polls into anything more earthshaking or permanent.

One of the more significant elections in BC's history—that of June 9, 1953—was therefore treated at the time as just another milepost down the long passage of parliamentary democracy. That Premier W.A.C. Bennett, chosen less than a year earlier to form a minority government, was gambling on an absolute

majority for his Social Credit party was noted in passing. What was not noted or surmised (nor could it be) was the virtual dominance the Socreds would have over BC for almost forty years. In fact, the *Victoria Times* was professionally cautious in granting Bennett the majority he got. *The Times'* Page One headline read, "Social Credit Re-elected, Initial Count Indicates." Even when we consider the fact that the single transferable ballot (a short-lived form of multiple-choice) was in effect, *The Times* did appear to be parsimonious in discounting early indications of a Bennett victory. In addition, the headline itself somehow seemed to be disapproving. If lines of type can be anthropomorphized, the *Times'* main head for June 10, 1953, was a haughty dowager sniffing at some boisterous urchin.

But what about this British Columbia that the press has so faithfully documented over the years? Born in 1871 of a railroad marriage with the rest of Canada, it included the original colony of Vancouver Island, which was more than fifty years old when the century turned. Long since joined with the mainland colony and the rest of the rugged territory west of the Rockies, the sprawling "provinceful of rock and rain" administered from Victoria took on the twentieth century with characteristic gusto and bravado.

The 1901 census showed 178,657 souls in BC, with more arriving every day. Most of these were of British descent. They had Old Country values (as did the other immigrants of European stock who settled here), and that meant non-whites were treated as second-class citizens. The Natives were exploited, patronized, torn asunder from their traditional lands and tucked into odd corners of the province. In 1900, white fishermen who were on strike violently protested the presence of their Japanese counterparts on the Fraser River. In 1907 came anti-Chinese riots and demonstrations that helped bring on an act of parliament excluding Chinese immigrants from Canada. This blemish of intolerance against Asians was to remain for much of the century.

Meanwhile, sturdy British Columbia lads had marched off to war as 1900 rolled around (more specifically, they took a train and then a boat), and were dying in South Africa. During the rest of the century, we were to fight in two world wars and a number of lesser ones. Apart from the familiar battlefields of the major conflicts—Ypres, Vimy Ridge, Juno Beach, the Falaise Gap, the Gustav Line—British Columbians also did their duty in such obscure locations as Paardeberg, the Ebro River and Taewha-Do.

Politics (really another form of warfare, with somewhat less blood) was an equally persistent theme of the century. In Victoria, the legislature was briefly led by several forgettable premiers (Joseph Martin, Edward Prior, William Bowser, Harlan Brewster, John MacLean, David Barrett, Rita Johnston) and a few memorable ones. Among the latter was Richard McBride, who took over as Conservative leader of the province in 1903 and stayed until 1915. The youngest (at thirty-two) to achieve the office, he was second only to W.A.C. Bennett in longevity.

An energetic extrovert who glad-handed his way around the province, McBride was the right man for the times. He was responsible for BC's first and only foray into the navy business, somehow briefly acquiring two submarines in the early months of the Great War. He also liked to spend the voters' money and embark on grand projects—a characteristic still common in the corridors of power in BC's capital city.

Bennett, who lasted from 1952 to 1972 before turning the reins of Social Credit over to his son, Bill, had the most impact of all the premiers. After gaining the premiership following a bizarre election in 1952, he consolidated his power a year later and prodded BC to maturity during the latter half of the century.

Also, this discussion of BC politics cannot be complete without mention of Bill Vander Zalm, Socred premier from 1986 to 1991. The words of a political rival, "charisma without substance is a dangerous thing," described The Zalm (as the more irreverent newspapers called him) to a Z. Eventually, he was forced to resign over conflict-of-interest allegations surrounding the sale of some property to an Asian businessman. (It is interesting to note that BC politics have now run the gamut from A to Z. BC's second premier, Amor de Cosmos—born William Smith—changed his name to reflect his love for mankind, while Vander Zalm once owned an enterprise called Fantasy Gardens.)

With politics came scandals, and the taint of malfeasance hung heavy over the waning months of Vander Zalm's administration. His cabinet's peccadilloes were pretty small beer, however, when compared with the case of Robert Sommers. As minister of lands and forests in the Bennett cabinet of the fifties, "Honest Bob" Sommers was responsible for dispensing forest management licences to the province's timber companies. Because they were, quite literally, licences to print money, they were hotly sought after. Too hotly, it turned out, for Sommers was convicted of bribery and conspiracy in the issuance of the licences and sentenced in 1958 to five years in prison. He was the first minister of the Crown in the history of the British Empire and Commonwealth to serve time for bribery.

From the very first day in 1955, when the allegations first came to light, *The Times* and *The Sun* were relentless in their pursuit of the story—bringing Sommers to remark bitterly that the coverage was "the most dirty and slanted in the history of BC." It wasn't, of course. The newspapers were just doing their job. That this slice of history was particularly juicy was not the messengers' fault. Actually, 1955 was a good year for Vancouver papers, scandal-wise. They also sniffed out allegations that Police Chief Walter Mulligan was mixed up in graft and corruption. Four months after he was fired, an inquiry found Mulligan guilty of accepting bribes from bookmakers.

Almost forty years later, the braying of the press reached another crescendo after the New Democrats formed the government in 1991. Led by *The Sun*, the papers pounced on revelations that the NDP had stiffed little old ladies and pensioners playing bingo in Nanaimo. It seemed the Nanaimo Commonwealth Holding Society (an arm of the party) had diverted charity proceeds from the bingo games for its own purposes. A guilty verdict was attained in court (without naming names), and the outcry forced the resignation of Premier Mike Harcourt in 1995. (The voters didn't care, apparently; they re-elected the NDP under Glen Clark the following year.)

Although scandals can fairly be described as disasters in their effect on those concerned, they don't have the impact of the man-made or natural variety. In a province blessed with a surfeit of vertical geography, there have been disasters aplenty during this century. They are sober reminders of the frailty of existence on the edge of the continent.

Earthquakes, avalanches, fires, a major flood, the remnants of a typhoon—all were manifestations of Mother Nature's cold heart. On the cruel seas that wash our shores, numerous marine disasters resulted in extensive loss of life. Underground, man's penchant for ripping out the province's natural riches led to disasters of another kind. Mine cave-ins and explosions, especially in the early part of the century, often led to grim newspaper stories of tragedy and bereft families.

In 1956, a Trans-Canada Airlines passenger plane slammed into Mt. Slesse near Chilliwack. As air disasters go it was bad—sixty-two dead—but the horror was magnified when the papers reported that among those aboard were some professional football players who, only hours earlier, had participated in the all-star game in Vancouver. The Mt. Slesse death toll matched that of a 1910 tragedy, when Nature shrugged and brought a slide down on a railroad work crew struggling to clear the line in Rogers Pass. Other tragedies, such as the collapse of the new Second Narrows Bridge under construction over Vancouver's Burrard Inlet in 1958, indicated that modern man was not immune from the heavy slap of fate. In the latter part of the century, the logging industry's insistence on clear-cutting wide swaths of mature BC forest was—to some—a man-made disaster of another kind.

But trees mean jobs, and that means prosperity. Aided by a network of rail lines and Socred-engineered highways, BC's Big Three resource industries—forestry, fishing and mining—provided a solid foundation for a booming economy that only occasionally stumbled over the rough ground of a recession. The decade-long Great Depression of the thirties was only a bitter memory, somewhat muted by the distractions of the Second World War, when the economy took off in the last fifty years of the century.

Through it all, the press took notes and wrote history as it happened. Mostly, those reporters and editors who toil in the trenches of journalism remain faceless and nameless, but from out of the past some giants come to mind: Bruce Hutchison, Hal Straight, Ross Munro, Benny Nicholas. There were consummate reporters like Torchy Anderson and Jack Brooks. (*The Sun*'s Brooks writing flawless, one-sentence paragraphs on a tight deadline was a sight to behold. As he finished each sentence, a copyrunner would rip it out of his typewriter and scoot to the city desk. Meanwhile, Jack had scrolled another sheet into his machine and pounded away virtually without pause.)

Among the photographers, Victoria's Jim Ryan and Bill Halkett, *The Sun*'s Brian Kent and *The Province*'s Bill Cunningham could capture the decisive moment as well as anyone. Yes, let's not forget the cameramen, because they were as ubiquitous as the reporters. Whether it was a shot of the Prince of Wales (later to abdicate as King Edward VIII) touring a Trail smelter in the twenties, the precise moment Roger Bannister passed John Landy during the Miracle Mile at Empire Stadium, or local yahoos rioting after a Stanley Cup game, the images amplified the words and often told their own stories.

But the twentieth century has many more tales than these to tell, including royalty's attraction for BC and our own wonderful world of sports. For the remainder of this book, these will be included in a blend of text, pictures and headlines that will give the reader a window into history in the making. In the headlines especially, the fabric of this century is woven and preserved for future generations. One hundred years from now, someone else can "read it in the paper."

POLITICS AND EXPECTATIONS

« 1900 – 1909 »

THE DECADE IN HEADLINES
« 1900 »

SEMLIN'S EXIT

Lt.-Gov. Thomas McInnes "administers the coup de grace," as *The Colonist* puts it, by unilaterally firing Premier Charles Semlin and his government. The political crisis will eventually lead to McInnes' dismissal.

The Colonist, February 27, 1900

SALMON ARE SCARCE

Under this innocuous headline, *The World* discusses the tense Fraser River sockeye situation. Buried in the story is the vow by a white fishermen's union on June 30 for "twenty-five cents or no fish" will be delivered to local canneries.

Daily World, July 3, 1900

THE FIN DE SIECLE STORE

The Hudson's Bay Company opens its four-storey "emporium" on the corner of Granville and Georgia streets in Vancouver. In 1893, the first HBC store in the city was located on Cordova Street.

The Province, December 15, 1900

OUR SOLDIER HEROES HOME

On the last day of 1900, Vancouver newspapers lead the cheering as the Royal Canadian Regiment returns from voluntary service in the South African War.

The Province, December 31, 1900

For British Columbians, New Year's Eve of 1899 was more gladsome than usual. Not only were they parting with an old year, they were discarding a pioneer century that saw them become full members of Confederation. So the expectations that normally accompany the onset of a new January were brightened by hopes about the next one hundred years. Out with the nineteenth! In with the twentieth! On the slight knoll rising above Victoria's Inner Harbour, the spanking new Legislative Buildings (opened for business in 1898) were a shiny symbol of a province with the brightest of futures.

The *Daily Colonist* reported that the streets were more crowded than usual on the last night of 1899, "with the booming of guns, tooting of steam whistles, blowing of horns and…perfect bedlam" being much in evidence.

Alas, reality set in rather quickly. The first day of the new century was showery and windy in the capital city. Furthermore, it stayed that way for most of January and February, with a little bit of sleet and snow thrown in just to remind the politicians, merchants and plain, ordinary citizens that it was wintertime on Vancouver Island, grand presumptions notwithstanding.

Inside the legislature on February 27, 1900, the mood was as rebellious as the weather. For just the day before, Lieutenant-Governor Thomas McInnes—the supposedly impartial, hand-picked representative of the Crown—had abruptly dismissed Premier Charles Augustus Semlin.

Having resigned as ordered, Semlin still had one cannon shot to fire across the Imperial bow. Rising in the House that fateful afternoon, Semlin declared that the lieutenant-governor's action was unconstitutional, and proposed adoption of a resolution which read, in part, "That this House…begs hereby to express its regret that His Honour has seen fit to dismiss his advisers as in the present crisis they have efficient control of the House." After a debate as spirited and partisan as it was long, the legislators adopted the motion by a vote of 22–15.

They had, in effect, censured the Queen.

The editorial writers at the time were generally in favour of McInnes' decision. *The Colonist* called Semlin's resolution "highly improper," while in Vancouver, the *Daily World* sniffed that he "played battle-door and shuttle-cock with the position he found himself in, and violated all constitutional usages."

At five minutes after eight in the morning, all is serene on one of Victoria's main streets. This view, circa 1900, is looking north on Douglas at Yates.

Thus one of BC's juiciest political scandals came to a full boil. McInnes' highhandedness, although not strictly unconstitutional (according to some interpretations), certainly stretched the British North America Act to its limits. Add one more ingredient not forgotten by the honourable members that February day: Semlin was the second premier to be tossed aside by McInnes without benefit of dissolution or the wishes of the electorate. By the time summer arrived and the weather improved, McInnes' chosen successor to Semlin had lost an election and McInnes himself was out of a job. On June 21, after the House in another resolution had formally asked that McInnes be removed, Prime Minister Sir Wilfrid Laurier named Sir Henry Joly de Lotbiniere as lieutenant-governor of BC. In replacing McInnes, Sir Wilfrid himself was breaking somewhat new ground. Removing a vice-regal representative "whose official conduct has been subversive of the principles of responsible government" was unprecedented.

The politics of early 1900 were not the only momentous events to occupy the thoughts of the young province. For in far-off South Africa, a colonial war was being fought and British Columbians were in the thick of it. In fact, on the very Tuesday that legislators voiced their displeasure at McInnes, the Royal Canadian Regiment (whose "A" company was made up of BC and Manitoba volunteers) acquitted itself with honour at the capture of Paardeberg. According to one contemporary account published in Edinburgh, the battle began with the splutter of musketry:

"Someone was up and doing early. It was the Canadians. They were acting on the principle of the early bird that catches the morning worm. Supported by the Gordons, Cornwalls and Shropshires, they were advancing, building a trench in the very teeth of the enemy, and at fifty yards' range were saluting him with such deadly warmth as to render his position untenable."

That the regiment's gallantry was instrumental in the surrender of the Boers was later confirmed by Field Marshal Lord Roberts. The commander-in-chief went

The Daily World.

Vol. XXV., No. 9,746.　　VANCOUVER, B. C. MONDAY, DECEMBER 31, 1900.　　PRICE FIVE CENTS.

The World's Want Adlets are perused by a greater number of readers than those of any other publication in the West, and therefore produce the best results.

VANCOUVER'S WELCOME TO THE BOYS IN KHAKI

Defenders of Canada's Name and Fame Greeted by Cheering Thousands—Patriotic Enthusiasm Was Let Loose at the C. P. R. Depot To-day—The Heroes Marched Through Lines of Excited People Who Cheered to the Echo—A List of the Soldiers Who Returned—Luncheon at the Theatre Royal—Parade and Presentation To-Night.

WELCOME HOME.

THE HEROES

VANCOUVER.
PTE. H. E. SIEBERGALL.
PTE. J. J. SINCLAIR.
PTE. H. J. ALLAN.
PTE. H. M. BONNER.
PTE. S. S. HARRISON.

NEW WESTMINSTER.
CORP. G. THEBOULD.
LANCE CORP. A. D. COHMAN.
PTE. J. P. SMITH.

VICTORIA.
PTE. H. SMITHERS.
PTE. W. H. BRETHOUR.
PTE. C. LEEMAN.

At the Station.

BUCCOTTISTS

At the Theatre Royal

The poem leading off this long account of veterans returning from the South African War reflects the unabashed patriotism of the era.

THE DECADE IN HEADLINES
« 1901 »

EXPLOSION AT UNION

With a series of staccato paragraphs, the disaster at the Union mine in Cumberland is reported. The next day, the *Free Press* says all hope is lost for the 60 entombed miners. Later, the death toll is set at 64.

Nanaimo Free Press, February 15, 1901

VOYAGE OF THE PELICAN

The Native war canoe that was to become famous as the *Tilikum* sets sail on its round-the-world odyssey. Both *The Colonist* and *Victoria Times* describe the vessel as the "Pelican."

The Colonist, May 21, 1901

WELCOME TO ROYALTY

The Duke and Duchess of Cornwall and York arrive in Vancouver to a fulsome, patriotic welcome. *The Province* devotes 11 of its 16 pages to the arrival of the future King of England and his consort. The royal pair later visits Victoria.

The Province, September 30, 1901

out of his way to praise the Canadians for their role in the battle.

Back home, editorial hearts throbbed with patriotic fervor. The *Victoria Times* reported there was "intense excitement throughout the city. The fire hall was the first to give the note of demonstration, its bells and whistles being taken as a keynote of general acclaim." Flags and bunting quickly made their appearance.

(The very next day, February 28, Ladysmith was relieved after a Boer siege of 120 days, sparking further celebrations. On Vancouver Island, the nascent mining settlement of Oyster Harbour south of Nanaimo had its name changed to mark the occasion. In the next decade, BC's Ladysmith would become better known for its involvement in the great miners' strike of 1912–14.)

Quite a start to a new year, a new decade and a new century.[1] And there was plenty more to come. The next ten years would be larded with beginnings and endings, underground and offshore disasters, more political twists and turns, strikes, crime, racism and rioting. New enterprises would be formed, to grow into familiar names and images: Canadian Pacific Steamships, Cominco, BC Telephone Co., BC Packers, Vancouver Stock Exchange.

There were also four provincial elections during the decade—an above-average number for British Columbia. The first was June 9, 1900, when McInnes' choice to replace Semlin, Joe Martin, sought the approval of the electorate and his fellow MLAs. Although gaining personal re-election, Martin was not well liked (the legislature voted 28–1 against him February 28 when he was chosen by McInnes). Realizing he could not muster enough support to govern (this was in the days before party loyalties), Martin resigned.

Thus ended the short BC career of "Fighting Joe" Martin, who later became a Member of Parliament in Great Britain. After the 1898 election, he was only the MLA from Vancouver when McInnes discarded his first premier, John Turner. In this anarchical period of provincial politics at the turn of the century, Turner was having problems forming a government, but it was hardly a firing offence. McInnes obviously thought otherwise and informed Turner August 8 "that I have decided to no longer delay in calling for other advisers."

Just as his successor, Semlin, did following his own removal, Turner protested that the dismissal was unconstitutional, but to no avail. Martin became the attorney-general in Semlin's government, but his feud with another cabinet minister, Francis Carter-Cotton (who, incidentally, was editor of the *Vancouver News-Advertiser*), became so strident that Semlin fired him. Joining the opposition in a crucial vote defeating a redistribution bill, Martin supplied the chopping block for McInnes' second swing of the axe.

With Martin out of the picture, James Dunsmuir, scion of the coal-mining dynasty, became the next premier on June 15, 1900, six days before Laurier removed McInnes. Although much more warmly regarded than Martin, Dunsmuir was a reluctant leader. After a decent interval, he resigned November 21, 1902 (only to return for another three-year stint in the legislative precincts as lieutenant-governor, 1906-1909).

His successor, Edward Gawler Prior, lasted less than seven months and was dismissed by Lieutenant-Governor Joly de Lotbiniere (without any outcry) for conflict of interest in the awarding of government construction contracts. This brought to the plate the young, personable, gladhanding Richard McBride. Finally, after four premiers in less than five years, British Columbia finally got it right.

McBride, when he was sworn in June 1, 1903, was the youngest premier (at thirty-two) in the province's history. He called an election for October 3, declaring that he was a Conservative and that the election would be fought along party lines. It was, and McBride's Conservatives won twenty-two of forty-two seats, to seventeen for the Liberals.

The advent of party politics coincided with an upsurge in prosperity—railway construction, mining and shipping activity, increased immigration, development of a forest industry—and McBride gradually became the symbol of his native province. He easily won elections in 1907 and 1909, and would go on to serve as premier until 1915. Until W.A.C. Bennett established his Social Credit dynasty in 1952, Richard McBride was the most significant political figure produced in British Columbia.

Meanwhile, the gentleman who started this train of events by trashcanning Semlin, Thomas McInnes, faded away into private life. His motives for discarding constitutional government can still be debated, although with hindsight a hundred years removed, it is fairly obvious he was a simple meddler impatient with democratic imperfections.

No matter. While the political situation gradually sorted itself out, British Columbians would receive several other jolts that hit much closer to home.

The first of them, the death of Queen Victoria, January 22, 1901, in England, was as wrenching as the loss of a favourite relative. To British Columbians, the Queen was virtually the reason for their existence: the provincial capital was named Victoria in her honour, and it was her choice of the name, British Columbia, over New Caledonia that constantly reinforced their Empire heritage. At the end of the century, British Columbians still celebrate the holiday—Victoria Day—that honours a reign founded in an earlier one.

Thus the mourning, both public and private, was for a particularly beloved mother who presided over a fractious, far-flung brood for sixty-three years. The day following her death, solemn black borders adorned the newspapers' front pages. Black armbands became a fashion statement. Editorialists grieved with unusual eloquence. In Vancouver, *The World* observed that all businesses were closed the day of her death except for the saloons. "As a woman, she was an example of every woman within the four corners of the earth," it said in an editorial.

In Victoria the main entrance of the legislature was draped in black, as were other public buildings. "She died as she had lived and she was Royal lady to the end," *The Times* wrote. "There was no superfluous lagging upon the stage."

While the Queen's death touched all, there were other, more personal tragedies to endure. In this seaboard province clinging to the edge of the continent, where rocks and shoals and forested islands coexist grudgingly with the surly Pacific, marine disasters can be expected at any time. In the early years of this century, especially, they became a recurrent theme.

One of the worst calamities in BC waters occurred between January 22 and January 25, 1906, when the passenger steamer *Valencia* sailed smack into Vancouver Island near Pachena Point. Although some survivors eventually reached safety, there was extreme loss of life. Because of inadequate record-keeping and no apparent master list of passengers and crew, published estimates of the death toll over the years have ranged from 115 to 136 (an imprecision that still drives historians and editors crazy).

Apart from the lives lost, two other questions have occupied the minds of marine chroniclers. The first—why the *Valencia*, which was bound from San Francisco

THE DECADE IN HEADLINES
« 1902 »

ANDREW CARNEGIE OFFERS VICTORIA

The millionaire philanthropist, in his determination not to die rich, adds Victoria to his roster of free libraries. The only catch to the $50,000 bequest is that the city spend $5,000 per year for upkeep. In June, the voters approve and three years later, Victoria joins Vancouver (1903) and New Westminster (1905) as recipients of Carnegie's largesse.

Victoria Times, March 24, 1902

A GHOSTLY CHARNEL HOUSE. DEADLY FIRE DAMP PREVENTS RESCUE

Using four headline decks, *The News* reports the "frightful explosion" at the Coal Creek mine near Fernie. Final death toll: 128.

Nelson Daily News, May 22, 1902

THE 'ALL RED' CABLE COMPLETED

Final link of the Pacific telegraph cable from Vancouver Island to New Zealand occupies the entire front page of *The Times*. A *Colonist* editorial says the event "proves the British race predominant in the civilization of the world...." The "All Red" refers to the linking of the British Empire around the globe.

Victoria Times, October 31, 1902

JAPS CAN NOT VOTE

The Imperial Privy Council rules in London that BC can refuse the franchise to Japanese residents. The ruling comes in the case of Tomey Homma, who tried to vote despite his ancestry. In an editorial, the paper says, "We are relieved from the possibility of having our polling booths swamped by a horde of Orientals...."

The Colonist, December 17, 1902

The Daily News-Advertiser.

VOLUME XXVIII. No. 20.   VANCOUVER, BRITISH COLUMBIA, WEDNESDAY, JANUARY 23, 1901.   WHOLE NUMBER, 5014.

VICTORIA THE GOOD

Passes Peacefully Away After More Than Six Decades of Righteous Rule, Vacating the Imperial Throne of Britain for a Dignity Not Earthly.

An Early Day of a New Century Sees the End of a Reign Fulfilled with Effort and Achievement for the Welfare of Mankind.

Mourned Almost as a Mother by the Millions of a World-Encircling Empire, As Woman and as Queen Both Great and Good.

THE LAST BULLETIN.

Cowes, Isle of Wight, England, January 22, 1901, 6.55 p.m.——The Queen is Dead.

A RECORD REIGN.

Sixty-Three Years of Progress and Prosperity, Under the Guiding Hand of Queen Victoria the First.

"She wrought her people lasting good; Her Court was pure, her life serene; God gave her peace; her land reposed, A thousand claims to reverence closed, In her, as mother, wife and Queen. And statesmen at her Council met Who knew the seasons when to take Occasion by the hand and make The bounds of freedom wider yet, By shaping some august decree, Which kept her throne unshaken still, Broad based upon her people's will, And compassed by the inviolate sea."

Thus wrote, and wrote truthfully Alfred Tennyson, greatest and worthiest of the laureates of the greatest and worthiest woman ruler of modern time, if not of all time, Victoria, Queen of Great Britain and Ireland, the Dominion of Canada, the Commonwealth of Australia, Empress of India and mistress of the hearts of myriads penned alike of their British citizenship and of their allegiance to a good and gracious Queen.

EARLY YEARS.

As Child and Maiden in an English Home

THE ROYAL EDUCATION.

THE CORONATION.

THE CONDITION OF THE PEOPLE.

ACCESSION

Victoria the Good Ascends the Throne.

POLITICS.

Changes of Ministry. — The Corn Laws.

to Victoria, Vancouver and Seattle, was sailing north into dangerous waters instead of eastward through Juan de Fuca Strait—has an apparently straightforward answer: the ship's captain, Oscar Marcus Johnson, was guilty of a serious error in navigation.

The second question is not so easy. This is the contention by some that vessels that could have helped save those aboard while the *Valencia* foundered for almost three days made no serious attempt to do so. *The Vancouver Province* gave full-page prominence to the lack of rescue efforts from both land and sea. "Why Did They All Run Away?" asked one headline on a story interviewing a survivor. Despite several inquiries, the only solid conclusion was that the *Valencia* ran ashore through the faulty seamanship of Captain Johnson. No action was taken against those mariners who allegedly did not do their utmost to effect a rescue.

Earlier in the decade, on August 15, 1901, the Canadian Pacific Navigation Co.'s *Islander* hit an iceberg in the southern approaches of the Lynn Canal and sank, with the loss of forty lives. This was in the same treacherous stretch of Alaska Panhandle geography that would claim the *Princess Sophia* and all 343 aboard in 1918. On the stormy night of January 8–9, 1904, the Puget Sound Navigation Co.'s steam packet *Clallam*, bound from Port Townsend, Washington, to Victoria, became disabled "in a howling tempest" in Juan de Fuca Strait. She foundered and sank with the lights of Victoria in sight, while tugs tried to tow her to safety, and fifty-six died.

While those who go down to the sea often face peril, those who go underground in BC are also subjected to dangerous conditions. This was never more apparent than on Vancouver Island and in the Kootenays, where, at the turn of the century, the coal barons were eager to exploit the rich seams.

On February 15, 1901, an explosion at Cumberland on Vancouver Island reportedly knocked people to the ground over a mile away. Underneath the town, "in a grave as deep as a 50-storey building," sixty-four men were trapped in the Union mine. Fire and deadly gas drove rescue teams from the pit. Escape routes were cut off by cave-ins. The next day, as aftershocks rippled through the drifts, the mine was flooded to prevent the fire from spreading into the main seam.

Down the Island, at Ladysmith, more mining tragedies were to come, in 1903 and 1909. But they could almost be termed insignificant when compared with the disaster at Coal Creek near Fernie in 1902. On May 22, another frightful explosion claimed 128 lives. Once again, deadly "fire damp"—a lethal mixture of methane gas and coal dust—had ignited. The coal inside the tunnel of No. 2 Colliery became so hot it coked. There was no hope of any rescue attempts. The injured miners who made it out of the shaft were cared for, and the grim task of recovering the dead began. Eventually, 91 of the 128 bodies were buried in makeshift coffins (and some hideous human remnants in sealed baskets). Coal Creek is BC's worst mining disaster of this century.

Safely removed from the dust, backbreaking labour and terror of the shafts and pits, the mining bosses and the boardroom warriors concentrated on the profit picture. On the Island, the Dunsmuir empire founded by Robert was passed on to his sons, Alexander and James. Until 1910, when James sold out, the Dunsmuirs' great Wellington seam was one of the best coal producers on the continent's West Coast. In the Kootenays, the romantic gold-seeking prospectors had been replaced by the pragmatists, who saw growth in such nonglamorous metals as silver, coal, lead, zinc and copper. They also recognized the value of the right merger at the right time.

THE DECADE IN HEADLINES
« 1903 »

THE PRINCESS VICTORIA

"The sound of a strange steamer whistle" heralds the arrival of the CPR's newest passenger ship on the West Coast. On August 29, she sets a record of three hours, 31 minutes for the Victoria-Vancouver passage.

The News-Advertiser, March 28, 1903

CONSERVATIVES IN THE MAJORITY

Much to the delight of the paper, Premier Richard McBride's Conservatives form the government in the first B.C election fought under party banners.

The Colonist, October 3, 1903

LED LIKE A LAMB TO THE SLAUGHTERHOUSE—HOW CANADA WAS SACRIFICED

Mincing no words in headline or story, the Vancouver daily gives a jingoistic account of how BC lost the Alaska Panhandle decision.

The Province, October 20, 1903

THE DECADE IN HEADLINES
« 1904 »

WESTMINSTER BRIDGE OFFICIALLY OPENED

The combination wagon and railway bridge across the Fraser River causes great rejoicing in the Royal City. The crossing remains New Westminster's link to the Fraser Valley until the arching Pattullo Bridge is completed in 1937.

Daily Columbian, July 23, 1904

PACIFIC EXPRESS HELD UP NEAR MISSION CITY

The daring start to Bill Miner's Canadian career is told in considerable detail. Although Canada's first train robbery is just outside Mission to the east of New Westminster, the paper chose to put a Vancouver dateline on the story.

The Columbian, September 11, 1904

On January 27, 1906, the Consolidated Mining & Smelting Company was born. This mouthful—more familiarly known as Cominco—had its beginnings at the turn of the century, when the Canadian Pacific Railway decided to become a major force in southeastern BC. Attracted by the land-grant provisions of a railway charter in the West Kootenays, it bought out the owner, an American named Frederick Heinze. Included in the sale was a small smelter at Trail Creek, which Heinze was anxious to unload because he couldn't get enough ore to keep it running.

Although the company's Montreal directors were uneasy about the capital outlay for the nonproducing smelter, their man on the spot—another young American, named Walter Aldridge—had a brilliant flash of insight that directly affected the bottom line. He acquired Canadian rights to a revolutionary lead-extraction process that negated the need to ship the ore to the US for final processing. The electrolytic method worked so well that the new industry of lead-refining (and a rebuilt smelter) put Trail on the world map. By 1905, the big copper, gold and lead-silver mines at Rossland and Moyie became prime acquisition targets for the CPR's Aldridge. Finally, all the pieces fit together in 1906 with the incorporation of Cominco.

The railway had control of the new company, with fifty-four percent of the stock, but the biggest financial and commercial players in Canada at the time were also involved. This did not go unnoticed by the local paper. In breaking the story, the *Trail News* dryly observed that "Toronto capitalists" had taken over. The huge mineral mountain called the Sullivan Mine was added to the mix in 1910, and its lead-zinc product became one of the cornerstones of Cominco's prosperity. The company's mighty smelter still exists, a monolith brooding on the hill above downtown Trail.

The CPR, meanwhile, was already stretching its tentacles to embrace seagoing as well as landlocked concerns. On January 12, 1901, the Canadian Pacific Railway Co. bought controlling interest in the Canadian Pacific Navigation Co. CPN and its forty coastal vessels were absorbed into CP Steamships on May 5, 1903; over the years CPS would add forty-seven more ships. Among them was the *Princess Victoria*, which arrived in Vancouver in 1903 from her builder minus her upper works, but still imposing enough to draw praise from the local press. The enthusiasm was not misplaced: After her superstructure was finished, the *Victoria* began setting the standard in speed and comfort for the Victoria-Vancouver run.

Maintaining this tradition, the Princess boats flew the CPS flag from Puget Sound to Alaska, only relinquishing their hold in the 1960s, when changing demographics, widespread use of the automobile, labour problems and rising costs brought an end to this era of elegant transportation.

But while the gleaming white Princesses graced many a brochure, it was the rival Union Steamship Co. that handled a lot of the dirty stuff. Its working steamers serviced the coastal logging camps and canneries for many years, poking their bows into virtually every navigable cranny from the turn of the century onward. Such struggling communities as Prince Rupert, Powell River, Ocean Falls and Port Alice owed much to the regular visits of the coastal ferries.

In 1896, the CPR had acquired the Columbia and Kootenay Steam Navigation Co., and by the 1900s was operating a separate division called the BC Lake and River Service. The *Minto*, which sailed the Arrow Lakes for fifty-six years, and the *Moyie* on Kootenay Lake were the flagships of a sternwheeler fleet that helped bring settlers and commerce to the Kootenays and the Okanagan.

When the steel ribbon knitting Canada together reached tidewater in 1885, the

CPR established a footprint in British Columbia that was to get broader and deeper as the years passed. The transcontinental railway was complemented by the building and acquisition of branch lines. We have already had a glimpse in this chapter of the company's expansion into shipping and mining. Vancouver, once a haphazard collection of structures "with the mark of the forest still on it" (in the words of old-time newspaperman James Morton), owes its prosperity to the lifeblood and sinew initially supplied by the railway.

So it is no surprise to note that Canadian Pacific soon moved to exploit every part of the hog except the squeal, so to speak. It built not one, but three successive Hotels Vancouver to accommodate those who rode its trains and steamships, and on January 20, 1908, opened the Empress Hotel on reclaimed land fronting Victoria's Inner Harbour. Designed by architect Francis Rattenbury, who was also responsible for the new Legislative Buildings and several other grand Victoria edifices, the new hotel quickly became the centre of society. The day the classic, chateau-style building opened, the first guests were an invited group of newspaper men and women. Kings, queens, lesser royalty and famous commoners have graced its corridors and banquet rooms throughout the century. For a number of years, *The Sun*'s Victoria bureau maintained an office deep within the bowels of the lower level.

While British Columbia was saying farewell to puberty, growth was even more accelerated south of the border. Not one, but four railroads served Washington and Oregon, bringing men, money and an insatiable demand for lumber. It didn't take long for the timber hustlers to discover the untapped stretches of virgin forest in BC. Encouraged by a helpful government bureaucracy that issued timber-cutting licences almost on demand, the Americans kick-started the BC woods industry. (Criteria for obtaining a licence soon tightened considerably.) Although the names of most of the Americans who moved in on the province would be unfamiliar today, some are still recognizable: Weyerhaeuser, Rockefeller, Bloedel.

Along with the demand for building materials came a thirst for the printed word. America's ever-burgeoning population was becoming more educated, leading to a boom in reading. Newspapers and magazines flourished, making newsprint a growth commodity. Sir Wilfrid Laurier's Liberal government in Ottawa reached a deal with the Americans that allowed for free entry of pulp and paper into the United States. Soon the mills were shipping more and more of their products south. Among them was the Powell River Paper Co. Born in 1909, it rolled out the first paper in Western Canada on April 12, 1912. Near the end of the century, Powell River's mill was still a major producer.

All this growth, virtually unregulated, eventually brought problems. Some of these were political: Laurier would lose a federal election over the reciprocity issue. In BC more and more forest fires were being touched off by careless logging operators. When the town of Fernie was flattened by fire in August, 1908, public concern deepened. The lack of control in the woods, plus confusion and infighting over the proliferation of timber licences and leases, forced the government to institute an inquiry. Among the commission's recommendations to be passed into law was the formation of a Forestry Branch, formally responsible for the administration and protection of BC forests. The first chief forester would be another name familiar to British Columbians: H.R. MacMillan.

As with timber, foreign interests helped solidify the telephone industry in BC. By 1900, capital supplied by Yorkshire woollen manufacturers in England was

THE DECADE IN HEADLINES
« 1905 »

FULL TEXT OF PETITION OF INDIANS

After patting itself on the back for breaking the story, *The World* reports that a delegation of BC Natives, led by Chief Joe Capilano, is preparing to leave for England. The petition to King Edward VII appeals for a more humane land-settlement policy.

The World, July 4, 1905

THE DECADE IN HEADLINES
« 1906 »

FIFTY LIVES LOST TO-DAY IN WRECK OF VALENCIA

Combining sketchy details with a cryptic telegram from a lighthouse keeper, *The Province* reports the loss off Vancouver Island of the ocean liner bound from San Francisco to Vancouver.

The Province, January 23, 1906

MINING AND SMELTER MERGER

Reporting the genesis of the Consolidated Mining & Smelting Co., *The News* gets right to the point: "A number of Toronto capitalists have incorporated..." begins its opening sentence.

Trail News, January 27, 1906

HISTORIC SCENE AT DRILL HALL

The last surviving Imperial garrison in Canada closes down. Canadian troops now occupy the Esquimalt defence establishment, which had housed British soldiers since colonial days.

The Colonist, May 9, 1906

VICTORIA MEMORIAL

A "garden of children"–2,000 of them—floods Stanley Park for the unveiling of the memorial to Queen Victoria. The memorial, which is actually a stylish drinking fountain, is partially financed by the school children's fundraising.

The News-Advertiser, May 23, 1906

used to finance expansion of a piecemeal telephone system on the mainland. On March 14, 1904, the present BC Telephone Co. was formed (under Canadian control), folding the Vernon and Nelson Telephone Co. into the Victoria system—the first in the province—along with companies in Nanaimo, Vancouver and New Westminster. Later that year, on October 29, Vancouver and Victoria were linked by a land and submarine cable that passed through the US San Juan Islands.

Yet another American, a young New Yorker named Henry Doyle, could take credit for the formation of the BC Packers' Association. Now known as BC Packers Ltd. (after a number of reorganizations), the association was sorely needed following the traumatic salmon crises of 1900 and 1901. As reported in *The Province*, Doyle persuaded forty-five canning companies to join together in a combine. On May 20, 1902, the new association, backed by Toronto money, was formed and immediately shuttered several canneries. The overabundance of fishboats on the Fraser River was trimmed and dispersed. With BC Packers in control, rather than dozens of individual canneries competing for the catch, the fishermen found their bargaining power severely restricted.

Capitalism's heavy tread, heightened social awareness and concern for inadequate working conditions helped unionism take its first halting steps in the early years of the century, triggering scattered work stoppages at Vancouver Island and Kootenay mine sites. Although the Big Strike of 1912-14 was still years away, the working class was becoming restless. This was no more evident than on the Fraser in 1900.

For the salmon fishermen, it wasn't so much the conditions surrounding their jobs as the desire to make a living wage. In the 1900s as well as the 1990s (and many decades in between), the annual return of this great species of fish to its spawning holes generated conflict, crisis and heavy-handed government intervention.

In June of 1900, the newly formed BC Fishermen's Union demanded "twenty-five cents or no fish," while the cannery operators offered prices as low as fifteen cents. On June 8, the Fraser sockeye fishery was shut down by waterborne pickets. Japanese-born fishermen (who heavily outnumbered the whites) supported the BCFU and did not waver for almost two weeks. Finally, intimidated by the knowledge that they owed their very presence in Canada to the canneries, their own Steveston-based union accepted an offer of twenty cents per fish.

The wrath of the white fishermen now descended upon the Japanese. Expecting bloodshed, negotiators for the cannery owners managed to persuade three local magistrates to call out the militia. After dutifully sailing around to Steveston from Vancouver's Burrard Inlet, a detachment of the 6th Duke of Connaught's Own Rifles was joined by a contingent from New Westminster. Together, they managed to maintain order. By July 30, the union and the canneries had settled on a flat, season-long price of nineteen cents.

Peace lasted only for a year. The following July, another strike idled the fleet, the difference being that the 1901 dispute occurred at the start of one of the great salmon runs in BC history. Expecting a glut, the canneries offered only twelve-and-a-half cents per fish caught before July 27, and ten cents afterward. The fishermen wanted a fixed price of fifteen. There was some scattered violence, especially against the Japanese, but the canners wouldn't budge. After less than three weeks, the fishermen capitulated in late July and sailed to meet the salmon.

Even with the whole fleet catching fish, however, the run surged past. There were so many salmon caught that the cannery workers couldn't keep up. Each boat's catch was limited to two hundred per day, but the canneries still threw thousands away. Hundreds of thousands more clogged the Fraser, and the river steamers had trouble pushing their way through the mass of fish. The stench from the rotting bodies of the dead sockeye hung over the Lower Mainland for days.

Failure of the 1901 shutdown to stampede the canneries diminished considerably the influence of the BCFU. It was eroded even more by the entry of BC Packers on the scene the following year. And not far below the surface, the residue of racial resentment lingered long after the stench of decay had dissipated. One typical opinion of the Japanese colony at Steveston appeared in *The Province* in the summer of 1901. In a Page One story, it noted that the "Japs" were not popular because they sent their money out of the country "and then came down on the canneries to make provision for them during the winter." One source claimed the advances paid to the Japanese were becoming so large they affected some canneries' financial health.

The antipathy toward Oriental immigrants turned ugly in 1907 with the formation of the Asiatic Exclusion League in Vancouver. Although there was nothing out of the ordinary about such an organization (many similar groups had waxed and waned along with anti-Orientalism in the past), this one would make a lasting impression.

The League staged a parade the evening of September 7, a Saturday. While bands played patriotic airs and an ever-swelling crowd sang along, the procession wended its way through downtown streets to Vancouver's City Hall, which at the time was situated close to Chinatown. After a round of pro-Anglo-Saxon speeches, a mob swept into the nearby Chinese neighbourhood. The rioters smashed windows, wrecked property and looted stores, then moved on to Japtown a few blocks away. Unlike the passive Chinese, however, the Japanese fought back to protect their property, so the damage was not as extensive.

Laurier's federal government apologized to Japan—with which it had a trade treaty. A young deputy labour minister named William Lyon Mackenzie King made two trips to BC to assess the damage claims from both Japan and China (the Japanese eventually received $9,036 and the Chinese, $25,000). During his first trip, however, King uncovered evidence of conspiracy to import Oriental workers by such leading industrial concerns as the CPR and James Dunsmuir's Wellington Colleries. Thus the rumours that big business was importing cheap alien labour to take the place of whites was more or less confirmed.

Although chauvinistic behaviour was easily apparent and somewhat expected at street level, it was no less prevalent in political ranks. In 1902, a Royal Commission investigating Chinese and Japanese affairs in BC suggested the head tax on most Chinese entering the country be increased to $500 from $100. In 1904, it was. (Almost twenty years later, in 1923, the Dominion Parliament enacted the ultimate anti-immigrant legislation, which had the effect of excluding all Chinese from Canada.)

In Victoria, the legislature, when not indulging in the game of revolving premiers, passed a string of racist bills between 1900 and 1908 designed to curb the influx of Asians. Generally known as Natal Acts (from Natal in South Africa, which required immigrants to pass an educational test), they attempted to place various restrictions on newcomers ranging from comprehension of English to length of hair, proof of British citizenship and knowledge of a European language. All were disallowed—by the lieutenant-governor, the federal government or the courts— for various reasons, not the least of which being trade considerations.

THE DECADE IN HEADLINES
« 1907 »

IMPORTANT OPENING TODAY

Opening of the Vancouver Stock Exchange gets a prominent position on Page One of *The World*. After a three-paragraph intro, the paper then reprints President C.D. Rand's "eloquent" speech.

The World, August 1, 1907

VANCOUVER WAS IN THROES OF SERIOUS RIOT LAST NIGHT

A rally and a parade protesting the influx of Asian immigrants turn ugly as a mob rampages through Vancouver's Chinese and Japanese districts. Anti-Asian sentiment was high during the early decades of the century.

The News-Advertiser, September 7, 1907

The placid exterior of the Legislative Buildings, depicted in this 1905 photograph, gives no hint of the turmoil that often erupts inside.

The newspapers were not immune to this condition. In January, 1901, *The Province* called the Act to Regulate Immigration "a very acceptable New Year's gift from the government to the people of the province." It also had the habit of calling Japanese "little brown men." During the Boxer Rebellion of 1900, the *News-Advertiser* placed such judgmental headlines as "The Arrogant Orient" and "Shanghai Prevaricator" over routine dispatches about the fighting between Western forces and the rebels in China. The publisher of *The World*, Louis D. Taylor, was one of the stronger supporters of the Asiatic Exclusion League (and, when he became mayor of Vancouver in 1910, vowed to "clean up" Chinatown). In Victoria, a 1901 *Times* editorial on Chinese immigrants called them Mongolians who were not as intelligent as white men. It said this "undesirable class" became "panic-stricken and unmanageable in times of crisis as has been repeatedly proved and in all respects are inferior to whites."

In 1903, the press temporarily suspended its distrust of Asians, turning its scorn on both Britain and the United States over the Alaska Panhandle decision.

This remote finger of real estate, which cuts off the northern portion of the mainland from the Pacific Ocean, was a consequence of a boundary treaty between Britain and Russia in 1825. When the US bought Alaska in 1867, a series of minor border incidents illustrated the fuzziness of the 1825 agreement. Then, when the Klondike gold rush in Canada's Yukon Territory erupted in 1897, the exact location of the boundary became a vital concern because Skagway, at the head of the Lynn Canal deep in the panhandle, was the best jumping-off place for the miners.

Both Canada and the US laid claim to Skagway (as well as other parts of the region) and—even though the Klondike stampede eventually dissipated—it was agreed in 1903 that an international tribunal of "six impartial jurists of repute" would decide the question. Three Americans and two Canadians were joined by Britain's chief justice, Lord Alverstone. On October 20, the panel's decision was announced, and it was almost total victory for the Americans. Lord Alverstone had sided with the US, agreeing that the compromise boundary should be drawn to give it the heads of the inlets, including the towns of Skagway and Juneau. Furthermore, on the particularly emotional point of the Portland Canal at the southern end of the disputed area, Lord Alverstone also accepted the American position: He agreed to split possession of four islands at the mouth of the canal rather than leave them BC territory, as everyone seemed to expect.

The bitterness that arose over the decision was remarkable. That Lord Alverstone was a diplomatic pawn of the Foreign Office intent on removing a source of irritation between Great Britain and the United States is a view still widely held. The two Canadians on the tribunal were so shocked they refused to sign the award. Cartoonists had a field day with grinning Uncle Sams, unctuous John Bulls and forlorn Canadas wearing only a barrel. "Led Like A Lamb To The Slaughter," rasped the headline over *The Province*'s Page One story about the decision. In an editorial, *The Colonist* wrote that "the first feeling that wells up is one of rage … Lord Alverstone … deliberately proceeded to sign away from Canada the most valuable portion of the territory claimed in order to placate the United States."

Meanwhile, the citizenry became alarmed and diverted for a few years by an American immigrant named Ezra Allen Miner, more commonly known as Bill. Like many personalities of the nineteenth century, Bill Miner's origins are shrouded in myth and the fog of time, but reasonably reliable sources indicate Ezra was born in Michigan in 1846. As a teenager, he apparently changed his name to William A. (for Allen) and embarked upon a fifty-year career of stagecoach and train robberies, along with sundry other crimes. After serving a nineteen-year stretch in California's San Quentin Prison, Bill Miner sidled into Princeton, BC, in 1903. Less than a year later, on September 10, 1904, he and two partners held up the CPR's Pacific Express near Mission. They scooped up $7,000 in gold dust and cash, plus $300,000 in bonds and securities. It was Canada's first train robbery.

Miner got away that time, but blundered when he pulled another robbery on the CPR line at Ducks (now Monte Creek, near Kamloops) on May 8, 1906. Fleeing with just $15 (it was the wrong train), Miner and two cohorts were soon arrested. He was sentenced, after a speedy trial in Kamloops, to life imprisonment at the penitentiary in New Westminster.

This is where Bill Miner's Canadian capers get really interesting. The lockup in the Royal City, on a hill east of downtown overlooking the Fraser, was not the forbidding fortress that was eventually phased out in 1980. In those years, the prison was a ramshackle affair, and Miner escaped easily on August 8, 1907. His departure and subsequent disappearance was so easy, in fact, that rumours began circulating that he had got a little help. Some eighteen months later, on March 3, 1909, *The Daily Columbian* in New Westminster added fuel to the rumours with a story alleging that a CPR detective was involved. It seems the Canadian Pacific was rather anxious about recovering those bonds allegedly stolen in 1904. The controversy had even reached the House of Commons a month earlier (J.D. Taylor, managing director of *The Columbian*, was also an MP). Despite an equivocal statement by Prime Minister Laurier that left the question of connivance up in the air, no inquiry was held. Meanwhile, Miner, who had safely made it back to America, resumed his train-robbing ways. He died in a Georgia prison infirmary September 2, 1913, aged sixty-six.

At the end of the decade, some BC residents were getting used to another diversion that had more lasting power than the transitory depredations of itinerant train robbers. For several years, a noisy contraption had been careering about the roads and scaring man and beast alike. It was called the automobile.

The first Stanley Steamer (gasoline-powered vehicles were not yet common)

THE DECADE IN HEADLINES
« 1908 »

EMPRESS HOTEL OPEN TO PUBLIC
Speeches, visiting dignitaries and extravagant praise for the CPR mark the opening of this BC landmark.

The Colonist, January 20, 1908

IMMIGRATION ACT IN FORCE
The "Natal Act" passed by the legislature seeks to limit Asian immigration by imposing strict educational requirements. The act is later overturned.

Victoria Times, February 11, 1908

THE DECADE IN HEADLINES
« 1909 »

BIG BRIDGE DECLARED OPEN

Lady Grey, wife of Governor General Earl Grey, cuts some ribbons with "a dainty golden penknife," and the original Granville Bridge over False Creek in Vancouver is open to traffic.

The World, September 6, 1909

A DISASTROUS ACCIDENT ON THE GREAT NORTHERN

The wreck of a work train kills 22 Japanese in the Royal City's Sapperton area. *The Columbian* describes the accident as one of the worst in the history of the railway.

The Columbian, November 28, 1909

navigated along Vancouver streets in 1899. On May 26, 1902, the *Victoria Times*, in its City News In Brief roundup, reported that "Dr. E.C. Hart has imported a very neat little automobile built for two," which he demonstrated on the Victoria Day weekend. The same year, a Locomobile made its appearance in Vernon, and a Wolseley (painted a flaming scarlet) startled residents and livestock in Spences Bridge. By 1907, a Peerless touring car had conquered the Cariboo country.

This strange, smelly, clanking amalgam of moving parts would, in short order, dominate the province's way of life. In 1909, newspaper ads extolled the charms of such makes as the Franklin, and by 1917, auto dealers were holding trade exhibitions to show off their models. The very shape of our cities would become a function of traffic flow, and the term "urban sprawl" would be coined to describe suburbs held in thrall by the internal-combustion engine.

Politicians would heed the call of the open road and build election strategy around the promise of blacktop and more blacktop. But for now, an even smellier, noisier machine was taking precedence. In the next decade, the steam locomotive would claim the attention of both legislator and working stiff alike to an extent not known since the first railroad arrived twenty-five years earlier.

---

1 The author does not subscribe to the theoretical nonsense that there was no "Year 0." The twentieth century began in 1900, not 1901, because our Gregorian calendar is an artificial record that came into existence long after there was a "first" century. People lived in Year 0; they just didn't know it.

COAL, STEAM AND DEATH

« 1910 – 1919 »

At the start of the second decade of the twentieth century, an arms race spawned by the inferiority complex of a European monarch was on the verge of becoming an unstoppable juggernaut. Germany's Kaiser Wilhelm was a mixture of arrogant Prussian and envious Anglophile. And even though he attended the funeral in London of his uncle, Edward VII, in 1910, he seemed determined to test the English resolve over domination of the sea.

It wasn't long before newspapers were running stories about Britain's battle-ship estimates and Wilhelm's vision of a Germanic Empire. But the events of August, 1914, and the great struggle that was to follow were almost beyond prediction, so British Columbians plunged into the new decade with little concern over the ominous accounts trickling out of London and Berlin.

They read, instead, stories and advertisements about the ebullience of a growing province that seemed destined to become ever richer. The boom that had gathered momentum during the first seven years of Richard McBride's premiership enabled his government to boast about a cash surplus of $5.9 million in 1910. The 1911 census tabulated a population of 392,480, which was more than double the 1901 figure.

Even the construction of a canal through the Isthmus of Panama was a feat worthy of optimism and investment. Shortened distances to Europe and, it was expected, lower transportation charges, boded well for BC's substantial export industry. In 1913, work started on the building of the Ogden Point docks in Victoria's outer harbour, in order to take advantage of the new opportunities.

One unremarked aspect of this growth, however, was its focus on that part of the province hugging the US border. The other, greater fraction of BC was relatively empty and ripe for exploitation. In the minds of politicians and construction contractors, this would best be accomplished by building railroads. After all, it worked for the CPR, whose transcontinental line to Vancouver was the catalyst for a money-coining empire that eventually stretched from the Crowsnest and Kicking Horse passes to Vancouver Island. So when the Grand Trunk Pacific Railway's first scheduled passenger train steamed into Prince Rupert on April 8, 1914, the future indeed seemed bright.

Prince Rupert, a townsite on an island at the mouth of the Skeena River, had

THE DECADE IN HEADLINES
« 1910 »

AWFUL AVALANCHE OF DEATH

In a story saturated with hyperbole and purple prose, the twice-weekly *Mail-Herald* reports the death of several CPR workers under a snowslide on the Rogers Pass. The slide occurred shortly before midnight, so the account in the next day's *Mail-Herald* is a triumph of reporting – despite the language.

Revelstoke Mail-Herald, March 4, 1910

EXHIBITION GATES SWING OPEN TO PUBLIC

Opening of the "first annual Vancouver exhibition" at Hastings Park (later to become the Pacific National Exhibition) attracts such notables as General Baden Powell, founder of the Boy Scout movement, and Canada's prime minister, Sir Wilfrid Laurier.

The World, August 15, 1910

LOCAL AVIATOR MAKES AEROPLANE AND FLIES

Three days after the event, *The Times* reveals the successful flight of local inventor William Gibson on his own machine. Gibson had tried to keep his accomplishment secret, but witnesses spread the word of this early airborne sortie.

Victoria Times, September 6, 1910

CHILLIWACK IS ON RAILWAY MAP

A three-column story on Page One of the weekly *Progress* hails the opening of the BC Electric Co.'s interurban line between Chilliwack and the Lower Mainland. "Monday the 3rd of October will rank as the greatest day in the history of Chilliwack," intones the opening sentence.

Chilliwack Progress, October 3, 1910

AGREEMENT IS CONCLUDED

The Songhees Indian Reserve in downtown Victoria is purchased by the provincial government. Each of the 43 families in the tribe is to get $10,000. The land, on the northwest side of Victoria Harbour, comprises 115 acres.

The Colonist, October 25, 1910

THE DECADE IN HEADLINES
« 1911 »

BANK ROBBERY IS A CONTINENTAL RECORD

A haul of approximately $250,000 by a group of safecrackers who tunnel into the Bank of Montreal puts New Westminster on the crime map. Despite the headline, the story did not specify the nature of the "record."

The Columbian, September 15, 1911

CANADA EMPHATIC FOR EMPIRE TRADE

In the "free trade" federal election that is of great interest to BC's fledgling forest industry, reciprocity with the US is rejected and Robert Borden replaces Sir Wilfrid Laurier as prime minister.

The World, September 21, 1911

Arrow Lakes paddlewheelers Rossland, Bonnington *and* Minto *are tied up at Arrowhead in 1912.*

illusions of its own. Established for the sole purpose of being the Grand Trunk's terminus, it did have some advantages: A good harbour, proximity to Alaska and a better connection with Asia than that of Vancouver. The GTP's president, Charles M. Hayes, claimed ships in the Asiatic trade could be unloaded at Prince Rupert and have their goods well on the way eastward on Canada's second transcontinental link long before the same vessel could reach Canadian Pacific's railhead in Vancouver.

The small city of Prince Rupert is still with us, of course. It is a major hub of the fishing industry and home to the world's largest salmon cannery. New facilities on Ridley Island, completed in 1985, make the city a major export centre for coal and grain. But the GTP never realized its goal of obtaining a regular trans-Pacific steamship service for the port. This overly optimistic outlook (not uncommon among railroad advocates at the turn of the century) also extended to projections of traffic volume and land sales along the 1,500-kilometre right-of-way. By 1919, operating expenses far outstripped revenues and the line lay virtually idle. The GTP and its parent, Grand Trunk Railway Company of Canada, went into receivership and eventually became part of the government-owned Canadian National Railways.

So where did this leave Fort George, the old Hudson's Bay Company post at the juncture of the Fraser and Nechako rivers? The promised arrival of the GTP was sure to transform Fort George into the great metropolis of the north. Promoters and land speculators conjured up visions of prosperity and even more railroads. It

would become a transportation hub to rival Winnipeg, Chicago and New York. Newspaper ads pronounced Fort George as the "Spokane of the North" and offered land at $1 an acre. For the northern Interior, the future, it seemed, had arrived.

Reality, however, got there first. Of all the railroads that were supposed to be laying track or surveying routes, only the GTP made it before continuing on toward Prince Rupert. All the others, with such exotic and far-flung names as Pacific and Hudson's Bay, Ashcroft, Barkerville and Fort George, and Bella Coola and Dunvegan, vanished without a trace into that black hole reserved for fanciful schemes.

(Fort George became incorporated as Prince George on March 6, 1915. Following a deal reminiscent of the purchase of the Songhees reserve in downtown Victoria in 1910, part of present Prince George is on former Carrier Native land. The railroad bought the reserve for $125,000 and relocated the band in 1913.)

Today, the region is served by two railroads—CN Rail (nee CNR) and BC Rail (nee Pacific Great Eastern). But from 1914 to 1952, this gateway to the Peace River country had to get along with one. The PGE, so grandly proclaimed in 1912 as the BC government's preferred railroad between the Lower Mainland and Fort George, took a long time to get where it was going.

The decision to grant a charter for the "Please Go Easy" to the railroad contracting partnership of Foley, Welch and Stewart was not Premier McBride's finest hour. Already he had drawn some heat for guaranteeing construction bonds of up to $35,000 per mile in 1909 for the Canadian Northern Railway. This guarantee was made during an election campaign, and can be considered another instance of bribing voters with their own money. So another government adventure in rail-laying raised several eyebrows.

It wasn't that a railroad between Vancouver and Fort George was a dumb idea. The Cariboo and other parts of the province further to the north had long desired a direct connection to the populous south. Indeed, several influential London-based consortiums had made known their interest in building such a link. But the untested Foley, Welch and Stewart got the charter. That John W. Stewart, one of the

THE DECADE IN HEADLINES
« 1912 »

PARACHUTE DROP STARTLES CROWD AT HASTINGS PARK

Canada's first (and only the third ever) parachute descent "from a speeding biplane" is the highlight of an aviation show in Vancouver. The chutist, Charles Saunders, lands "waist deep in mud."

Vancouver Sun, May 24, 1912

CHIEF FORESTER ASSUMES OFFICE

H.R. MacMillan arrives in Victoria to take the reins of the newly organized BC Fforestry Branch. It is the start of a career that will make the MacMillan name synonymous with forestry in the province.

The Colonist, July 18, 1912

CUMBERLAND MINES ARE CLOSED

Three days after the great Vancouver Island mine strike starts, *The Free Press* catches up with the story.

Nanaimo Free Press, September 15, 1912

HAIL TO OUR GOVERNOR GENERAL!

The Duke of Connaught arrives by train to the cheers of thousands in "loyal Vancouver." *The World* is full of details about the new Governor General's crowded program, while an editorial praises his service to the Empire.

The World, September 18, 1912

partners, was a known Liberal sympathizer was another puzzlement, for McBride was a Conservative premier. Granting of the charter put a whole new twist on the meaning of patronage.

The partners were very good at building railroads (Canadian Pacific, GTP and Canadian Northern could be found on their resumes), but inexperienced at actually running one. This lack of smarts, combined with under-capitalization and the arrival of the Great War, quickly spelled doom for the brave enterprise. In February, 1918, just six years after the legislation that gave birth to the PGE, the provincial government took it over. The end was rather messy. With Stewart off fighting the war and the company now located in Seattle, the cabinet had a frustrating time settling the matter. Finally, the PGE was signed over "lock, stock and barrel," as *The Colonist* put it, late on a Saturday night in Seattle. The partnership agreed to pay up to $1.1 million compensation for failing to meet its commitments, $500,000 of it immediately.

The "Prince George Eventually" struggled on for a few more years as a government concern, actually laying some track as far as Quesnel. But in 1921, cabinet interest waned even further, and the project was shelved. Until 1949, when construction resumed, the PGE was a railway from nowhere (Squamish) to nowhere (Quesnel). The rail connection to North Vancouver was decades away, and passengers and freight had to travel down Howe Sound via ferry and barge to reach civilization.

As the Grand Trunk and the PGE were faltering, so was the Canadian Northern Pacific (as it was known in the legislation guaranteeing the bonds). Under the guiding hands of railroad veterans Donald Mann and William Mackenzie, and thanks to McBride's financial help, the BC stretch of the Canadian Northern was actually completed in 1915, making it Canada's third transcontinental line. Four years later, in 1919, its Union Station opened near the east end of Vancouver's False Creek, but the railroad as a viable entity was long gone. On November 16, 1917, the Dominion government took control of the faltering carrier. It would be the first BC line to be folded into the CNR in 1918.

Meanwhile, the CPR, which was in no danger of going broke, was doing some fine-tuning on its main line. In 1909, the spiral tunnels that were later to become famous and photogenic were completed through two separate mountains, substantially reducing the grade up the Kicking Horse River in the Rockies. That done, the railroad turned its attention to a second problem: Rogers Pass in the Selkirk Range. Snow conditions were so severe each winter that maintaining the line was a constant and perilous battle. With traffic increasing rapidly, the expensive bottleneck had to be eliminated.

Bottom-line pragmatism aside, a dreadful disaster on March 4, 1910, added new impetus to relocation planning. That night, at the tail end of a particularly bitter winter, yet another slide buried the tracks. As a work gang of sixty-three men (many of them Japanese) laboured to clear the blockage, another, more massive avalanche struck around midnight. Of the sixty-three men working on the cut, sixty-two died. "So sudden was the disaster that the men had no time to make for safety, and died an awful death," the *Revelstoke Mail-Herald* reported the next morning, adding that the force of the tons of ice and snow lifted up a rotary plow and deposited it several feet away.

Work on a tunnel beneath Mt. Macdonald, which would put the line under Rogers Pass instead of over it, began in July, 1913. With Foley, Welch and Stewart

Crunch! Even in 1914, traffic accidents are bound to happen. This one occurs at the corner of Connaught and Granville in Vancouver.

as contractors, the eight-kilometre-long tunnel—longest in North America at the time—was completed in the summer of 1916. The Duke of Connaught, Governor General of Canada, was an honoured passenger on a special flat car hauled through the bore on July 17. Later named the Connaught Tunnel in his honour, it opened for regular traffic December 9.

While railroad operators and contractors laboured to stitch the province together with a network of steel rails, the BC Electric Railway Company was quietly expanding the public transit monopoly it had established at street level. Formed April 15, 1897, to run streetcars, lighting and utilities, the BC Electric, as it came to be known, kept expanding right up to the eve of the Great War. Already well-established in Victoria and on the Lower Mainland, the company extended its interurban reach all the way to Chilliwack, at the upper end of the Fraser Valley, in 1910. A new head office was opened in 1911 at the corner of Carrall and Hastings streets in Vancouver, with the interurban depot occupying the ground floor.

Although the streetcars and long-distance trams were gradually replaced by buses after the Second World War, and the intercity lines abandoned, BC Electric continued to move people around (and supply their electrical needs) until 1961, when it became part of a new Crown corporation called the BC Hydro and Power Authority.

(The first publicly owned street railway in the province was in Nelson. In 1899, this East Kootenay town rivalled Trail as a mining hub, boasting a transit line that operated sporadically until the town assumed control in 1914. With eight kilometres of track and two streetcars, it was called the "smallest streetcar system in the British Empire.")

The boom that looked so permanent in 1910 began showing some signs of distress by 1912, despite all the big talk about railroads and industrial expansion. Even the forestry industry, prime distributor of wealth in the province by 1914, began to falter as the situation in Europe and its implications began to impinge upon local concerns.

To this unstable brew can be added one more ingredient: labour unrest.

Early in the century, the socialist philosophy and confrontational tactics of the Industrial Workers of the World crossed the border into southern BC from the United States. This form of radical unionism targeted unskilled and itinerant workers, such as those toiling on the railroads, and in the forests and mines. The class struggle and the revolution were the twin messages the IWW (or Wobblies, as they were popularly known) offered the working man.

Strikes in 1912 and 1913 against the Canadian Northern and the Grand Trunk

THE DECADE IN HEADLINES
« 1913 »

TEKAHIONWAKE'S VOICE IS STILLED
Poetess Pauline Johnson, called Tekahionwake because of her Iroquois blood, dies of cancer in a Vancouver hospital. After permission is received from the minister of defence in Ottawa, her remains are placed in Stanley Park, which was a military preserve at the time.
The World, March 7, 1913

AVIATOR BRYANT FALLS TO DEATH
A long story with much detail chronicles the crash of John Bryant's aircraft onto a downtown Victoria roof during a flying exhibition. The fatal crash is reportedly the first in Canada.
The Colonist, August 6, 1913

NANAIMO NOW QUIET, TROOPS PREVENT FURTHER DISORDER
The arrival of troops helps stem several days of violence by striking mine workers. The unrest is part of the Vancouver Island strike, which began the previous September.
Victoria Times, August 15, 1913

Out in the open for a group photograph in 1913, these are the type of men who toiled underground during the turbulent early years of BC's mining industry.

Pacific attracted little notice (although the legendary Wobbly bard, Joe Hill, allegedly showed up in Yale to lend support). They did, however, impede construction significantly, especially on the GTP. In April, 1911, the "Battle of Kelly's Cut" in Prince Rupert—a violent clash between contractors and a construction union inspired by the visit of an IWW organizer—ended one strike by the workers.

Later in the year, Wobbly organizers and sympathizers were in full cry when a slowdown in construction contracts added to the number of unemployed at loose ends in Vancouver. Outdoor gatherings had been banned, but the IWW defied the order on January 28, 1912. Police surrounded the demonstrators and moved in. As the mob fled, many were beaten; twenty-four were arrested. According to *The Province*, these included "known" and "rabid socialists."

This new militancy was even more evident on Vancouver Island, where a coal miners' strike was to blossom into one of the century's longest and most bitter confrontations between labour and management.

In 1911, the United Mine Workers of America began organizing on the Island. Although the miners had been going on sporadic strikes (and dying from appalling working conditions) since the mid-nineteenth century, their efforts lacked cohesion until the UMWA arrived. Soon all those eking a perilous living from the pits—from coal diggers to lump pickers—were primed for action.

It came September 15, 1912, when workers struck in Cumberland. The Ladysmith miners followed. The issues were union recognition and unsafe practices. Canadian Colleries (now owned by Mackenzie and Mann of the Canadian Northern) locked out everybody and started evicting families from the company housing. Although replacement workers kept the coal moving, the fledgling union hung tough. It wasn't easy. In February, 1913, five months after the strike began, the *Vancouver Sun* published a poignant account of life in Ladysmith. It said, in part:

"Oh, it's very quiet in Ladysmith. The streets are deserted, the men are subdued, holding on, following meekly, turning the other cheek, obeying implicitly, the suggestions of the quiet, young fellow who is their leader. Yes, Ladysmith, beautifully situated, commanding a view of the bay, with wooded hills beyond, is quite silent, brooding, although she shelters 700 striking miners, most of whom own their own homes, whose children have been born in that town and love it.

"As you go away from the little town you notice that it becomes a hill, a column of smoke idly drifting over it gives it a sinister appearance and involuntarily you exclaim, 'It looks like a volcano.'"

Eventually, that volcano erupted. By the summer of 1913, frustration had eroded discipline, although the Big Strike had by then affected every pit on the Island. Violence, vandalism and confrontation spread through Ladysmith, Cumberland, Extension, South Wellington and Nanaimo. Some imported strikebreakers and their families were stoned and chased into the woods. Gunshots and dynamite blasts became common. The Nanaimo rioters rampaged out of control and the BC Provincial Police detachment was overwhelmed.

On August 14, Attorney-General William Bowser ordered in the militia. Two days later, there were 1,000 troops from Victoria and the Lower Mainland in the area. Included were the Seaforth Highlanders, Duke of Connaught's Own Rifles, Victoria Fusiliers and the British Columbia Regiment. Mass arrests—some at the point of a bayonet—brought the situation under control. By the end of the month, most of the units had been withdrawn. The strikers hung on for another year, but the sand was draining out of their resolve. In August, 1914, the cash-short UMWA suspended strike pay and the strike was over. Many of the unemployed, with no job to return to (even if they weren't blacklisted), joined the army and headed for Flanders Fields. The coal kept moving.

The dispute achieved nothing, except to deepen the gulf between capitalism and labour. More than eighty years later, that bitterness and distrust would still be with us, kept alive by a left-wing provincial government that shamelessly exploited class warfare.

Another consequence of the Big Strike was the emergence of an ardent unionist and socialist named Albert (Ginger) Goodwin. Blacklisted in Cumberland for his UMWA activities, he drifted into the Kootenays, where for a few shining, revolutionary years, he was at the forefront of the labour movement. Ginger Goodwin would become a martyr in 1918, shot dead not far from Cumberland, but before he died he would run for the legislature and take 1,500 Trail smeltermen out on strike against Cominco.

Goodwin would lose both the election and the strike. And he would lose his life because—evidence suggests—of his anti-war and anti-conscription rhetoric. Despite bad teeth, a bad stomach and bad lungs, Goodwin was rated fit for military duty. When he didn't report, he was branded a draft dodger and hunted down. The official story is that Dan Campbell, a cashiered BC provincial policeman hired as a special constable, confronted the fugitive July 27, 1918, on a trail near Comox Lake. Goodwin raised his rifle to fire and Campbell killed him in self-defence.

According to Susan Mayse, who wrote *Ginger: The Life and Death of Albert Goodwin*, that is baloney. After carefully examining the Goodwin mystique, she presents the conclusion that Campbell murdered Goodwin from ambush, and that he was hired to do precisely that. Despite the fact Campbell never went on trial for his homicide, the labour movement found him guilty. On August 2, 1918, a one-day general strike was called to protest the callous means by which Ginger died. Although only partially successful elsewhere, it got the attention of the public—and repatriated war veterans—in Vancouver.

The streetcar operators, longshoremen and others walked away from their jobs, effectively paralyzing much of the Lower Mainland. This martyrdom of a draft evader outraged the veterans. A group of them marched on the Labour Temple at the corner of Dunsmuir and Homer and engaged in a raucous afternoon of vandalism, fistfights and epithets.

THE DECADE IN HEADLINES
« 1914 »

BATTLE FOLLOWS ROBBERY OF BANK

A Wild West shootout on the main drag of New Hazelton between citizens and bandits is crisply reported by the local paper. Three robbers are killed during the affray.

Omineca Miner, April 7, 1914

CELEBRATED ARRIVAL OF FIRST TRAIN FROM EAST

Thousands welcome the inaugural Grand Trunk Pacific train service from Winnipeg, which establishes a second transcontinental rail link.

Prince Rupert Daily News, April 8, 1914

WILL NOT LET KOMAGATA MARU TOUCH THE SHORE

A boatload of "Hindoos" from India is turned away in Vancouver harbour. The *Komagata Maru* finally leaves with her immigrants still aboard on July 23, ending one of the most controversial racial incidents in BC history.

The World, May 23, 1914

THE DECADE IN HEADLINES
« 1915 »

FIFTY ARE KILLED AT BRITANNIA BY SNOWSLIDE

A "terrible accident" at a Howe Sound mine shortly after midnight gets brief but prominent play on Page One of *The Province*. The next day's edition includes more details, pre-slide pictures of the site and a revised death toll of 56.

The Province, March 22, 1915

PACIFIC COAST CHAMPIONS WIN STANLEY CUP IN THREE STRAIGHT

Less than four years after being formed, the Vancouver Millionaires win the Cup by defeating the Ottawa Senators. It is BC's first national hockey title.

News-Advertiser, March 26, 1915

THE INCORPORATION ACT

The legislature passes an act incorporating Prince George as a municipality. The *Herald* reports the details of the act without comment.

Fort George Herald, April 8, 1915

RIOTERS WRECK CITY PREMISES

An anti-German demonstration in downtown Victoria follows the news of the sinking of the *Lusitania* a day earlier. Several German-owned or -operated businesses are trashed by a mob of 500. The sinking of the innocent ocean liner is "murder most foul," rages a *Colonist* editorial.

The Colonist, May 8, 1915

UNIVERSITY CLASSES ASSEMBLE FOR WORK

The University of BC opens without fanfare in temporary quarters at the corner of 10th and Laurel in Vancouver. The move to a permanent site at Point Grey is years away.

The Province, September 30, 1915

Ginger Goodwin was a brief comet in the early days of unionism. Perhaps the last words on his life and death should come from the Kootenay town where the Cominco smeltermen staged their abortive strike fashioned from Ginger's despair. "Goodwin deserves no sympathy nor do those who think as he does," the *Trail News* wrote in an editorial. "Canada is at war and has called its young men to the colours. He was one of them, and his persistent evasion of his duty brought the natural consequence … He was a bright man and could have made a name for himself."

While the coal-mining sector was being rent asunder by violence and dissent, the forest industry was getting untracked. The Forest Act of 1912 was the government's giant step toward putting BC's most important resource under regulatory control. Establishment of the Forestry Branch placed all activities in the hands of a single agency. This included systematic and consistent assessment and collection of royalties and stumpage fees. Attention was given conservation, more efficient fire protection and an active sales policy.

An Ontario-born Yale graduate named Harvey Reginald MacMillan was hired as BC's first chief forester. He assembled a professional field staff and introduced the concept of tying royalty rates to the price of lumber. As a further aid to conservation, H.R. (as he came to be known) also succeeded in having amendments passed that graded logs according to quality. In the few short years before the war changed everything, logging and sawmilling became big business. In 1913, the forest industry passed mining as the largest employer in BC.

It got a helping hand from American publishers. The US demand for Canadian paper remained so strong that free entry of newsprint and pulp was legalized that year. This followed the failure of Canada to ratify a reciprocity treaty allowing free exchange of a wide range of goods. Fighting a federal election with the help of the slogan "No truck or trade with the Yankees," Robert Borden's Conservatives replaced Laurier's Liberals in 1911. It made little difference in the short term to BC's pulp mills. With Powell River Paper leading the way, investment ballooned to $13 million in 1913 from zero in 1900.

On July 31, 1914, the shingled roof fell in, not only on the lumber industry, but on the railroads, the construction sector and any business that depended on capital to live. The London money markets, which controlled the world's credit system, staggered under the weight of the European crisis. It became almost impossible to buy or sell stocks or bonds, or borrow money. With the onset of war four days later, shipping shortages became critical and lumber and fishery exports suffered. Canadian markets also dried up. Except for a crash shipbuilding program (using Douglas fir) and a flurry of activity in 1917-18 harvesting coastal spruce for use in aircraft construction, the BC forest industry virtually shut down for the duration. MacMillan resigned as chief forester in 1916. After some wartime work for the feds, he started his own export agency. This eventually grew into the corporate timber giant known as MacMillan Bloedel Ltd.

The *Komagata Maru* incident left a brief stain on BC's consciousness only days before the war began. With 376 East Indians aboard, the Japanese-registered vessel sailed into Vancouver harbour May 23, 1914. The passengers were mostly Punjabi Sikhs, and their militant leaders were determined to test Canada's immigration laws, which essentially barred East Indians. While the lawyers fenced their way through the legal process (with no result that changed anything), the *Komagata Maru* lay brutally isolated in Burrard Inlet. Except for twenty who had proper

Awaiting the axe, a majestic grove of Sitka spruce in the Queen Charlotte Islands dwarfs the humans who have come to cut the trees down in 1918. The Charlottes' spruce trees were used in aircraft construction in both world wars.

papers, no one was allowed to leave.

Hungry, thirsty and desperate, the "mutinous Hindoos" violently repelled a force of police and immigration officers who tried to board the vessel in June. Finally, HMCS *Rainbow* was called in from Esquimalt, although there was no provision in the Naval Service Act for naval aid to the civil power.

As she steamed through the First Narrows on the sunny morning of July 21, the city watched and waited. "Every street end, every window, every possible van-

THE PAPER THAT PRINTS THE FACTS

LATE EDITION

The Vancouver World

THE ONLY INDEPENDENT NEWSPAPER IN BRITISH COLUMBIA

THE PAPER THAT PRINTS THE FACTS

TWO CENTS

NEWS STANDS AND TRAINS FIVE CENTS

EIGHTEEN PAGES — VANCOUVER, B. C., MONDAY, AUGUST 10, 1914 — PAGES 1 TO 18

MOBILIZATION OF VANCOUVER TROOPS EFFECTED TODAY

NORTH SEA CLOSED

GERMANY PREPARES TO INVADE GREAT BRITAIN

TWENTY-FIVE HUNDRED MEN NOW UNDER ARMS

Regiments Forming the Twenty-Third Infantry Brigade Under Col. Duff-Stewart Ready, Aye Ready

TROOPS TO GUARD ALL VULNERABLE POINTS

Enlistment Proceeding Rapidly—Overseas Contingent Growing—Use Skating Rink

Vancouver is today an armed camp. Two thousand five hundred men, the officers and privates in the ranks of all those regiments which constitute the 23rd Infantry Brigade under the command of Colonel J. Duff Stuart, stand ready to do their duty to their country, whatever that duty may mean.

Every regiment, every corporal's guard, is complete. The order for mobilization was issued Sunday night by Col. Stuart, and this morning street cars and automobiles bore the hundreds of officers and soldiers to headquarters in preparation for a war that may last twenty years or as many months.

The 104th Regiment, at New Westminster, Col. J. D. Taylor commanding, is similarly commanded to mobilize.

They Welcome War.

War, it seems, is as welcome to the sturdy veterans and the beardless youngsters as a raise of wages in peace time. Those fellows volunteered. No war lord stood over them with flattened sword or drove them by ponderous frown to enlist. They are volunteers, volunteers in the army to defend their country's honor.

(Continued from Page 10.)

CITIZEN SOLDIERS

The militia organizations of the city and district have all been ordered out for active service by the mobilization orders issued today. They are:

Sixth Duke of Connaught's Own Rifles.

Seventy-second Seaforth Highlanders.

Eleventh Irish Fusiliers.

One company of the Canadian Army Service Corps.

Eighteenth Field Ambulance Corps.

The Sixth Field Company of Canadian Engineers of North Vancouver.

One Hundred and Fourth Infantry, North Vancouver and Chilliwack.

Rainbow May Convoy Two Sloops of War From San Diego To Esquimalt

VICTORIA, Aug. 10.—Out of a maze of conflicting reports in regard to the naval situation on the Pacific coast, two facts stand out pretty clearly. One is that the presence of the much-discussed German cruiser Leipzic in the waters adjacent to the west coast of Vancouver Island is no bugaboo but a grim actuality. The other is that the only effective fighting ship on the coast, H. M. Canadian cruiser Rainbow, is not here just now to give battle to the threatening invader. About the only naval defense which the sunset doorway of the Dominion can offer to the kaiser's warship, aside from the land defenses at Esquimalt, which command the Straits, now rests with the two new submarines recently purchased from the Chilean government.

(Continued on Page 2)

ELDER STATESMEN LAY WAR PLANS BEFORE MIKADO

PEKIN, Aug. 10.—German cruisers are said to be searching the Yellow Sea and causing British, French and Russian merchant vessels to remain in the various ports. From Shanghai reports were received today that the British Pacific fleet had passed toward the north, accompanied by two French cruisers.

(World's Special Service)

TOKIO, Aug. 10.—Two German cruisers which came out of Kiaochau bay a few days ago appeared Sunday off the south coast of the main island of Japan. They had been chasing a British merchant vessel, which after a hot race sought refuge in the harbor of Shimidzu, in Shizuoka Prefecture, only a hundred miles south of Tokio.

(Continued on Page 2)

GERMANY ON EVE OF REVOLUTION

PARIS, Aug. 10, 5.50 a. m.—A special to Figaro from Brussels says that two strangers who arrived from Berlin, which city they had left with some difficulty, declared they had witnessed an agitation against the emperor in the German capital. They said that in the Avenue of Tilleuls they heard cries of "Down with the Emperor" and "Down with the Crown Prince."

AUSTRIA AND FRANCE FORMALLY AT WAR

LONDON, Aug. 10.—The French ambassador at Vienna has asked for his passports, according to the London Daily Telegraph.

The Austro-Hungarian ambassador was still in London today, and the British government seems disposed to leave the initiative to Austria-Hungary in the question as to whether war is to be declared between the two countries.

The delay of the French government in asking Austria-Hungary to declare her intentions is understood in London to have been due to the fact that the French fleet in the Mediterranean was engaged in convoying Algerian troops to France. France, therefore, was not ready to cope with the situation in case the reply of Austria-Hungary proved unsatisfactory, but on the completion of the transportation of French troops yesterday the note of inquiry was addressed to the Austro-Hungarian ambassador in Paris.

Britain's Most Powerful Floating Fighting Machine

The Iron Duke, the last word in super-dreadnoughts and the pride of the British navy. This monster is the flagship of the great armada which is now holding the German navy in a corner of the North Sea. The Iron Duke could use up ammunition at the rate of $50,000 worth a minute if all her guns were brought into play at one time.

GERMAN LINER CAPTURED ON ATLANTIC

Kronprinz Wilhelm Prize of His Majesty's Cruiser Essex

(Associated Press, World's Leased Wire.)

NEW YORK, Aug. 10.—From two sources today came a report in New York that the North German Lloyd liner Kronprinz Wilhelm had been captured by the British cruiser Essex and taken to Bermuda as a prize. The liner Narragansett reported having heard a wireless message to this effect and the manager of the Royal Mail Steam Packet, whose ships run to Bermuda, says he had heard a similar report.

The report was given some credence here in view of the announcement by the Canadian government, made at Ottawa last night, that the Essex had advised the Bermuda station that she was bringing in a prize. The name of the captured vessel was not disclosed in the government's announcement.

Since the beginning of the war the Essex has been cruising between Bermuda and Halifax. The message which the Narragansett is said to have intercepted, read as follows:

"Bringing in Kronprinz Wilhelm as a prize."

The manager of the Royal Mail Steam Packet said he had ever reason to believe the report was true. He would not say where he had heard it, but it was believed that the British consul was his authority.

Rigorous censorship is being enforced in Bermuda and no confirmation of the report could be obtained at Hamilton.

The Kronprinz Wilhelm, named in honor of the heir to the German throne, was launched in May, 1902. She is 663 feet long, of 66 feet beam, 23,600 tons displacement and 30,000 horsepower. She has a speed of 23 knots and at the time of her launching was one of the fastest and largest vessels afloat. She has accommodations for 1715 passengers and a crew of 552.

A despatch from San Juan, Porto Rico, last night said the German cruiser Karlsruhe had arrived there Sunday, taken on enough coal to permit her steaming to Hamburg, and would leave today. The Karlsruhe is believed to be one of the German cruisers which have been harrying French and British vessels leaving New York for European ports.

THOUSANDS OF GERMANS KILLED AND WOUNDED 1700 MEN CAPTURED

BRUSSELS, via London, Aug. 10, 5.20 p.m.—The commander of the forts at Liege, according to an official announcement, reports that all the forts are intact. The soldiers manning them are in fine health and spirits and are amply supplied with provisions and ammunition. There is no cause for alarm.

LONDON, Aug. 10.—A telegram from Charleroi, Belgium, to the Daily Mail, despatched on Sunday night, says a force of French troops arrived in time to participate in a fine success of General Leman's Belgian division over the German troops investing Liege.

The correspondent adds:

"The French succeeded in reaching the town of Liege, and working behind the Germans, cut off their retreat.

"The Germans are said to have lost 8000 killed and wounded, while 1700 of them were captured. I give the figures under reserve."

ROME, Aug. 10.—Germany has made further overtures t another European country; this time it is Spain. The Germans have made lavish promises to Spain in exchange for co-operation in attacking France, these taking the form of territorial expansion in Morocco and elsewhere. Spain, however, refused to entertain the proposal.

BOYS CHEERED OFF BY MOTHERS AND SWEETHEARTS

(Registered in Accordance with the Copyright Act of Canada.)

LONDON, Aug. 10.—Yeterday saw England at prayer. Fifty thousand people in the evening assembled around Buckingham Palace and sang "God Our Help in Ages Past," with wonderful solemnity before the King and Queen emerged.

The scenes as the troops go off to the front are inspiring, particularly in the west country districts.

"You didn't try to keep him back," said a friend addressing a girl who laughingly bade her lover goodbye. "Never, never," came the reply, "he'd never marry me if he didn't fight for the King now."

Mothers assemble at the market places cheering their sons as they march off. "Do you duty, my lads," they shout. The farewell tears are kept back until the lads are gone. This is the universal spirit.

Developments so far are wholly satisfactory to the authorities, and the pessimists are confounded.

Canada's magnificent gift of food following the promise of troops has thrilled the nation enormously. It is valuable as checking the rise of prices and relieving great and threatening distress.

T. A. McKENZIE.

INCREASE R. N. W. M. P. BY FIVE HUNDRED MEN

The R. N. W. M. P. have inserted in the advertising columns of all city papers a notice calling for five hundred ex-service men to re-enlist in that body for one year's service. Major Snyder is recruiting for his old corps in Vancouver. The office he has opened is at Room 1, 525 Pender street.

The call is a result of an order issued from the headquarters of the corps at Ottawa, instructing Commissioner Perry, commanding officer of the R. N. W. M. P. to increase his establishment by the number of men stated. While preference is given to ex-R. N. W. M. P. men in the call, there is nothing in the order from Ottawa to prevent men otherwise adapted from offering.

ADMIRALTY ORDERS FISHING FLEETS TO REMAIN IN PORT

LONDON, Aug. 10—The North Sea was again closed to the fishing fleets today. The harbor master at Scarborough received a message from the admiralty instructing him to tell the masters of fishing vessels not to go out until further notice.

SAN JUAN, Aug. 10—The German cruiser Karlsruhe took on board 900 tons of coal here yesterday and sailed at night for an unknown destination. As she left the harbor she put on full speed and her lights were all extinguished.

Her captain reported that he was in an engagement last Friday night off the Bahamas, when the Karlsruhe was pursued by four English and French cruisers. When he first sighted the lights the captain thought it was a schooner until a shot was fired. He said he believed one of the cruisers was disabled as the pursuit was abandoned and the other war vessels appeared to be assisting her.

NEW YORK, Aug. 10.—The captain of the Atlantic Transport liner Minnetonka, in today from London with 127 cabin passengers, reported that his ship had been chased by a war vessel from a point some distanc east of Nantucket lightship to nearly within sight of land.

The Minnetonka flies the British flag. When the pursuing warship, whose identity could not be made out, was sighted, the liner put on full speed. At nightfall, with the craft still following, all lights on the liner were extinguished. By daylight the warship was out of sight.

Not far off the coast of the United States, the Minnetonka was in communication with the British cruiser Essex, which asked if any German cruisers had been sighted.

In mid-ocean the Minnetonka was in wireless communication with the British cruiser Drake. On Saturday the liner passed at a distance two American war vessels bound east. They were believed to have been the Tennessee and the North Carolina.

Among the cabin passengers on the Minnetonka was Owen Wister, the novelist.

KAISER HOPES TO SUCCEED WHERE NAPOLEON FAILED

(Registered in Accordance with the Copyright Act of Canada.)

LONDON, Aug. 10.—The military correspondent of the Times today forecasts a serious attempt of the Germans to invade this country. Last copies of the Berlin Lokal Anzeiger brought to English by fugitives plainly intimate that the German navy will take the offensive in co-operating with the army against England.

"We must be prepared for a desperate enterprise on the part of the entire German navy, and for the attempted co-operation of the German army against us, not only from the North Sea but from the Baltic," says the Times. "For such a gambler's throw we are probably well prepared."

The correspondent declares that from the soldier's point of view the time to strike such a blow is within the next fortnight.

Sober military critics here insist that excessive importance must not be placed upon the Belgian Alsace victory. Many Belgian reports are evidently exaggerated, particularly concerning the number of Germans wounded. The Alsace advance is important in proving the morale of the French army, but is not a deciding factor in developments. The main French and German armies will not be ready until Friday. What the past week's fighting has done is to destroy the legend as to German invincibility, and gives France more time to complete her preparations.

F. A. MACKENZIE.

WORLD'S CANDIDATES SHOULD BE WELL PLEASED THIS WEEK

Special Request for Another Chance at 50,000 Extra Vote Ballots Granted—50,000 Extra Votes for Each and Every $19 Worth of Subscriptions Turned in Before This Saturday Night—Also Three $105 Scholarships To Be Given for Best Work Done Before Saturday.

BEGIN WORKING FOR $19 CLUBS TODAY

Many Candidates Get Disappointments Because They Wait Until Last Few Days of Special Offers—Procrastination is the Theif of Votes.

Owing to the excitement over the war last week, a great many candidates have requested that we give another opportunity to secure the 50,000 extra vote ballots, as conditions were not favorable for good results last week. We are willing at all times to assist the candidates in every possible way, consequently we will give every candidate one more opportunity to work for the 50,000 extra-vote ballots. This week will will allow 50,000 extra votes for each and every $19 worth of subscriptions turned in before 10 p.m. Saturday night, August 15, or mailed by out-of-town candidates up to midnight Saturday, August 15. This will be the last opportunity to secure the 50,000 extra-vote ballots; there will be no more after Saturday. It makes no difference how many extra votes you have secured during the previous 50,000 offers, it will pay you to secure every possible extra vote ballot and lay up a big reserve for the close of the campaign. If you have not made a start so far, it will pay you to get busy, for this is your last opportunity to secure the 50,000 extra vote ballots which count up so fast for the valuable prizes.

Scholarship Offer Closes Saturday.

Do not overlook the fact that there will be three $105 3-months' business scholarship prizes given out for the best work done last week and this—the offer closes this Saturday night, and the winner will be announced next week, when we have heard from all the out-of-town candidates with letters bearing the postmark of Saturday, August 15.

Photos Wanted.

In a very short time we will begin publishing the pictures of the leading candidates, together with a short write-up.

Candidates who are working for the prizes would do well to get their photos in as soon as possible, for it takes several days to prepare them for publication.

Your Photo Free.

Candidates who call at Berry's popular confectionery and ice cream parlor, 104 Hastings, west, will be given absolutely free a ticket good for one photo at one of the well-known art studios in Vancouver.

War dominates Page One of The World *in the first month of the conflict. The coverage will remain intense until the Armistice.*

On parade at Hastings Park, female troops undergo inspection in 1915.

tage ground was thronged with expectant crowds, the waters of the harbour were like a regatta day, and all deadly still," the *Rainbow*'s captain, Walter Hose, recalled in 1919. With the light cruiser's six-inch and 4.7-inch guns brooking no argument, the Sikhs agreed to go away. They were supplied with food and sailed for India on July 23. The *Rainbow* shadowed the *Komagata Maru* through Juan de Fuca Strait and watched her disappear over the rim of the Pacific.

Within days of the *Rainbow*'s return to Esquimalt, the Dominion of Canada found itself at war. The call to Imperial arms on August 4 was immediately and enthusiastically answered. On August 10, mobilization orders were issued to militia groups on the Lower Mainland. "Vancouver is today an armed camp," said *The World* in its Page One story. It listed as "ordered to active service" several elements, including the 6th Duke of Connaught's Own Rifles, 72nd Seaforth Highlanders and the 11th Irish Fusiliers.

"Ready, Aye, Ready," said *The World*. The first units headed east from Vancouver by train August 22. On August 26, Victoria's first detachment of volunteers arrived on the *Princess Mary*. Eventually, more than 43,000 British Columbians would serve overseas. A smaller fraction manned coastal defences, patrolled vital installations and kept an eye out for saboteurs and German sympathizers. Detachments of the Rocky Mountain Rangers, based in Kamloops, guarded the CPR's main line.

Once the Canadian volunteers had been swallowed up by the British Expeditionary Force, actual details of the fighting were not widely available at first. In our modern era of instant, electronic dissemination of news, the manner in which dispatches from the front reached the public in 1914-18 would seem intolerable. But communications then, despite wireless radio and the telegraph, were not what they are today. Censorship, common in any military endeavour, played a large part.

Thus it took some months for the carnage along the Western Front to become common knowledge outside military circles. The newspapers concentrated, instead, on optimistic generalizations about the ebb and flow of the fighting. Eventually, however, the accounts became too gloomy to go unremarked. When the casualty lists became so long that those at home in BC realized their sons and husbands were dying in great numbers, along with other Canadians, at Ypres, the Somme, Passchendaele and Vimy Ridge, the Great Adventure lost much of its romance.

Meanwhile, the press had a sea frontier of its own to cover, and did so with an enthusiasm that sometimes had little to do with the facts. The bogeymen that had the West Coast in a ferment were the German cruisers *Leipzig* and *Nurnberg*. Part of the squadron commanded by Admiral Graf von Spee, they were roaming the Pa-

THE DECADE IN HEADLINES
« 1917 »

THIRTY-FOUR LOST LIVES AT COAL CREEK

Another explosion in the mining area near Fernie is reported on Page 3 of the far-off *Times*. In 1902, 128 were killed in a Coal Creek explosion.

Victoria Times, April 5, 1917

HAPPENINGS IN BRIEF: APPOINTMENTS GAZETTED

The appointment of Helen McGill as the first female provincial court judge in BC warrants one sentence in a roundup of items. Similarly, *The Victoria Times* gives the news three lines of type at the end of a "New Appointments" listing on Page 5.

The Colonist, July 19, 1917

DAILY NEWSPAPERS OF CANADA LINKED BY GREAT LEASED WIRE

The formation of The Canadian Press, a national news-gathering cooperative, is compared by *The World* to the completion of the transcontinental railroad. It is indeed a singular event in the evolution of the press in BC and Canada, leading almost immediately to faster and easier dissemination of news.

The World, September 2, 1917

B.C. PROHIBITION LAW BECOMES EFFECTIVE — MONDAY

On the Saturday preceding the enforcement of prohibition, *The World* reminds its readers of the new liquor regulations.

The World, October 1, 1917

1500 MEN QUIT AT CONSOLIDATED SMELTER

Union activist Ginger Goodwin leads his men out on strike, demanding an eight-hour day. They return to work under the previous conditions on December 21 and Goodwin, branded a draft dodger, becomes a fugitive.

Trail News, November 15, 1917

cific when the war started, immediately fuelling rumours and false reports of imminent depradations. The pair never did sail together in the summer of 1914, but that didn't stop the newspapers from hinting at confrontation between them and the gallant *Rainbow*.

"Rainbow May Have Met Enemy" was a typical headline based on sketchy details about gunfire off San Francisco. When obviously British wooden fittings and doors were found in the sea off the California coast, the press jumped to the conclusion that the *Rainbow* had been sunk. She had, in fact, jettisoned flammable material just in case she did go into battle. (It must be remembered there were four daily newspapers in Vancouver in 1914. Page One stories about naval battles seemingly just over the horizon from Cape Flattery couldn't hurt in the constant struggle to capture readership.)

In Victoria, *The Times* was particularly bullish about the *Rainbow*'s chances against any enemy cruiser. "The *Rainbow*, a faster boat and mounting two six-inch guns, is more than a match for the German boat," it boasted on August 1. "If Britain engages in war it will the business of the *Rainbow* to get this German boat." In reality, HMCS *Rainbow* would be no match for either the *Leipzig* or the *Nurnberg*. Although the *Rainbow*'s main armament was indeed larger in calibre, the enemy ships' four-inch guns had more striking power and greater range. They were also faster and their crews better trained.

The *Leipzig* did take on coal at San Francisco, and the *Rainbow* may not have been far away at the time, but they never met. The *Leipzig* never ventured any further north than Cape Mendocino, and the *Nurnberg* was thousands of miles away that summer. Nevertheless, the poor *Rainbow* was kept steaming up and down the coast—from Prince Rupert (exposed, vulnerable and nervous) to Mexico—in response to different orders and false reports of mysterious cruisers standing in toward shore. When it was determined that the two shadowy warships had rejoined von Spee's squadron off Chile (to be subsequently sunk off the Falkland Islands), naval life at Esquimalt grew less hectic.

The naval scare also led to British Columbia having its own navy for three days that August. According to Volume One of the official history of Canada's naval service, Premier McBride acquired two submarines built in Seattle because, basically, BC was at panic stations.

In late July, the subs, laid down for the Chilean navy, were rejected because they were not built to specifications. Stuck with the unsold pair, the owner of the Seattle shipyard, a certain J.V. Paterson, mentioned at a get-together at Victoria's Union Club that they were available. When McBride was approached, he liked the idea because the thought of the untested *Rainbow* trying to guard BC's long coastline was a sobering one.

Through the naval establishment at Esquimalt, he attempted to get the federal government to commit itself to purchasing the submarines. Ottawa stalled. By August 3, time was of the essence, because President Woodrow Wilson was about to sign a US neutrality proclamation forbidding any fitting out or arming of any vessel that "shall be employed in the service of either of the said belligerents." McBride, fearful that further delay would result in the subs being quarantined, endorsed a cheque for $1.15 million drawn by the Province of British Columbia on the Canadian Bank of Commerce. Early in the morning of August 5 and without clearance, the two submarines slipped away with Paterson and the Canadian representative, W.H. Logan (who had been at the Union Club meeting), aboard.

The Soldiers' World

Is issued gratis each Thursday with The Vancouver World, and is NOT sold separately. It is meant for World readers to mail with or as a letter to their soldier friends. Postage three cents for one page—weight of this sheet, one-half ounce.

The Soldiers' World

OVERSEAS EDITION

WITH COMPLIMENTS OF THE VANCOUVER WORLD.   VANCOUVER, THURSDAY, OCT. 24, 1918—PAGE 13   ISSUED EVERY THURSDAY

TWELVE DEATHS DURING THE DAY

Influenza Takes Heavy Toll of Patients Suffering From Disease at General Hospital.

FOUR MORE DEATHS ARE REPORTED AT COQUITLAM

Volunteer Nurses Are Proving of Great Help in Meeting Situation.

Open Soup Kitchens to Relieve Present Stress

VETERANS WANT INDIANS' LAND

To Ask Government to Redeem and Irrigate Reserves Whose Chief Crop is "Thistles"

BEST LAND IS HELD BY SIWASHES, UNCULTIVATED

Suggest Government Should Clear Quarter of Each Forty-Acre Tract.

POLICE INQUIRY NEXT THURSDAY

Commission Opens, But Unable to Proceed, as the Mayor Is Absent—Soldier Wants Royal Commission.

DR. WESBROOK DEAD

President of the University of B.C. loaned away on Sunday last. He was 50 years of age and had been ailing since February.

PUCK CHASERS ARE LOYAL LOT

Sixteen Pacific Coast Hockey Players Have Joined Colors —Five Millionaires on Roll.

FOSTER SPIRIT OF CAMARADERIE

Colonel W. P. Purney, President of Great War Veterans' Association, Arrives From East.

SAYS VETERANS MUST ALL STAND TOGETHER

Wants Soldier Representatives Placed on Government Committees.

MANY APPEAR IN MILITARY COURT

Correction in Order-in-Council Regarding Carrying of Papers Leads to Several Fines.

ALL SATURDAY GAMES ARE OFF

Influenza Also Prevents Football Meeting Tonight—Cameron Case to Come Up at First Meeting.

TAX SALE NEED NOT SO PRESSING

Buyers of City Bonds Ready to Assist Council Over Payments to be Made on Loans.

FREIGHT HANDLERS ARE BACK AT WORK

Shipments Again Handled Almost in Normal Manner.

CALL FOR NURSES IS SENT OUT BY COUNCIL

COMMISSIONERS ARE TAKING NO CHANCES

Will Not Continue Shipmasters' Inquiry While "Flu" Rages.

INVEST FIVE THOUSAND IN VICTORY LOAN BONDS

Decision of Exhibition Board Associated on Sound Financial Basis

ARGUMENTS ENDED IN SIX-CENT FARE CASE

Judge Reserves Judgment in City vs. B.C.E.R. Action.

SOUTH VANCOUVER RATEPAYERS' ASSOCIATION REPLIES TO LETTER RECEIVED FROM PREMIER

Deprived of Franchise

FIVE SCHOOLS ARE CLOSED AS CHILDREN NOT AILING

WARDENS REPORT MANY PHEASANTS

Birds Are Very Plentiful in Nearly All Districts—Receive Instructions From Dr. Baker.

THIRD HULL WILL BE LAUNCHED NEXT WEEK

Mrs. Frank Davey to Christen Schooner Helen Lyall.

WILL CHECK UP SALES OF SUGAR

Supervisor Arthur Nelson to Keep Closer Tab on Purchases Made for Manufacturing.

CARIBOO DISTRICT IS PRODUCING GOLD

Famous Old Mining Area Gives Great Promise.

CHINAMAN'S CRUELTY

Cuts Bill of Live Bird and is Fined $25 and Costs.

MRS. McMILLAN DIES

This special page, produced each Thursday, is intended for overseas distribution among BC troops.

THE DECADE IN HEADLINES
« 1918 »

PROVINCE NOW OWNS RAILWAY

The Pacific Great Eastern is signed over to the BC government in Seattle after it runs into financial difficulties and defaults on obligations.

The World, February 23, 1918

PREMIER BREWSTER PASSES INTO THE GREAT BEYOND, AND CLOSES A BRILLIANT LIFE OF SERVICE

BC's 18th premier succumbs to pneumonia in Calgary while returning from an Eastern conference. It is the second death of a BC politician within seven months. Former premier Richard McBride died August 6, 1917.

Victoria Times, March 1, 1918

MRS. SMITH WILL HOLD FLOOR TODAY

The first woman member of the BC legislature —Mrs. Ralph Smith—makes her maiden speech. At the 1921 session, she becomes the province's first female cabinet member.

The Colonist, March 1, 1918

CHANGE OF TIME IN FORCE TOMORROW; CLOCKS TO ADVANCE

The Times puts a brief notice on Page One on April 13, the day before Daylight Saving Time is introduced in Canada, while an editorial praises the new system, saying, "Its value in terms of recreation, sport and health are potent."

Victoria Times, April 14, 1918

GIANT TELESCOPE BEGINS CAREER

The Dominion Astrophysical Observatory in Saanich, north of Victoria, has its "official" opening, although it has been functioning for some days beforehand.

The Colonist, June 11, 1918

Five miles south of Trial Island, just outside Canadian waters, they met an escort vessel carrying two RCN officers. After an inspection, the boats were declared satisfactory, and the cheque was handed over to Paterson. Later in the day, naval headquarters in Ottawa signalled the Esquimalt base to prepare to buy the submarines. "Have purchased submarines," was the terse reply. Thus BC became the only province to own its own warships. The Dominion government assumed responsibility August 7 and the subs, named CC1 and CC2, were placed at the disposal of the Admiralty. It took some weeks to get them fit for active operations (they had no torpedoes, for instance), but they remained on the West Coast for almost three years before being transferred to Halifax.

None of this made the papers until later. The first mention of BC's instant navy appeared in a two-paragraph item on Page One of *The World*, August 5. The other dailies didn't catch up to the story for a number of days, and the facts weren't fully known until the Davidson Commission Concerning Purchase of Submarines issued its report in Ottawa in 1917 (from which the naval history obtained the details mentioned in this account).

Overseas, BC's most important contribution to the war was Gen. Sir Arthur Currie, who was given command of the Canadian Corps on the Western Front in June, 1917. An immigrant from Ontario, Currie became a successful insurance agent in Victoria and joined the militia in 1897. Eventually, he rose to command the 50th (Highland) Regiment. It was this appointment that led to a blemish on Currie's career that was not public knowledge until long after his death in 1933. Lured by the high profits of land speculation, Currie had switched from insurance to real estate—and took a bath as the market collapsed.

Deeply in debt, Currie misappropriated $10,833.34 earmarked for regimental uniforms to pay his own bills, then left for the war as a brigade commander. Although Currie's misuse of the government allowance (which could easily have led to charges of fraud and theft) was known to his superiors, he nevertheless became commanding general of the largest armed force Canada had ever assembled. Under Currie, one of the most successful generals of the war, the Canadians won a number of notable victories, including Passchendaele and Mons. Shortly after his promotion, he repaid the funds he diverted in 1914.[1] Sir Arthur Currie never returned to BC after the Armistice and settled in Eastern Canada.

When the war ended, thousands gathered in downtown Victoria, Vancouver and other communities. The night of November 11, 1918, was noisy and joyous, punctuated by whistles, bells, sirens and bands. In Vancouver, hit hardest by a particularly virulent epidemic of Spanish influenza that autumn, 25,000 still streamed toward the city's centre to mingle and rejoice. The epidemic, first reported in early October, had begun to abate by mid-November. Hundreds of deaths were recorded across the province.

The emotional release of the Armistice was also tempered by the aftereffects of a stunning marine tragedy. On the night of October 25-26, 1918, the Canadian Pacific Steamships' *Princess Sophia* slipped off a reef that had held her captive in the Lynn Canal for two days, and foundered. There were no survivors among the 343 passengers and crew. The loss of the *Sophia* was the worst disaster involving British Columbia shipping.

The steamship was one of the finest employed by CPS on its northern routes. She left Skagway late in the evening of October 23, bound for Vancouver. The wind was rising and soon heavy snow squalls cut visibility to near-zero—fairly common

Victoria Daily Times

WEATHER FORECAST

For 36 hours ending 5 p. m. Sunday: Victoria and vicinity—Strong winds or gales, mostly easterly and southerly, unsettled and mild, with rain. Lower Mainland—Easterly and southerly winds, fresh to high on the Gulf, unsettled and mild, with rain.

NO MEETINGS TO-NIGHT

All engagements are cancelled owing to prohibitory Order-in-Council against public assemblies.

VO 53. NO. 100   VICTORIA, B. C., SATURDAY, OCTOBER 26, 1918   TWENTY-TWO PAGES

DISASTER OVERWHELMS PRINCESS SOPHIA

PRINCESS SOPHIA LOST WITH ALL HANDS, ON VANDERBILT REEF; RELIEF SHIPS COULD NOT ASSIST

Steamer Had Been Exposed to Northern Winds Since Stranding; Rough Sea Was Pounding Vessel and Passengers Had Not Been Transferred to Relief Ships in Lynn Canal

The worst marine tragedy in the history of the Pacific Coast occurred last night when the Canadian Pacific steamship Princess Sophia, which on Thursday morning crashed on Vanderbilt Reef, Lynn Canal, hammered by a terrific gale, was driven across the jagged reef and lost with all hands.

Two hundred and sixty-eight passengers who were aboard the ill-fated steamship when she piled up were dashed to almost instant death.

In addition to the passengers, the Sophia carried a crew of seventy-five.

The first news of the terrible disaster was received here late this afternoon, having been flashed out from the United States wireless station at Juneau and picked up by the Canadian Government wireless service here.

"There were no survivors, the wireless message stated. Everything possible was done to aid the passengers, who on the vessel breaking up, were hurled into the seething waters whipped up by the Alaska gale.

The vessels which had been standing by were powerless to render aid. The ship, apparently, was hurled right across the reef, and those aboard her were precipitated into the raging waters.

Ashore on Thursday

The Princess Sophia crashed on the rocks at Vanderbilt Reef at 3 o'clock on Thursday morning during a heavy snow squall while on her way south from Skagway.

She took aboard at Skagway the previous night two hundred and fifty passengers composed almost wholly of Alaskans, who reached White Horse from the interior points of Alaska with the close of river navigation.

The vessel held fast, and it was at first anticipated that she would be released on the high tide occurring at 4 o'clock on Thursday. All efforts, however, failed, and as the vessel hung perilously on the reef a northerly fresh breeze sprang up in the Lynn canal causing the ship to pound hard.

A bad sea was kicked up, making it impracticable to launch the lifeboats and transfer the passengers to the craft which had hurried to the scene immediately the S. O. S. call had been flashed broadcast.

Among the vessels which have been standing by the ship since she piled up on the rocky ledge are the light-house tender Cedar and the Peterson, both owned by the United States Government, and a large number of smaller craft, mostly fishing vessels, of which there are hundreds in Northern waters.

The auxiliary schooner King & Winge, the vessel which rescued the Karluk party, of the Stefansson Expedition, from Wrangel Island, has also been hovering near in an effort to render assistance to the stranded passengers.

Many Would Be Rescued

In view of the fact that such a large number of vessels were standing by the officials of the steamship company are inclined to the belief that in the event of the Princess Sophia slipping off the reef a large number would have been picked up.

Shipping men who know the northern waters say that a bad sea is kicked up with a fresh breeze from the north and it is contended that it would be impossible to attempt the transfer of passengers while the wind remained in that quarter.

Apart from the item of heavy gales the news that the C. P. R. steamer was ashore comparatively little information has since filtered through regarding the ship and her load of human freight.

Although Vanderbilt Reef is only about forty miles distant from Juneau the means of communication are said to be very poor.

No Confirmation Yet.

Capt. J. W. Troup, manager of C. P. R. Coast steamships, on being notified of the wireless report to the effect that the Sophia had slipped from the reef at once attempted to get into telegraphic communication with Juneau and other points, but up to a late hour this afternoon had received no confirmation of the reported marine tragedy.

The wireless message from which the report emanated was flashed from Juneau to Ketchikan and relayed from Prince Rupert. The message was picked up by the Dominion Government wireless here.

Hardly Conceivable

"It is hardly conceivable. I cannot believe it," said Capt. J. W. Troup when seen this afternoon while endeavoring to get into telegraphic communication with Juneau to secure confirmation or denial of the rumor.

"The company," he added, "did everything to render immediate assistance to the Sophia's passengers by sending the Princess Alice, the best steamer available. The Princess Alice did not reach the scene of the disaster until early

to-morrow morning, after making a fast run up the Coast.

The Princess Alice, Capt. Slater, left Vancouver on Saturday night. She is equipped with powerful wireless but no direct message has been received from the ship that might throw any light on the reported disaster.

The only news channel available is the wireless as the telegraphic cable to Skagway is said to be out of commission.

A Fine Vessel

The Princess Sophia is one of the finest vessels engaged in the Northern t-ade. She is a steel screw steamship of 2,320 tons gross and 1,466 tons net register, and was built in 1912 at the Paisley yard of the liow. McLachlan Co., Ltd. The vessel was originally designed for the Queen Charlotte Islands service, but on her delivery in this Coast she was transferred to the Alaska trade.

Capt. F. L. Locke, her master, is one of the most experienced navigators in the service of the C. P. R., who has been master of vessels in the Northern service for many years.

The human cargo which the Princess Sophia transported out of Skagway was probably the most varied group or crowd that ever sailed away from the North. They were among the last of the Alaska exodus.

Eager to get "outside" to escape the rigors of the winter hundreds of old-timers intent upon having a good time with their hard-earned gold, at the first sign of snow, caught the last of the river boats out of Fairbanks and Dawson.

Between October 16 and 21 some 850 people rushed Whitehorse and Skagway, and it was a despondent multitude when it was learned that practically no steamship accommodation was available.

Over 300 of the Alaskan travellers were accommodated on the G. T. P. steamship Prince Rupert, which made a special trip North for the purpose.

As the Prince Rupert backed away from the Skagway dock her crowd sent up ringing cheers, but the crowd standing on the wharf realizing, no doubt, that they might be stranded there all winter, refused to respond and watched the vessel steam away in silence.

Most of those left behind had the misfortune to catch the Princess Sophia.

S. S. PRINCESS SOPHIA

AUSTRIAN GOVERNMENT IS GETTING READY TO DEMOBILIZE FORCES

London, Oct. 26.—An official statement, according to which the demobilization of the Austro-Hungarian army is being prepared, has been published by the newspapers of Vienna, an Exchange Telegraph dispatch from Copenhagen says.

Basel, Oct. 26.—Vienna newspapers are publishing articles relative to preparations for the demobilization of the army.

Zurich, Oct. 26.—Prince Frederick Lobkowitz and Baron Madherny, who represent the strongest anti-German tendencies at Vienna, have left that city for Switzerland charged with a mission about which no details have been given, according to The Neuste Journal of Vienna.

Sailors Balked and Arthur Henderson Did Not Cross to France

London, Oct. 26.—(Reuter's)—Rt. Hon. Arthur Henderson, his secretary, and Camille Huysmanns, Belgian Socialist, were unable to reach France yesterday with Albert Thomas and M. Vandervelat, because the crew of their ship refused to sail if they were aboard. The men said that they would not sail with Pacifists and pro-Germans. Mr. Henderson and his two companions left the ship and hailed a taxicab, but the driver refused to take them and they had to carry their luggage to the station. Mr. Henderson subsequently stated in London that he was going to Paris to meet Samuel Gompers in connection with the organization of a world labor conference after the war.

German Submarine Activity Past Week Almost Negligible

London, Oct. 26.—The German submarine activity reached such a low state this week as to be almost negligible as a war measure, notwithstanding that many more U boats are hunting in the Atlantic and the Mediterranean. The British Admiralty looks upon this situation as part of the German peace offensive. It is believed at the Admiralty that if Germany elects to fight to the end of her resources her greatest submarine effort may be expected late in December and in January.

Two Regiments at Village in Croatia, Hungary, in Revolt

Basel, Oct. 26.—One of the newspapers of Vienna says two infantry regiments stationed at Karlowitz have revolted.

Karlowitz is a village in Croatia-Slavonia, Hungary.

Winnipeg Workmen are Fourteen to One in Favor of a Strike

Winnipeg, Oct. 26.—The strike committee of the Trades and Labor Council, of Winnipeg and Transcona, has received the official reports of the various unions on the proposed general strike as a protest against the "no strike" mandate of the Dominion Government. The proportion in favor of a general strike is given out as fourteen to one in a total vote polled of 12,000. Some 5,000 votes are yet to be received and the complete returns are not expected until the middle of next week. No immediate action will be taken pending further negotiation with the Government authorities.

Berlin is Awaiting Declaration of Terms by Entente Nations

London, Oct. 26.—The German Government is not contemplating at the present time any further note to President Wilson, says an Exchange Telegraph dispatch from Copenhagen. It is probable that the Government will make a declaration in the Reichstag to the effect that Germany is awaiting the peace conditions of the Allies.

TURN BACK THE CLOCKS

To-day is the last day of the Daylight Saving period. Clocks must be turned back an hour at 2 o'clock to-morrow morning. Make sure by turning them back before you retire to-night.

ITALIANS ADD TO BAG OF PRISONERS

Report Issued at Rome Tells of Capture of 2,000 More

Rome, Oct. 26.—In their successful assaults against the Austrians along the Piave and west of that river, the Italian forces have captured more than 2,000 prisoners in the last twenty-four hours, the War Office announced to-day.

Washington, Oct. 26.—Violent fighting continues to-day on the line where Italian forces, with the British troops co-operating, launched a new offensive against the Austrians yesterday. A Rome dispatch to the Italian Embassy here says the Fourth Army franctrated attempts of the enemy to reconquer territory lost yesterday, and further attempts are being made.

The message adds that the Italian troops are continuing to advance along the lower Mati, in Albania, and that the Albanian tribesmen are taking up arms against the Austrians and fighting under the Italian colors.

JUNKERS GIVE IN ON ALSACE QUESTION

At Least Solf Says Germany Agrees to Regulation as Wilson Proposed

Amsterdam, Oct. 26.—"As for Alsace-Lorraine, it is at once clear that as these territories are expressly mentioned among President Wilson's fourteen points, we agree to the regulation of these questions," said Dr. Solf, the German Foreign Secretary, in addressing the Reichstag on Thursday, (in the address referred to President Wilson said that "the wrong done to France by Prussia in 1871 in the matter of Alsace-Lorraine, which has unsettled the peace of the world for nearly fifty years, should be righted.")

"Moreover, having accepted President Wilson's programme as the basis of the entire peace work," the Secretary continued, "we will loyally and in the sense of complete justice and fairness fulfill the programme in all directions and at all points."

Washington, Oct. 26.—The question of Alsace-Lorraine is purely a German internal question, declares Karl Hauss, the new Governor of Alsace-Lorraine, in a statement published in The Strassburg Gazette. The statement is a reply to declarations made in the Reichstag by Dr. George Ricklin, a Deputy from Alsace-Lorraine, and amounts to a Government manifesto. It has been issued in agreement with other Deputies in Alsace-Lorraine.

The statement of Hauss declares that the future of Alsace-Lorraine must be decided by a vote of the population and that it is an internal question for Germany, with which a peace conference could have nothing to do. It concludes by saying that a new era is opening for Alsace-Lorraine which will enable the two provinces to form a point of reconciliation between France and Germany, "and to collaborate in establishing a compromise between two civilizations called to work in common for the safety and prosperity of humanity."

FUEL SITUATION IN ONTARIO MADE WORSE BY PRESENT EPIDEMIC

Toronto, Oct. 26.—The outbreak of Spanish influenza has demoralized labor conditions in the mining districts from which Ontario draws its supply of fuel. Most discouraging reports have reached the Ontario Fuel Administration within the last few days and the administration considers it necessary to notify the province that every coal dealer in the province has even now begun a critical turn and that a serious fuel emergency exists in Ontario.

A Citizen's Loan.

BRITISH GAIN NORTH AND SOUTH OF VALENCIENNES AND FRENCH ON OISE-AISNE FRONT PUSH FORWARD

Germans Have Lost 7,000 Square Miles of Belgian and French Territory Since July 18; Coalfields in North France Recovered by Allies

London, Oct. 26.—British forces continue to progress between Valenciennes and Tournai, according to Field-Marshal Haig's report to-day. The village of Maulde, on the front north of Valenciennes, was taken last night. South of Valenciennes British troops gained two successes on the border of the Mormal Forest to-day, capturing Mount Carmel and Englefontaine. British patrols progressed north of the railway between Valenciennes and Le Quesnoy.

The statement reads as follows:

"Early to-day we carried out a successful minor operation on the borders of the Forest of Mormal, capturing the hill known as Mount Carmel and the village of Englefontaine, with a number of prisoners. Farther north our patrols have made progress at certain points north of the Le Quesnoy-Valenciennes railroad.

"A determined counter - attack launched by enemy troops yesterday evening against our positions on the railway northeast of Maing was met by the troops of the 51st Division with the bayonet and repulsed with heavy losses. Our line was advanced yesterday between Valenciennes and Tournai and the villages of Oromes and Maulde captured."

Paris, Oct. 26.—On the Serre front, southwest of Marle, French troops last night captured the village of Mortiers after violent fighting. The War Office announced this afternoon. Between the Oise and the Serre the French forces maintained contact with the enemy.

The statement follows:

"During the night there was heavy artillery fighting between the Oise and the Serre. Contact was maintained with the enemy all along the front north of Mortiers, which fell into their hands after a violent fight in which they took 167 prisoners, including two officers.

Held Their Gains.

"East of the Souche the night was marked by energetic reactions on the part of the enemy infantry. Rather lively fighting occurred, especially in the outskirts of Petit Caumont. In spite of German counter-attacks our troops maintained their positions east of the village.

"The battle continued until the end of the day between Sissone and Chateau Porcien. Our troops, breaking up the resistance of the Germans, carried the strong positions organized in 1917 and which the Germans had continued to reinforce between Banogne, Recouvrance and the Herpy mill on a front of seven kilometres, attaining a depth of three kilometres at certain points. Our troops pushed forward their line as far as the road from Recouvrance to Conde-le-Herpy. More to the right French troops captured the Herpy mill and several centres of resistance. We took a number of prisoners and a considerable quantity of material.

"There was no change in the situation on the rest of the front."

Washington, Oct. 26.—Summarizing the situation on the Western battlefront to-day, General March, Chief of Staff of the United States Army, said the Germans have evacuated or lost 7,000 square miles of Belgian and French territory since July 18; that 400 square miles have been freed during the past week and that all the coalfields in Northern France have been reconquered except a five-mile tract where the advance of the Allies now is being pressed near the Belgian border.

General March pointed out that the Franco-American line from the Meuse to the Oise stood virtually parallel to the great railway line near the Belgian border and constituted a threat against that line throughout its entire length.

EVE OF CANADA'S GREATEST DRIVE FOR VICTORY FINDS CITY READY TO BUY BONDS

Backed by a record of unceasing patriotism, and with her Victory Loan organization perfected, Victoria, on the eve of the launching of the greatest financial drive in Canadian history, is ready to start on Monday a whirlwind attack which will not end until all barriers have been thrown down, and the $5,000,000 objective has been reached.

In spite of all opposition, everything humanly possible, says R. F. Taylor, Chairman of the Local Committee, has been done to make the campaign a supreme triumph. It only remains for the people of the city to buy bonds and to do it in a way which will cause the least possible delay and friction to those in charge. Without the support and co-operation of the individual citizen, the most perfect organization will fail. "Let every man and woman on the Island," said Mr. Taylor this morning, "know exactly how far he or she can go, when the drive starts. And let them go the limit. If this has been decided beforehand we shall win. Remember, the work is great, and the time is short. But I am sure Victoria, as always, will keep faith."

Everything is Ready.

"Everything we can do has been done," said Mr. Taylor. "The organization of every unit is complete. We have received the most hearty support in all quarters, and no single request made by me has been refused. And I have been carried out in a manner that gives me confidence now, at the last minute, that our Island will come up to the scratch.

A Citizen's Loan.

"We have a most energetic body of canvassers," continued Mr. Taylor. "These have been fully instructed in the details of the Loan. But I would appeal to the citizens to assist them in all ways. It will be impossible for them to answer all the questions asked, but such interrogations will be cheerfully answered at the central office. Again, I people request the can

(Concluded on page 2.)

COUNT APPONYI IS REPORTED TO BE NEW HUNGARIAN PREMIER

London, Oct. 26.—Count Apponyi has been appointed Hungarian Premier in succession to Dr. Wekerle, according to a Vienna dispatch to the Politiken, of Copenhagen, forwarded by the correspondent of the Exchange Telegraph Company.

CAMP SHERMAN, ILLINOIS, FREE OF IN

Kravelo, Sixty Miles Northeast of Nish, Taken by Serbians

London, Oct. 26.—Kravelo, sixty miles northeast of Nish, has been occupied by Serbian troops, says a Serbian official statement issued here to-day. In the same region Serbian troops crossed the Tsrnitsa River.

German Telephones.

Hamilton, Oct. 26.—The Hamilton Board of Control has agreed to join with the other Ontario cities which are opposing the increase in rates proposed by the Bell Telephone Company.

A stunning marine disaster takes precedence over news from the Western Front in the final weeks of the war.

Hard aground, the Princess Sophia *awaits her fate in Lynn Canal. All 343 aboard die when she eventually slips off the reef and sinks.*

THE DECADE IN HEADLINES
« 1918 cont'd »

PRINCESS SOPHIA SLIPS OFF LEDGE AND GOES TO BOTTOM

The CPR steamship had gone aground two days earlier and was believed to be in little danger. The official death toll is 343.

The World, October 26, 1918

ENTENTE TRIUMPHS

With one of the biggest and blackest streamers in its history, *The Times* proclaims armistice in the Great War. The news sparks huge demonstrations in the city as well as the rest of BC.

Victoria Times, November 11, 1918

VICTORIA CROSS WON BY LIEUT.-COL. PECK WHO DID BRILLIANT WORK AT FRONT

"Col. Peck seems to have been one of the big men of the Canadian army, an army which is full of much splendid material," says the *News* in printing the official *London Gazette* announcement. Peck, who is MP for Prince Rupert's riding of Skeena, wins the Empire's top honour for his gallantry under fire at Cagnicourt, France, on September 2. (BC's VC winners are listed in Appendix D.)

Prince Rupert Daily News, November 20, 1918

weather conditions in Alaskan waters at that time of the year. Shortly after 3 a.m. the next day, the *Princess Sophia* ran aground on a mid-fjord reef some fifty kilometres northwest of Juneau.

High tide failed to free the liner and she remained stuck while rescue vessels struggled to reach the area. By the 25th, the storm had worsened to such an extent that the attending fleet of small vessels was advised to abandon any thoughts of rescue and seek shelter. Sometime between 6 p.m., when darkness and gale-whipped snow obscured the scene, and daybreak the next morning, when her mast was seen sticking out of the sea, the *Princess Sophia* slipped out of the embrace of the reef and went to her doom. As darkness fell, a last, weak radio transmission from the ship had said, "Just time to say goodbye. We are foundering."

The maritime drama pushed much of the war news off the front pages. The *Victoria Times* and *The World* were the first to report the final act of the tragedy, but all the dailies kept their readers abreast of developments from the time the first news of the grounding was received on October 24.[2] Sadly, they also noted the arrival in Vancouver of the *Princess Alice*, "a veritable floating hearse" with 157 coffins, on the same day word was received of the Armistice.

Fifteen months earlier, the province had marked the passing of Sir Richard McBride, its longest-serving premier. McBride, who had been knighted for his service to the country, died August 6, 1917. He had been ill for some time, and had resigned as premier on his forty-fifth birthday, December 15, 1915.

William Bowser assumed the premiership, but lasted less than a year. He called an election for September 14, 1916, only to preside at one of the biggest reversals in British Columbia's political history. Bowser's Conservatives, who had won thirty-nine seats under McBride in 1912, were swept away by the Liberals, who took thirty-six seats to nine for the governing party. Harlan Brewster became premier November 23, but died suddenly of pneumonia while returning from a trip to

Ottawa. He was succeeded on March 6, 1918, by John Oliver, who would guide BC through the victorious final months of the war and well into the twenties.

But the decade wasn't all war and strife and politics. There was also renewal and progress to go along with the failures and disasters. On the sporting front, a new leisure activity promised relaxation and exercise, while women took some significant strides out of the dark ages of male dominance.

With men naturally concentrating on more momentous happenings, the women quietly collected some impressive victories. On April 5, 1917, they were enfranchised in BC, which meant women were now "persons" in law and could vote. The *Victoria Times* chose Page 7 for the story. It also spared three lines of type on Page 5 to announce the appointment July 19 of Helen McGill as the first female judge in BC. (As with *The Times*, *The Colonist* buried the news in a roundup of brief items. The Vancouver papers apparently ignored the appointment altogether.) On March 1, 1918, Mrs. Ralph Smith made her maiden speech on the floor of the legislature. She was BC's first female MLA, and would later become the first cabinet minister.

The influence of women's suffrage also reached into that last male bastion, the saloon. After years of rallies, petitions and marches, the temperance movement—with women and the evangelical clergy in the van—succeeded in getting a referendum on prohibition on the ballot for the 1916 election. The prohibitionists won narrowly, and BC went dry on October 1, 1917 (although for only a few years).

By this time, many females and their male companions had taken up the indoor pastime of ice skating. A new spectator sport was also available: ice hockey. Frank and Lester Patrick, the brothers who brought this about, built arenas in Vancouver and Victoria that included the first artificial ice plants in the country. Although both cities claim credit for bringing indoor ice to the outdoor sport of skating, reports in the press during December of 1911 give the nod to Frank's Vancouver arena (at 10,500 seats, "the globe's largest indoor sports emporium"). On December 21, the ice plant worked to perfection and the public came to skate. Lester's 4,000-seat Victoria arena opened to the public on Christmas Day. It hosted the first hockey match played on artificial ice in Canada, January 3, 1912.

If this riotous decade was a theatrical production, a fitting last act might be the return of 1,400 veterans of the war. They arrived in Vancouver on January 23, 1919, aboard the *Empress of Asia* after sailing directly from Liverpool via the Panama Canal. The 40,000 dignitaries and citizens who greeted the surviving warriors did so with joy tempered by relief.

Unlike the return of another generation from the South African War nineteen years earlier, the mood was different. In 1900, the boys were returning from a colonial adventure. Kids' stuff, almost. The Great War was a grown-up man's war, a killing conflict that produced more survivors than heroes. France and Belgium had been a maelstrom of blood, mud and death, a war to end all wars. Peace—and life—was precious in British Columbia in 1919.

---

1   J.S.H. Matson, publisher of *The Colonist*, was a good friend of Currie (and indeed was his boss when he entered the insurance business). Because of their relationship, Matson must have known about Currie's debt, but not a word appeared in his newspaper.

2   Pierre Berton, in his book *Starting Out*, perpetuates the myth that a journeyman editor named T. Harry Wilson placed his paper's "exclusive" on the sinking under Shipping Notes on the Marine Page. Cute, but false.

THE DECADE IN HEADLINES
« 1919 »

EMPRESS OF ASIA BRINGS VANCOUVER'S WARRIORS HOME

Some 40,000 citizens cheer the return of nearly 1,400 veterans of the Great War. After sailing from Liverpool via the Panama Canal, some of those aboard noted that there was only one white cook and that the cheese "moved quite well without help" at times.

Daily World, January 23, 1919

THE TWENTIES:
TO THE
PRECIPICE

« 1920 – 1929 »

The post-war decade that became the Roaring Twenties south of the border progressed at a somewhat more sedate pace in British Columbia. Despite growing connections across the Pacific and to the east and south, the province was still wont to go its own way. Its alienation from the rest of Canada was not entirely extinguished by participation in the Great War, nor was its penchant for the weird and unusual.

Oh, a few things manufactured in America trickled northward: flappers, saddle shoes, jazz, bobbed hair (for the women), slicked-back hair (for the men), raccoon coats. Some British Columbians succumbed to the world-wide mah-jongg craze. The younger set danced the Charleston at the Alexandra in Vancouver ("Home of Refined Dancing") or surrounded by greenery at the new Crystal Garden in Victoria. Those who didn't know the steps could learn at one of the dance studios advertised in the papers. Others listened to syncopated swing on their phonographs and that new medium, the radio. On the movie screens, they ogled Clara Bow (the "It" Girl), or swooned at the image of Rudolf Valentino. Charlie Chaplin, Greta Garbo, Mary Pickford and Douglas Fairbanks offered evenings of comedy, romance, adventure and escape. In October of 1928, real talking pictures started to replace the silent versions in BC theatres.

The first licensed private commercial broadcasting stations in British Columbia were at *The Province*, *The Sun* and *The World*. *The Province* beat the other two by going on the air first—March 13, 1922. Initial radio programs consisted of musical selections for a few hours each evening except Sunday, and they were picked up on crude receiving sets with earphones. Receiving licences cost $1 (a government levy not discontinued until 1953).

The World, after boasting about its high-powered station atop Spencer's department store in downtown Vancouver, flogged $25 "crystal detector receiving sets" supplied by the Trans-Canada Radiovox Co. Readers were assured that the sets were easy to install at home. Soon, however, the mysteries of this new medium were unravelled, and radios became available without the added complications of antennae, ground connections or special telephone headsets. Within a few years, the press was carrying ads for such brands as Stewart-Warner, Marconi, Atwater Kent and Westinghouse Radiola.

THE DECADE IN HEADLINES
« 1920 »

POLICE 'RED COATS' WILL BE RETAINED
The Dominion Police and the Royal North-West Mounted Police are amalgamated into the Royal Canadian Mounted Police. The new force gradually assumes some duties in BC that were once the responsibility of the Provincial Police.
The Province, February 1, 1920

ORDER OPENING OF OUTER DOCKS
The ship-docking complex at Ogden Point in Victoria's outer harbour is open for business.
The Colonist, October 13, 1920

AIRCRAFT FROM SOUND BRINGS LAST MINUTE MAIL FOR ORIENT
The first official air mail in Western Canada is delivered by float plane from Seattle to Victoria.
Victoria Times, October 15, 1920

PROVINCE ENDORSES GOVERNMENT CONTROL
Most of Page One is devoted to the voters' overwhelming rejection of prohibition in favour of government control of liquor sales. BC's "dry" experiment — approved in 1916 by a narrow majority — lasts only a few years.
The Colonist, October 20, 1920

THE DECADE IN HEADLINES
« 1921 »

GOVERNMENT CONTROL OFF TO A GOOD START IN CITY, BEER QUESTION IS SETTLED

"The good ship British Columbia was safely launched at 11 a.m. today on a sea of foaming liquor, 500 barrels deep," begins *The World*'s Page One story as it records the opening of government liquor stores.

The World, June 15, 1921

LARGE CROWD AT DEDICATION

A paragraph is added to international history, says *The Province*, as it describes the dedication of the Peace Arch on the Canada-US boundary just north of Blaine, Wash. The event, commemorating 100 years of peace between the two countries, attracts a crowd of 10,000.

The Province, September 6, 1921

HUDSON'S BAY CO.'S STORE WELCOMES PUBLIC TO-DAY; INAUGURAL LUNCHEON

That commercial icon of Canada's West—the HBC—opens its new Victoria store on Douglas Street.

Victoria Times, September 19, 1921

Commercials and sponsored programs did not become commonplace until the early 1930s, because Canadian regulators lasted much longer than their American counterparts in preserving the "purity" of the airwaves. The newspapers abandoned their stations after a few years (cost of programming was certainly a factor), when it was determined they didn't increase circulation as much as was hoped. But the papers did devote editorial space to radio news and schedules. In the thirties, special radio sections in some weekend editions were a harbinger of the space later devoted to television entertainment.

Meanwhile, such names in the news as Peter Verigin, Brother XII and *Beryl G* could be found in the various dailies during the decade, as would Winston Churchill, Percy Williams and the Prince of Wales, among others. But along with the famous visitors, local heroes and the ever-changing cast of political characters, there was progress.

Modest at first, the prosperity that replaced a brief post-war slump grew until it was virtually out of control at decade's end. If the twenties really "roared" in BC, they did so in 1929 before the Great Crash abruptly shut everyone up. Until then, however, there was solid, if not spectacular growth. The forest industry recovered nicely from the uncertainties of the previous decade and expanded on the local and world fronts. Exports of wood products rose, thanks in part to the Panama Canal. Vancouver gained importance as a port, as did Victoria. Wheat from the Prairies was funnelled into grain terminals in Burrard Inlet and began filling ships' bottoms. In Victoria, the Ogden Point docks were completed in 1920, making the capital city accessible to deep-sea trade from Europe via the Canal. The agriculture industry—thanks to a farmer-premier—expanded.

Vancouver grew, too, to the west and southward toward the Marpole district (named after a CPR superintendent), as the forests that once ringed the city were replaced by housing and streets. Burnaby was on the verge of assuming its role as a suburban bedroom community. On southern Vancouver Island, Victoria's growth was closer to stagnant than riproaring. The Saanich Peninsula drew some interest, but Victoria seemed to be accepting its twentieth-century destiny as a one-industry town: politics.

In the legislative corridors, the Liberal government of Premier John Oliver started the decade on a shaky note. The substantial majority gained in 1916 shrank to only three after the 1920 election (25 Liberals, 15 Conservatives, 3 Socialists and 4 independents). Oliver was a man of the soil. A farmer from Delta with only a basic education, his rough clothes and rustic ways caused many an urbane snicker in the Legislative Buildings during his career as an MLA.

The Liberal-leaning *Victoria Times* liked him, however. "He is a true type of the self-made man," it said in an editorial. "Without the advantages of early mental training and instruction enjoyed by many of his confreres in public life, he has forged to the front by virtue of marked natural ability." When chosen premier to replace the late Harlan Brewster, Oliver still wore the tweeds, cloth cap and sensible boots of the landsman venturing into the city.

For a while, the voters didn't mind. If the 1920 results were a wake-up call, however, the 1924 election was a slap in the face. Despite road-building programs, agricultural reform and a tentative start toward social assistance, the Liberal majority government turned into a minority one. Arrayed against the 23 Liberals elected were 17 Conservatives and 8 from splinter parties (Oliver lost his own seat and had to win a by-election). The pesky Provincial Party, a mixture of malcontents unhappy with the prevailing political situation, took three seats. This is the sort of splinter group that drives mainstream parties crazy by siphoning off vital votes. In 1924, Oliver managed to stay in the premier's seat by gaining the support of three Labour MLAs and the lone independent.

Party loyalties notwithstanding, the House unanimously passed a resolution in December of that year asking Ottawa to denounce all treaties curbing Canada's power to halt Asiatic immigration. Amendments to the federal Chinese Immigration Act in 1923 and 1924 (among which were the elimination of the head tax and and a tighter definition of "merchant") were so sweeping "that the door to the North Pacific had been slammed in the face of the Chinese," as the *Victoria Times* put it.

BC's legislators wanted more, however. The sponsor of the resolution, Provincial Secretary William Sloan, said the problem was now the Japanese, whose "natural increase in numbers was alarming." In a detailed *Times* story brutal in its frank discussion of white bigotry (Sloan was quoted, for instance, as boasting he had never worn a shirt laundered by a Chinese), the point was finally made that the legislature was upset because trade treaties with Japan were usually the basis for Dominion rejection of BC's own anti-immigration statutes.

The resolution had little outward effect, and the Japanese question, which had been simmering since their actions during the 1900 and 1901 Fraser River salmon strikes, remained a sore point until 1941, when Japanese-Canadians' presence in BC was deemed a threat to the war effort. As for the Chinese, the federal restrictions ensured that only eight entered Canada legally between 1924 and 1947.

As the voters changed their attitude about governments, they also did so on the matter of liquor. Sober second thoughts—if you'll pardon the expression—brought about a reversal of the prohibition vote of 1916. British Columbians who had so cheerfully rejected demon rum back then voted even more enthusiastically for its return in 1920. And, as *The Colonist* noted with muted surprise in its Page One story, the women who led the fight against booze in 1916 campaigned actively for the stuff four years later.

Apparently, it all depended on how the question was phrased. What men and women were voting for in 1920 was moderation—through government control of sales. On June 15, 1921, the experiment was launched "on a sea of foaming liquor," in the words of *The World*.

Thus the lasting legacy of Premier Oliver (apart from having a town named after him and at least one school) would seem to be the BC Liquor Control Board, which still has the last word on the province's drinking habits. (A strange byproduct of the new LCB regulations was the hotel beer parlour. The government did not want the return of the saloon, so it mandated that these drinking establishments be confined to hotels, sell only beer and allow no standing at the bar. Even stranger was the issue of women in the parlours. Legally, they were allowed to drink beer, too, but temperance advocates, upset at the weaker sex being tempted by these iniquitous dens, threatened to force another plebiscite. So the hotel operators agreed informally to keep women out. This more or less worked until July, 1927, when "agitation on the part of certain ... licensees," as *The Province* put it, resulted in a new protocol allowing separate rooms for women.)

Getting your own parlours in which to drink beer while being safely segregated from the smelly, noisy male was, one supposes, a victory of sorts for women. But it was small potatoes when compared with other advances. On October 18, 1929,

THE DECADE IN HEADLINES
« 1922 »

PUBLIC CAUTIOUS ON CHANGE IN RULE OF ROAD

The change to right-hand drive in BC brings "no more accidents than usual," *The Times* observes in its January 2 edition. It also notes that many motorists intend to leave their cars at home until the switch becomes familiar.

Victoria Times, January 1, 1922

ON PILGRIMAGE TO VARSITY GROUNDS

To a marching song of dubious rhyme and metre, nearly 1,200 UBC students tramp from downtown Vancouver to the university's designated Point Grey site. The march, which will become known as the Great Trek, is in protest over government inaction and the crowded conditions of the students' temporary quarters.

The Province, October 28, 1922

MAKE WOMEN LIABLE TO SERVE ON JURIES

An amendment to the provincial Jury Act adds women to those persons eligible for duty.

The Colonist, December 15, 1922

The Daily Colonist.

(ESTABLISHED 1858)

WEATHER FORECASTS	COLONIST TELEPHONES
Victoria and Vicinity—Easterly and southerly winds, partly cloudy and mild, with showers.	Business Office 11
	Circulation 12
Lower Mainland—Easterly winds, mostly cloudy and mild, with showers.	Job Printing 197
	Editorial Rooms 50
	Editor 2111

NO. 264—SIXTY-SECOND YEAR   VICTORIA, BRITISH COLUMBIA, THURSDAY, OCTOBER 21, 1920   TWENTY PAGES

PROVINCE ENDORSES GOVERNMENT CONTROL

Government Control Endorsed by Electors

More Liberal Liquor Regulations Is the Demand of Victoria Voters Who Repudiate Prohibition Act—New Principle Given Majority of 4,195 in the City

CITY PLEBISCITE RESULTS

Division	Prohibition	Govt. Control	Spoiled	Absentee
One	696	1,164	10	275
Two	860	1,788	27	28
Three	1,405	2,257	29	93
Four	902	1,664	25	114
Five	1,228	2,413	34	32
Total	5,091	9,286	125	542

Majority for Government Control, 4,195.
Total ballots cast, 14,502.

Victoria, by the overwhelming majority of 4,195 for the principle of Government control of liquor, participated yesterday in the Province-wide repudiation of the existing Prohibition enactment, and voiced its desire for a change in the present system of dealing with the liquor traffic.

Never before in the history of the city has such a majority been registered as the public expression of opinion on an issue submitted to the people. The result was a surprise even to the supporters of the Government Control principle; it was a stunning blow to the "drys," who were confident that the Prohibition Act would be supported even in the face of what they admitted was an active and aggressive opposition.

When the returns, not alone from Victoria and adjacent polling districts, but from all over the Province, kept coming in telling of a tremendous slump towards more liberal liquor regulations and wholesale condemnation of the existing conditions, there was gloom at the Prohibition headquarters.

Majorities Everywhere

Every ward in the city gave a substantial majority for Government Control, as will be seen from the accompanying table setting forth the figures in detail. The vote polled was a remarkable expression of the keen interest taken by Victorians in the issue.

The total ballot cast was 14,502 out of a total on the list of 18,992 names. It was seventy-five per cent of the total possible vote. In view of the fact that the women's vote—the vote relied upon by the Prohibitionists to carry their cause to victory—is nearly one-half of the total, it is apparent that Government Control received very strong support from the fair sex, despite the emotional appeals made during the campaign to enlist the sympathy of that element for the dry column.

Throughout the day at every one of the five polling stations there was a steady stream of voters on foot, or in vehicles, wending their way to the polls. Returning Officer Captain Carew-Martin, had all his arrangements made for the voting and the lack of confusion and rapidity with which the ballots were handled speaks volumes for the efficient manner in which he dealt with his onerous duties.

Keen Interest Shown

The Prohibition Party and the Liberty League were early in the field getting out the vote. But it was apparent that the great bulk of the electors did not require urging. They were out in force and early, over forty per cent of the vote. It is estimated having been registered by noon. The fact that the afternoon was a holiday assisted in making the vote a record one.

It was the first time that the great bulk of the women exercised the franchise and they took full advantage of the opportunity. During the afternoon when the stores and business places were closed the polls were swarmed by young girls who were casting their first ballots, and they appeared to thoroughly enjoy the experience.

At the five polling places a total of sixty-two booths were receiving ballots and when the polls closed and the count commenced the tally was quickly made, no booth having more than 256 ballots to count. Before 5 p.m. the city result was known.

The public interest in the outcome was manifested after the close of the poll when a large and enthusiastic crowd gathered on Broad Street in front of The Colonist and cheered to the echo every bulletin telling of the success of the Government control principle. The enthusiasm increased as returns from outside points came in, in every case showing defeat for Prohibition. When it was reported that Vancouver, like Victoria, was polling almost two to one for Government control the dense throng let itself lose and the welkin rang.

Absentee Voting

It was the first time that the principle of absentee voting has been tried in the Province. Under it an elector away from the riding in which he resides and where he registered his name on the voters' list, may vote in the riding in which he happens to be at the time of voting. He less than 542 such absentee votes were recorded here yesterday, the bulk at the Number One polling station, Yates Street, that being the most central location. This system proved a godsend to hundreds, who were thus enabled to spend the day in the country and yet be enabled to record their vote by calling at the nearest polling station in their vicinity and voting for Victoria. By reason of the absentee votes, the actual and final polish of the city's vote will not be known until this afternoon.

final count of ballots by the returning officer must commence not later than eight days of the election day, and at this count the absentee ballots will be tallied. But in view of the sweeping nature of yesterday's vote for Government control, no absentee vote, however strongly it may go for Prohibition, can in any degree effect the result.

For Government Control

In the adjacent electoral ridings of Esquimalt and Saanich the vote went just as strongly for Government control as in the city. Owing to the scattered nature of the polling places in Esquimalt, it was not possible to get all the returns, but those received showed the attitude of the electors of these sections.

There were no untoward incidents marking the day's polling, the utmost order being maintained throughout.

Terrorism in Ireland Will Be Suppressed

Sir Hamar Greenwood Makes Prediction in Speech Answering Mr. Henderson in Regard to Reprisals — Rule of Island by Assassins to Be Terminated

LONDON, Oct. 20.—A motion made by Mr. Arthur Henderson in the House of Commons today calling for a public inquiry into reprisals in Ireland was withdrawn this evening after a heated debate. The Government, which had firmly resisted the demand for the inquiry, had a large majority in the House at the time of the withdrawal.

While admitting armed forces of the crown had suffered provocation, the Government's policy Mr. Henderson asserted, seemed to him to aim at stamping out Nationalist opinion and breaking the spirit of the Irish people.

The defense of the Government, set up by Sir Hamar Greenwood, Chief Secretary for Ireland, was that "while the Sinn Feiners put the emphasis on the reprisals, I put it on the provocation."

He insisted that no case has been made out for what he characterized as Arthur Henderson's insulting resolution demanding an inquiry into the reprisals by the police and soldiers in Ireland. He incidentally remarked that American spy no longer embrace ing immigration from Ireland because it did not desire to admit the vast total of disturbing elements in the republic, and he declared his intention to rule Ireland from end to end, including Ulster, in search for guns.

Unsupported Assertions

Sir Hamar Greenwood, declared Mr. Henderson, had not produced a single case to justify his motion. He stoutly defended the Government forces against the charges, and declared a great majority of the cases were alleged against policemen or soldiers acting in self-defense.

The Chief Secretary detailed the circumstances of the murder of Inspector Brady. He admitted there had been reprisals in this case. Three shops belonging to notorious Sinn Feiners had been burned, he said, and seven of their shops smashed. He was convinced, however, that the persons who suffered from the reprisals had possibly helped in the murder of the inspector. He regretted the reprisals but declared these men had no right to complain.

Reign of Terror

"The difficulty is," continued the Chief Secretary, "that there is a reign of terror which exists throughout the country. The Irish republican army, constituting all brigades, companies and platoons scattered throughout the country, with branches in England, Scotland and Wales has terrorized, until recently, nearly the whole of Ireland." I am

Continued on Page 3

CALLS ASSERTIONS VULGAR MENDACITIES

OTTAWA, Oct. 20.—Hon. C. C. Ballantyne, Minister of Marine and Fisheries, today characterized the alleged statements of William Duff, member for Lunenburg, at Lethbridge, as "vulgar mendacities." He had no further comment to make on them.

HUNCHUN INCIDENT RAISES COMPLICATION

PEKING, Oct. 19.—The recent raid by bandits upon Hunchun, a small frontier post in Eastern Manchuria, contiguous to both the Korean and Siberian borders, which at the time attracted little notice, promises to develop into a diplomatic controversy between China and Japan, involving the Korean border district south of Hunchun.

The difficulty is threatened through the sending by Japan of troops into Chinese territory, ostensibly for the protection of Japanese citizens. It was declared in Tokio that the Chinese Foreign Ministry had committed itself to allowing Japanese forces to co-operate with Chinese troops on Chinese soil in the disturbed district, but subsequently refused to agree to the sending of Japanese reinforcements to Hunchun.

ELECTION DECEMBER FOURTH, IS TIP

Government to Announce Early Contest Within Next Few Days, Is the Gossip in Inside Circles—Getting Ready

Whether or not British Columbia is to have an early election will be decided within the next few days. December 4 is the date mentioned, but if that is the present intent of the Government there is no indication of it.

Premier Oliver, when asked last evening if it was true that the Government would immediately make announcement of an election, and if December 4 was the date to be fixed, stated, as he had done on previous occasions when the possibility of an early contest was mooted, that he had nothing to say, but he intimated that the rumor that an announcement would be forthcoming today was incorrect.

Undoubtedly the result of yesterday's vote on the liquor question will have to be digested by the Government. It is no secret that whatever might be the personal opinions of the Government on that question, a victory by the Prohibitionists was fully expected by the members of the Cabinet. The overwhelming manner in which the electors relegated prohibition to the discard and supported Government control comes as a more or less disconcerting incident to the political powers that be.

A Possibility

That an early election, one called before the next session of the Legislature, was on the tapis is indicated by the warning Hon. J. W. deB. Farris, Attorney-General, gave the faithful in Vancouver the other day when he advised them to be ready for an early contest. Further, the Government has not overlooked the necessity of an active publicity campaign, and, it is stated, a Mr.

Continued on Page 19

NO AGREEMENT IS IN SIGHT

Parties to Coal Mines Dispute in Britain Have Made No Further Approaches to Effect Settlement

SOME HOPES BASED ON MR. BRACE'S PLAN

Secretary Ashton, of Manchester Miners, Believes Conference Would Have Good Results—Railwaymen Differ

LONDON, Oct. 20.—The day brought no new developments in the coal strike. Neither side to the dispute made any approach to the other, and no outside mediation was instituted.

It is still hoped that the proposal of William Brace, president of the South Wales Miners' Federation, may eventually lead to renewed negotiations, but it is admitted that it must first be adopted officially by the miners' executive, which has so far been impossible, as members of the executive are scattered all over the country.

Advocacy by some extremists of withdrawing the pumping staffs from the mines finds few supporters among the miners generally. Robert Smillie and other leaders are strongly against it.

Renewed efforts were made at the Ministry of Labor today through negotiations by the parties concerned to avert a strike on railroads and in the transport industry. The negotiations, however, were adjourned until tomorrow.

Railway Men Divided

The National Union of Railwaymen, the executive committee of the Transport Workers and the Parliamentary committee of the Trades Union Congress, all held meetings this morning to consider their attitude towards the coal strike, but thus far no decisions have been taken. After approximately two hours of discussion, James Henry Thomas, general secretary of the railwaymen's union, said the whole situation had been reviewed and adjournment taken until Thursday. The executives of the Transport Workers and the Trades Union Congress continue their meetings this afternoon.

A sharp difference of opinion prevails among the railroad men. Mr. Thomas personally desires peace, it is declared, but has a strong minority of the organization's executive against him.

The national council of the Independent Labor Party adopted a resolution today expressing grave apprehension over the attitude of the Government toward the miners, "conveying as it does an aggressive challenge to the whole working class movement."

The resolution requests the Labor party to convene a special conference.

One effect of the strike will be an increase in the cost of living owing to the decline in the value of the pound sterling and the increased cost of inward bound freights, caused by the diminution of exports, declared Arthur Chamberlain, Chancellor of the Exchequer, in answering a question in the House of Commons today.

Official estimates of the number of persons thrown out of employment in other industries as the result of the coal strike are lacking, but newspaper estimates place the number at 100,000 at least, with the total growing steadily.

Reports from Morrison, Wales, state that many of the steel workers there who have been made idle by the strike have decided to emigrate to Canada at an early date.

Thomas Ashton, general secretary of the miners at Manchester, today said that if the Premier called the mineowners and the miners' officials into conference regarding more production out of the mines, the first meeting would give the Premier all guarantees to increased output he needed.

The miners' leaders were willing. Mr. Ashton said, to attend such a conference.

BANDITS MAKE RAID ON HOUSE IN THOROLD

ST. CATHERINES, Oct. 20.—Five masked bandits early yesterday morning entered the boarding-house at Thorold, Ontario, where Vasil Sungari lived and gagged the boarders. Sungari had saved up $3,000 and had intended to leave for Italy today. The bandits demanded the money, but as Monday was Thanksgiving and a holiday, Sungari had not been able to draw his savings from the bank, and the robbers got only $100 and a gold watch from the other boarders.

Magdia's Aid to China

MANILA, Oct. 20.—Approximately $250,000 has been raised in Manila for the famine-stricken Chinese Provinces. The army transport Merritt, which sails for China tomorrow, will carry several hundred tons of food supplies to the starving Chinese. Major-General Francis J. Kernan, commanding the Department of the Philippines, donated all of the vessel space on the Merritt for the relief cargo and sent an officer to superintend the distribution and supply.

MODERATION PLAN RECEIVES SUPPORT OF VAST MAJORITY

Electors in Nearly All Cities and in Great Number of Smaller Places Declare Against Present Prohibition Act and in Favor of Sale Through Government Agencies

LARGEST CENTRES MOST EMPHATIC

Vancouver Gives Record Majority of 10,176 for Proposed New System—Total in Province Is Expected to Reach Close to 30,000—Heavy Vote Is Polled

VANCOUVER, Oct. 20.—British Columbia today voted overwhelmingly in favor of Government control of the sale of liquor. At this hour, 10 o'clock, the majority in favor of Government control totals well over 15,000. Moderationists, however, claim that when the final figures are in, the majority in favor of Government control will total close to 30,000. The Moderationists, who supported Government control of the sale of liquor, have scored a great victory, and the defeat of the present "dry" act is conclusive.

All the cities on the Lower Mainland and Vancouver Island returned large majorities in favor of the repeal of the present act, the outstanding surprise of the voting being the large "wet" majority recorded in this city, of 10,176.

New Westminster and Prince Rupert registered a vote favorable to Government Control. Kamloops, Nanaimo, Fernie and Rossland did likewise.

A record vote was polled, not only in the cities and towns, but in the rural districts as well. The women took part in today's voting following an active part in the campaign, it was admitted that the women would exert influence in favor of the present regulations, and the result appears to indicate that a large number of the women voters endorsed the proposed new regulation of Government Control.

Strenuous campaigns were waged by both the prohibitionists and the moderationists, and both sides were equally confident as to the result of today's balloting.

The first referendum on the prohibition party in British Columbia was taken in 1916, and resulted in a small majority for the Drys. The vote then was 41,806 for prohibition and 38,103 against. The civilian vote was "dry," but the vote of the soldiers overseas gave a "wet" majority.

William Savage, president of the prohibition party in British Columbia tonight said to the Canadian Press that the result of the referendum showed that there had been a conclusion in the public mind on the term "Government Control." Particularly was this so with regard to the women's vote. The women thought it meant a system whereby the Government would take better control of the liquor traffic than it had done under the present act. "We shall have to wait an experience of the new system," he concluded.

ISLAND GIVES BIG VOTE FOR CONTROL

Vancouver Island's vote on the plebiscite yesterday, so far as returns from outside sections were received last night, shows Government control was overwhelmingly approved by the electors. The details, by ridings, are as follows:

Riding	Prohib'n	Govt. Control
Victoria	5,091	9,286
Saanich	1,684	3,028
Esquimalt	291	1,064
Cowichan	547	1,434
Nanaimo	854	1,936
Newcastle	806	1,057
Comox	436	1,078
Alberni	484	746
*The Islands	...	...
Totals	9,993	19,609

*No returns.

ISLAND'S VOTE IS FOR CONTROL

Practically Every Point on Vancouver Island Records Its Support of Government Control

Vancouver Island registered its verdict on the liquor plebiscite yesterday in no uncertain fashion for Government control as opposed to the present Prohibition regulations. From practically every point, from Victoria in the south to the northern parts of the Alberni ridings came returns showing the majority of the electors favoring the principle of Government control.

Owing to the scattered nature of the up-Island ridings complete returns could not be got last night, but most of the points reported. The returns so far received from the outside ridings on the Island, with the exception of The Islands riding, whence no returns have yet been received, are given below:

Esquimalt

	Prohib'n	Govt. Control
Esquimalt Mun.	244	468
Colwood	15	52
Strathcona Lodge	13	57
Otter Point	10	15
Port Renfrew	2	28

Six more polls to hear from.

Saanich

	Prohib'n	Govt. Control
Oak Bay	227	563
Ward Four	179	703
Ward Five	84	174
Ward Six	93	240

Four more points to hear from. The total was 3,028 for Government control and 1,684 for Prohibition.

Cowichan

	Prohib'n	Govt. Control
Duncan	266	651
Shawnigan Lake	27	53
Somenos	31	95
Crofton	5	59
Cowichan Station	58	140
Cowichan Lake	14	78
Cobble Hill	82	137
Westholme	9	84
Chemainus	67	111

Nanaimo

	Prohib'n	Govt. Control
City	854	1,936
Ladysmith	295	468
Northfield	36	120
Cassidy	20	61
South Wellington	45	160
North Wellington	24	86
Extension	13	86
South Cedar	48	66

Other points to hear from.

Alberni

	Prohib'n	Govt. Control
Port Alberni	173	149
Alberni	141	129
Coombs	19	20
Errington	15	32
Parksville	25	58
Tofino	2	43
Nootka	...	17
Ucluelet	4	32
Uchucklesit	16	25
Sidney Inlet	...	9
Clo-oose	3	15
Qualicum	30	79

Several more points to hear from.

Comox

	Prohib'n	Govt. Control
Courtenay	151	294
Comox	25	63
Grafton	...	23
Cumberland	127	601
Headquarters	12	62
Merville	19	94
Campbell River	26	78
Quathiaski Cove	23	51
Oyster River	...	24
Alert Bay	29	31
Saturna Island	19	38

Other points to hear from.

The Islands

No returns were forthcoming from polling places in The Islands electoral district last night.

RESULT SURPRISES PREMIER OLIVER

Had Expected Prohibition Act Would Have Been Sustained —Major Gillespie, Liberty League President, Delighted

"There is nothing I can say except that I am very much surprised," stated Premier Oliver last evening when informed of the outcome of the vote on the Plebiscite throughout the Province.

"What are the figures?" queried the Premier.

When informed that Victoria had gone in favor of Government control by over 4,000 of a majority, that Vancouver polling against the Prohibition Act is like fashion and that returns from all over the Province showed the people to be overwhelmingly in support of government control and adverse to the act which has been in force for the past three years the Premier remarked:

"I can only repeat, I am surprised. I expected that the Prohibition Act would have been approved by the electors. That is all I care to say."

The Premier asked that in view of the expression of public opinion on the matter, the necessary legislation to repeal the existing Act and to bring into effect the principle of government control will be brought down by the Government.

"The will of the people will have to be met. The Government, if it had not been prepared to meet the wishes of the majority of the electors, would not have submitted the plebiscite to them," he said.

Major Gillespie's Views

"The result of today's vote on the Plebiscite is exactly what I expected it would be when the people of this Province had opportunity to express their wishes on the liquor question," said Major Gillespie, president of the Liberty League, of the organization which opposed the Prohibition efforts in the campaign.

"Throughout the Province the issue was keenly fought out, and the result should not at rest once and for all any question of how it matter. Where the people stood on this important subject."

"The Liberty League was not standing when the issue of Prohibition versus government control by any other system of dealing with the liquor question. Our aim was to maintain, to the extent of our efforts, the liberty of the subject, who will remain in being as an organization, and will be prepared to resist to the utmost, not alone Prohibition legislation that infringes upon the liberty of the subject, but any other restriction of the liberty in any way that liberty in any other important matter affecting the welfare of the people."

Detailed Returns

VANCOUVER—Final official figures: Wet, 23,942; dry, 13,744. Majority, 10,176.

Alberni Bay—Government control, 22; Prohibition, 13.

Courtenay—Government control, 264; Prohibition, 151; spoiled, 3.

Roberts Creek—Government control, 7; Prohibition, 2.

Darcy—Government control, 21; Prohibition, 16.

Lac la Hache—Government control, 22; Prohibition, 1.

Powell River—Government control, 786; Prohibition, 140; spoiled, 4.

Cherry Creek—Prohibition, 1; Government control, 9; absent, 2.

Duck's Range—Government control, 14; Prohibition, 7; absent, 4.

Rose Hill—Government control, 7; Prohibition, 4; absent, 2.

Tappen—Government control, 19; Prohibition, 21.

Harper's Camp—Prohibition, 16; Government control, 24.

Fort Fraser—Government control, 187; Prohibition, 87.

Britannia Mines—Government control, 86; Prohibition, 42.

Squamish—Government control, 107; Prohibition, 32.

Yuskin—Prohibition, 5; Government control, 14.

Golden—Prohibition, 95; Government control, 181.

Alhambra—Prohibition, 5; Government control, 9.

Beavermouth—Prohibition, 2; Government control, 8.

Pritchard—Government control, 33; Prohibition, 10.

Aberdeen—Prohibition, 2; Government control, 9.

Georgetown—Prohibition, 4; Government control, 16.

Nicholson—Prohibition, 19; Government control, 5.

Continued on Page 15

Italian King's Estate

ROME, Oct. 20.—King Victor Emmanuel has estimated the value of his estate at 92,000,000 lire, which at the present rate of exchange amounts approximately to $3,680,000, in compliance with the new law establishing a tax on patrimony. The tax the King will pay will amount to about 1,000,000 lire. The estate of the Queen is valued at only $160,000.

The end of BC's short-lived experiment in prohibition claims a substantial portion of The Colonist's *front page.*

the Privy Council in London affirmed that women were "qualified persons" within the meaning of the British North America Act. The ruling reversed a Supreme Court of Canada decision and made them eligible for appointment to the Canadian Senate. The year before, on February 22, 1928, Mary Ellen Smith conducted the affairs of the legislative chamber as Deputy Speaker—"for the first time in the history of representative government anywhere in the world," *The Sun* noted. Mrs. Smith had already blazed new political trails by becoming the first female MLA in 1918, and the first female cabinet minister in 1921.

"Honest John" Oliver died in office August 17, 1927, at the age of seventy-one. Although diagnosed earlier with cancer, he was asked to stay on by his supporters. Gallantly, he did, living long enough to pilot an old-age pensioners' bill through the House that would enable BC to implement federal legislation. This wasn't much—$20 a month for people over seventy, with a strict means test—but it affirmed Oliver's commitment to social programs.

The premier-designate was John Duncan MacLean. He took over the reins August 20, 1927, and lasted exactly one year. Despite its minority status, the government had done relatively well, and MacLean had high hopes that the prosperity of the late twenties would help keep the Liberals in power with a solid majority. He was wrong. In the election of July 18, 1928, there occurred another one of those bewildering reversals of fortune. The Conservatives swept back into office with thirty-five seats to twelve for the Liberals (and one independent). Simon Fraser Tolmie became premier on August 21, just in time to preside over the collapsing economy of 1929, and the start of the Great Depression.

About this time, the mysterious Brother XII intruded upon the consciousness of Vancouver Island. As the legend grew, so did the press coverage, until it is generally accepted that Brother XII (otherwise known as Edward Arthur Wilson) was an evil, sexually deviant con man who bilked his followers out of thousands of dollars.

Bruce McKelvie, a veteran newspaperman, provided a number of bylined pieces for *The Province* promising "revelations that will startle the public." Purple prose about "weird occult doctrines" aside, the historical facts seem to be that Wilson, having declared himself the Twelfth Brother (the other eleven being mystical, divine beings), established colonies in 1928 at Cedar, south of Nanaimo, then on De Courcy Island just offshore across Stuart Channel.

The Brother's Aquarian Foundation was theosophical in nature and attracted the more mature cultists, along with their money. One of them, Mary Connally, eventually decided she was being had and took Wilson to court in 1933, alleging fraud. She was awarded $35,600. Wilson hired a lawyer but never appeared in person. Instead, he and his consort, a certain Madame Zee (who was rumoured to be even nastier than him), left town. The colony by this time had broken up and Brother XII never surfaced again.

Unlike the Aquarians, with their overtones of faddism and chequebook redemption, the Doukhobors were a serious, devout, pacifist—and stubborn—religious sect that held steadfast to the principle that man is a vessel of God, and nothing should intrude between the soul and the divinity.

They were agrarian and communistic and so committed to individual awareness that they denied the right of any external authority to control their actions. This last belief has got them into a lot of trouble in Canada.

The Doukhobors emigrated from Russia near the turn of the century to escape persecution by the czar. They settled in Saskatchewan, where they were soon quar-

THE DECADE IN HEADLINES
« 1923 »

HEAVY DEATH TOLL IN CUMBERLAND EXPLOSION

The Victoria morning paper prints the first sketchy details of the night-shift disaster in Mine 3 of the Canadian Colleries seam. Three days later, it reports "14 white men and 17 Orientals" killed.

The Colonist, February 8, 1923

GREAT CONCOURSE GREETS HARDING

A crowd estimated at 30,000 jams Vancouver's Stanley Park to hear US President Warren Harding speak. His visit—a stopover on a cruise from Alaska to Seattle—is the first time a sitting American president has come to Canada.

The World, July 26, 1923

Christmastime in 1925, and a group of Sun *newsboys are treated to dinner at the Oaks Cafe.*

THE DECADE IN HEADLINES
« 1924 »

MILLION DOLLAR VIADUCT OFFICIALLY OPENED TO-DAY

The highway section of the Johnson Street Bridge is completed, linking Victoria to its western suburbs. The bridge had been opened earlier to rail traffic.

Victoria Times, January 11, 1924

MYSTERIOUS WIRELESS SIGNALS ARE HEARD AGAIN IN VANCOUVER

Point Grey wireless operators are picking up coherent groups of signals, and the speculation is that they are coming from Mars. However, a leading British scientist in town for a conference debunks the theory.

The Province, August 21, 1924

B.C. LEGISLATURE UNANIMOUS IN DEMAND THAT CANADIANS CONTROL ORIENTAL INFLUX

Despite federal legislation virtually outlawing Chinese immigration, the House formally asks Ottawa to renounce trade treaties (especially with Japan) that inhibit BC's anti-Asian initiatives.

Victoria Times, December 17, 1924

relling with various levels of government over schooling, land claims and taxes. In 1908, they began following their leader, Peter The Lordly Verigin, to a new promised land, the valleys of BC's Kootenay country.

Among the members were the Sons of Freedom, a splinter group of zealots who believed any compromises with authority were contrary to true belief. It was the Freedomites who first paraded nude to demonstrate the purity of righteous living. In 1922, the relatively peaceful coexistence with the province's legal infrastructure ended when Doukhobor parents withdrew their children from school. After a number of parents were fined and property seized, nine schools in the Brilliant area were torched over the next few years.

These were the first acts of arson connected with the sect in BC. Following the ninth burning in 1925 (to protest a jail sentence), Premier Oliver had an angry confrontation with Doukhobor activists in Grand Forks. Defending the Canadian justice system, he told one protester, "The laws would probably be more right if you were dead, than you are now." The next day in Nelson, Oliver suggested to another group of Doukhobors that they leave the country if they did not want to obey British Columbia's laws. Soon, homes and other community property were in flames. The apparent culprits were the Sons of Freedom. Thus they had added arson as a protest weapon to go with nudity. In the thirties, dynamite was included as the Freedomites embarked on many years of destructive dissent.

In the midst of the school-burning spree, Peter Verigin was murdered. On October 29, 1924, a railway coach in which he and several others were riding was blown up. One of the nine persons killed was John McKie, the MLA for Grand Forks. The death of the charismatic Verigin prompted *The Sun* to praise his vision. He was "a man of attractive and impressive personality ... A big man, physically and mentally," it said. Although Verigin had many enemies, both inside and outside the Doukhobor community, and the papers offered various scenarios about assassination plots, the case has never been solved. He was succeeded by his son, Peter Petrovich Verigin, quite a different man from Peter the Lordly.

When British Columbians were voting for the return of liquor, Americans were bracing themselves for life without it. At 12:01 a.m. on January 17, 1920, the National Prohibition Act (popularly known as the Volstead Act) came into effect to enforce the 18th Amendment to the US Constitution. This was the one that made the manufacture, possession, importing, exporting, delivery, barter or sale of liquor illegal. Almost instantly, the smuggling of booze across the border became a huge and profitable calling for a number of Canadians.

The inshore waters of British Columbia and Washington State are perfect for smuggling. Only an artificial line drawn on a chart separates the Canadian Gulf Islands from the American San Juan Islands. Commercial or pleasure craft can flitter or chug across the Haro Strait separating the two archipelagos with little hindrance or control. There are so many inlets, islands, obscure passages and hidey-holes that enforcement of any border regulation is virtually hopeless.

So it was easy for enterprising, seagoing businessmen of the twenties to turn a fast profit. Almost anything that floated, from scows, fishboats and schooners to freighters, speedboats and luxury yachts, could be used. Sometimes, there were several trips a day. On the Island, ardent spirits would be moved from Victoria warehouses to vessels anchored in the Inner Harbour, or waiting in the many inlets off Gordon Head or the Uplands. From Vancouver, the "exports" usually headed for a Gulf Island rendezvous. There were two types of cargoes: The straight goods from BC brewers, distillers and bonded warehouses, which were illegally destined for Washington State ports, or excise-exempt alcohol, which was legally loaded for fictitious foreign destinations, then transferred at sea to US bootleggers.

Transshipment from one vessel (Canadian) to another (American or foreign) would be made in the aforementioned protected waters, or at sea off Vancouver Island, at a latitude and longitude known as Rum Row. Fast, dark boats running without lights would deliver the forbidden payload to the San Juans or Puget Sound. The vessels accepting Rum Row cargoes were more substantial (although often just as fast). Their destinations were Portland or California ports.

This is not to say these smugglers were allowed to conduct their activities unimpeded. The US agencies charged with enforcing customs laws had their successes. But the sheer hopelessness of plugging all the ingress points made their efforts largely ineffectual. Enforcement was also compromised by human frailty and venality. US agents were often open to bribery and corruption. Some actually engaged in bootlegging with the liquor they had seized.

Dodging or dealing with Prohibition officials was one thing. Escaping from hijackers was another. Rumrunners were a particularly tasty target for those preying on their crooked brethren, especially on the high seas. Boats full of smuggled hootch were regularly knocked over by these pirates—and death was sometimes a byproduct. The most celebrated hijacking case of the twenties was that of the *Beryl G*, a nondescript craft that was found blood-soaked, empty and crewless. Although the bodies of William Gillis and his seventeen-year-old son were never recovered, a long manhunt ended with two Americans being charged with murder. Harry Sowash and Owen Baker were extradited and tried in Victoria. They were hanged at dawn on January 14, 1926. *The Sun* reporter covering the double execution at Burnaby's Oakalla Prison wrote that the pair went to their deaths without emotion. "Step on it, kid; make it fast," Sowash told the hangman just before the trapdoor was sprung.

Another sensational court case arising from the illicit liquor trade was that of Henry Reifel, the province's leading booze baron. With his sons, Reifel owned Brewers and Distillers of Vancouver Ltd. It was also understood that Henry was BC's leading bootlegger and rumrunner. On July 7, 1934, the US government charged Reifel and his son George with smuggling $10 million worth of liquor into the country between 1928 and 1933. Uncle Sam also instituted a civil action against

THE DECADE IN HEADLINES
« 1925 »

COUGARS WIN STANLEY CUP
Lester Patrick's Victoria squad defeats the Montreal Canadiens for the "world hockey championship."

The Colonist, March 30, 1925

CRYSTAL GARDENS WELL PATRONIZED ON OPENING DAY
Its glass roof sparkling in the spring sun, the Crystal Garden at the foot of Douglas Street is open to the public. Called an "amusement palace" by *The Times*, this Victoria landmark features a large swimming pool surrounded by indoor greenery.

Victoria Times, June 8, 1925

THE DECADE IN HEADLINES
« 1926 »

TWO HIJACKERS HANGED AT DAWN; BID EACH OTHER CALM FAREWELL

Owen Baker and Harry Sowash, convicted in the murder of two rumrunners, are strung up at Oakalla Prison. The double execution ends the celebrated *Beryl G* hijacking case.

Vancouver Sun, January 14, 1926

the family (and other co-conspirators), demanding $17.25 million for customs evasions, taxes and penalties. The Reifels settled out of court a year later for $500,000, plus $200,000 in bail that Henry and George forfeited for nonappearance on the criminal charges.

The senior Reifel had also caused a stir in 1926 when he candidly admitted before a government commission that $100,000 in political contributions had been paid out by brewers in two years. This panel was appointed to probe charges of bribery and corruption in the Canadian customs and excise service. The brewery owner, a very tough witness, duelled verbally with commission counsel over cheques written for "assurance and protection." His statement about the $100,000 in "campaign funds" prompted *The Province* to remark in an editorial that the "plain name (of protection and assurance) is bribery and corruption."

The law-enforcement body that initiated the successful investigation of the *Beryl G* case, the BC Provincial Police, was a low-key, low-profile force that had been around since 1858. In the early twenties, the provincial cops' noses became somewhat out of joint over the emergence of the Royal Canadian Mounted Police on their turf. The RCMP came into being on February 1, 1920, as a replacement for the Royal North-West Mounted Police and the Dominion Police (Dan Campbell was a temporary constable in the small Dominion force when he killed Albert Goodwin). Even before the merger, however, an expanded RNWMP presence in BC in 1919 raised a few eyebrows. Mandated to enforce all federal laws, the feds quickly poured in men, money and equipment.

When the RNWMP became the RCMP in 1920, they kept the scarlet dress uniforms of the old Mounties. To the public and the press, this red badge of the law was much more interesting than the drab image of the Provincials. The new Mounties were also more approachable, an outlook that helped turn a campaign against narcotics into a Page One event early in the decade. With undercover Mountie agents supplying tips, the papers embarked on a publicity blitz about the evils of the drug trade—especially in Vancouver. "The menace to the youth of Vancouver today is not whisky, it is DOPE," *The Sun* warned in announcing a series on drug peddling.

The trouble was, all the narcotics agents started bumping into each other. Co-operation was almost nonexistent. In scenarios straight out of a Hollywood script academy, undercover operatives of the BCPP, Mounties and city police sometimes investigated each other. As with most "wars" on drugs, nothing much happened in court until August of 1923, when the BCPP helped nail two RCMP agents for illegal possession of opium and opium pipes in Victoria. They were charged and convicted.

The increasing tension among all the bodies supposedly keeping the peace in the province led to the appointment of a Royal Commission on the drug enforcement question. However, when the commissioner, a lawyer from Toronto named J.P. Smith, refused to include the Victoria convictions in his terms of reference, a frustrated attorney-general's department charged the RCMP in BC with incompetence, then withdrew from the hearings in a dispute over examination procedures.

When Smith concluded, on February 14, 1924, that there was no evidence of RCMP trafficking in narcotics, nobody was surprised. The inquiry had already "resolved itself into an official farce," *The Colonist* barked. "Commissioner Smith has not removed the cloud which has gathered over the methods of law administration in question." Not only that, the two Mounties charged and convicted in Victoria

Taking a break during a tour of BC in 1927, the Prince of Wales (second from left) is flanked by Cominco executives as he visits the company's Trail smelter.

were then pardoned by the Governor General on March 10.

Nevertheless, the Mounties got the message. Later in the year, the RCMP presence in BC was sharply reduced, and the BCPP (now attired in a natty combination of khaki and green) took over many of the duties of the federal force. The war on drugs sank without a trace.

Some pretty interesting people also visited during the twenties, including the usual royal personage. This time it was the Prince of Wales (who would later abdicate as King Edward VIII). In August of 1927, he and a younger brother, Prince George, dropped in on Vancouver and Victoria before taking the CPR's Kettle Valley route eastward through the Kootenays. The royal party arrived the day after Oliver's death. The welcoming crowds in Vancouver were large and enthusiastic, but the loss of the premier cast a shadow over the visit. Official functions in Victoria involving His Royal Highness were cancelled. Although the heir to the throne had visited Canada a number of times before (he owned a ranch in Alberta), the papers still managed to gush about "the world's darling of youthfulness and romance."

Two British politicians added more spice to our international guest book. In 1922, MP Neville Chamberlain visited Victoria. Chamberlain, who later would gain undying notoriety as the British prime minister who appeased Hitler, admitted out loud that governments are sometimes not popular. The man who succeeded him in the early months of the Second World War, Winston Churchill, had a more positive message in 1929—and drew a more frenzied welcome.

Long before he became the incandescent symbol of British courage in the dark days of the Nazi onslaught, Churchill was a dynamic figure in world politics at a relatively young age. The former cabinet minister's first official duty in BC was to open the Diamond Jubilee Provincial Exhibition at Queen's Park in New Westminster on September 2. Unfortunately, most of the exhibition's buldings had burned down earlier in the year and were replaced by tents. This didn't deter Churchill from making a rousing speech, nor a huge crowd from attending.

Winnie then gave a lecture to a packed house at the Vancouver Theatre (later named the Lyric) the next day. Greeted by waves of applause and cheers, the unmistakable figure with "his shining pate, his cutaway coat, wing collar and cravat" warned in his address that the Empire must guard its children—from Singapore to Palestine. As a somewhat overwhelmed *Province* reporter wrote: "The speaker drove his points home one after another in a speech clear and direct and yet flashing with

THE DECADE IN HEADLINES
« 1927 »

FORMAL OPENING OF DRYDOCK FEATURE OF JUBILEE CEREMONIES

The Esquimalt dry dock, second largest in the world, is officially opened by BC Chief Justice J.A. Macdonald. The dock is 1,150 feet long, 149 feet wide and 40 feet, 5 inches deep.

The Colonist, July 1, 1927

THE DECADE IN HEADLINES
« 1928 »

NEW B.C. GOVERNMENT WITHIN MONTH

With votes still being counted the following day, *The Times* reports a Conservative landslide in an election that sees a new premier, Simon Fraser Tolmie, chosen. His Tories took 35 of the 48 seats.

Victoria Times, July 18, 1928

WILLIAMS OF VANCOUVER WINS WORLD SPRINTING TITLE AT OLYMPIC GAMES

Percy Williams' brilliant victory on the world stage sparks a paroxysm of laudatory coverage by the BC press. Two days later the "Vancouver boy" (he is 20) stuns the world again by winning the Olympic 200-metre race.

The Province, July 30, 1928

FLYING BOAT REACHES VANCOUVER WITH TRANS-DOMINION AIR MAIL

The first sack of air mail to cross Canada directly arrives in Vancouver out of the dusk of a Saturday evening. RCAF Squadron Leader A. Earle Godfrey lands his plane at Jericho Beach air station after a flight from Ottawa of 32 hours.

Vancouver Star, September 8, 1928

NEW TRAFFIC SIGNALS WORK WITHOUT A HITCH

Vancouver drivers are unfazed by the city's first automatic traffic control at Main and Hastings streets. The signal, a combination of a semaphore and a bell, is eventually replaced by traffic lights and a central control system.

Vancouver Sun, October 17, 1928

brilliant phrases. His wit, his apt illustration and ready delivery carried his audience with him from the time he stepped on the platform, and as he concluded, picturing the greater Empire of the future, he roused the assembly to a high pitch of patriotism."

The famous British statesman also visited Grouse Mountain and, according to some reports, painted a view of English Bay. Continuing to Victoria, he was greeted by an ovation of several minutes at a Canada Club luncheon in the Empress Hotel. In his speech to the gathering of nearly 800, he noted that British Columbia, from its favourable position on the Pacific rim, had a unique chance to channel the flow of burgeoning Asiatic trade.

If Churchill was a visiting hero, then Percy Williams was a local one. The obscure Vancouver sprinter stunned the world, his countrymen and the press by winning two gold medals at the 1928 Amsterdam Olympics. *The Province* reported that "a riot of cheers" swept the stadium when Williams won the 100-metre sprint on July 30. Two days later, he posted another sensational win, this time in the 200-metre race. As *The Province* put it, the "city is agog with pride" at the performance of this Vancouver "schoolboy" (he was twenty at the time).

"Let us praise Percy Williams," it said in an editorial after his 100-metre win. "It is the classic race of all the races—that beautiful competition of strong, young manhood, impetuous, flashing, sudden, brief and glorious—the race that the old Olympians themselves held in chief honour. And it has been won, to the great glory of Canada, and surely to the honest pride of Vancouver, by one of our own boys, Percy Williams." On September 14, the Olympic hero rode alongside Premier Tolmie through the streets of Vancouver to the cheers of a wildly excited throng. It was perhaps the last hurrah of the twenties.

Churchill's rhetoric about Empire and young Percy's flashing heroics were delivering a message of well-being and superiority far removed from the fragile balloon that was the North American economic picture. As 1928 and 1929 unfolded, people were living beyond their means to a degree not heretofore known. Credit, that beckoning, fairy artifice that is still luring the unwary to a debtor's nightmare, had made its appearance. In Vancouver, Victoria, New Westminster, the bigger towns and the smaller villages, people were spending and acquiring to an unprecedented extent. Much of this was on the "never-never," the pay-later system that retailers and banks encouraged. This circus atmosphere of endless gratification extended to the stock market, where British Columbians joined in the giddy trading of shares.

The growing hysteria activated the greed glands of the brokers, promoters, member firms and other sharks that hung out at the Vancouver Stock Exchange. Ignoring the exchange's own rules, many firms advertised juicy bargains in the daily press. Regular readers of the financial pages could find strident pitches from brokers for such forgettable stocks as Gibraltar Oils, Capitol Oil, Premier Gold Mining Co. and Lorne Gold Mines Ltd. Crooked traders and bucket shops (which accepted money from gullible investors for trades that were never completed) skimmed a lot of gravy from the speculative sector. Trading volume on the VSE soared from 17.3 million shares and a value of $1.9 million in 1926 to 143 million and a value of $133.5 million in 1929.

Some brokerages set up duplicate trading boards so that the public could catch the action at first hand. As 1929 reached a crescendo, high-speed tickers were installed in an effort to keep up with the volume recorded in New York. It was a bull market that went on and on. It seemed these magical quotations, with their

THE VANCOUVER DAILY PROVINCE

3 CENTS Per Copy

THIRTY-FIFTH YEAR—NO. 126. WEATHER SYNOPSIS: GENERALLY FAIR AND WARM. VANCOUVER, B.C., WEDNESDAY, AUGUST 1, 1928. —26 PAGES. CIRCULATION TUESDAY... 83,077 PRICE THREE CENTS. Five Cents on Trains, Boats and in Country.

BATTLE OF THE GIANTS Britain Sees First
Skirmishes Between Free Traders and the "Squarders" — Page 2.

CANADA VOICES ITS PRIDE
Flood of Congratulatory Cables Pours in on Percy Williams — P. 3.

This Is Aim of **TO STABILIZE CHINA**
New United States Pact—Plans to Regulate Oriental Tariffs — P. 14.

Percy Williams, Vancouver Boy, Captures Second World Title by Brilliant Victory in 200-Metres

"World's Fastest Humans" Trail Slim Young Vancouver Mercury In Sprints at Olympics

PERCY WILLIAMS.

JACKSON SCHOLTZ.

CHARLES BORAH.

CHARLES PADDOCK.

BORAH, Jackson and Charles Paddock, the great trio picked at the great New York trials as the American sure-winners of all the sprint events at the Olympic games, have been outrun at the Olympic games by Percy Williams, the "baby of them all," in age and experience. Above, the local lad is shown at the tape, ready for the gun, at a race here before he won his Canadian laurels at Hamilton. Jackson V. Scholz, former 200-metre champion, was [illegible] in this, his third Olympiad. Charles Borah, United States favorite to win, was eliminated in the preliminaries on Tuesday. The Southern California University star, only two years older than Williams, is a nephew of Senator William E. Borah. Charles Paddock, long known as the "world's fastest human," made world's records in all distances from 100 to 300 yards and from 150 to 300 metres, but age told against him today, and he finished badly, unable to stay with the leaders. He was visibly in distress as he neared the tape.

SIX KILLED IN WELLAND CANAL LOCK

Fifteen Others Injured When Steel Gate Drops From Crane.

FEAR TOLL WILL BE LARGER YET

Five-hundred-ton Structure Thought to Be Still Holding Some Victims.

ST. CATHARINES, Ont., Aug. 1.—(CP)—The crash of the steel gate of lock number 6 of the new Welland Canal at Thorold, Ont., just before noon today, caused the deaths of six workmen, and injuries, some of which may prove serious, to fifteen.

The accident was caused by the boom of one of the cranes slipping when an effort was being made to raise the 500-ton steel gate into place on the west side of the lock. Two cranes were at work at the time, one handling either end of the heavy gate. The crane nearest to the head of the lock held, but the boom of the crane at the lower end slipped. The huge gate crashed into the steel-gate fabric at the east end of the lock and, smashing the steel work, fell to the bottom of the lock, crushing the workmen as it fell.

Two of the dead have been identified as F. Smalco and J. McArthur, both of St. Catherines.

Prior to the accident today the toll of death during the construction of the canal, which was begun fifteen years ago, has been about ninety.

COURTNEY HOPS FOR AMERICA

HORTA, Azores, Aug. 1.—After many delays and one false start last week, Captain Frank T. Courtney, British flyer, hopped off from here this afternoon for Newfoundland. He plans to refuel there and to continue to New York.

His passenger in the huge Dornier-Wahl plane was E. B. Hosmer, Montreal millionaire, who was with him when he made an attempt to cross the Atlantic last year. He then got only as far as Spain.

Weather conditions today are reported extremely favorable for the flight.

CITY THRILLED BY WILLIAMS

Cables of congratulation are once more beginning to flow across the ocean to Percy Williams at Amsterdam from proud fellow citizens, who are enthusiastic over his second success at the Olympic games—the 200-metre event. When public officials were informed by telephone of his new achievement, their expressions of admiration of his prowess knew no bounds.

When Acting Mayor F. E. Woodside heard of Percy's second victory this morning he exclaimed:

"Well, now, isn't that marvellous. That boy is a wonder. I'm going right down to the telegraph office and send him some more congratulations on behalf of the citizens of his home town. I'm ready to keep right on sending them. Just imagine, the whole world

(Continued on Page 21, Col. 8.)

Sonnysayings

By FANNY Y. CORY

Some ladies dest went by an' ast me if I was listenin' to the little angels singin'? They looked sort ob 'stonished when I telled 'em I was dest tryin' to 'member all the naughty words Grandpa said when I knocked my soup into his lap.

Americans Stunned at Rout of Their Athletic Stars

Discouraging Blows Dealt In One Olympic Event After Another.

The following despatch is written by Frank Getty, United Press staff correspondent at Amsterdam, and is intended for consumption of United States readers. It reveals the bitter disappointment at the American failures in the feature events at the Olympic games.

AMSTERDAM STADIUM, Aug. 1.—A near rout of America's star track men was continued at the Olympic games today when Charley W. Paddock was eliminated from the 200-metre dash in the first semi-final.

Pessimism Over Paddock's Elimination Intensified By Other Defeats.

Percy Williams of Canada, Rangley of Great Britain and Schuller of Germany qualified in this semi-final—the first section.

Williams is the 20-year-old school boy, who won the 100-metre dash on Monday, defeating such United States stars as Bob MacAllister of New York and Frank Wykoff of California.

PESSIMISM OF U.S. WAS INCREASED.

American pessimism over Paddock's elimination was increased a moment later when Henry Cumming jr. of the Newark A.C. was eliminated in the

(Continued on Page 8, Col. 5.)

Two Killed by Sheriff.

RAVENNA, Ohio, Aug. 1.—(UP)—Two men were killed and a third was seriously wounded in a battle with Sheriff J. P. Perry and Deputy George Dussel at Lovers Lane, near here today.

Perry said he and Dussel surprised the men stealing chickens.

Ira Clogston, 25, and Harry Gipe, 26, both of South Newberry, near here, were killed and Ralph Brown, 25, their companion, was wounded.

Street Sale Price Increases

Effective today the street sale price of The Vancouver Daily Province is increased to 3c per copy. Saturday and Sunday price will remain 5c per copy.

Increasing production costs force us to make this increase in price, of which a portion goes to the newsboy.

Vancouver is one of the last cities on this continent to increase the price on the street.

Vancouver Boy Gains Sensational Win, Leaping Ahead of World's Best Sprinters in Sensational Finish

Double Sprint Victory Not Achieved Since 1912

Williams Nearly Mobbed by Delirious Crowd in Stadium—Spectators Broke Onto Field

AMSTERDAM, Aug. 1.—Percy Williams' track achievements have given twenty points to Canada's Olympic total and put the Dominion in third place.

The standing at the end of the fourth day of the Olympiad is: United States, 123¼; Britain, 35; Canada, 28; Finland, 23; Germany, 22¼; Sweden, 21; South Africa, 14; Ireland, 10; France, 5; Haiti, 5; Italy, 4; Philippines, 3; Norway, 3; Japan, 2 and Holland, 1.

By R. T. ELSON,
Staff Correspondent The Daily Province.

AMSTERDAM, Aug. 1.—A scene of riotous joy was enacted in this great stadium here today when Percy Williams, Vancouver's brilliant schoolboy flash, achieved a second glorious victory in winning the 200-metre championship, after winning the 100-metre event on Monday.

The whole Empire wildly acclaimed the young winner, who in every heat had beaten the much-vaunted American track stars.

The Canadians in the stands broke through the police barriers and draped Williams with the Union Jack. P. J. Mulqueen, Canadian Olympic president, fought his way through a force of police and kissed the Canadian victor.

Williams came through today as no other sprinter in history, because of the fact that he fought off the greatest sprinters the world has ever seen. Most of his opponents were three or five years older and one of them was three times an Olympic champion. He remains modest in his victory.

After the race he said: "I can't say how I won. I just ran. I am glad all competition is over, and I want The Daily Province to be sure to tell mother, Mr. Graham Bruce and the High School of Commerce." Mr. Bruce was Williams' coach at the high school.

Percy adds that when he gets home, he hopes to have some fun hunting.

It is a grand and glorious day for Canada here.

PERFORMED REMARKABLE FEAT.

Williams performed the remarkable feat of winning both of the Olympic sprints, as he captured the 100-metre crown on Monday.

Williams won by a yard from Rangeley of Great Britain. There was uncertainty over the placing of the other runners, but the officials decided Scholz and Koenig of Germany tied for third place. Fitzpatrick of Hamilton was fifth.

BRITISH EMPIRE TRIUMPHS.

Again the British Empire triumphed in the astounding victory of the Vancouver sprinter, who has carried away the major glory of the Olympiad so far. Williams preceded his feat of taking the 200 metres final by winning the semi-final of the same event. He defeated the world's greatest sprinters, among others the German ace, Helmut Koenig and Jackson Scholz of the United States. It was the first double sprint victory since 1912.

Williams flashed a spectacular finish to overtake Koenig in the last fifteen metres.

Williams, as in the 100 metres, had tremendous speed left for the final dash after trailing the leaders until near the finish. The curly-haired Canadian boy was unbeatable.

Williams was nearly mobbed and was photographed with the Canadian flag draped around him. His time was 21 4-5 seconds.

(Continued on Page 20, Col. 1.)

HOIST ALL FLAGS IN CITY TO HONOR PERCY WILLIAMS, WORLD'S FASTEST SPRINTER

LET'S hoist all the flags in Vancouver! Percy Williams' performance in winning further honors for Canada today was decidedly a more brilliant feat than even his sensational victory in the hundred on Monday inasmuch as Charley Paddock, heralded all over the United States as the "world's fastest human," and his teammate, Jackson Scholz of New York, went down to ignominious defeat. The victory is further accentuated by the fact that while Williams is competing in his first world test, both Scholz and Paddock are former Olympic champions, Paddock in the 100 metres and Scholz in the 200. Furthermore Scholz is joint holder with Archie Hahn of the Olympic record for the 200 metres, 21.6 seconds.

The Daily Province building was bedecked with flags in honor of Williams' victory as soon as the news was received. The Hotel Vancouver flags were also hoisted.

(Continued on Page 21, Col. 7.)

PLANS FOR WILLIAMS STIR CITY

Bert Tennant Calls Sport Organizations to Friday Meeting.

Fund Gets Good Start—Tribute Paid to Splendid Trainer.

Granger Fund.

T. S. Dixon	$50
Geo. Snider	$10
P. D. Gordon	$25
Mrs. N.	$ 5
Dave Crawford	$10

With Percy Williams heaping further honors on the city of Vancouver by today adding his second triumph of the Olympic games—the 200 metres—Terminal City sport lovers will have a real opportunity of showing their appreciation of that honor.

The Province believes suitable recognition should be made, not only to Williams but also to Bob Granger, auburn-haired coach, who persisted in his efforts and finally arrived at Amsterdam to continue his coaching and assist in carrying the Vancouver lad to world championships in the two sprint events, an accomplishment that has not been equalled since the Olympic games of 1904.

In connection with Granger a fund has been started, headed by T. S. Dixon, president of the Vancouver Board of Trade, to bring Williams' trainer back to Canada in fitting style and in decent comfort. Officials in Amsterdam are loud in their praise of Granger and his protege. Subscriptions to this fund of $500 will be acknowledged by The Province and cabled to Amsterdam.

PERCY IS TAKEN TO VANCOUVER'S HEART.

Ever since Williams made his first amazing run, Vancouver has taken this wonderful boy to its heart. Scores of times daily, by telephone and personal message, The Province is asked what can be done for this lad when he comes home to show the appreciation of his fellow-townsmen. Olympic rules on their face provide against grants of money or goods to Olympic winners. It appears that no contribution can be made to Williams without endangering his amateur status. On the other hand, it would seem that no Olympic rule could prevent a committee representing Vancouver's citizens from arranging for this lad's future and providing him with a university education. Another important thing is to keep him a citizen of Vancouver, for he is certain when he returns to be inundated with offers, some of them professional, to go to populous centres of the United States.

In order to start the ball rolling, Bert Tennant, president of the Vancouver branch of the A. A. U., has called a meeting of sport organizations, service clubs and others interested, in the Board Room of The Daily Province on Friday evening at 8 o'clock. All wishing to have a part in this organization are asked to be present.

Vancouver should most certainly do herself proud in welcoming Canada's greatest athletic marvel of the day and in securing him a good start in life."

ROMAN INSIGNIA AS EMBLEM OF VICTORY.

Acting-mayor Frank E. Woodside, announced this morning that he would present a suggestion at this meeting that Percy be presented with the ancient Roman insignia of the victor—a chaplet of golden laurel wreaths mounted on a suitable shield and centred with the maple leaf, with a plate below describing his achievements at the Olympic Games of 1928. He will also suggest a tiny button-hole replica to be worn by Percy as a constant reminder of the pride Vancouver took in his victories. Ald. Woodside suggests that the cost of such gift be raised among the citizens of Vancouver.

GREAT SIGNIFICENCE NOT FULLY REALIZED.

The following letter was received by Acting-mayor F. E. Woodside this morning from Mr. A. E. Tennant, vice-president of the Canadian Olympic committee:

"Your Worship—

I wish to tender to you and the City Council my sincere thanks for the interest you are taking in Percy Williams.

"I do not think we yet realise the great significance of the honors which Percy Williams has won and which he has brought to Canada and your fair city. His feats have been wonderful and he has proven what can be done by clean sport. This is a national event of great importance and I think the whole of the Dominion should pay their homage to our hero.

"America recently had brought before it a young man whose initiative won for him great fame and I think Williams' magnificent triumph at Amsterdam in winning the 100 and 200-metre events in competition with the world's best, is worth similar recognition by our country and the city. It should also act as an impetus to all our young boys and young men to interest themselves in clean amateur athletics. Sincerely,

A. E. TENNANT."

BOB WAS FINAL SPORTS ARBITER.

The following appreciation of Bob Granger by the father of a Vancouver boy has been sent to The Province for publication:

"How many people in this wonderful city near the sea knew anything about Bob Granger until his name and mention of him had been cabled from Amsterdam by a boy who loves him well? How many knew of Bob Granger

(Continued on Page 3, Col. 2.)

The newspaper's own reporter, Bob Elson, describes the "riotous joy" accompanying Percy Williams' second Olympic victory.

THE DECADE IN HEADLINES
« 1929 »

PROVINCIAL EXHIBITION OPENED BY RT. HON. WINSTON CHURCHILL; TREMENDOUS CROWD IS PRESENT

Churchill, a distinguished British statesman even at this early date, gives a rousing speech at Queen's Park in New Westminster. The Diamond Jubilee exhibition is held despite the loss of several buildings in a disastrous fire on July 14.

The Columbian, September 2, 1929

ARE ELATED AT DECISION OF COUNCIL

Women are pleased that the British Privy Council has declared them "persons." The ruling was made as part of a judgment allowing females to sit as Senators in Ottawa.

The Colonist, October 18, 1929

PANIC ON WALL STREET BRINGS LOSS OF BILLIONS; WORST CRASH IN HISTORY

Black Thursday, the market collapse that is a precursor to the Great Depression, gets Front Page attention from Vancouver's leading paper.

The Province, October 24, 1929

arcane coding and precise fractions, would never drop in price.

Well, they did. On two black days at the end of October, 1929, the speculative excesses on the trading floor, fanned by easy credit, drove the New York Stock Exchange to its knees. The thud of suicidal market players hitting the pavement was drowned out by the screeching of the economic engine suddenly going in reverse.

The first crash, on Black Thursday, October 24, saw a staggering volume of almost 13 million shares traded on Wall Street. The book losses were in the billions of dollars. That was the day the bubble burst. BC's biggest paper, *The Province*, was sufficiently alarmed to treat the market situation as a disaster on Page One. The *Vancouver Sun* was more low key, but both newspapers ran stories during those fatal five days emphasizing "rallies" and positive news.

More sanguine than most commentators was *The Sun*'s regular financial writer, A.J. Smith. This opening sentence of his October 25 report pulls no punches about the crisis' effect on the city: "Chilly winds of financial adversity, more or less world wide in their range, blew upon the Vancouver Stock Exchange Friday during the early hours of trading here and forced some new lows in popular favourites." No one could escape the storm surge of losses. Financial pages reported panic dumping of shares in Toronto, Montreal, Chicago and other exchanges. Wheat prices plunged in Winnipeg grain trading.

Five days later, on Black Tuesday, October 29, Wall Street had another fatal spasm. This second bear hug from the market ended any brave talk of recovery. That day, the frenzy at the VSE was given a prominent position on Page One of *The Sun*. In New York, Black Tuesday's disastrous "correction" resulted in a record 16.4 million shares traded, with a paper loss of billions of dollars more. In its lead editorial of October 30, titled Bulls And Bears And Lambs, *The Province* mused that, although the peculiar processes of Wall Street are intimately related to the daily business of making our living in the world, "there is no help in a wringing of hands about the stock market."

"For business must still be done at the old stands," it concluded, "and we shall do it better if we do not worry overmuch because the bulls and the bears have made a feast among the lambs." Brave words. Beyond the horizon of the anonymous editorial writer's vision, however, the Great Depression and those beasts called Poverty, Unemployment, Bankruptcy and Violence lay in wait.

THE THIRTIES: DIRTY AND DEPRESSED

« 1930 – 1939 »

The cabinet of Simon Fraser Tolmie didn't have a clue about the length and depth of the economic calamity unravelling around it. The government's timid response to the first signs of convulsions ensured that the Conservative party would be one of the major victims of the thirties.

Tolmie, like Oliver, came from rural stock. Despite his political wanderings, the family farm in Saanich remained his home throughout his life. The MP for Victoria since 1917, Tolmie was chosen provincial Tory leader in 1926. But he remained in the Commons until Premier John MacLean called the 1928 election. Perhaps the rarefied debates in Ottawa were too far removed from the soil of BC, because the situation at the turn of the decade was beyond his understanding.

Tolmie's lacklustre collection of ministers stumbled through three legislative sessions without devising any constructive solutions to the financial and unemployment problems facing them. While they governed by platitude, bread lines formed almost immediately and kept growing. The banks that had encouraged so much borrowing in the twenties started foreclosing. The ordinary folk who saw their futures swept into the gutter as part of the detritus of Wall Street no longer bought houses or cars or big-ticket items—let alone stocks. A glut on the world grain market, plus a drought on the Prairies, had a serious impact on the ports of Vancouver and Prince Rupert.

Homes went on the block for non-payment of taxes. Working men, accustomed to making an honest buck for honest toil, went on relief by the thousands and suffered the indignity of accepting pennies a day to feed their families. If businesses didn't close down, they cut employee rosters to the bone. Nobody could afford to go anywhere. At the Empress Hotel in Victoria, it wasn't unusual for the staff to outnumber the guests. Tolmie's answer to the crisis was a tax of one percent on all incomes over $12 a week.

It didn't take long for the unrest to reach critical levels (you get that way waiting in queues for handouts). There were strikes at canneries, lumber operations and mines when owners tried to cut wages. On February 22, 1932, when there were 67,000 unemployed in BC, 6,000 men, women and children staged a hunger march in the rain in Vancouver. This open manifestation of working-class anger was just the beginning. The protests, marches, rallies and violence would finally escalate

THE DECADE IN HEADLINES
« 1931 »

GREAT RECEPTION FOR SIAMESE ROYALTY TO-DAY

The King of Siam, Prajadhipok, lands in Victoria after a trans-Pacific voyage aboard the *Empress of Japan*. He is the first reigning monarch to visit Canada.

Victoria Times, April 16, 1931

POLICE SEIZE THOUSANDS OF SWEEPSTAKE TICKETS IN RAID ON CITY OFFICE

A phoney lottery scheme with gross receipts of $1.6 million—a huge amount at that time—is broken up by Victoria police.

The Colonist, April 22, 1931

PRINCE OF WALES CABLES AIRPORT CONGRATULATIONS; 20,000 AT FIELD OPENING

The future King of England leads a host of laudatory messages as Sea Island Airport and Seaplane Harbour opens in the Vancouver suburb of Richmond. It will eventually become known as Vancouver International Airport.

Vancouver Sun, July 22, 1931

into ugly confrontations as the Great Depression ground its painful way toward 1939.

Into this cauldron of despair, the Kidd report on government finances in 1932 dropped a bomb that had all the finality of an eviction notice for the Tolmie cabinet. Commissioned by the Conservatives as another one of their weak-kneed responses to the economic crisis (with the expectation that nothing would ever come of it), the Kidd committee laid out a detailed, devastating critique of what was wrong with politics in British Columbia. Largely overlooked by succeeding generations, this analysis and the solutions it proposed are as relevant today as in the 1930s.

The members of the committee—George Kidd (chairman), Austin Taylor, W.I. Macken, A.H. Douglas and R.W. Mayhew—were all prominent businessmen. They concluded that, as a public enterprise, the BC government was a failure. Here are the opening paragraphs of *The Province*'s Page One story on the committee's recommendations, released August 30, 1932:

"Party politics, patronage and self-interest are largely responsible for British Columbia's present intolerable load of taxation, its mounting debt and its gross extravagance in most branches of government, according to the report of the Kidd businessmen's committee issued today.

"The central recommendation of this committee, about which all its detailed proposals are built, is that politicians should stop squabbling over party advantage and the spoils of office, should hold an immediate session of the Legislature and unite in putting government on a sound basis."

Its other recommendations included a 28-seat legislature, a six-man cabinet, sale of the Pacific Great Eastern Railway, closure of the University of BC (which was facing a funding crisis because of the lack of government money), replacing the provincial police force with the RCMP (which happened in 1950), slashing the civil service payroll and elimination of the party system.

The *Vancouver Sun* called the report "a thorough, capable businessman's analysis," but claimed it was "senseless ... to hope for improvement for the present 'do-nothing' group in Victoria." *The Sun* was right. The committee's solution was very strong medicine and Tolmie refused to swallow it. Although the cabinet made vague noises about studying the document, insider reports in the press indicated the government planned to do little.

There was some cabinet angst over the elimination of parties, because Tolmie had already sent out feelers to the Liberal Opposition about formation of a coalition government. Why a premier with a House majority of more than twenty seats would seek help from the opposite benches is not clear, but Tolmie apparently thought such a cooperative effort, as in wartime, would help focus energies.

In any event, Liberal leader Thomas Dufferin Pattullo laughed and laughed. He knew the Conservatives were in big trouble, and preferred to take his chances in the next election. Tolmie knew, too, because he strung out his mandate to the very last inch, not calling an election until late in 1933. On November 2 of that year, Tolmie and the Conservative party disappeared. The election results gave Duff Pattullo's Liberals 34 of 47 seats. There was a new official Opposition party—something called the Co-operative Commonwealth Federation—with seven seats.

One thing about Premier Pattullo: He was no hand-wringing sissy worrying about what the voters and the opposition would think. Although he had obviously read the Kidd report along with every other politician in the province, he wasn't about to scrap the party system now that his party had a huge majority. Nor was he interested in coalition government with the ragtag remains of the opposition. There were, however, things that would be done, but only in his own inimitable, pragmatic manner.

Duff Pattullo, who was born in Ontario, was a newspaperman, civil servant and municipal politician before being elected an MLA in 1916. He was somewhat of a dandy, but kindly and courteous when the need arose. His charm masked a steely interior. When he became leader of the Opposition and then premier, Pattullo was well versed in how other jurisdictions were attempting to handle the economic disaster that followed 1929. In particular, the New Deal of Franklin Delano Roosevelt in 1933 impressed him because FDR's vision of state intervention ran parallel to his own. (Roosevelt's brief visit to Victoria in October of 1937 warmed the premier's heart so much that he soon made a reciprocal, unofficial call on FDR at Hyde Park. "We'll see you soon," Eleanor Roosevelt had told Pattullo as the presidential pair departed Victoria aboard a US warship.)

In the spring legislative session of 1934, Pattullo introduced a New Deal of his own that was draconian in its scope and severity. The Special Powers Act decreed that the government have total control of all matters in the province. These included private and public business, property and civil rights, municipal institutions, the borrowing and lending of money, transportation and communications, and "generally all matters of a merely local or private nature in the province."

British Columbia's collective jaw dropped. Following introduction of the bill on March 17, more than one newspaper summed up its sweeping powers in one exclamatory word—Dictatorship! Reports from Victoria said the morning headlines "made the capital's flesh creep." Although the opposition members only numbered a puny baker's dozen, they nevertheless conducted a long, bitter and ringing attack in the legislature. Tom Uphill, the CCF member from Fernie, brandished a huge Nazi swastika at the government benches. Gerry McGeer, Independent Liberal (and mayor of Vancouver) called the premier "Franklin Pattullo."

Through it all, Pattullo contended that, because the difficulties facing BC were so grave, the government must have discretionary powers in order to deal with any emergency and avert chaos. The act, he insisted, would not interfere with any constitutional guarantees. In the end, of course, the Liberals' comfortable majority ensured that the bill passed with only minor modifications.

When the session ended, the incomparable Bruce Hutchison, who was then approaching his prime as Canada's foremost political correspondent, wrapped up the historic debate with a Page One essay for *The Province* that was both profound and elegant. "Yes, the first instalment of the New Deal ends in a gigantic question mark—so big, so grim and alarming that most members don't want to contemplate it," he wrote. "The question, of course, is what the Pattullo government proposes to do now, and if the government really knows it certainly hasn't told anyone."

"Don't imagine, poor, wondering citizen, that the Pattullo government has failed to realize its position," he continued. "It knew, as the Legislature adjourned and left it here in lonely grandeur, that it must make good in a big way during the next year or go under."

Although the worst fears of the opposition and the press were not even remotely realized, Pattullo did use the blank cheque of the Special Powers Act to play hardball during the rest of the decade. The premier insisted throughout the Depression that

THE DECADE IN HEADLINES
« 1932 »

NUDE DOUKHOBOR GIRLS RACE POLICE IN THRUMS ORCHARD

The newspaper's correspondent has some fun with the three female protestors, "laughing gaily," who join a Sons of Freedom march briefly before donning their clothes again. On a more serious note, 118 naked fanatics are arrested that month and sentenced to three years in prison.

Vancouver Sun, May 3, 1932

NEW DRIVING FEE DUE SOON

The Times, along with other BC newspapers, warns motorists that driving licences are now compulsory at the cost of $1 each. The permits went on sale May 9 and take effect June 1.

Victoria Times, May 9, 1932

COUNCIL CHEQUE TO GOVERNMENT MARKED "N.S.F."

The Page One story says the bounced cheque by the municipality of Coquitlam is perhaps the first in BC history. In the same May 31 edition, it also details Burnaby's financial woes as the Depression begins to take hold.

The Columbian, May 30, 1932

McNAUGHTON FOUGHT FOR HOURS IN HEAT TO WIN HIGH JUMP

Although preoccupied on Page One by the failure of Percy Williams—the 1928 Games hero—*The Sun* does describe how Vancouver jumper Duncan McNaughton wins his gold medal at the Los Angeles Olympics.

Vancouver Sun, August 1, 1932

JOHN BENNETT TAKES CHARGE AT MUNICIPAL HALL

The BC government assumes control of the affairs of Burnaby after the municipality defaults on a $25 debt payment. In a later editorial, the weekly *Broadcast* advises Bennett—a defeated Vancouver mayoralty candidate—to steer a safe middle course as Burnaby's custodian.

Burnaby Broadcast, December 31, 1932

THE DECADE IN HEADLINES
« 1933 »

STERILIZE UNFIT

A majority of MLAs indicate they favour sterilization of the mentally unfit. A bill authorizing the procedure is passed into law April 7.

Vancouver Sun, April 1, 1933

McLARNIN KAYOES CORBETT TO CAPTURE WELTER CROWN

Vancouver's Jimmy McLarnin decks Young Corbett with one punch in the first round to win the world welterweight boxing title. *The News-Herald* splashes the story on Page One and adds a short, congratulatory editorial.

The News-Herald, May 29, 1933

SMASHING LIBERAL VICTORY IN B.C. ELECTION BATTLE

The new morning paper devotes most of Page One (in an eight-page edition) to the initial Liberal win in an election conducted in two stages. The Liberals amass 34 seats out of 47.

The News-Herald, November 2, 1933

BC must maintain fiscal autonomy in order to counter meddling from Ottawa. On June 1, 1937, the Liberals comfortably won re-election with 31 seats, but Pattullo's obstinacy was beginning to alienate even his own party. For Duff, the thirties and his premiership were drawing to a close.

Meanwhile, somewhat removed from the corridors of power, the Great Depression managed to become, from time to time, slightly less depressing. At the 1932 Olympics in Los Angeles, Percy Williams failed to repeat his heroics of 1928, but another Vancouver athlete brought home a gold medal. He was high jumper Duncan McNaughton. Then on May 29, 1933, Jimmy McLarnin, of Union Street in Vancouver, knocked out Young Corbett in the first round at Wrigley Field in Los Angeles and became world welterweight boxing champion.

Royalty arrived and departed. King Edward VIII, whom BC got to know so well as the Prince of Wales, abdicated in 1936. Earlier, a foreign king—the first reigning monarch to visit Canada—sailed into Victoria on the *Empress of Japan* on April 16, 1931. He was Prajadhipok, the King of Siam. His Highness was slightly indisposed, so official functions were curtailed before he and his consort, Queen Rambai Barni, continued to Vancouver and then eastward via rail.

Toward the end of the decade, the successor to Edward, King George VI, stepped from another train at Vancouver's CPR station on May 29, 1939. His trip across Canada with Queen Elizabeth was the first visit to the Dominion by a reigning British king. In Vancouver and Victoria, the love affair with the Empire's ruling family was obviously unaffected by the distractions of the Depression.

"May it please your Royal Majesties," wrote *The Province* in an editorial. "This is British Columbia, a green and pleasant land, rugged and rich. And this is Vancouver, great seaport of the Western Empire. We believe one of the world's cities of destiny. Nowhere in your Dominion of Canada will your welcome be warmer or more heartfelt. Your royal great-grandmother named this land British Columbia and British it is and will remain."

Some 40,000 kids got out of school to see the Royal couple. They joined the 600,000 people (according to one estimate) who lined the route of the royal procession. Thousands more thronged to the corner of Burrard and Georgia streets, where the city's third Hotel Vancouver, which had opened for business only days earlier, was playing host to George and Elizabeth.

In Victoria, "the crowds roared themselves hoarse" and ships sounded bells, whistles and sirens as the pair arrived on the *Princess Marguerite*. *The Colonist* (which once proudly called itself *The British Colonist* in its masthead) said in an editorial that "the presence of the King and Queen in our midst raised the people's pride to an elevation higher than ever in the past, because they saw in them a new vision of the privilege of forming a part of a wide Empire, an Empire in which these Majesties stand for ideals of power, of dignity, of freedom and of love."

The citizenry was also titillated by the sensational Francis Rattenbury murder case in Britain. Rattenbury was well known in the province as the designer of the Legislative Buildings, the Empress Hotel and other Victoria landmarks. The press was full of stories about a classic love triangle, but only one person was convicted, on May 31, 1935, of Rattenbury's murder. He was George Percy Stoner, a nineteen-year-old chauffeur who was having an affair with Rattenbury's forty-two-year-old wife, Alma. Although Mrs. Rattenbury was accused along with Stoner, she was not convicted of any charges.

Another notable name for the obituary writers to lay to rest was Texas Guinan, who died in Vancouver's General Hospital November 5, 1933. For those readers in the under-fifty crowd who thought Oprah, Letterman and Geraldo were such big names, Guinan was easily their equal in chutzpah. Famous in the twenties and thirties as a speakeasy operator and entertainer, she coined such Americanisms as "Hello sucker," "Big butter and egg men" and "Give the little girl a great, big hand." Guinan was in town to share her pungent and pithy vocabulary with Vancouver audiences when she was stricken with "intestinal trouble." According to the *News-Herald* (which was also partial to colourful language), "a dog howled outside the hospital" the night Texas Guinan died, aged forty-nine.

While many of the province's jobless were facing the barren prospect of life in a relief camp, Sons of Freedom Doukhobors by the hundreds were being transported to a penal colony. In July, 1931, the federal government, in a fit of vengeful prudery and intolerance, amended the Criminal Code so that nudity in a public place carried a mandatory penalty of three years' imprisonment. The religious fanatics against whom the amendment was directed, the Sons of Freedom, reacted with all the fervor of martyrs and began removing their clothes in unprecedented numbers. On May 6, 1932, it took an efficient Nelson magistrate just two hours to sentence the first wave of nude lawbreakers—118 of them—to a total of 354 years in prison. Eventually 600 received the mandatory three years. The federal pen at New Westminster had no room for them all, so Piers Island, just outside Swartz Bay on Vancouver Island, was selected. Two enclosures were built (one for men, one for women) and the Freedomites basically fended for themselves for thirty months before being released.

Shortly after the prisoners returned to the Kootenays, there were some scattered bombings, and the number of burnings rose sharply over a two-year period. No doubt the arsonists were protesting government actions, but by this time the Sons of Freedom had been disowned by Peter the Purger Verigin, so part of their dissent was directed at him.

The son of Peter the Lordly had become known as Peter the Purger because of his violent moods and his vow to strengthen the community by purging. In contrast to his father, Peter the Purger was only interested in personal power. He also drank and lied. In 1932, Verigin did time in prison for perjury, and again in 1934, for assault. A drunken brawl in a Nelson beer parlour, also in 1934, resulted in a fine (it seems the patrons of this drinking establishment were loath to show respect by baring their heads in his presence).

Like a great many individuals and companies in BC, the main Doukhobor community went bankrupt in 1937. With the provincial government looking on impassively, the Doukhobors' two major creditors foreclosed on more than $3 million in assets because of nonpayment on a $360,000 debt. Then, suddenly realizing that thousands of angry Doukhobors were about to be evicted and turned loose on an unsuspecting public, the government made a deal with the creditors that allowed the community to remain (on property which now belonged to the province). Much of this happened without the input of Peter the Purger. He had taken ill in 1938 and died of cancer, February 11, 1939—the day after Pope Pious XI passed away.

There was more than one community and one faith being tested by the ravages of the Depression. Vancouver would become the focal point for all the rage, hopelessness and frustration, but the effects were province-wide. Belleville Street, which fronts the legislature in Victoria, was a favourite gathering place for placard-wav-

THE DECADE IN HEADLINES
« 1934 »

FEMALE WORKERS ARE TO BE PROTECTED UNDER LAW

Minimum wage standards will apply to women (except domestics, farm labourers and fruit pickers), according to a bill introduced in the legislature. The bill, which becomes law in a matter of weeks, is more detailed than legislation passed in 1918.

The News-Herald, March 16, 1934

DICTATORSHIP IN B.C.

As the Depression deepens, a Special Powers Act gives the Pattullo government sweeping control over the province's affairs. The bill passes after two weeks of bitter debate and editorial outcry—although none as sweeping as *The News-Herald*'s stark, black headline.

The News-Herald, March 16, 1934

LAST ACT OF LEGISLATURE GIVES TO GOVERNMENT CONTROL OF MARKETING; INDUSTRIAL CODES ARE POSSIBILITY

In less than half an hour, the Natural Products Marketing Act is rammed through without debate. The act, which establishes the BC Marketing Board, is dismissed by *The Colonist* as "half-baked" and "precipitate," making possible bureaucratic interference with the law of supply and demand.

The Colonist, March 29, 1934

VANCOUVER-SEATTLE AIR SERVICE OPENS

The inauguration of airline service on the Dominion Day long weekend between the Pacific Northwest's two major cities is reported on Page 9, with a picture. Earlier, however, *The Sun* noted that the new service linked Vancouver with the entire North American continent.

Vancouver Sun, June 29, 1934

THE DECADE IN HEADLINES
« 1935 »

VANCOUVER WALKS TO WORK AS SNOW BLOCKS STREETS; 17½ INCHES IN 24 HOURS

The worst snowfall in the city's history disrupts transportation and many services. The weight of the snow collapses the roof on the Forum at the PNE.

The Province, January 21, 1935

STONER FOUND GUILTY OF RATTENBURY MURDER AS CO-DEFENDANT GOES FREE

A young chauffeur is convicted in London of slaying Francis Rattenbury, who designed the Legislative Buildings and the Empress Hotel. Rattenbury's wife, Alma, is acquitted.

The Colonist, May 31, 1935

ing demonstrators. One casualty far removed from the placid protesters of Victoria was the mining settlement of Anyox, located on the remote central coast. When the price of copper sank through the bedrock in 1935, this company town was closed down. Among the families making their uncertain way south to Vancouver were the Boyds.

Denny Boyd, long-time columnist for *The Sun*, recalled in that paper's Centennial Edition in 1971 how it felt to grow up in Depression Vancouver. Here is an excerpt from his reminiscences:

"We were on relief for a year, three of us living on $29 a month. Fortunately, my father had two married sisters living here and they helped out with Sunday dinners and food packages. My father got a job loading trucks at the salt works. He developed boils in his wrist, which became infected from the salt. The wrist festered and swelled horribly but he didn't dare take a day off for fear of losing the job.

"For us, a big night out was a streetcar trip to The Old English Fish & Chips. When it became time for me to go into Grade One at Cecil Rhodes School, I needed new shoes. There was no money for them, so my mother applied for relief shoes. What arrived was a pair of genuine jet-black, high-cut clodhoppers, with eyelets and hooks and copper toecaps. Having worn sensible shoes since my first baby steps, I loved these stout stompers but they made my mother weep."

Families trying to exist on $29 a month could perhaps grasp the dilemma facing Canada and its nine constituent provinces. The problem was debt. In 1933, the Dominion Bureau of Statistics estimated that the provinces owed $1.225 billion. Which doesn't sound like much to today's BC residents, who are co-existing with a provincial government debt in the vicinity of $30 billion. But in 1933, newspapers were three cents a copy, coffee was 32 cents a pound, a 16-oz. tin of Libby's pork and beans was available for five cents, and you could buy a 25-lb. sack of potatoes for 23 cents at the Piggly Wiggly. A five-room "modern stucco bungalow" in Point Grey was listed in *The Sun*'s real estate section for $2,500. A debt surpassing $1 billion in those hard times was serious money.

British Columbia owed $18.755 million in treasury bill paper in addition to a floating debt of $4 million. That was the provincial picture. At the municipal level, the total was worse. While Pattullo fought for favourable refinancing terms from Ottawa, he did little to help the cities and towns meet their own financial obligations. Although the government provided some money for local relief programs, some centres complained that the guidelines were too tough or inconsistent.

On December 20, 1932, with no money in the bank, no help from Victoria and the jobless on every street corner, the municipality of Burnaby went broke. It defaulted on payment of a $25 interest coupon on a $6,000 debenture. Prompted by an application for intervention by the BC Bond Dealers Association, council voluntarily sought the appointment of a provincial government administrator. He and his successors would direct the affairs of Burnaby until January, 1943, when a new municipal council regained local autonomy. Although the most visible municipality to crumble under the weight of the Depression ("third largest place in BC," as the weekly *Burnaby Broadcast* once proclaimed on its masthead), Burnaby was not the only one. Both the city and district of North Vancouver were taken over in the same manner, as were Merritt and Fernie.

Vancouver had to make a special deal with the legislature in 1935 to escape a similar fate. After much debate, manoeuvring and political compromise, Pattullo's Liberal government agreed to amend Vancouver's city charter legislation so that it would not follow the same humiliating path as Burnaby. Although the cabinet would not give the city outright cash ("If any direct aid had been granted, every municipality would have demanded the like and the government would have been in an impossible position," said one negotiator), it agreed to guarantee Vancouver's borrowing up to a prescribed limit as well as ease its tax situation.

The relief-camp phenomenon was the dirty laundry of the thirties. Under provincial, then federal control (and managed for a time by the defence department), the camps were an attempt to channel the jobless away from the hobo jungles and urban areas (where they panhandled shamelessly) into a controllable environment. In BC, there were more than 230 such camps, with an inmate population exceeding 18,000 at its peak. These men, who rode the rods from the chilly Prairies to the more amenable climate of coastal BC, established their jungles—transient squatters' quarters—in such railroad towns as Kamloops, Penticton, Grand Forks and Hope. They were gaunt, sickly, unkempt and desperate. If they wanted anything more than a job, it was food.

Some local efforts were made to feed the dispossessed, but these foundered on the shoals of inadequate budgets. When the higher levels of government took over the responsibility for these men (100,000 persons were out of work in 1933), they attempted to establish a public works program that would get them out of the towns and cities and into the bush. The target was mostly the single, unemployed male. Some were put to work building the Big Bend, a gravel highway around the northern loop of the Columbia River. Others built bridges, cleared the land for rural airports or used their picks, shovels and wheelbarrows to improve roads in remote areas of the province.

Life was harsh in the relief camps. They were poorly—and sometimes fraudulently—administered. Conditions were primitive, food was scarce and pay almost nonexistent. These "slave compounds" were Fascist measures designed to bring the working class to heel, according to left-wing orators.

It didn't take long for the hopeless vista offered by existence in the camps to ignite rebellion. The Relief Camp Workers' Union was formed to fight for better conditions and a living wage. They were getting maybe 20 cents a day in the camps, and some thought 25 cents a hour was a fairer deal. A sawmill worker in Vancouver, with a real job, made that kind of money. The RCWU was supported by the Communist party and the CCF.

Vancouver, because it was the end of the line in more ways than one, became the focal point in 1935 for the strife and rhetoric. The jobless decided to go on strike against camp conditions. Word was passed from camp to camp and eventually some 1,800 men grabbed freights heading for the coast. There were plenty of meetings. On March 31, the diminutive Tim Buck, Canada's top Communist, told 5,500 shivering faithful at Denman Arena (boards had been laid over the artificial ice) that the authorities "herd the young men into slave camps because they are afraid of them. Because if they are left in the city, they would become the spearhead of the struggles of the working class."

Three weeks later, on April 23, a parade of some 1,000 strikers and sympathizers turned violent. The demonstrators invaded the Hudson's Bay Company store on Granville Street and caused an estimated $5,000 in damage and losses. Later that night, they clashed with police at Carrall and Hastings streets. Mayor Gerry McGeer read the Riot Act at the Cenotaph in Victory Square. It was the first time the Act—official notice that an assembly was unlawful—had been read since 1912.

THE DECADE IN HEADLINES
« 1936 »

COAL HARBOR SWEPT BY FLAMES; ARENA TOTAL LOSS
As the Denman Arena burns down, *The News-Herald*, a morning paper, provides its readers with details of the fire as fresh as 2:30 a.m. The 25-year-old structure, built by hockey's Patrick family, is never replaced.
The News-Herald, August 20, 1936

EDWARD VIII ABDICATES DESPITE ALL ENDEAVORS TO CHANGE HIS PURPOSE
The capital city is "profoundly moved" by the King's desire to renounce his throne and marry a divorced woman. In a long editorial, *The Colonist* advises its readers not to view the event as a tragedy, but to embrace the continuity of the monarchy.
The Colonist, December 10, 1936

THE DECADE IN HEADLINES
« 1937 »

SLICED BREAD SOLD BY PURITY BAKERS

The inaugural sale of sliced bread in BC makes Page 2 of *The Sun*. On the same page as the five-paragraph story is a three-column advertisement from Robertson's Bakeries— suppliers of the bread. *The Province*, which didn't carry the ad, buried the story at the bottom of its "Modern Kitchen" page.

Vancouver Sun, July 19, 1937

PRESIDENT ROOSEVELT WARMLY WELCOMED

The visit of the US chief executive to Victoria is the top story in BC's daily press. A long, laudatory account in *The Colonist* fails to mention the reason for the 90-minute visit— which apparently is little more than a "good neighbour" luncheon stop on a presidential tour.

The Colonist, September 30, 1937

CROWD ESTIMATED AT 30,000 PRESENT AS PREMIER PATTULLO OPENS GREAT NEW FRASER SPAN

The new bridge between downtown New Westminster and the south shore of the river is opened in a driving sleet storm by the span's namesake. *The Columbian* marks the occasion with a 20-page Souvenir Bridge Edition.

The Columbian, November 15, 1937

DRASTIC LABOR BILL IN HOUSE

The far-reaching Industrial Conciliation and Arbitration Act is introduced, debated and passed in three days. For the first time in BC, workers have the right to organize, bargain collectively and demand arbitration of disputes.

Vancouver Sun, December 7, 1937

The following Sunday, 13,000 people jammed into Denman Arena to support the strikers. The rally, sponsored by the women's wing of the CCF, drew some tough words from Harold Winch, who wasn't all that interested in peace and quiet. "A lot are going to die before this thing is through," cried the demagogic MLA with the flashing eyes and long, dark hair. "If the authorities are going to use the mailed fist and the iron heel, it is time that the people took off their gloves also."

In June, the malcontents shifted their sights from the provincial level to Ottawa. They organized a freight-train assault that would take the jobless all the way to the Dominion capital. There, they would demand a meeting with Prime Minister R.B. Bennett. From Vancouver, more than 700 striking men rode the boxcars eastward, passing through the towns and cities of BC and Alberta without major incident. By the time they reached Regina on June 14, the numbers had swelled to 2,000. Then the Bennett government ordered the CPR and CNR to keep the transients off their trains.

While the men simmered in Regina, holding rallies, accepting handouts and making plans to resume the trek in trucks, an advance delegation of eight leaders continued to Ottawa. There, they were insulted and rudely dismissed by Bennett. On July 1, 1935, after the leaders had returned to Regina, RCMP and city police tried to arrest them as they addressed a large demonstration. Thus began the Regina Riot. One city cop was beaten to death, more than 100 persons were injured, and 130 arrests were made. When calm was restored, the authorities returned two loads of strikers to BC on special trains.

The birth of the CCF in 1932 offered a new political alternative to the voters and workers of BC and the rest of Canada. Methodist clergyman J.S. Woodsworth's blend of agrarian populism with the activist elements of academe, the pulpit, trade unions and the urban jungle produced a brand of socialism that would have a distinct effect on this province's electoral future.

Despite such intemperate calls to violence as those of Harold Winch, however, the revolution ran more gentle through the thoughts of these left-wing reformers than in the fevered minds of the Communist Party of Canada. To the press and the entrenched political structure, there wasn't all that much difference between the two. A Red was a Red was a Red, no matter what label the rabble-rousers chose to use. To the unemployed working stiff, whose quest for social justice didn't go much further than a steady job and a square meal, the political label of the "revolution" wasn't nearly as important as results.

In truth, neither the CCF nor the Communists had any profound effect on the course of the Depression. (The appeal of the CCF would be more relevant to post-Depression politics, but that is the stuff of another chapter.) Both parties sponsored rallies and organized marches, but for entirely different reasons. The CCF sought change for a troubled Canada, while the Communists viewed the country as just another arena in the world-wide crusade against capitalism. When the trek to Ottawa was beaten back by the nightsticks and guns of the establishment police in Regina, the more militant of the disaffected had to wait a while for the next cause to come along.

And that next cause turned out to be the Spanish Civil War, which began in July of 1936 when the Republican government was challenged by the military. Supported by the rich, conservative and politically powerful Roman Catholic Church, the Spanish Army under General Francisco Franco attacked. Thus began this bloody prelude to the Second World War: Franco's Fascism vs. left-leaning republicanism.

Flushed out by tear gas, the jobless who occupied Vancouver's post office in 1938 head down Hastings Street in a riotous frame of mind.

The Republicans pleaded for volunteers. Eventually, six international brigades were formed, including the Mackenzie-Papineau Battalion from this country (Mackenzie and Papineau were leaders of the 1837 rebellions in Upper and Lower Canada). Among the 1,448 volunteers were many veterans of the relief-camp front. They joined up despite official Canadian sanctions against doing so. It must be remembered that there was an air of appeasement polluting international diplomacy at the time. Also, Canada was pockmarked with anti-Communist, anti-Jewish and pro-Fascist sentiments.

Adolph Hitler in Germany and Franco in Spain were admired by many. It didn't help Mac-Pap organizers that some of them were Canadian Communist Party members. Of the volunteers, only a fraction were Communist sympathizers, and the efforts of a hostile RCMP and senior government functionaries to smear the whole lot with a Red brush rankled many of them. "It was the Depression, the world was collapsing, capitalism wasn't working," one former volunteer recalled in 1996. "The world was being divided into Fascists on one side and socialists and Communists on the other. I wasn't a member of any political party, but my sympathies were with the unemployed and the underprivileged."

As the history books have recorded, Franco's Fascists won this vicious little war in 1939, and the surviving Canadian volunteers were harassed even before they began returning home. On February 11, *The Province* reported a warm welcome for thirty-one of the veterans at Vancouver's CPR station the night before. The federal reaction was more hostile, however, and those who fought in Spain have never received the recognition or pension benefits so easily obtained by veterans of other wars.

On the home front, the last serious confrontation between the unemployed and the authorities occurred June 19, 1938. On that Sunday morning, RCMP and city police attacked six hundred squatters at the federal post office in downtown Vancouver. They had been there since May 20. That spring, there had been more

THE VANCOUVER DAILY PROVINCE

44th YEAR—NO. 72 | OFFICIAL FORECAST: FAIR AND WARM. | VANCOUVER, B. C., MONDAY, JUNE 20, 1938—26 PAGES ★ ★ ★ | PRICE 3 CENTS On Trains, Boats and in the Country, Five Cents

Pattullo Rejects Pleas Of Jobless; Damage By Riot Set at $30,000

JOBLESS MEET PATTULLO—Representatives of the single jobless and Premier T. D. Pattullo met in conference at Hotel Vancouver this morning. At the head of the conference table is Premier Pattullo. Facing the camera, left to right, are Ernie Cumber, John Matts, secretary of Relief Project Workers' Union, and R. W. Campbell. With backs to camera, left to right are, J. Jamieson, a court stenographer and Norman Harris, leader of the men from the Art Gallery.

"You Will Get Food If You're Eligible," Premier Tells Unemployed Delegation

ALL PARLEYS FAILURES

PREMIER T. D. Pattullo today refused all proposals advanced by a group of Protestant ministers, a delegation of C. C. F. members of the Legislature and a delegation of single unemployed.

(1) He told C. C. F. House members there would be no special session of the Legislature and no emergency relief projects. The conference was marked by heated clashes with Dr. Lyle Telford and Mrs. Dorothy Steeves.

(2) The Premier bluntly rejected a demand by Protestant ministers for grant of emergency food rations for single unemployed and creation of a conciliation committee.

(3) He told a delegation of "sit-downers" there would be no further government relief projects.

4. Significant of the Premier's stand was his statement to the ministers: "There comes a time when too much sympathy can be shown the men. That time has now come in Vancouver."

Conference of the jobless and the Premier broke up twenty minutes after it started with no progress having been made.

Premier Pattullo reiterated his stand that no emergency relief will be given during the summer months.

Demands of the men were:

1. Emergency relief for single unemployed.
2. Works programme.
3. Guarantees that there would be no discrimination against demonstrators.

"You are not in a very good position to dictate anything," remarked Premier Pattullo. "You have already been advised of the position taken by the government and it is not going to alter."

WERE ILL ADVISED.

"You were very ill advised to do what you did," he informed the delegates at the start of the meeting. "Why did you do what you did despite everything? Why did you send those men to Victoria when you knew I would meet you here?"

"It is a question of food," replied John Matts, secretary of Relief Project Workers' Union.

"If you are eligible to get food you will," answered the Premier. "If you are not you won't."

Other jobless delegates were R. W. (Doc) Campbell, Ernest Cumber, J. Jamieson and Norman Harris, former leader in the Art Gallery.

Campbell informed the Premier "the boys" had exhausted every constitutional method to win assistance from governmental authorities.

"Private industry can not absorb all of these men," he asserted. "Therefore it is the duty of the government. Unemployment is here to stay and the government has got to provide a works programme or you will have this situation from year to year. Immediate relief will have to be granted and a works programme started."

"1000 Men Await Answer"

The Premier told the men that the whole works programme is now underway.

"If the unemployed are eligible to receive work, they will get it," he declared.

"There are a thousand men waiting for your answer," Matts told the Premier. "What action follows depends upon your answer. These are good men. They want work."

"They've come from all parts of Canada," Premier Pattullo charged. "Then they gang up and act contrary to the law and expect us to feed them."

Harris interrupted to remark that statistics taken by Relief Project Workers' Union showed a majority of the men had been in British Columbia three years. He urged that some guarantee of work be given.

"We are not going to guarantee every man will be given a job," the Premier said. "It will destroy initiative."

He asserted that 1500 of the men came from the prairies during the past three weeks.

Ask "Constructive Attitude"

The C. C. F. delegation, composed of Dr. Lyle Telford, Mrs. Dorothy Steeves, E. E. Winch and Harold Winch, urged emergency relief, re-opening of camps and a long-term public works programme.

Mrs. Steeves, spokesmen for the group, said "we are here to urge the government to take a constructive attitude instead of following what we think is a destructive policy."

"The government has already made a statement of policy and does not intend to change it," replied the Premier.

"You mean," asked Mrs. Steeves, "that regardless of any catastrophe, the government won't change its policy?"

I didn't say that," said the Premier sharply.

(Continued on Page 2.)
See PATTULLO.

COUNCIL SPLIT ON RIOT ISSUE

Plan to Put Matter Squarely Before B. C., Ottawa.

Sharp division in the City Council over tactics employed in Sunday's "sit-down" and subsequent damage to stores was evidenced today as aldermen angrily debated the situation and discussed steps to impress governmental authorities with the seriousness of the crisis here.

Discussion of the disturbances came after Mayor G. C. Miller announced that he had had an interview with Premier Pattullo and had received assurance that the province would sponsor a city application for a $1,200,000 works loan to relieve unemployment under the federal $30,000,000 low-interest self-liquidating works scheme.

FAVORS PROTEST.

There was only half-hearted support for a motion of Alderman Helena Gutteridge favoring a protest to Premier T. D. Pattullo and the federal minister of labor, Hon. Norman Rogers., for actions in dealing with "single homeless men" and urging speedy action to provide work for the jobless. The measure also urged temporary relief until a works programme is adopted.

Ald. Gutteridge's resolution was finally laid over in favor of a memorial which will be prepared this afternoon by special committee headed by Mayor Miller.

The memorial, which will be placed before City Council for approval on Tuesday, is calculated to cover all angles of the relief situation here and to place the issue squarely before provincial and federal authorities.

"It will have to be something better than to go into a filing cabinet," commented Ald. H G. Wilson, who proposed the document.

OTHERS DISAGREE.

While Ald. Gutteridge defended the men's actions, contending they had been provoked beyond endurance, other aldermen took a less lenient view.

Ald. Gutteridge contended the council should censure both governments for their delay, and their action of Sunday.

"It is our responsibility to see this city is not made the battleground for the two governments," she exclaimed. "It is our business to tell both bodies it is a disgrace which the city of Vancouver is not prepared to tolerate. Vancouver citizens have shown their sympathy is definitely with the men."

She added more than $300 was collected on behalf of single jobless at the meeting on Powell

(Continued on Page 2.)
See COUNCIL.

Twenty-two Held After Postoffice and Art Gallery Sit-Downers Routed

DELEGATION AT VICTORIA

SITUATION AT A GLANCE.

Thirty-nine persons, including five policemen, injured when constables evicted jobless from Postoffice and Art Gallery Sunday morning.

Property damage totalled $30,000, chiefly plateglass windows.

Twenty-two jobless arrested.

Delegation of 100 unemployed landed at Victoria this morning, but Provincial Government refused to grant them an interview.

Business as usual!

Vancouver swung back into commercial stride this morning after a week-end marked by bitter street fighting and destruction of $30,000 in private property.

Early Sunday morning, acting on secret orders from Ottawa, Royal Canadian Mounted and city police used tear gas to rout unemployed sit-down strikers from the Postoffice and Art Gallery.

Thirty-nine persons, including five constables, were injured in the brawling which followed the assault on the Postoffice. Many others received superficial hurts.

The fleeing jobless, maddened by gas and galvanized by blows from police truncheons, stormed east along Hastings and Cordova streets, smashing windows in business houses as they ran. Damage to plateglass and window displays at Woodward's Ltd., where seventy ground floor panes were shattered, was estimated upwards of $15,000.

SITUATION STILL TENSE TODAY.

Twenty-two men were under arrest when the smoke of battle cleared Sunday. The rest of the jobless remnants of an army of 1200 that withstood siege in the public buildings since May 20 nursed their wounds in Ukrainian Hall.

But today the situation is still tense.

One hundred jobless, cheered on by 8000 sympathizers, went to Victoria on the Sunday night boat and today deployed about the locked Parliament buildnigs despite Premier Pattullo's warning that they would be denied an interview with provincial authorities.

Violence seemed certain to flare again immediately after the boat left when the crowd massed outside the Postoffice and six more windows were broken. The crowd dispersed at the request of Harold Winch, M.L.A., but as jobless and curiosity-seekers swung along Hastings street, hoodlums smashed two new panes at Woodward's Ltd.

Unemployed leaders announced that they were ready to send 200 more men to Victoria if they don't get "work and wages."

As merchants on Hastings and Cordova streets ruefully repaired windows and made inventories of damaged stocks, Mayor George C. Miller said that no more sit-down strikes will be tolerated in this city.

Police maintained a close guard over business areas to prevent a recurrent outbreak of vandalism.

When news of the disorder spread through the city Sunday morning, thousands swarmed down town, gazed in awe at the litter of glass that had cascaded to the sidewalks, examined the dress dummies and display goods that had been hurled into the streets and poked exploratory fingers through the gaping windows until warned off by constables on guard.

Traffic choked the streets in

(Continued on Page 2.)
See JOBLESS.

Action Photos—

Two full pages of action pictures of jobless riot, Pages 10 and 12.

Eye witness stories from postoffice and Art Gallery. Page 11.

Comment from all over Canada, Page 13.

Details of damage to downtown stores. Page 9.

Interview with Steve Brodie in hospital, Page 16.

City to ban future sit-downs, Page 16.

Story of mass meeting on Powell street grounds. Page 13.

C.C.F. members demand resignation of whole Legislature, Page 7.

Death Toll Set at 40 as Train Plunges Into Flooded Creek

No Canadians On Board as "Olympian" Is Wrecked Near Miles City, Montana.

(By Associated Press.)

MILES CITY, MONT., June 20.—Bodies of eleven persons were recovered today from the wreckage of sleeper B of the Milwaukee Railroad's "Olympian," bringing to twenty-three the number of bodies recovered from the train which early yesterday plunged into a creek near here. It is believed the wreck caused the death of at least forty persons.

Railroad officials said the seven bodies were all that were in the submerged car, but they believed there were two or three more bodies pinned under the wreckage.

The bodies were brought to Miles City by train.

With them were four other bodies which had lain all night on the bank of Custer Creek, 26 miles east of here, where the wreck occurred early on Sunday morning.

Sixteen bodies were recovered yesterday and last night.

NO CANADIANS.

Train porters said "five or six" other persons were swept away.

The list of known dead, injured and missing, issued by the company, included the names of no Canadians. Many of the dead, however, were from coast cities in Washington.

Eleven bodies recovered yesterday were brought to Miles City mortuaries last night. The body of a woman believed to have been a passenger on the train was recovered from the Yellowstone River near Glendive, fifty miles from the scene of the wreck.

Last night railroad authorities said twelve bodies had been brought to Miles City, but later it was said one of the bodies was that of an embalmed corpse.

(Continued on Page 2.)
See TRAIN WRECK.

FOUR NIPPON SHIPS SUNK BY CHINESE

Victory Claimed In Bombing Raid.

SHANGHAI, June 20.—The Chinese reported officially today that four war vessels of the Japanese fleet in the Yangtse River were sunk above Anking in a raid by eight heavy bombers.

A statement issued in Hankow said the Chinese planes managed to outfight and outspeed twelve Japanese pursuit ships to carry out the attack.

A Japanese naval communique confirmed the raid, but denied any ships were sunk. The communique said the Chinese planes were driven off by a heavy anti-aircraft fire after a bomb slightly damaged a troop transport.

The Chinese said several attempts to land Japanese troops on the south bank of Yangtze above Anking had been blocked.

Before receipt of the report of the Chinese attacks, a Japanese naval spokesman said warships preceded by mine-sweepers were twenty miles upstream from Anking, or 195 miles by water from Hankow.

5000 NEW JOBS PLANNED IN B.C.

Road Work Total for Year Is Set at $3,000,000.

By BRUCE HUTCHISON.
Daily Province Staff Correspondent.

VICTORIA, June 20. — Five thousand new jobs will be created in British Columbia this summer by public works, under the Federal and Provincial governments, according to official figures issued at the Legislative Buildings.

As finally totalled up, and including latest Federal Government appropriations, public works in British Columbia this year will cost $3,010,000.

PLANS DETAILED.

This includes $1,500,000 to be spent by the Provincial Government on its roads: $300,000 on the Pacific Highway; $360,000 on mining roads and trails; $600,000 on the Big Bend Highway; $200,000 on the Yahk-Kootenay Park; $40,000 on Spanish Banks, and $10,000 on Stanley Park.

NOT FOR STRIKERS.

Road work will absorb about 4000 men for the summer and over 800 young men will be placed in government forestry and mining camps.

In addition the Federal Government is employing some 300 men in defensive works in this province. The Provincial Government will also keep from 8000 to 10,000 men employed on road maintenance work.

The labor department explained that it does not suggest that road-building jobs are open to the sit-down strikers, but it believes that the creation of 5000 new jobs will relieve the labor situation and make other jobs available to the men now idle in Vancouver.

WHAT HAPPENED HERE?—Hastings street presented a gruesome sight—in fact even the officers were fooled when they rushed up to these figures. The decapitated forms drew awed gasps from the first spectators to see them, and probably started the rumor that a woman had been killed in the riots. They turned out to be dummies pulled from the show windows of Woodwards Ltd.

LEADER STANDS FIRM—Steve Brodie, leader of the jobless sit-downers in the Postoffice, is shown during the fight. He is putting his hands over his head to protect himself as a plainclothesman swings at him with a length of rubber hose.

A BEATING HALTED—An R. C. M. P. officer steps over the form of Steve Brodie, unemployed leader, to protect him. This picture was snapped a few minutes after Brodie was pushed from the building by officers. It was Brodie who gave to officers the men's decision to remain in the building despite police warning that they would be ejected.

The most dramatic incident of the Great Depression—the Post Office Riot—is examined in great detail the next day in Vancouver's leading newspaper.

jobless than usual in the city, despite encouraging signs that the economy was improving. These were mostly single men, swelled by a large contingent from the Prairies who had been released from interior BC forest camps. Premier Pattullo did not endear himself to this latter group. "They've come from all parts of Canada," he charged during the crisis. "Then they gang up and act contrary to the law and expect us to feed them."

This obdurate attitude, which was underscored on May 17 by a labour ministry announcement that no more relief would be available for the transients, was in large part the impetus for subsequent events. Three days later, 1,500 marched on the Georgia Hotel, the art gallery and the post office. They were quickly induced to leave the hotel (essentially being bribed by city council), but at the other two buildings they squatted and remained. Negotiations didn't get anywhere, nor did threats. The men wanted relief for the single unemployed, a meaningful works program and no discrimination against the demonstrators. The various levels of officialdom just wanted them to go away.

For one month, the occupation continued, until the Dominion government stepped in. Because the post office was a federal building, the RCMP were ordered to clear out the squatters. After an ultimatum was ignored, the Mounties struck, using tear gas and clubs. When the first gas bomb exploded within the Post Office, the men broke windows in order to get some fresh air. They also started trashing parts of the interior, and approximately $30,000 in damage was done.

At the art gallery, the occupants noted the heavy city police presence in the neighbourhood, not to mention a few tendrils of tear gas in the air, and heeded advice to leave quietly. Not so at the federal facility, which was emptied in ten minutes of violent action. "The fleeing jobless, maddened by gas and galvanized by blows from police truncheons, stormed east along Hastings and Cordova streets, smashing windows in business houses as they ran," *The Province* reported the next day. "Damage to plate-glass window displays at Woodward's Ltd., where 70 ground-floor panes were shattered, was estimated upwards of $15,000."

There were twenty-two arrests and thirty-nine persons injured, including five policemen. The next day, June 20, Pattullo met with representatives of the jobless, the CCF and the Protestant clergy in the Hotel Vancouver. He stubbornly rejected all their entreaties, reiterating his stand that there would be no emergency relief during the summer months.

Pattullo accused the clergymen—representing the Anglican, Baptist and United churches—of meddling, and delivered a parting shot to the CCF: "Just to make a long story short, I am not going to sit here all day and argue with you. Obviously, you are out to criticize the government."

Thus ended the Great Depression in British Columbia, for all intents and purposes: To the acrid stench of tear gas and the echo of police truncheons smacking into flesh is added the image of a courteous but adamant premier convinced that his path is the right one.

Within weeks, the Vancouver unemployed had been dispersed throughout the province. Some got temporary jobs, while others helped fight a big forest fire on Vancouver Island. New factories began opening and an intensive program of public works delivered more jobs. The forest industry, which managed to survive the darkest years, got welcome news in November of the year. Under a new Canada-US trade deal, prohibitive and restrictive American conditions (including one that would require every stick of lumber to be stamped with the country of origin) were eased.

THE DECADE IN HEADLINES
« 1938 »

600 MEN FIGHT TO CONTROL BLAZE AT CAMPBELL RIVER

The most troublesome fire of a disastrous summer in the woods gets the attention of the media. This Vancouver Island fire is called "the most serious in the history of the province" by Premier Pattullo. Firefighters finally get the upper hand after almost a month of effort.

Nanaimo Free Press, July 16, 1938

B.C. MILK ACT LEGAL; INDEPENDENTS LOSE IN PRIVY COUNCIL APPEAL

A Fraser Valley farmers' challenge to the Natural Products Marketing Act is dismissed by the Empire's highest legal tribunal. Several attempts have been made over the years to overturn government control of agricultural marketing.

Vancouver Sun, July 27, 1938

MRS. MARY SUTTON, 76, 'FIRST' ACROSS BRIDGE

The first pedestrians try out the brand-new Lions Gate Bridge between Vancouver's Stanley Park and the North Shore. Two days later, motorists are given access to the Empire's longest suspension span.

Vancouver Sun, November 12, 1938

The Vancouver Sun **EXTRA**

Only Evening Newspaper Owned, Controlled and Operated by Vancouver People

FOUNDED 1886 VOL. LIII—No. 279 | OFFICIAL WEATHER FORECAST Cool: Scattered Showers | VANCOUVER, BRITISH COLUMBIA, SUNDAY, SEPTEMBER 3, 1939 | Price 5 Cents | Trinity 4111

BRITAIN AT WAR!

Ottawa Rushes Preparations

Cabinet Meets As Australia Declares War

By British United Press

CANBERRA, Sept. 4 (2:30 a.m. Monday) — Australia declared today that a state of war exists between her and Germany.

By Canadian Press

OTTAWA, Sept. 3.—Dominion cabinet ministers, aroused early by the dread but not unexpected news that Great Britain and the Empire are at war with Germany, hurried through foggy streets today to meet Prime Minister Mackenzie King in the Privy Council chamber at 10 o'clock (6 a.m. Vancouver time).

Mr. King, advised by the Canadian Press a few minutes after the flash was received that Great Britain had declared war, lost no time in communicating with his ministers, who had been warned to be ready for such an emergency.

Hon. Ian Mackenzie, minister of defense, was the first to arrive for the council. He reached the meeting at 9:45 a.m. Shortly afterwards Hon. C. D. Howe, minister of transport; Hon. Ernest Lapointe, minister of justice; Hon. J. G. Gardiner, minister of agriculture; Hon. Norman McLarty, postmaster-general, and Hon. T. A. Crerar, minister of resources, arrived.

Mr. Lapointe who, as acting Secretary of State, will have charge of any press censorship in Canada, said the cabinet has taken power to establish a censorship but could not say whether plans to put in effect have been completed.

So far, however, no censorship applies to the press and the minister declined to comment on reports of the censoring of cables and telegrams at Montreal.

It is understood, it was learned from other sources, that a subcommittee of the cabinet on censorship has been set up under the chairmanship of Mr. McLarty.

The Prime Minister appeared fresh and unworried as he entered the Council chamber after chatting for a few minutes with reporters.

He said he is not sure what procedure will be followed when Parliament meets Thursday. Whether a formal declaration of war will be made by Canada is one of the matters of detail yet to be worked out.

Only a few people watched the minister enter the East Block. A small girl with a dog on a leash played around the door as Mr. King and his colleagues began their deliberations.

As usual, Royal Canadian Mounted Policemen were on duty at the doors, but about the only other spectators were a few newspaper reporters and motion picture photographers.

All is in readiness for speedy action along whatever lines the government proposes to move, now that Canada, as a partner in the British Commonwealth of Nations, stands literally if not technically at war with Germany.

It was indicated that necessary Orders-in-Council are ready for merely inking in dates and the formality of adoption to put into affect the various wartime measures which may be needed pending the meeting of Parliament Thursday.

Lord Tweedsmuir, the Governor-General, is at Government House ready to co-operate with the government in speeding orders through. No radical steps will become generally effective.

While it is accepted by all political parties and authorities that when Britain is at war Canada is at war, the actual declaration of

Please Turn to Page Two
See "Canada at War"

Churchill in Cabinet

LONDON, Sept. 3.—It was officially announced that Rt. Hon. Winston Churchill has been appointed First Lord of the Admiralty in the new war cabinet.

Today At a Glance

LONDON: Prime Minister Neville Chamberlain proclaimed by radio to the British Empire and to the world at 2:15 a.m. Vancouver time, that Britain is "at war" with Germany.

BERLIN: Germany rejected Britain's demands for withdrawal of German troops from Poland, blamed Europe's war on the British Cabinet and announced that Fuehrer Adolf Hitler today personally was taking the field of battle with Germany's eastern army. The German Army High Command announced German troops smashing deeper into Polish territory.

PARIS: France demanded a German reply to her ultimatum by 8 a.m. Vancouver time.

WASHINGTON: White House and state department officials reported that President Roosevelt and Secretary of State Hull were keeping in closest touch with European war developments. President to broadcast at 7 p.m. Vancouver time.

BUDAPEST: Hungary declared her neutrality.

WARSAW: Poland attempting to reinforce the Polish-Rumanian pact of assistance. Lithuanian troops shot down a heavy German airplane. Poland assured Lithuania that her neutrality would be respected.

MOSCOW: Soviet Russia's capital calm. Populace permitted to follow factual accounts of European events in newspapers and radio.

TOKYO. — Japan will remain neutral because of the Soviet-German non-aggression Pact, newspapers reported.

ROME: Italy, so far neutral, in accordance with Mussolini's statement that Italy will take no military initiative.

PARIS: France revealed that she considered herself at war with Germany at the moment that Prime Minister Chamberlain involved Britain in the conflict, although she was not legally at war with the Reich until the expiration of her ultimatum at 5 p.m. (9 a.m. Vancouver time).

CANBERRA, Australia. — The Australian government declares "State of War" between Australia and Germany.

EDITORIAL

Fighting For a Just Cause

You are to be proud today of your citizenship in Canada and the British Empire.

Was there ever a war so just as this one to which we are solemnly committed?

Has there ever been, in the world's history, a more noble event than for Britain and France, as they decide today, to come promptly to the relief of their ally, now in dire need of succor?

Selfish interest might have called for our two allied peoples to save their own skins, even at the sacrifice of their treaty undertakings. It is something akin to this sentiment that is relied upon by the isolationist peoples of the world today, as they seek to justify a position of aloofness.

We belong to an Empire and we belong to a breed which honors its commitments. Poland's fight, and what it stands for, is our fight today.

In Germany, the Allied Front, for what it means, will not be completely understood. The Sun has already noted that the German mistake of 1914 is being repeated 25 years later. And for the second time the lesson must be brought home to the German people. Another generation has been led away—this time by Hitler and a gang of cold-blooded adventurers who already have committed every crime of rapacity and oppression that is listed in the calendar.

In London, this noon, Mr. Chamberlain stood in his place in Britain's Parliament, as chosen head of the free people of this Empire, announced that we are at war with Germany. His was a tragic and difficult task; and we shall all of us face difficult tasks before this conflict is ended. But today we have a great satisfaction. It is that with infinite restraint and patience, we in this Empire, through our chosen leaders, have sought to intervene by every peaceful means that could be summoned to our aid. We have tried to appease and placate and advise; in every way, over a long period, we have thrown our weight and influence on the side where right is not the sole prerogative of might. We have given "last warnings" and have delayed more precious hours to allow those warnings to sink in with full effect. But Herr Hitler, holding to his record of duplicity and grab, has chosen to go unheeding the other way.

Thus, we have arrived, sadly but still firm in resolve, at today's fateful decision. We shall have no fear of the outcome. That is not the British way. It is a part of the propaganda of the Hitler-Stalin ideal that the democratic way of living is to be swept aside for that nameless shambles of ruthlessness and disorder which has reduced the peoples of Germany and Russia to practical serfdom. Don't be fooled by this nonsense! We are facing days of personal worry and national trial, but the calmness and common-sense of mankind will ultimately prevail. There shall be no other end.

Again we say we have a just cause and a clear national conscience. Last Sunday, the clergy of Vancouver and other cities in our land led the people in prayers that we might be delivered from the horror and suffering of another war. Today, we shall devoutly pray again for guidance and for victory over the evil forces which stalk through the world, seeking to ruin the liberty and decent way of life of mankind.

WAR BULLETINS

MOSCOW, Sept. 3. — The appointment of a new Soviet military attache to Berlin was announced today in line with Soviet Russia's swiftly changing foreign policy. The new appointee is M. A. Purkaieff.

BUDAPEST, Sept. 3. — Proclaiming a state of emergency, the Hungarian Government today issued decrees drastically limiting civil rights.

LONDON, Sept. 3.—The air-raid precaution animals committee attempted to call a halt today on the destruction of pet dogs and cats by owners wishing to save them from a more brutal death by bombing. The committee said it had made arrangements for the emergency care of animals.

Please Turn to Page Four
See "Bulletins"

World Radio Broadcast By The King at 9 a.m.

By British United Press

LONDON, Sept. 3.—The British Broadcasting Corporation announced that the King will address his subjects in a world-wide broadcast at 6 p.m., London summer time (9 a.m. Vancouver time).

The King and Queen heard Prime Minister Chamberlain's war declaration over the radio in their private apartments at Buckingham Palace.

NEW YORK, Sept. 3.—The American network broadcasting companies announced that they would rebroadcast a radio address of the King to the Empire at 9 a.m. Vancouver time.

Poland Invades Germany

Counter-Attack Sweeps Over Border Into East Prussia

By EDWARD BEATTIE Jr.
By British United Press
Special to The Vancouver Sun

WARSAW, Sept. 3.—Polish troops have entered Germany.

Polish troops, counter-attacking, crossed into East Prussia in the vicinity of Deutscheylau.

East Prussia is the province of Germany separated from Germany proper by the Polish Corridor.

The Poles are attempting to cut off the German army which has advanced south into the Corridor from East Prussia, has reached the Cze River, about 20 miles south of the southeast corner of East Prussia and is trying to contact the German army driving across the Corridor from West Prussia.

The Polish radio also announced the recapture of Zbaszyn, a town due west of Warsaw on the German frontier in the province of Pznania.

TOWN FALLS

The Polish spokesman confirmed that the army from West Prussia has taken the town of Sepolno, on the west side of the Corridor and that the eastern army has captured Zbaszyn and Myztniec on the southern border of East Prussia. Poles, not expecting an attack, had not been at the border to protect them, he said.

The spokesman said that the town of Wielun had been practically burned out by a "deluge" of incendiary bombs dropped from German planes.

There is heavy fighting along the border of the Polish district of Czestochowa.

(Berlin said German troops had taken that important industrial city).

CITIES BOMBED

An official communique early today said that 12 hours after Poland had accepted a German proposal that both refrain from bombing open cities, German bombers had showered death and destruction on "not less than 24" Polish cities, killing and wounding 1500 persons.

Germany approached Poland through the Netherlands government Friday night, the communique said. Poland accepted at once. Saturday German bombers raided from dawn until dusk, it added.

"The German government Friday night contacted Poland through an intermediary, the Netherlands government, with a proposal not to bomb open cities," the communique said.

"The Polish government declared its agreement. Nevertheless, German fliers, on Sept. 2, bombed not less than 24 cities, including such a holy city as Czestochowa, which is entirely in flames, the textile centre of Lodz, the bath resort of Busco, and many others, causing not less than 1500 deaths and wounding."

HOSPITAL DESTROYED

A spokesman said that incendiary bombs dropped by German planes had destroyed the hospital at Velunje on Friday, and Saturday air raids on Lublin killed 30 persons, including five children, and injured 58. News of new bomb victims was arriving hourly.

The German Embassy staff is

Please Turn to Page Two
See "Fighting"

Chamberlain Tells Empire of Decision

France Joins in Declaration Against Germany; Prime Minister Predicts 'A Liberated Europe and Hitlerism Destroyed"

By WEBB MILLER
Special to The Vancouver Sun
Copyright, 1939, by British United Press

LONDON, Sept. 3.–Great Britain went to war against Germany today–25 years and 30 days from the time she entered the conflict of 1914 against the same enemy.

A brief announcement by Prime Minister Neville Chamberlain that went by radio to all outposts of the Empire sent Britain to war in fulfillment of her pledge to help Poland if that nation was invaded by Adolf Hitler's Nazis.

The French government set its deadline at 5 p.m. (8 a.m. Vancouver time) but announced from Paris that France considered herself automatically at war with Germany the moment Chamberlain made his pronouncement.

"This country is at war with Germany," Chamberlain said in slow, measured tones. "You can imagine what a bitter blow this is to me that all my long struggle to win peace has failed."

A radio hook-up to all places under the Union Jack was made and Chamberlain stepped to the microphone in No. 10 Downing Street to speak the fateful words.

"We have a clear conscience," declared the Prime Minister. "We have done all that any country could do to establish peace, but the situation has become intolerable, and we have resolved to finish it.

"Now may God bless you all and may He defend the right, for it is evil things that we shall be fighting against — force, bad faith, injustice, oppression and persecution. Against them, I am certain, the right will prevail."

"God Save the King" was played on the BBC's Empire hook-up as Chamberlain concluded.

Wounded Polish Airman Battles 12 Nazi Planes

WARSAW, Sept. 3. — Lieutenant Pausiniski of the Polish Air Force was hailed in Warsaw today as an early hero of the war.

Taking off in a combat plane, Pausinski attacked a squadron of 12 German bombers. He shot down one of the attacking planes after a thrilling dogfight, witnessed by thousands of residents of Warsaw.

Several bullets fired by the German planes struck Pasinski's plane, damaging its wings and wounding the Polish flier.

Despite his wounds and the dangerous condition of his plane he made a successful landing from an altitude of about 2500 feet.

'Russia Will Be Neutral'

MOSCOW, Sept. 3. — (5:30 p.m.). Foreign circles today are convinced that Soviet Russia will remain neutral in the new European war, but there was no official comment on Britain's declaration that a state of war exists between the United Kingdom and Germany.

It was unofficially reported, however, that service has been suspended on eight principal domestic airlines.

Throng in Downing Street

The curbstones of Downing Street were thronged as Chamberlain spoke. Cabinet ministers and important members of Parliament hurried to the Prime Minister's residence. Soon the entire south side of Downing Street was crowded with men and women waiting to be told that they were at war.

France, committed to the same stand as Britain in regard to the defense of Polish sovereignty, is expected to go to war, too.

An ultimatum, calling for a reply by Germany to Britain's demand that the Reich withdraw troops from Poland, was the technical step that committed the British to war. A government communique announced that unless such a reply was forthcoming by 11 a.m. (2 a.m. Vancouver time) today a state of war would exist.

The German reply did not arrive before the deadline.

Half an hour before the deadline set in the British ultimatum expired the German embassy here still was waiting word from Berlin.

"There is no news," the German embassy announced as the clock crawled toward war. "We are in constant communication with Berlin."

Apparently there was no slackening in Germany's invasion of Poland. Warsaw said there had been 1500 casualties from German air raiders. The Poles fought back and claimed that their troops had penetrated East Prussia, the isolated piece of Germany that is cut off by the Polish Corridor.

War Machine Moves

Great Britain moved quickly to set her war machine moving. The King convened the Privy Council at 11:45 a.m. (3:45 a.m. Vancouver time) to announce that a State of War exists.

The House of Commons passed the National Service Bill under which the government can conscript all men between the ages of 18 and 41 for military service.

Instructions regarding air raid warnings went out over the British Broadcasting Company system.

The formal notification that Germany must reply by 11 a.m. was delivered in Berlin by Sir Nevile Henderson, British Ambassador. He delivered that notification at 9 a.m.

Please Turn to Page Two **See "Britain at War"**

MR. CHAMBERLAIN: "Now may God bless you all and may He defend the right, for it is evil things that we shall be fighting against—force, bad faith, injustice, oppression and persecution. Against them, I am certain, the right will prevail."

The onset of the Second World War is announced in an extra edition of The Sun.

BC wood products got an easier ride across the border.

Two familiar forestry personalities also appeared on the scene in the thirties. Harold Foley, a graduate of Notre Dame at South Bend, Indiana, joined the Powell River Co. in 1936 and reorganized it just in time to take advantage of the newsprint boom of the forties. Walter Koerner, whose family were refugees from Nazi Germany, joined with his brothers in forming the Alaska Pine Co. in May of 1939. They had found a way to treat hemlock, a little-regarded wood, so that it was commercially desirable. The product was christened "Alaska pine" and the Koerners became rich. Walter Koerner and Harold Foley both became major philanthropists in BC.

With the Depression apparently on the backburner and the jobless becoming less visible, the news editors and editorial writers started to pay more attention to foreign news. Hitler had been gobbling up European body parts for some time, while Britain practiced a diplomatic policy of benign appeasement. But after Prime Minister Neville Chamberlain sold out Czechoslovakia at Munich in September of 1938 (and returned to London to declare "peace in our time"), few doubted a showdown was inevitable. In the summer of 1939, Britain issued an ultimatum to Germany, which had invaded Poland: Withdraw or war will be declared.

War it was; on September 3, an Extra Edition of *The Sun* told Vancouver the momentous news. "We belong to an Empire and we belong to a breed which honours its commitments. Poland's fight, and what it stands for, is our fight today," it said in a Page One editorial. "...We shall devoutly pray again for guidance and for victory over the evil forces which stalk through the world, seeking to ruin the liberty and decent way of life of mankind."

Vancouver's own regiment, the 72nd Seaforth Highlanders of Canada, was mobilized that month, as were other BC units. On December 15, the Seaforths left Vancouver for Eastern Canada on the first stage of the trip overseas. Readers of *The Sun* and *The Province*, however, weren't allowed to know this officially because of censorship restrictions. Both papers printed detailed stories of the regiment's final parade through downtown streets without mentioning it ended at the CPR station. *The Province* also printed an eight-page supplement on the Seaforths ("unique in newspaper history") that week, so anyone not clued in on the departure date knew something was going on. *The Sun* made do with pictures of each serviceman.

All the "hush-hush" of December 15 drew the Page One ire of *The News-Herald*, which ridiculed censorship laws that attempted to keep secret the movement of 900 soldiers. "These men might have been marching to a prison camp instead of beginning the most glorious adventure that their enthusiasm could conceive, and their young hearts imagine," it said in an editorial, calling the secrecy childish and the censorship board "amateurs."

Ten days later British Columbians celebrated a rather subdued Christmas. In Vancouver particularly, there was many an unoccupied chair at the festive table. For several of those households, that chair would remain empty for an eternity.

THE DECADE IN HEADLINES
« 1939 »

HOTEL VANCOUVER OPENS DOORS TO FIRST GUESTS

The third version of the city's landmark hotel opens on the corner of Burrard and Georgia. Lt.-Gov. Eric Hamber, who heads the list of dignitaries at the event, calls the hotel the best in North America.

Vancouver Sun, May 25, 1939

STANLEY PARK GUNS MANNED

In a roundup of war preparedness developments, *The Sun* reports the activation of Vancouver's coastal defence guns as well as the installation of searchlights and the construction of new emplacements on Point Grey.

Vancouver Sun, August 26, 1939

LOCAL MEN LEAVE FOR ACTIVE DUTY ON COAST

The 2nd Searchlight Battery, 102nd Battalion, leaves in two drafts for wartime duty in Prince Rupert as *The Citizen* barely contains its pride in reporting the departure. After more training, the battery will join the coastal defence forces.

Prince George Citizen, October 3, 1939

FIRST AUTOMATIC PHONE EXCHANGE OPERATING

With Page One full of war news, *The Sun* reports the arrival of dial telephones—nine years after their installation in Victoria—on its local section front.

Vancouver Sun, December 2, 1939

NEW B.C. HIGHWAY TO BORDER NAMED 'KING GEORGE VI'

A new route between the Pattullo Bridge and the US border honours the monarch who visited BC earlier in the year. The King George Highway is now a vital artery in the suburban city of Surrey.

Vancouver Sun, December 13, 1939

THE FORTIES: THERE'S A WAR ON

« 1940 – 1949 »

'BLOODLESS REVOLUTION' ACHIEVED IN OKANAGAN

Central selling of the fruit crop is debated at the annual BC Fruit Growers Association convention in Penticton. The plan to make BC Tree Fruits Ltd. the sole agency is endorsed the next day.

Vancouver Sun, January 11, 1940

AERIAL FERRY OPERATES OVER FRASER RIVER

On a Front Page dominated by war news, the New Westminster daily reports the opening of the Boston Bar aerial passenger ferry—first of its kind in Canada.

The Columbian, March 15, 1940

NEW GROUP OF ANTIPODES AIRMEN REACHES CANADA

The British Empire Air Training Scheme gains impetus as Australians and New Zealanders arrive. *The Sun*'s story focuses on two Maoris in the contingent, and notes that "they speak perfect English." Under the scheme, Empire airmen hone their wartime skills at Canadian bases.

Vancouver Sun, October 25, 1940

As the deceptive month of January ushered in 1940, a great many British Columbians had to concentrate on the fact they were at war. Sure, there was the marching of soldiers and sailors, tearful departures and various shortages. Everyone noticed those things. The Seaforth Highlanders had to turn away dozens of volunteers when they recruited a replacement battalion for the regiment that had sailed to England. But the drama and anticipation of the previous September, which saw the Seaforths and the Canadian Scottish Regiment mobilized and the coastal defence guns at Stanley Park manned, had been replaced by something akin to indifference.

The French and German armies still glared at each other across the Maginot and Siegfried lines. This was so patently non-newsworthy that BC's dailies were examining the Russo-Finnish conflict in great detail and running stories about the cold winter in Britain. Business reporters noted that the terminal facilities in Vancouver lay idle because Prairie wheat was being shipped—at lower cost—to US ports.

On Vancouver Island, the Esquimalt naval base bustled with censored activities, while the pride of Victoria, the Canadian Scottish, prepared themselves for war. Downtown, the legendary Billy Tickle and his orchestra still played the national anthem at 10 p.m. precisely in the lounge of the Empress, shutting down Victoria for the night. Shipyards in all the West Coast ports were preparing to handle a surge of government orders. The first Dominion War Loan ($200 million at 3.5 percent) was floated by Ottawa. These recurring appeals for money to finance the war would later be called Victory Loans.

On January 10, *The Sun* reported that the Japanese population in Vancouver had risen 15 percent—to 8,647—in five years. Alderman H.D. Wilson was alarmed by the figures. "I attribute the increase to the Orientals' ability to survive where an Occidental will fail in business, because they have different standards of living and a tendency to evade or circumvent labour legislation," he told the paper. Wilson also claimed the Japanese were making very serious inroads on Vancouver's commercial life. Within two short years, his overt intolerance would be echoed by others during the wholesale removal of the Japanese in 1942.

The lazy complacency of this decade's opening weeks, however, didn't fool *The*

THE DECADE IN HEADLINES
« 1941 »

CONSTRUCTION OF R.A.F. STATION PUSHES FORWARD

A few months before completion, the new Royal Air Force base at Patricia Bay north of Victoria is revealed to reporters. The station is turned over to the federal transport department in 1948 and eventually becomes the Pat Bay Airport.

The Colonist, October 11, 1941

ALARMS TIGHTEN BLACKOUT RULES

One day after the Japanese attack on Pearl Harbor, war jitters hit the BC coast and blackout measures go into effect. The following day, the rival *Sun* warns its readers that the "jolly game" is serious now.

The Province, December 8, 1941

HART BECOMES B.C.'S PREMIER

The change in leadership following the resignation of T.D. Pattullo is pushed to Page 2. The aftermath of Japan's attack on Pearl Harbor dominates the front pages of most BC dailies.

The Province, December 9, 1941

Sun's editorial board. In a prescient editorial early in the month, the paper predicted that the "unpredictable war" would soon spread to Norway, Belgium and Holland. In April, it did, when the Nazis struck at Norway. The Low Countries were next, on May 10, when "Blitzkrieg" (lightning war) became part of British Columbia's vocabulary. Hitler's Panzer divisions obliterated Belgium and Holland, swept around the left flank of the Maginot Line and trapped the British Expeditionary Force. May was also the month that a new synonym for "miracle" entered our language: Dunkirk. Some 338,000 British and French troops were safely snatched from the jaws of the Wehrmacht and returned to England, and a war that could have been over in days would last another five years.

Winston Churchill replaced Neville Chamberlain as prime minister of Great Britain and leader of the free world. From the Houses of Parliament at Westminster, he snarled defiance at Hitler with a blend of bulldog bravado and eloquent syntax that raised the image of politicians to a rarefied level. Back home in the relatively minor league of Victoria, Premier Thomas Dufferin Pattullo was fretting about "better terms" from Ottawa and losing the confidence of the electorate.

There are few humans as blind to potential disaster as politicians. The gene that compels them to seek office has an evil twin. This is the one that whispers in their ears that everything is well, there is no problem, the muttering out there is just sour grapes. These folks we elect to govern our affairs have a form of tunnel vision that does not permit extraneous doubt to get in the way of any rosy projections.

Despite Pattullo's performance as a virtual one-man band during the previous decade and the relatively easy victory in the 1937 election, his continued harping on provincial rights (read: BC First) at a time when the future of the Empire was at stake did not endear him to his constituents. Didn't he know there was a war on? Even Pattullo's own cabinet—including his right-hand man, John Hart—were drifting away. But the premier, sure that his policies would bring a resounding victory, called an election for October 21, 1941, and campaigned on a platform that didn't really offer anything new except vigorous prosecution of the war. Which is right up there in the motherhood league with denouncing crime.

As elections in BC are wont to be, the results were shocking. Pattullo's party won only twenty-one seats out of forty-eight. The Conservatives, pronounced dead in the thirties, came to life again with twelve and the CCF got fourteen. Even more shocking, the socialists led in the popular vote with 33.36 percent to the Liberals' 32.94 percent, one of the rare instances in this century that a party with the most votes didn't lead in seats won. All this arithmetic added up to minority government, as far as Pattullo was concerned. Others weren't so sure, including Hart, his finance minister. The C-word, which had been submerged ever since Pattullo clamped his iron hand on BC's affairs in 1933, popped up again. A coalition government of the right, many said, would help the war effort and, not incidentally, keep the CCF at bay. There were even hints before the election that coalition thinking had come out of the closet—a suspicion that made Pattullo's subsequent estrangement from Hart more bitter.

Despite the evidence before him that the citizens had grown weary of his brand of leadership, Pattullo vowed to carry on. He went to Ottawa for a conference on federal-provincial affairs (which he helped wreck by his obstinacy) and returned to find the trusted John Hart favouring a Conservative call for an "all-party administration." Pattullo fired Hart as finance minister on November 17. Two weeks later, the Liberal party met in convention and voted December 3 for a form of coalition.

With British Columbia and the rest of the world still digesting the Japanese attack on Pearl Harbor two days earlier, Pattullo resigned as premier on December 9. He went out with a whimper, not a bang, after failing to maintain control with a "ghost" cabinet. Bruce Hutchison, now writing for *The Sun*, neatly summed up the situation with this trenchant sentence: "To the right sits the newly formed ghost government of Pattullo, the frail shadow of a shadow, the battered political scarecrow which now scares nobody and will soon collapse—a mere morning coat, striped trousers and top hat stuffed with straw." Grandiose in his dreams and often charming in his manner, the bedrock of BC granite that was Duff Pattullo retired to the backbenches of the legislature and sat there until he was defeated in the 1945 election by a CCF candidate.

Hart became the new premier and would remain in that post until after the war. At the age of sixty-two, he had become a savvy and respected fiscal administrator. As early as 1917, Hart had served as finance minister in the cabinet of Harlan Brewster. During his association with Pattullo in the thirties, he performed ably in the same portfolio, and took it on in 1941 when he became premier. The war years, however, did not call for the expertise or mindset of a bank manager as much as they did for a humanist and a diplomat. Actually, John Hart probably could have done little to stem the outflow of anti-Japanese sentiment that was rising in the province even before the Coalition government was formed. But his parroting of the xenophobes' demand to rid BC of all Japanese did stain his administration.

Following the fall of France, the long summer of 1940 saw the Battle of Britain fought in the skies over England. The losses sustained by the Royal Air Force in this vicious toe-to-toe slugfest with the Luftwaffe added impetus to a program devised in 1939 to train pilots and aircrew in Canada. Called the British Common-wealth Air Training Plan, it provided for the establishment of facilities across the Dominion to handle recruits from all over the Empire. By the autumn of the year, newspapers were reporting the arrival of Australian and New Zealander trainees at a "West Coast Canadian port" (Vancouver). Although most of the stations for the BCATP (also called the British Empire Air Training Scheme) were on the Prairies and in Ontario, there were several in BC. These included Patricia Bay and Comox on Vancouver Island, and Sea Island, Vancouver, Boundary Bay and Abbotsford on the mainland. At war's end, the plan had trained 131,000 airmen—72,835 of them Canadians.

On the sea frontier, the first fighting ship of the war from a BC builder was laid down April 11, 1940, at Burrard Dry Dock Co. in Vancouver. Exactly three months and seven days later, HMCS *Wetaskiwin*, a Flower class corvette, was launched. She was commissioned December 17, 1940, the first of fifty-three frigates, corvettes and minesweepers to be built by five BC shipyards. The venerable Yarrows Ltd. in Esquimalt led the way with twenty-two warships.

With Hitler's easy conquest of continental Europe, Canada became Britain's principal ally and resource, so Prime Minister Mackenzie King's vision of a limited partnership died on the beaches of Dunkirk. Some form of conscription was necessary, and on June 21, 1940, the National Resources Mobilization Act mandated the callup of draftees for home guard duty. The problem of what to do with legitimate conscientious objectors was solved by an Ottawa bureaucrat, who suggested putting them to work in Canada's national parks. The plan was in place the following spring, and Kootenay and Glacier parks in British Columbia became part of the "alternative service" network.

THE DECADE IN HEADLINES
« 1942 »

FLAG SIGNALS START OF LOAN DRIVE
Parades, rallies, flag-waving and patriotic exhortations mark the start of the second Victory Loan campaign of the war. The drive begins the day after Singapore falls to the Japanese.
Vancouver Sun, February 16, 1942

TAYLOR HEADS JAP REMOVAL
The federal government establishes the BC Security Commission to handle the removal of ethnic Japanese from the West Coast. Vancouver businessman Austin C. Taylor is named chairman.
The Province, February 27, 1942

UNITED STATES TROOPS INVADE DAWSON CREEK TO BUILD ALASKA ROAD
The weekly *News* reports the beginning of the Alaska Highway.
Peace River Block News, March 9, 1942

TAXES AND GAS RATIONING PUT MOST OF CITY IN LINEUP
The day that gasoline rationing—the first such restriction of the war—goes into effect in Canada, *The News-Herald*'s story concentrates on motorists queuing to fill their tanks the day before. March 31 is also the deadline for filing income tax returns.
The News-Herald, April 1, 1942

CADETS PARADE, WHITE ENSIGN HOISTED AS CANADA'S NAVY COLLEGE COMMISSIONED
The opening of Royal Roads establishment on Juan de Fuca Strait west of Esquimalt earns a Page One picture and a long story on Page 2.
Victoria Times, October 21, 1942

THE DECADE IN HEADLINES
« 1943 »

EXPLOSION AND FIRE TAKES FIVE LIVES – WHOLE BUSINESS BLOCK DESTROYED

Downtown Dawson Creek turns into a fiery hell as a US Army truck crammed with high explosives catches fire and blows up. *The News*, which bills itself as a weekly, is actually publishing every two weeks at the time, so it reports the disaster in its February 25 edition.

Peace River Block News, February 13, 1943

VANCOUVER BLACK MARKET EXPOSED

With wartime rationing comes the black market in scarce commodities. *The Sun* sends a reporter to purchase items without benefit of ration coupons, then publishes his revelations (with pictures) prominently on Page One.

Vancouver Sun, April 8, 1943

In an act of official stupidity and folly, the doomed Winnipeg Grenadiers and Quebec's Royal Rifles of Canada sailed secretly from Vancouver October 27, 1941, for Hong Kong. The overwhelming Japanese assault on the Crown colony in December and their subsequent brutal treatment of Canadian prisoners is still a source of pain and bitterness for the descendants of those who were sent to a tragic fate on an indefensible island. In an editorial criticizing such inept war planning, *The Sun* commented: "No stuffed shirts or bombproof brass hats of the 'safe-enough' school. We want men who understand the speed of modern warfare."

As we have seen, BC papers had a lot of things to report in December of 1941. It was one of the newsiest months of the war. Pearl Harbor, Hong Kong, Coalition and Pattullo's demise all jostled for headline space. But out in the Lulu Island community of Steveston, only one event had any significance. That quiet Sunday morning of December 7, the streets of this Japanese fishing village were peaceful and half-empty. The residents, many of whom had lived in the little community at the mouth of the Fraser River for more than half their lives, listened to the radio bulletins with a growing sense of unreality and uncertainty. The bad things that were happening were so far away, and Canada was their home. A lot of the older people did not easily understand English, so the news had to be explained to them by their children, educated in BC's schools.

Japan's rape of Manchuria and China in the late thirties had brought a recurrence of anti-Oriental feeling in the province, and both the Japanese-Canadians and their non-naturalized brethren were already feeling uneasy. Now this stunning news about their homeland's unprovoked attack on America had them all wondering about the future. "I trust the Canadian government will give us justice," one of them told *The Province*. "As for the Japanese here, the worst thing that could happen to us would be a military order that cuts us off from our livelihood," said another.

The worst thing did happen to the approximately 23,000 persons of Japanese descent in BC. Already, they had been forced to carry registration cards. Now, with Canada declaring war on Japan even before the United States, events began to move swiftly. Japanese newspapers were shut down, as were their schools. Some forty men were interned at once. The West Coast fishing fleet was immobilized "for security reasons." Rumours of infiltration, subversion and treachery, prevalent earlier in the war, gathered momentum, and municipal and provincial politicians began demanding action (even though the RCMP, after close surveillance of the Japanese, declared there was no security threat).

Emotional reaction to the fall of Hong Kong on Christmas Day was violent. The military, the press and the politicians were bombarded with appeals—some of them hysterical—for action against the local Japanese. On January 14, 1942, in one of those half-measures so typical of Prime Minister King's style, a partial removal of Japanese nationals without Canadian citizenship was ordered. This fudging on the issue lasted until February 15, when the British Empire's bastion of Singapore surrendered. Panic was the operative emotion. The apparently unstoppable Nipponese juggernaut was expected to hit the British Columbia coast at any moment. The slowness of the aliens' removal brought bitter complaints.

"What is particularly aggravating is that meantime the Japanese in our local areas have been exulting over the victory of their countrymen at Singapore and there is wide complaint amongst our people at their cocky and insolent attitude," a *Sun* editorial said. "*The Sun* trusts that within the next few days there will be an end of these incidents which allow the Japanese to snap their fingers at Canadian authority."

The ugly spectre of racial riots in BC's major cities occupied the minds of King's cabinet. The only answer was total withdrawal: On February 27, Ottawa announced the evacuation from the "protected areas" of all Japanese—men, women and children. The BC Security Commission, chaired by Vancouver businessman Austin Taylor, was formed to handle the details. A curfew was put into effect, the Japanese were forbidden to drive and property (in addition to the fishboats) was seized. Trainloads of aliens headed eastward; by November of the year, the Japanese were gone from the West Coast.

Where did they go? From such holding areas as the livestock building on Vancouver's PNE grounds, many went to camps in Jasper National Park.[1] Others laboured on the Yellowhead-Blue River and the Hope-Princeton highways. Former ghost towns were reborn to harbour gangs of forest workers. Eventually, the Japanese were spread out across Canada at a number of sites. Under an official policy of dispersal laid down by the federal government after the war, each province had a quota to assimilate. On April 7, 1948, *The Sun* again found time to lecture those returning to the coast. Despite having every opportunity to become Canadians, it said, the original trouble with the Japanese was that "they coagulated in their own colonies and retained their social identity."

This deliberate erasure of an entire segment of BC society has been debated by historians, politicians and laypersons over the years. Callous as they may seem in times of peace (and to those who have no conceivable idea of the impact war has on civilians), the decisions made in 1942 sprang from a very real fear. This sea-bound province, so far away from any outside help, has always overreacted to threats from the Pacific. The panic over German raiders in the Great War is one example. In addition, the events of the Second World War reinforced a perception that had always prevailed among the white population. As occupiers with a predominantly British ancestry, they were sensitive to any threat from alien quarters. The Natives of BC were quickly subjugated and put in their place, as was only natural in a colonial setting, so any other race impinging upon the white man's right to occupy the province would generate suspicion. The Asians (both Japanese and Chinese) were too clannish, too different, too industrious to be trusted. They were a threat in 1942 just as they were in the early 1900s.

Another group of chronic outsiders, the Doukhobors, continued to vex the authorities throughout the forties. The registration requirements of the 1940 mobilization act prompted some arrests of Sons of Freedom scofflaws, but the majority of Doukhobors accepted the principle with equanimity. In 1943, however, when a new Selective Service program emphasized government control of industrial workers, they refused to go along. When the military attempted to force the issue at Brilliant on December 12, an ear-splitting "No!!!!" (as *The Province* described it) from the assembled 3,500 sect members was so resounding that the army officers retired in confusion. To emphasize the rejection, the Freedomites burned down the Brilliant jam factory, once the jewel of the community (and owned by the provincial government since the Doukhobors' bankruptcy in 1937).

Thereafter, the sect did its own thing in the Kootenays. The blind eye cast by officials had a practical aspect: Doukhobors were often the only source of manpower in the Interior valleys because most other males had gone off to war. Despite this government restraint, the Sons of Freedom followed up the Brilliant fire with

THE DECADE IN HEADLINES
« 1944 »

INVISIBLE SPECS MAKE DEBUT IN VANCOUVER
Contact lenses become available for the first time. Because of the cost ($175) and "the slight inconvenience wearing them entails," their use is recommended only in special cases.
Vancouver Sun, September 15, 1944

B.C. SHIP MAKES ARCTIC HISTORY
The RCMP patrol vessel *St. Roch* completes its epic Halifax-Vancouver voyage across the top of the world. The 7,600-mile trip takes 86 days.
Vancouver Sun, October 16, 1944

6 HURT, 2 HELD AS 'ZOMBIES' DEMONSTRATE IN 5 B.C. TOWNS
The national debate over sending Zombies—conscripted troops who refuse to fight—overseas sparks a wave of protests in BC. Despite rioting in other parts of Canada, Vancouver and Victoria remain calm.
The News-Herald, November 25, 1944

'SMOKEY' SMITH WINS V.C.
The hometown paper spreads the Victoria Cross award to Pvt. Ernie Smith across the top of Page One. Smith is the second New Westminster soldier to win the Empire's highest award for bravery. Coincidentally, the first winner, Maj. Jack Mahony, returned to a hero's welcome in the Royal City two days earlier. (BC's VC winners are listed in Appendix D.)
Columbian, December 19, 1944

THE DECADE IN HEADLINES
« 1945 »

EMILY CARR, FAMOUS VICTORIA BORN AUTHOR AND PAINTER DIES

The untimely death of the 73-year-old interpreter of Native life rates a Page 6 obituary in one of her hometown papers.

The Colonist, March 2, 1945

17 MEN INJURED IN SHIP BLAST HERE

The detonation aboard the *Greenhill Park* at Pier B-C in downtown Vancouver sweeps most other news off Page One as both *The Sun* and *The Province* respond with details and pictures of the noon-hour tragedy. Death toll is later set at eight.

Vancouver Sun, March 6, 1945

'FAMILY' CHEQUES MAKE COUNTLESS HOMES HAPPIER

Arrival in the mail of Canada's first family allowance payments rates a long story on Page 5. The allowances run from $5 per month (one child under six) to $59 for a family of five or more children.

The News-Herald, July 20, 1945

ALL VANCOUVER OUT TO GREET SEAFORTHS

The city's beloved First Battalion Seaforth Highlanders returns from the war to a tumultuous welcome from 100,000 citizens. *The Sun*, in the opening paragraph of its Page One story, likens the return to the triumphant march of Caesar's legions, while *The Province* runs a dramatic eight-column picture with the overline, "Journey's End For Vancouver's Seaforths."

Vancouver Sun, October 7, 1945

more burnings in 1944. A group of them paraded nude in Nelson in April, and again in Vancouver on May 7. The following day, some of them stripped in court. Incidents of arson and dynamiting flared up again in the summer of 1947, emphasizing the deep schism within the sect. One of the orthodox leaders, John J. Verigin (there was a power struggle in progress through much of the decade) sought police protection for his followers and the removal of the Sons of Freedom from the Kootenays.

Finally, the Hart cabinet appointed Judge Harry Sullivan as a one-man commission to probe the whole Doukhobor mess. From October 14, 1947, until he abruptly suspended the hearings on January 7, 1948, Sullivan presided over a succession of fractious, hostile, argumentative witnesses intent on smearing each other and championing their own brand of religious fanaticism. The fact that a major Doukhobor cooperative facility had been blown up only days earlier was a major factor in Sullivan's decision.

"The regrettable fact is that even while these hearings were in progress, not less than six outrages of extreme gravity have been committed," the judge told the courtroom. He described the wave of terrorist incidents as "due to crime and insanity, and the work of certain agitators." On April 14 his report was tabled in the legislature. Judge Sullivan recommended immediate disciplinary action, including lengthy prison sentences for the guilty. (For a variety of reasons, the Freedomite perpetrators who were tried and convicted spent little time behind bars.)

With the Japanese-Canadian question more or less settled to everyone's satisfaction—except, naturally, the Japanese—the business of conducting war on the home front picked up speed. The blackouts that followed the attack on Pearl Harbor diminished to the level of "dimouts." Rationing became a fact of life. Gasoline was the first commodity to come under strict control, on April 1, 1942. Tea, coffee and sugar followed in May. Butter went on the list December 21, 1942, just in time for Christmas. Two years earlier, a *Vancouver Sun* editorial had called the butter shortage "fictitious," and said the market was being manipulated by Eastern interests.

"Meatless Tuesdays" made their appearance in May of 1943. In February and March of that year, beer and liquor were rationed. (Newsprint was also rationed later in '43, a development that made Page One of *The News-Herald*.) With all these controlled substances being much in demand, the black market raised its opportunistic head. In April of 1943, *The Sun* went into standard expose mode and revealed the extent of the illegal trade in everything from steaks to inner tubes.

Meanwhile, BC's shipyards had their warship contracts, but they were also busy sending cargo vessels down the ways. On March 4, 1942, *The Sun* noted that on one day in February, three 10,000-ton merchantmen were launched. "And that was only the beginning, folks, only the beginning," the paper's marine reporter wrote. Yards on False Creek and Burrard Inlet were finishing work on four more freighters that month.

Over on the Island, Yarrows and VMD also had their order books full. *The Times* reported in May that "the shipyards have been in continuous operation, with labour and capital cooperating in a smoothly balanced organization." It described the operation of one machine with this well-turned sentence: "Then, with a gentle sigh, a scarcely perceptible shudder, like an elderly maiden settling herself comfortably in her chair at an afternoon tea, the machine moves slowly and placidly and ruminatively chews off a hundredweight of iron, or imperturbably punches a hole of exact, predetermined dimensions through half an inch of solid steel."

17 MEN INJURED IN SHIP BLAST HERE

CLOUDY, WARMER
Official weather forecast: Partly cloudy, warmer in afternoon. Wednesday cloudy, slightly warmer with scattered showers. Monday's temperatures high 37, low 31.

The Vancouver Sun

RATIONED FOODS
Sugar—Coupons 52, 53 now valid.
Butter—Coupon 97 now valid.
Preserves—Coupons 39, 40 now valid.
All valid coupons in Book 5 good until further notice.

FOUNDED 1886 VOL. LIX—No. 140   MArine 1161   HOME EDITION   VANCOUVER, BRITISH COLUMBIA, TUESDAY, MARCH 6, 1945   ★★★C   PRICE 5 CENTS $1.00 per month BY CARRIER

AT HEIGHT OF BLAZE—Smoke envelops the ill-fated freighter Greenhill Park as a lumber laden scow burns beside it, following the explosions early today. The freighter was later towed out of the harbor through the Narrows as fire-fighters sought to extinguish the flames. —Picture by Sun Staff Photographer.

ONE OF THE VICTIMS—Tragedy is etched on the face of this local woman worker who rushed to the scene of the blast at Pier BC today. She is pictured bending over one of the victims. Other pictures on pages two and nine.

CHEMICAL SHIP BLOWS UP AT CPR PIER B-C

Downtown Vancouver was rocked by a series of blasts as the SS. Greenhill Park, loaded with chemicals, blew up at noon today, injuring at least 17 men who were working aboard the vessel.

Several other persons suffered injuries when they were struck by flying glass as the blasts shattered hundreds of windows in the business section of the city.

There were reports that some men may have been trapped aboard the ship, but these were not verified at press time.

Flames and smoke shot 100 feet into the air as the explosions of the chemicals set off some of the ship's ammunition and also sent ship flares soaring into the sky in an awesome display of grim fireworks.

Four blasts from the ship caused the waterfront to shudder under the impact and citizens by the thousands who were enjoying their lunch hour were shocked almost into panic.

Newspaper offices were deluged by phone calls as some wondered if there had been an air raid.

The Greenhill Park was being loaded with lumber at Pier B-C and the scow alongside, loaded with airplane lumber, was also set afire.

It was being loaded with cargo for Australia.

Windows Blasted From City Blocks

Some Persons Hurt by Flying Bits of Glass; Few Signs of Panic

Broken glass strewing the streets from the 400 block on West Pender as far as Thurlow and from the waterfront up to Dunsmuir, whole office blocks with scarcely a pane of glass left intact, was the picture today after the first confusion caused by the ship blasts at Pier B-C had subsided.

Several persons in the offices of the Vancouver Merchants' Exchange, Marine Building, suffered slight cuts from broken glass as the large plate-glass windows were blown "almost across the whole offices" in the first explosion.

NONE BADLY INJURED

None was injured sufficiently to require medical attention from outside, and were "patched up" by fellow-workers with the office first-aid kits.

No records were lost or destroyed in the Income Tax department's offices at 739 West Hastings, although all windows were blown out. No one was injured, according to officials.

POST OFFICE CARRIES ON

The Post Office reported only one large lobby window and several smaller ones broken. There was no disruption of service after the first shock.

Workers in the Wartime Prices and Trade Board offices, Marine Building, said the explosion sounded as though "every door in Vancouver was being slammed at once."

Glass flew everywhere, they said, but no one was hurt, except for superficial cuts. A few stenographers were blown out of their chairs by the blast.

Several large windows on the north side of the CPR Station were broken, it is reported.

About a dozen windows in the Immigration Building are reported broken.

EXTENDED TO SEYMOUR

Window damage also extended as far east as Seymour, according to early reports.

Many of the north windows of Spencer's store were smashed and several of the sales staff suffered from cuts.

While most shoppers kept their heads, a few showed signs of panic and some of the customers who were having an early lunch in the marine view dining room of Spencer's store stopped without waiting to collect hats or coats, in their rush to get to the main floor and outdoors.

Some buildings on Hastings lost their southern exposure windows.

LIST OF INJURED

Following is the list of those injured as a result of the blasts from the Greenhill Park:

Eleven from aboard ship and one street victim are in General Hospital. Those from abdard ship are

Donald Dailey.
Frank Simms.
James Barius, 3566 West Twentieth.
Frederick Lester, 1505 East Fifteenth.
Andrew Wangenstein, 8073 St. George.
Sandy McLean, 1772 East Twenty-second.
Joseph Klimek, 389 Blundell Road, Lulu Island.
Stanley Harris, 372 East Thirteenth.
Edward Sickerish, 2556 West Third.
John Adask, 2024 Arbutus.
Mike Stockinoff, 249 East Hastings.
Mrs. Louise Koven, 2990 West Twelfth, was struck by glass from a Cordova Street window.

Three are in St. Paul's Hospital from the ship. They are:

Jules Lantchier, chief cook of the Greenhill Park;
Don Smith, 250 Commercial, shock;
Alfred Combes, 2846 Trinity, shock and bruises.

Injured on the street and in St. Paul's Hospital are:
Clara Wagner, 1536 East Twelfth;
Thomas Adams, 4474 Quebec Street;
Eva Luis, 3334 Cambridge.

Treated for injuries in Spencer's store first aid station after the Cordova Street windows smashed from the impact of the blast are:
Mrs. H. MacMillan, about 65, 2846 Willingdon, severe shock and cuts on head.
Mrs. D. McLean, 2774 East Sixth, employed in the store.
Mrs. D. Naughton, employed in store.
Donald Douglas, 3, of 6267 Victoria Drive, cuts.

'Snow,' but Too Little to Measure

Vancouver had snow Monday, but it can't be proved by the weather records. Meteorological officials said the snowfall was too small to be measured.

Steadily increasing temperatures are in store, but the bureau which were ripped from the walls.

Huge piles of goods caught fire and firemen had to battle blazes in the storehouses and offices as well as along the pier itself.

The ship was towed into English Bay shortly after 1 p.m., and the Fireboat Carlisle was brought into action, playing water on the still burning vessel.

There were approximately 100 men, longshoremen, crew and shipyard workers, working on the Greenhill Park.

Some of the men dived over the side to safety.

Others went down ropes and some were even blasted to safety.

First aid organizations all swept into action to aid city authorities.

Most of the injured men from the ship are longshoremen. It is believed, who were working on the big 10,000-ton freighter when she blew up, spraying flaming ammunition over the heart of downtown Vancouver.

Thousands of spectators jammed the waterfront to watch city police, fire and ambulance departments battle the flames.

The men, believed trapped in the ship, are in the engine room.

Cook Blown Off Vessel

The force of the first explosion smashed the engine room.

The ill-fated vessel was the victim of a series of four detonating explosions, which smashed windows a mile away.

The first explosion came in hold No. 3. A few seconds later, the second blast blew out No. 2 hold.

The second explosion blew the cook from his galley out through a hatch onto the concrete pier. His name has not been obtained. He is suffering groin and abdominal injuries.

The third explosion smashed through the two hatches, but stopped short of No. 1 hatch forward.

It is this hatch—reported to be still crammed with explosives—which harbor tugs are fighting to isolate by towing the ship into midstream.

Four Men Still Missing

Joseph Bouchard, who had fourteen employees working on board the Greenhill Park, cleaning boilers, told The Sun shortly before 2 p.m. that four of his men were still unaccounted for.

He said he believed two more were in hospital.

When the new ship exploded amidships, her steel sides curled up like wet cardboard.

Main force of the shock was between the bridge and the funnel and as the fire burned unchecked the bridge slumped over into the gap in the ship's decks.

Debris was thrown for hundreds of feet and the shock smashed plate glass windows in nearly every building in the downtown section.

Quick work by small naval craft got another big ship, moored at the outer berth of the same pier, out to safety in the stream.

Every ambulance in the city was pressed into service as hospitals and aid crews bent every effort to assist the dying and injured.

Scarlet flares in the ship's cargo continued to pop intermittently as the blaze continued.

Like Fourth of July displays, they dropped into crowds among firemen, or on the decks of naval craft hovering about.

Rumors went the rounds that a further explosion, mightier than the first, would occur as soon as the flames reached the afterhold of the ship.

Police and military, taking no chances, moved the

Please Turn to Page Two   See "17 Injured"

Rivets Shoot Out of Ship's Steel Plates

Vancouver waterfront in the vicinity of the CPR docks today looked like nothing more or less than a scene from war-torn Europe.

As the Greenhill Park, her hull ripped wide open on both sides, lay at Pier BC, burning, she presented a picture not unlike a newsreel shot of the harbor at Naples.

PIER DAMAGED

Smoke poured, too, from Pier BC, which was badly damaged by the fire.

The dock and the network of roads around the Pier were littered with everything from rivet heads which were shot out of the ship's steel plates by the explosion to smashed bottles of pickles that were sent flying out of her No. 3 hold.

Hundreds of men in uniform, Red Cross nurses, police and firemen milled about the scene.

Army and navy trucks and ambulances were rushed to the dockside to assist the injured.

FIRST AID CENTRE

An emergency first aid centre was set up in a room below the pier.

There the injured men were treated by Red Cross nurses before being rushed to hospital.

Even as they lay there, the ship's cargo continued to explode and flares shot out over the docks.

The dock alongside was littered with cargo and debris.

WINDOWS SMASHED

Pier B.C., which bore the brunt of the explosion, was littered with broken glass and other fixtures which were ripped from the walls.

WAR NEWS IN BRIEF

WESTERN FRONT—U.S. forces officially capture Cologne; U.S. 3rd Army scores break-through to south, drive 25 miles toward Rhine. (Story and map on Page 8.)

EASTERN FRONT—Russian troops reach Stettin Bay, capture Polish citadel of Grudziadz on Vistula.

PACIFIC—Americans destroy 100,000 Japanese troops on Luzon; close in for kill on remaining trapped groups; U.S. Marines mass for all-out assault against last Japanese defenders on North Iwo.

ITALY—American and Brazilian forces advance in central sector southwest of Bologna.

AIR WAR—RAF hassles hit oil refinery northwest of Muenster, following up 1100-plane night raid on Chemnitz.

will be a few days before the city returns to the balmy 50-degree weather of last week. Rain is in the forecast for Wednesday.

THE DECADE IN HEADLINES
« 1946 »

SWEEPING CHANGES URGED FOR B.C. FOREST INDUSTRY

Chief Justice Gordon Sloan's report on lumber practices calls for a special forestry commission and a change in the tenure system as part of a wide-ranging series of recommendations.

Vancouver Sun, January 10, 1946

PROVINCE PAPER UNABLE TO PUBLISH

The start of the bitter, violence-marred strike of ITU compositors against its rival is the top story in *The Sun. The Province* is so wounded by the strike that it never regains its position as BC's biggest newspaper.

Vancouver Sun, June 6, 1946

COURTENAY CENTRE OF EARTHQUAKE

Several days after the occurrence, the weekly *Argus* provides some details of widespread damage caused by the quake (later estimated at 7.3 on the Richter Scale). A puckish subheadline, Lovely Smell Of Liquor Store, heads a paragraph about smashed bottles at the local outlet.

Courtenay-Comox Argus, June 23, 1946

Although the federal war cabinet had turned down a recommendation for a national program of wooden shipbuilding, it did approve an innovative method of aircraft construction. The glamorous Mosquito fighter-bomber was almost entirely built of Sitka spruce from the Queen Charlotte Islands. Everything except the engines, electrical fittings and other hardware was made of wood bonded together by a new generation of synthetic resin glue. "May their stings be long and powerful as the great trees from which they are constructed," said a 1942 *Sun* editorial praising the versatile aircraft.

Unlike 1914–18, when the timber industry played a minor role, BC's entire forestry resource was devoted to this war. A shortage of steel dictated the use of wood in much construction, including housing, manufacturing plants and military bases. The pulp and paper segment was hard put to keep up with demands ranging from pulp used in explosives to newsprint. As *The News-Herald* grumped, a lack of manpower in the plants meant smaller, more tightly edited papers and fewer copies printed. Midway through the war, in September of 1942, logging and lumbering were officially classified as essential industries.

Amid all this activity, BC Chief Justice Gordon Sloan conducted an inquiry into the forestry situation. One of his key recommendations, made public January 10, 1946, was to issue forest management licences in order to produce a sustained yield from the province's most valuable resource. In an editorial the following day, *The Sun* summed up the thrust of his report with the observation that BC must stop mining timber and start farming it. The FMLs became official policy in 1947 (and were changed to tree farm licences in 1966).

Women played a large part in BC's war effort. According to *The Times*, Victoria had the first female welder in the shipbuilding industry. Many others also found jobs in the shipyards, as well as in almost every aspect of lumber production. They made the tiny batteries that powered lifejacket lamps, and learned how to put teeth into saws. Many more took over driving chores that were once the prerogative of the male, from taxis and delivery vans to ambulances and salvage trucks. The BC Women's Service Corps, formed in 1939, was trained in mechanical repair, first aid, hospital duties and emergency field work. "Readily adapting themselves to the changed conditions, they have shown amazing ingenuity and skill in a great variety of crafts new to them," crooned *The Times*.

Overseas, BC-based units were getting in some pretty good licks at the Germans and Italians. In July, 1943, the Seaforth Highlanders were in action in Sicily, prompting prominent Page One coverage from Vancouver papers. Later in the year, the Seaforths were heavily involved in the Italian campaign. In October, 1944, the regiment had reached the Savio, one of the endless succession of rivers that run from Italy's spine down to the sea. There, on October 22, 1944, Pvt. Ernest (Smoky) Smith, from New Westminster, won the Victoria Cross for gallantry.

The Westminster Regiment, with many more Royal City lads in its ranks, fought in some of the same campaigns as the Highlanders with the 5th Canadian Armored Division. On the Melfa River, south of Rome, another New Westminster soldier won the Victoria Cross. He was Major J.K. Mahony, who led his Westminsters against a German counter-attack.

While the 1st Canadian Corps was slogging its way up Italy's boot, the Normandy landing of June 6, 1944, came and went. British Columbia's regards were sharply delivered on D-Day by "C" Company of the Canadian Scottish from Vancouver Island. They landed on the right flank of Juno Beach along with the Royal

Winnipeg Rifles. Because of the heavy hand of the censor, however, BC newspapers could only say "Canadian troops" were involved in the invasion.

In March, 1945, all Dominion troops were placed under Gen. Andrew McNaughton in the 1st Canadian Army. Among those joining the Seaforths, the Westminsters and the Canadian Scottish in "the dagger pointed at the heart of Berlin" were the British Columbia Regiment and the British Columbia Dragoons. This army would play a pivotal part in the liberation of Northwest Europe.

In the North Atlantic, the RCN ships that had been born in BC's shipyards fought and died to keep open the vital convoy routes to Britain. Among those lost was HMCS *Alberni*, the first corvette laid down by Yarrows in Esquimalt. She was torpedoed in the English Channel August 21, 1944. Closer to home, the Japanese patina of invincibility was punctured at the battle of Midway in June, 1942, even though enemy troops landed in the Aleutians the same month.

Helping to guard BC's convoluted coastline was the Fishermen's Reserve. Manned by hardy ex-fishermen and coastal skippers "who know the coast with their eyes shut," this fleet was a useful addition to Canada's inner defence ring. Among the trawlers, fish packers and other auxiliaries were a number of Japanese-Canadian vessels impounded after Pearl Harbor. "They are the best ships among the Japanese fleet … and in view of the added danger of attack they will be very useful," an RCN officer told *The Province*.

However, the fishermen's patrol was nowhere in sight the night of June 20, 1942. Shells from the Japanese submarine I-26 started falling around the lighthouse and radio-telegraph station at Estevan Point on Vancouver Island's west coast. It was the first armed attack on Canadian soil since Confederation. The same weekend, the Oregon coastal settlement of Seaside was also shelled from the sea. Neither attack caused any damage. Although the newspapers went into a Page One dither, the general mood was one of calm. The *Victoria Times* took pains to note that the citizens went quietly about their business, and *The Province* in an editorial accurately called the raid "a nuisance and nothing more" (while getting the date of the shelling wrong).

Despite the transitory nature of the incident, some people still insist on seeking a deeper meaning. Like the conspiracy theory that has grown up around the assassination of John F. Kennedy, attempts have been made over the years to put a sinister spin on June 20, 1942. One theory is that there was no submarine at all, that it was a government plot to scare everyone and apply pressure for better West Coast defences, or something. The trouble with many of the hypotheses trying to dredge a hidden motive out of the Estevan attack is their amateurism. An article in a leading BC yachting magazine in 1994 purporting to "expose" the '42 event was so poorly written that it was virtually unintelligible.

When the guns of Europe finally fell silent, there was some pretty serious rejoicing. After the obligatory Extra Editions and the screaming headlines of May 7, 1945 (VE-Day was officially designated on May 8), celebration stories took over the front pages. There was a bad riot in Halifax, but on Canada's other coast, we were mostly in a carnival mood. A giant parade in Vancouver the evening of May 7 was matched by an equally monstrous traffic jam as bunting-bedecked vehicles turned downtown into one braying, horn-tooting mess. Across Burrard Inlet, huge bonfires crackled on the West and North Vancouver beaches. In Victoria, the news of Germany's surrender touched off the celebratory wail of air raid sirens, followed by the usual cacophony of boat whistles and horns from the Inner Harbour.

THE DECADE IN HEADLINES
« 1947 »

CEILINGS OFF MANY GOODS, SERVICES

Wartime price controls imposed by the federal government are virtually ended. Restrictions on consumer credit are also lifted, prompting *The Sun* to predict a speedy return to "dollar down" merchandising.

Vancouver Sun, January 11, 1947

MOTORISTS PAY TO PARK CARS STARTING TODAY

Parking meters arrive in BC during the summer of '47. While Victoria frets over the legality of its parking bylaw, Vancouver debates the issue of single vs. double meters.

The Colonist, August 7, 1947

CHARRED RUINS, TENTS DOT KOOTENAY; FAMILIES FEARFUL

Another outbreak of Doukhobor violence and arson during August forces orthodox members of the sect to flee their homes. The day before, BC Att.-Gen. Gordon Wismer announces a police crackdown on the terrorism.

Nelson News, August 23, 1947

C.N. STEAMSHIP PRINCE GEORGE LAUNCHED

The weekly *Citizen* proudly announces the launching of the city's namesake three days after she slides down the ways at Yarrows in Esquimalt. The first large liner built in Canada in 25 years, the *Prince George* will end its life as a derelict, sinking while under tow in the North Pacific in 1996.

Prince George Citizen, October 6, 1947

"V-E" DAY EXTRA

The Daily Colonist.

(ESTABLISHED 1858)

"V-E" DAY EXTRA

VICTORIA, BRITISH COLUMBIA, MONDAY, MAY 7, 1945 — EIGHT PAGES

PEACE IN EUROPE

★ ★ ★ ★ ★ ★

GERMANY SURRENDERS

Western Allies, Russia Receive Capitulation

REIMS, France, May 7 (AP)—Germany surrendered unconditionally to the Western Allies and Russia at 2:41 a.m. French time today.

The surrender took place at a schoolhouse which is the headquarters of Gen. Eisenhower.

The surrender which brought the war in Europe to a formal end after five years, eight months and six days of bloodshed and destruction was signed for Germany by Col.-Gen. Gustav Jodl, who is the new chief of staff of the German army.

It was signed for the Allied Supreme command by Lt.-Gen. Walter Bedell Smith, chief of staff for Gen. Eisenhower.

It was also signed by General Ivan Susloparoff for Russia and by Gen. Francois Sevez for France.

Gen. Eisenhower was not present at the signing, but immediately afterward Jodl and his fellow delegate, Gen. Admiral Hans Georg Friedeburg, were received by the Supreme Commander.

The surrender was announced officially after German broadcasts told the German people that Grand Admiral Karl Doenitz had ordered the capitulation of all fighting forces, and called off the U-boat war.

Joy at the news was tempered only by the realization that the war against Japan remains to be resolved, with many casualties still ahead.

The end of the European warfare, greatest, bloodiest and costliest war in human history—it has claimed at least 40,000,000 casualties on both sides in killed, wounded and captured—came after five years, eight months and six days of strife that overspread the globe.

Arrogant German armies invaded Poland September 1, 1939, beginning the agony that convulsed the world for 2,319 days.

Unconditional surrender of the beaten remnants of Hitler's legions first was announced by the Germans.

The historic news began breaking with a Danish broadcast that Norway had been surrendered unconditionally.

The world waited tensely. Then at 9:35 a.m., E.D.T., came the Associated Press flash from Reims, France, telling of the signing at General Eisenhower's headquarters of the unconditional surrender at 2:41 a.m. French time (8:41 a.m., E.D.T.). Germany had given up to the Western Allies and to Russia.

London went wild at the news. Crowds jammed Piccadilly Circus. Smiling throngs poured out of subways and lined the streets.

Cheers went up in New York, Toronto and Montreal, too, and papers showered down from skyscrapers.

Grand Admiral Karl Doenitz in an order broadcast today ordered all his Nazi U-boats to cease hostilities, and reports from Stockholm said V-E Day might be proclaimed without a battle for Norway.

The Flensburg radio broadcast a three-day old order of the day by Doenitz to his submarine crews telling them:

"Crushing superiority has compressed us into a very narrow area. Continuation of the struggle is impossible from bases that remain."

Unconfirmed advices from Stockholm—repeated later by the Allied-controlled Luxembourg radio—said the Germans already had affixed their signature to Allied surrender terms for Norway.

Great Britain was clearly expecting a V-E Day announcement at any time. London began to dress up for the big occasion by draping flags on some downtown buildings.

Prime Minister Churchill was declared to be busy at his desk, but close-mouthed as to his plans. The British Cabinet stood by for any possible emergency session.

The political correspondent for The London Evening News said "Mr. Churchill is today expected to broadcast from the Cabinet Room at 10 Downing Street that the war in Europe is over."

Famous Figures Released

ITTER, Austria, May 6 (AP)—Former French Premiers Edouard Daladier and Paul Reynaud and Gens. Maurice Gamelin and Maxime Weygard were freed from months of Gernman political imprisonment yesterday when two battalion of the 36th "Texas" Infantry Division fought their way into Itter Castle.

The B.B.C. said that Kurt Schuschnigg, former Premier of Austria; Leon Blum, former Premier of France; and Martin Niemoeller, famous anti-Nazi German pastor; all were rescued by the Americans farther to the south near the Brenner Pass, after having been removed from the same prison that housed Daladier, Gamelin, Reynaud and Weygand.

The world-famous four French leaders were among a number of other famous persons who were liberated.

Among them were a sister of Gen. Charles de Gaulle, a former head of the French trade unions, and tennis champion Jean Borotra who, in a melodramatic fashion, got out of the castle at noon to bring word to American troops of the plight of those imprisoned.

Elements of the 12th Armored and 103rd "Cactus" Divisions and the 753rd Tank Battalion figured in the release of the famous figures.

Tonight they were en route to an American general's command post for a conference and dinner.

In Paris it was announced that Andrew Francois Poncet, former French Ambassador to Berlin and Rome, had been liberated by French troops in South Germany. Albert Sarraut, former president of the French Council, and Francisco Nitti, president of the Italian Ministerial Council, also were freed.

For all the Americans knew, as the tanks and footsloggers moved up through roads and hills alive with S.S. men offering last minute resistance, this was the last important engagement of the war, since back at Innisbruck arrangements were being made for all fighting in Austria to cease tomorrow.

The Americans lay at a farmhouse in the woods just below the castle at 2 p.m. when Borotra came up the road, accompanied by a guard, to tell how a German 88 gun had knocked out a 12th armored tank which had made its way to the castle last night and had shelled the castle this morning.

He led another company of the battalion back up the road to surround the German defenders.

"I've been waiting two years to get back into uniform," the famous bounding Basque said.

To get to the United States forces he waded a river, posed as a refugee, and came through the German lines.

Berlin announced April 5, 1943, that Daladier, now 60, and Gamelin, 72, had been claimed by the German Government and removed to German prisons to prevent "establishment of a counter-government" under Allied auspices.

Both had been held by the Vichy Government of Marshal Petain from shortly after the German defeat of France in 1940.

Reynaud, also arrested by Vichy in 1940, was taken by the Germans after the Allied invasion of North Africa in November, 1942.

Weygand, who remained loyal to the Vichy Government after his defeat in the field by the Germans, was arrested by the Germans later in November, 1942, as a hostage for Gen. Henri Giraud, who had escaped from a German prison and joined the Allies.

Gamelin, scholarly soldier once hailed by the Allied world as the best-trained French military man since Napoleon, was generalissimo in command of both the French and British Expeditionary Forces at the start of the war.

Symbol of Hope and Encouragement

—Copyright by Karsh

Throughout the Darkest Days of the War, the Quiet, Graceful Courage and Resolute Strength of His Majesty King George VI Was a Symbol of Hope and Encouragement to the Peoples of the British Empire.

King and Queen Refused to Leave London; Shared Dangers of Blitz

LONDON, May 6 (CP)—The King and Queen rejected plans to evacuate the Royal Family to the country from London when German invasion was considered imminent back in 1940, it was disclosed today. They wanted to share the dangers and hardships with their people.

Now peace has come to Europe, and with it the revelation that no King and Queen in Britain's history has been closer to his subjects at war. The only occasions on which the Royal Standard did not fly from Buckingham Palace or Windsor Castle, both within the Greater London air-raid area, was when the King was visiting his forces or inspecting war factories.

When bombs fell almost nightly on London during the blitz the King and Queen drove—sometimes in a splinter-proof automobile—to cheer the homeless amid ruins of their houses and in streets filled with still-blazing debris.

Six times enemy planes damaged the Palace. Their Majesties spent many nights in a deep underground shelter while enemy planes and later flying bombs were overhead.

In one daylight raid by piloted planes the King and Queen, watching through a window, saw the bombs fall from the raider. In another, the Queen's private apartments were wrecked. Of several thousand windows in the Palace only a few score were left unbroken. Windsor Castle, however, escaped damage from enemy action.

When the Germans indiscriminately bombed Coventry the King motored to the stricken city and walked through the streets with unexploded time-bombs lying about.

Five times His Majesty left Britain to visit his fighting men, and a few days before D-day motored to the south coast to review units of the invasion armada. It was just ten days after the first Allied soldier splashed on to the Normandy beaches that the King was there, and he visited Holland and Belgium last October. Previously he had inspected the British Expeditionary Force in France in 1939, and went to North Africa after the Allied landings, and later to Italy.

LED GREAT SHIPS OUT TO PRACTICE

Five times the King made the 700-mile journey from London to the north to inspect the Home Fleet, and led the great ships out to battle practice as they awaited an enemy who never came.

The King and Queen crossed to Northern Ireland by cruiser in June, 1942, to make their first inspection of the advance guard of the United States armies. At various times they reviewed units of the Canadian Army which prepared so long in southern England for invasion, and also visited R.C.A.F. squadrons.

Scores of Canadians were among the thousands of persons who received decorations from the King at regular investitures held in one of the magnificent rooms of Buckingham Palace. By the King's command everyone attending an investiture was allowed to bring two guests, so the Palace doors, guarded by the colorful Yeoman of the Guard, have been opened during the war to a greater cross-section of people than ever before.

The King, wearing uniform almost every day, kept in closest touch with the day-to-day progress of the war. He had frequent conferences with Allied leaders, and especially with Prime Minister Churchill, who has lunched with the King at least once a week during his Premiership, except when one or the other was away from London.

Refusing any special privileges, their Majesties and the Princesses hold ration cards and clothing coupons like anyone else, and have kept strictly within the allotted quotas. Flower gardens at the Palace and other Royal residences were given over to growing of food and production on the Royal farms was increased greatly.

Their Majesties, in tours of England, Scotland and Wales, visited hundreds of war factories, inspected parades, and talked to thousands of war workers and members of the services. There was little time for relaxation, but occasionally the King might be seen around Windsor Castle in a tweed lounging suit.

It was the King's hand, writing "George R.I." at the bottom of a parchment scroll of the Declaration of War at a Privy Council which placed the nation in war. The same Royal signature on another Privy Council scroll proclaimed the defeat of Germany.

Island Needs $2,000,000 In Bond Drive

With one week of the Eighth Victory Loan campaign remaining, Vancouver Island has still to subscribe bonds to the value of $2,034,600 to reach its minimum objective of $10,640,000. Victoria, with $5,058,300 against a quota of $6,300,000, lacks $1,741,700.

Officials began to look toward substantial oversubscription, since every unit on the Island is ahead of the corresponding time in the Seventh Loan, but they also pointed out the objective in the current campaign is higher than before, and that a considerable amount still remains to go over the top.

Official figures to the end of the week follow:

	Subscribed Seventh Loan	Subscribed Eighth Loan
Greater Victoria	$4,810,750	$5,058,300
Saanich, Esquimalt rural and Gulf Islands	642,950	688,300
Cowichan-Duncan	596,700	725,550
Courtenay-Comox	375,150	522,700
Nanaimo	704,900	861,900
Alberni-West Coast	514,050	535,200
Ladysmith	194,700	213,450
Totals	$7,839,200	$8,605,400

BULLETINS

COPENHAGEN QUIET

COPENHAGEN, May 6 (Sunday) (AP)—The Danish capital was quiet early this morning after a wild day of shooting and disturbances which included a brief but bloody battle between liberating British troops and German soldiers who were awaiting surrender.

ADVANCE ON PRAGUE

LONDON, May 6 (Sunday).—The Partisan-controlled radio at Prague said at 12:20 a.m. (P.D.T.) today that British and American tanks were "advancing" on the capital city, apparently the scene of a battle between Czech Partisan and German forces. The broadcast said "we salute the British and American tankmen who are coming to help Prague."

VANCOUVER, May 5 (CP).—James Wilson, 55, was killed when hit early today by an automobile that did not stop at the scene of the accident.

Japs on Run Before British

CALCUTTA, May 7 (AP)—Allied armies swung eastward toward Thailand Sunday, pursuing the Japanese retreating from their decisive defeat in the Battle of Burma.

The communique said the enemy was withdrawing toward Moulmein, across the Gulf of Martaban east of the liberated capital of Rangoon, with the British Fourteenth Army in pursuit.

In the pursuit, the British were driving beyond captured Pegu, 50 miles north of Rangoon nad near the head of the gulf, where the main railway swings back southeast 80 miles into Moulmein.

More than 110 miles north of Pegu, other forces fighting five miles east of Toungoo were headed toward the mountains of Karenni in Eastern Burma, blocking the way into Thailand.

The campaign to open Rangoon for the flood of Allied shipping was progressing speedily.

Arrest Nephew of Benito Mussolini

ROME, May 6 (Sunday) (AP).—A Swiss Telegraphic Agency dispatch from Berne quoting frontier reports, said today that Vito Mussolini, nephew of the fallen Duce, had been arrested by Partisans in Northern Italy along with several other Fascists.

Vito Mussolini was the editor of Popolo D'Italia of Milan, a Fascist newspaper.

Despite some confusion over the time sequence of the German surrender, The Colonist *declares peace in Europe with a "VE-Day" Extra.*

Then thoughts turned to the months ahead. The Allies were still at war with Japan, and before our boys could return to "civvie street" (with or without a war bride in tow), the remaining tentacle of the Axis had to be subdued. As one of North America's major West Coast ports, Vancouver knew it would play an important role in the escalation of the Pacific war. To complicate things just a little, the cautious and vote-conscious Prime Minister King had decided no serviceman need fight Japan without volunteering. On top of that, they were all entitled to thirty days' leave first.

This was almost too good to be true for certain elements of HMCS *Uganda*'s crew. The light cruiser was already on active duty in the Pacific when word arrived about volunteering. That as members of the RCN they were already volunteers meant nothing. That their captain pleaded with them to stay meant the same. A vote was required, so a vote was taken: 605-300 for going on leave.

Thus HMCS *Uganda* became the only warship in recorded naval history to vote itself out of a war. (Stuart Keate, who went on to a distinguished career as a newspaper publisher, was a young officer aboard the *Uganda*. He told the author, when we were both at the *Victoria Times*, that "sea lawyers" manipulated their shipmates because of uncomfortable tropical fighting conditions.) The ship sailed through the loophole so conveniently provided by the prime minister and slunk back to Esquimalt. Fortunately, the second atomic bomb of the war had just fallen on Nagasaki on August 9, the day before she arrived. So the press, preoccupied with the momentous prospect of Japan's imminent demise, didn't ask many embarrassing questions about earlier reports of the crew's "mutiny."

More air raid sirens and Extras signalled Japan's surrender August 14. In Vancouver, the celebration this time was more frantic and physical. *The Sun* reported that a "human cyclone" hit the streets. There were free kisses and free beers. Some shop windows were smashed. According to the paper the next day, seventy-five persons were injured. In Victoria, *The Colonist* reported that joyous street scenes were tempered by prayers as thousands thronged to the city's churches. August 15—officially VJ-Day—was designated a public holiday across Canada. It was over.

By 1945, the Coalition in Victoria had settled into a comfortable routine. The press, the public and the politicians themselves accepted two-party governance as a natural thing. Despite their differences, the Liberals and the Conservatives managed to prosecute the war from the troubled days of December, 1941, to the heady months of triumph. In October, Premier Hart led the Coalition candidates to an election victory that gave them thirty-seven seats. The CCF shrank to ten. Cracks in the facade were bound to appear, however, and they started to mar the serenity of the post-war period in 1947. John Hart, who was now sixty-eight, stepped down just a few days before the New Year. Succeeded by Byron (Boss) Johnson on December 29, Hart finished his legislative career as Speaker of the House.

Boss Johnson was not a career politician. He served only briefly as an MLA after the 1933 election before returning to private business. A strong supporter of the coalition wing of the Liberals, he returned to the House in 1945. After Hart announced his intention to resign, Johnson threw his name into the hat. Somewhat unexpectedly, he was chosen over the two other candidates, Gordon Wismer and Herbert Anscomb, because of his public personality and the perception he was less partisan as a Liberal than Wismer. However, the Tories were upset because Anscomb had been pushing for the job. During the 1948 legislative session, when a sales tax

THE DECADE IN HEADLINES
« 1948 »

B.C. SALES TAX MEASURE REACHES FLOOR OF HOUSE

The Coalition government introduces the "Social Security and Municipal Aid Tax Act," which provides for a three-percent levy on a wide range of transactions. The act, designed to finance increased social services, goes into effect July 1.

The Colonist, April 8, 1948

DYKES COLLAPSE AT DEWDNEY, AGASSIZ; EVACUATION UNDER WAY; TOWN ISOLATED

"The long-feared flood of the Fraser River struck in the middle of the night," begins the paper's opening sentence.

The Columbian, May 27, 1948

REGISTRATION FOR HEALTH SCHEME TO START IN JULY, PEARSON SAYS

Health Minister George Pearson reminds the province that every person must register under the new Hospital Insurance Act, which was passed in the same session as the sales tax legislation. Implementation date is January 1, 1949. The compulsory aspects of the controversial act (including collection of premiums) will help erode the popularity of the Coalition government in its final years in office.

Victoria Times, May 28, 1948

STREETCARS END SERVICE IN VICTORIA

After 68 years, the trolleys are no longer part of the transportation scene, having been replaced by a modern bus system. An Editorial Page writer called only A.H.S. offers this epitaph: "It has the finiteness of the last period at the close of the last sentence in the book."

Victoria Times, July 5, 1948

THE DECADE IN HEADLINES
« 1949 »

SALE OF MARGARINE IN B.C. NOW LEGAL

A 70-year ban on butter substitutes ends after Parliament passes a bill regulating sale of the product. The legislation specifies the amount of yellow colouring required and that the package be clearly labelled.

Vancouver Sun, March 24, 1949

SPIRITED DEBATE MARKS PASSAGE OF ALUMINUM BILL

The legislation empowering the BC government to make a deal with the Aluminum Co. of Canada for the development of a smelter is reported on Page 6. This is the genesis of Alcan's Kemano project.

Victoria Times, March 24, 1949

FIRST P.G.E. EXTENSION JOB LET FOR $634,029

The government awards the first contract in the $10 million expansion of the Pacific Great Eastern Railway from Quesnel to Prince George. Work on the line has been stalled since the early twenties.

Victoria Times, June 28, 1949

THRONGS SEE MEMORIAL ARENA GIVEN OVER AS KEYSTONE OF NEW, GREATER COMMUNITY

After four years of "doubt, bickering and hard work," Victoria's arena honouring the dead of the Second World War opens.

The Colonist, September 25, 1949

bill was introduced to pay for increased social programs, Anscomb and other Conservative members of the caucus made a nuisance of themselves by questioning aspects of the scheme.

The Colonist was also not amused. In an editorial, it said the tax was so far-reaching it covered "everything from automobiles to aspirins and from perambulators to penpoints ... In its present form, the bill is like an octopus with greedy, groping tentacles." Nevertheless it passed into law, as did equally unpalatable legislation establishing a compulsory hospital insurance plan.

But Johnson felt comfortable enough with the thrust of his government that he called an election for June 15, 1949. Once again, the Coalition scored big: thirty-nine seats to seven CCF and two others. It appeared the "socialist menace" had been put to rest. The Coalition partners had nothing to fear but themselves. Only twelve days after the provincial vote, a massive 193-seat Liberal victory in the federal election (with only 42 Tories returned) prompted both wings of the Coalition to ponder the sanctity of their wedding vows. There were also problems with the controversial hospital plan. Nevertheless, the Coalition muddled on, bickering and sniping like a dysfunctional family.

The beginning of the end would come in 1951, when the government benches pushed through amendments to the Elections Act providing for alternative voting, also known as the single transferable ballot. This new method of counting votes would be the last whimper of the two old-line parties, because the next election—in 1952—would consign them to oblivion for the rest of the century.

Meanwhile, political disasters aside, Mother Nature managed to shake her fist at the mewling MLAs and smug captains of industry as the forties drew to a close. Two earthquakes rattled the outer coast in the latter years of the decade. Courtenay on Vancouver Island suffered widespread damage when a tremor estimated at 7.3 on the Richter Scale struck June 23, 1946. Several buildings collapsed, including part of the elementary school (which, providentially, was unoccupied). A *Colonist* sidebar on the quake was headlined: "It Sounded Like A High Wind—Maybe Something Out Of Ottawa."

The biggest recorded earthquake in Canadian history, 8.1 on the Richter Scale, occurred offshore on August 21, 1949. It convulsed wide areas of the Queen Charlotte Islands. Embankments collapsed, trees were toppled and earth fissures severed roads. There were the usual tumbling chimneys, rattling dishes, swaying signs and panicky residents along the coast. In Prince Rupert, the *Daily News* reported "great excitement."

The Fraser River flood of 1948 lasted longer than any tremor and caused millions of dollars more in damage. The dikes collapsed at Dewdney and Agassiz in the Fraser Valley on May 27. As the New Westminster *British Columbian* observed, the swollen river was a "dirty brown snake meandering down through the luscious green carpet of the spring countryside." Hundreds fled their farms and homes as the Fraser rose week after week. Although Agassiz was hardest hit, 55,000 acres of the valley were inundated and dozens of bridges washed out. Damage in the valley was estimated at $15 million.

More dikes succumbed on Lulu Island, flooding parts of Richmond. Stories about looting and unsafe drinking water made the front pages. Sailors from HMCS *Naden* in Esquimalt joined army reservists to help in flood control and evacuation. The flood, the worst in the history of the river, persuaded the federal, provincial and municipal governments to embark in 1968 on a dike-upgrading program that would

TIDES AT SANDHEADS

Thursday, May 27	Time	Tide
Low water	3.19	10.1
High water	6.04	10.5
Low water	14.05	1.3
High water	22.16	13.6
Friday, May	**Time**	**Tide**
Low water	4.51	9.7
High water	6.36	9.8
Low water	14.44	2.2
High water	22.56	13.4

The British Columbian

88th YEAR — WEATHER FORECAST: Light rain. — NEW WESTMINSTER — THURSDAY, MAY 27, 1948

TEMPERATURES

New Westminster	75	57
Montreal	73	50
Toronto	68	40
Winnipeg	87	40
Regina	81	33
Prince Albert	57	28
Lethbridge	73	50
Edmonton	61	38
Victoria	64	50
Prince George	79	53

Dykes Collapse at Dewdney, Agassiz; Evacuation Under Way; Town Isolated

Mission Red Cross Ready To Give Care to Homeless

The long-feared flood of the Fraser river struck in the middle of the night and has forced hundreds to flee their homes. Damage already is running high at Agassiz, which is flood bound, and Dewdney peninsula where broken dykes let the rushing water flow over the farmlands and small communities.

A full scale evacuation is going on in the Dewney peninsula area where the Fraser river is roaring through a large break in the dyke. D. W. Stachan, former MLA for Dewdney, said this morning that all operations to repair the break have ceased, and a warning for residents to evacuate the area has been issued.

The break came at 8:30 a.m. when a whole section of the dyke collapsed under the strain of the volume of water. As the great wall of water rushed in on the low-lying land, the homes of 40 families were threatened. The break occurred in the same section that collapsed in the 1936 freshet, on the farm of Dugald McDoanld.

In Mission, Rex Cox, head of the Civilian Emergency Committee, has had all churches and halls cleared and made ready to receive the Dewdney evacuees. His committee has pressed 50 trucks into rescue service in the Dewdney area.

Premier Byron I. Johnson and his secretary, Percy Richards, in from Victoria this morning and left immediately for the Mission-Agassiz area by auto. The premier will inspect damage with provincial and federal engineers and aid in the organization of relief measures. They will make an inspection of all threatened areas.

Totally isolated by the flooding of the Lougheed highway and the cancellation of the Agassiz-Rosedale ferry, the Agassiz district is in great need of aid. An estimated 5500 sandbags were flown there by Cascade Air Service and two volunteer Seabee pilots during the night from Chilliwack airport.

Seven families, the Canous, Hayward, Reynolds, Swick and Walker families and relatives, had to move from their homes. They let their 200 head of cattle seek their own safety.

The flood, which swept through numerous breaks in the Agassiz dykes, has inundated an estimated 2000 acres of farm land. Unconfirmed reports stated that present plans call for the entire population of the town to be evacuated to higher land.

Further up the Fraser, eleven families were forced off Herling Island They are being provided with accommodation by the Chilliwack Red Cross.

In a fresh flood surge at 8:30 a.m. the Dewdney dyke near Nicomen slough broke and the raging Fraser swept in. Workers gave up the battle to strengthen the dyke late Tuesday night. A small break widened to 100 feet and within half an hour four feet of water covered most of the fields between the river and the CPR railway embankment.

As the flood situation worsened today, Nicomen island with its hundreds of cattle, is in peril. If the dykes go it is feared many cattle will be lost as there is no place for them to be taken.

Also the main inner farm lands of Dewdney around Hatzic lake and north of the railway are in danger if the railway embankment is threatened with erosion. The railway has sluice gates at several points and the company has the right to open them if the embankment is giving way. This would admit the waters to the inner farmlands.

CATTLE LEFT

Meanwhile most families are evacuating Nicomen island, leaving the cattle to their fate. The dykes were built to stand a river height of 26 feet and so far are holding, although seepage is increasing. Men are patrolling closely. The road to the Nicomen bridge was flooded but a sandbag barrier restored communications.

Only dyke battle now being waged is at Hammersley pumping station, 10 miles west of Agassiz, where efforts are being made to keep the main highway open. The Lougheed highway is already flooded at Harrison Mills.

Three schools have been closed in Matsqui as a precautionary measure, although the Matsqui dykes are all holding today. The schools closed are at Clayburn, Matsqui and Glenmore.

Abbotsford Red Cross is listing all available boats in case they are required for evacuation.

There is considerable seepage in Sumas and Matsqui areas and many fields show water. The Vedder river dykes are holding. Seepage had flooded a section on the Trans-Canada at Cottonwoods.

Canadian Army ordnance depot, North Vancouver this afternoon sent 30 men and three trucks with 6000 sandbags to Glen Valley, north of Aldergrove, where the dykes are threatened.

Eight Feet of Water

The flood in the town of Agassiz came at a bad time, shortly after midnight and within 20 minutes the water had flowed into the side streets of the town. Many residents and stores had to get goods out of their basements. The main street by the track was not flooded. Further away in the fields adjoining the river the water was eight feet deep. Vicious currents swirled all around the village. It was feared that all the town would be inundated but up to noon the water has risen only slightly.

A premature baby was born to Mrs. Steve Mahyr during the Agassiz flood. The child was delivered by a local nurse and mother and babe were rushed to Mission hospital.

Three cattle had been shot by noon today but more than 500 head have been herded to safer ground.

Plans to evacuate families by bus to friends in Vancouver had to be suspended when reports indicated the highway at Harrison mills might be washed out. It is already submerged.

Spreading waters around Agassiz have already inundated 5000 acres and the area is increasing.

The river guage at Mission read 21.9 feet this morning.

Barnston Island Evacuated

At Chilliwack Red Cross workers and work gangs are evacuating 17 families from the Glendale and Cottonwood Corners districts in the face of the rising waters. Overnight the river recorded a one-foot rise, sending water swirling over the Trans-Canada highway near Glendale, a western suburb of Chilliwack.

Reports say the Glendale district is completely isolated by some six inches of water. Work crews are in drastic need of boats and sand bags.

Chilliwack city is so far clear of danger, but municipal authorities report Ballam road, on the river's edge, flooded for one mile. More than 10 acres of land are flooded at Minto Landing, and road passage is nearly impossible.

Rumors of a break in the Atchelitz dyke have been termed false. All other municipal dykes are reported holding steady with work crews readying sand bags.

Fort Langley has been turned into an island by the rising waters, but homes are mostly built on high points, and no reports have been received of families being in danger. Wednesday afternoon the water swept over the Glover road to a depth of nine inches, and a resident told The Columbian today that road passage will be impossible by the early evening.

Evacuation is also underway on

(Continued on Page 2)

No Panic Despite Disaster

By STAN BURKE

AGASSIZ, May 27—Refugees from the Fraser floods are thronging the passable roads from Mission to Agassiz. Farmers on horseback are driving herds of cattle along the highway to friends on higher ground.

Evacuated families from Dewdney and Nicomen island have filled their household goods into trucks, cars and trailers and are moving to havens provided by the evacuation committees.

Despite the shadow of damage and disaster, all the people in this section of the Valley appear to be quite calm. Many stubbornly refuse to leave their isolated homes, to the distraction of the officials.

Commercial firms and merchants have closed down business in Agassiz and joined the truck pool. Nearly 150 trucks and cars have been made available to W. H. Hicks, chairman of the evacuation and relief committee.

Water covers the main streets of Agassiz town. Four boats with outboard motors are tied up to the posts of stores ready to evacuate people. Household goods are stacked on the railway station platform.

Stores are still selling groceries and residents are wading about to get supplies and call for mail. The Agassiz telephone office is jammed with residents trying to call through to relatives down the Valley. But there is no panic and everybody is doing his job as best he can.

Strangest sight of all was down near Mission where a family calmly donned bathing suits to reach their home outside the dyke. Waters wirled around the house and threatened to take it out at any time, but the bathing-suited mother, father and young son did not seem alarmed.

Servicemen's Homes Ready Next Winter

OTTAWA, May 27 (BUP)—A $20,000,000 Canada-wide housing program to provide new homes for married personnel of the armed forces to ease the civilian housing shortage will be "well completed" before next winter, Defense Minister Brooke Claxton announced today.

The program calls for the completion of 2350 new homes for service men and the defense research board, Claxton said.

PGE Increases Freight Rates

VICTORIA, May 27 (BUP) — John Hart, president of the government - owned Pacific Great Eastern railway, announced today a 21 per cent increase in freight rates on the line will be put into effect immediately.

FLOODS LOOK PUNY IF SEEN FROM PLANE

—Croton Photo Studio

AGASSIZ AREA GOES UNDER—Above are vivid views of the inundation caused by the flooding Fraser river in Agassiz district today. The Agassiz school just outside the town is surrounded by four feet of water. Below is one of the many roads in the district covered by water and virtually impassable.

'Dirty Brown Snake Twists Through Valley'

Floods in the lower Fraser Valley appear very puny from the air and give no indication of the hundreds of pygmy humans battling the waters at several communities from New Westminster to Hope.

At 6000 feet the mighty Fraser river is a dirty brown snake meandering down through the luscious green carpet of the spring countryside. At most places the sharp line of dykes bounds the river.

But at the flooded areas the brown water smears one to three miles inland into fields and around tiny blobs that are homes and farm houses. Dykes and roads disappear and hedges or windbreaks dwindle to meagre lines like tufts of grass sticking out of a lake.

Viewed from an RCAF plane the Fraser below the Royal City appears quite normal, except the dyke line near Ladner is almost under water. Smoke still plumes from the scores of sawmills, and countless booms of logs can be seen like little collections of toothpicks along the shorelines.

Broad inundations, however, are apparent in the upper Valley. Fort Langley is an island, with the Glover road washed out and the only access along River road from the east.

Hatzic and Dewdney flats near Hatzic have suffered the worst, with the river sweeping three miles inland. The highways are under water, the dykes long since lost, and specks of farm houses appear to be in the middle of a vast river.

The same ruthless penetration of the river is apparent near Chilliwack where many new islands have taken shape as the water creeps over the fields below Rosedale. The route of the Rosedale ferry and the road approaches have vanished. Agassiz peninsular is a splotchy pattern of water and clumps of trees where scores of families were forced to evacuate.

Above Agassiz the Fraser is confined in its narrower canyon and there are no broad inundations, although froth and debris can be seen coming down on the surface of the muddy water.

Eastward the towering Coast Range mountains are still laden with snow — and a lot of it is pouring daily into the swollen Fraser.

Youths Sent To Jail

Three youths charged with the breaking and entering of the Stubby Beverage Company, 717 Princess street, were sentenced by Magistrate H. L. Edmonds in police court this morning.

Robert Gordon Abbott, 18, was given two and a half years suspended sentence, this being his first offense.

The magistrate warned him of the seriousness of the charge and said, "You apparently were very good until recently and then got into bad company and then into trouble. I am being lenient with you to give you a chance to make good."

James Robert Draney, 22 and Irvine Forester, 19, both with past records, were sentenced to 26 months and two years, respectively.

Rev. White, 93, Passes

One of British Columbia's well known pioneer ministers, Rev. James Henry White, DD, died on Wednesday night at his home, 3790 Pine Crescent, Vancouver. A former minister of Queen's Avenue United church, he had served in many other Methodist and United churches in the province for 42 years, retiring in 1923. Born in Ontario, he was 93 years of age and was a son of the late Rev. Edward White, first minister of the church now known as Queen's Avenue United church. He had been residing in Vancouver for the past 18 months. Surviving him are his wife; one daughter, Mrs. J. C. McDonald, Chilliwack; three sons, Edward W., Victoria, George B., Vancouver and Arthur A., Ottawa; eight grandchildren and five great grandchildren.

Last rites will be held on Monday, at 3 p.m., in Queen's Avenue United church, Rev. W. B. Willan and Dr. A. M. Sanford officiating. Interment will be in Fraser cemetery.

Light Showers Are Friday Fare

Cloudy with scattered showers is the weather forecast for tonight and Friday. Winds will remain light with little change in temperature.

Hundreds Flee B.C. Lowlands

By British United Press

British Columbia recorded its second flood death today as rivers throughout the province ran wild, inundating thousands of acres of farmlands, destroying homes and causing damage that will run into millions before the waters subside.

Peter C. Barrett, 23, jumped into the swollen Twenty Mile Creek near Princeton and was swept down the rushing mountain stream.

Authorities said Barrett told friends shortly before he jumped that he was fascinated by the swirling waters.

In the Kootenay, the flood situation was still causing concern although workers had made some progress to stem the Mark creek which continued to flood through Kimberley.

Damage was mounting hourly and in the Kimberley area alone it was expected to pass the $500,000 mark. Approximately 60 homes were destroyed and some 600 persons were homeless.

Hundreds of residents throughout the province were evacuating their homes as waters slowly crept past danger levels. About 200 families were evacuated from near Prince George after the Nechako river overflowed.

In the Okanagan, the army rushed 100 sandbags to Summerland to curb the raging Trout creek. Reports from Penticton said so far there is no danger in the area.

Prince Rupert was cut off by rail and road as the Skeena pounded over its banks and flooded highways and rail lines.

Wm. Steele Dead at 65

A member of the New Westminster teaching staff for 29 years who retired in 1945, William Steele, 1011 Dublin street, died on Wednesday afternoon at his home. He was 65 years of age and came here from Scotland, his birthplace, 32 years ago. Surviving him are his wife, three daughters, Isobel Steele, at home, Mrs. F. E. Hogg, Arvida, Quebec, Mrs. Charles Carncross, city; four grandchildren; one brother, James, in Vancouver and two sisters in Scotland.

Industrial arts instructor, Mr. Steele taught in the Duke of Connaught high school, F. W. Howay junior high, Lord Lister and Richard McBride schools. He was a life member of the B.C. Teachers' Federation, member of King Solomon Lodge AF and AM, and past chief of the Sons of Scotland.

Last rites will be held on Saturday, at 1:30 p.m., in the chapel of S. Bowell & Sons, Rev. J. C. McLean-Bell officiating. Interment will be in Fraser cemetery.

Northwest Stamp Show Opens Here Tomorrow

Rare and highly interesting philatelic collections will be on display beginning tomorrow in New Westminster when the Royal City Stamp Club acts as host for the 8th Annual Congress and Exhibition of the Northwest Federation of Stamp Clubs. Collectors from the lower mainland, Vancouver island, Washington and Oregon will gather for the three-day meeting to be held May 28, 29 and 30. The exhibition will be open to the public at 1:30 p.m. Friday at the Dontenwill hall on Agnes near Fourth street.

Among the outstanding exhibits to be seen will be some of the well-known forgeries of the G.P Bainbridge collection. These clever fakes have received world-wide notice, having been shown in London, Vienna and other large cities.

Of particular interest to New Westminster residents will be three frames on the postal history of British Columbia as it affected the Royal city. They are from the collection of Gerald E. Welburn of Duncan.

Other exhibits include: a complete collection of Vatican city; airmail stamps, 97 percent complete, and a complete Newfoundland collection.

Official opening ceremonies will be held at 12:30 p.m. tomorrow when delegates gather at a luncheon in the Hollywood Bowl under the joint auspices of the city council, board of trade and the federation. Distribution of awards will be made at the grand banquet in the bowl on Sunday at 6 p.m.

With New Westminster perched uneasily on the banks of the Fraser, The British Columbian *treats the century's most devastating flood with utmost seriousness.*

cost more than $145 million.

Traumatized by war, shaken by earthquakes, dampened by floodwaters and diddled by politicians, British Columbia ended its first 50 years of the century in a dyspeptic mood. Surely things would calm down in the next decade. No way.

---

1 Canada's national parks were the dumping ground of choice for the nation's unwanted throughout the century. During the Great War, aliens of European descent were put to work in various parks. The unemployed during the Depression were followed by "conchies" and Japanese in the forties.

THE FIFTIES: DYNASTICALLY YOURS

« 1950 – 1959 »

This was probably the most pivotal decade of the century. Perched at mid-tide between 1900 and 2000, the fifties marked a transition in the affairs of British Columbia. Left behind were the forties, a world-wide struggle to the death and the teething problems of post-war recovery, to be replaced by stable government and an irresistible cascade of promises and expectations.

True, another war was to begin almost immediately, but its impact was diffused by an agenda of beginnings and endings, of high drama and low comedy. Tragedy, derring-do, grand schemes, scandals and magic moments so crammed these years that one almost had to take a deep breath and a soothing cup of tea when it was all over. If someone had to write a pilot script for The Decade That Had Everything, they'd pick the fifties.

As is often the case in democratic societies, political affairs took a front seat early in the show and occupied it to the very end. No one in the press or otherwise connected with the political scene, however, could guess the true import of a warm summer evening in 1952. For shortly after 9 p.m. on August 1 of that year, William Andrew Cecil Bennett was sworn in as premier of British Columbia—and the Social Credit dynasty was born.

It was perhaps the most logical denouement to a most peculiar election. The newspapers, the public and the candidates were little prepared for the confusion that followed election day, June 12. For the first time, British Columbians had cast their vote via the single transferable ballot. Passed into law in 1951 as a deathbed wish of the crumbling Coalition government, this alternative voting method was designed to ease the Liberals and Conservatives back into a two-party system (and, incidentally, keep the CCF from coming first). Tabulations for 212 hopefuls in 48 ridings was so difficult and time-consuming, however, that it took almost a full month for the final results to be announced.

When they were, the CCF indeed did finish in second place, with eighteen seats. But Social Credit was first, with nineteen, while the Liberals had only six and the Conservatives, four. Obviously, the Socreds were the main beneficiaries of the transferable vote. Under this system (wisely junked by Bennett once he had a majority government), candidates on each ballot are chosen in order of preference. A candidate with more than 50 percent of first-choice votes is declared elected. If this

THE DECADE IN HEADLINES
« 1950 »

THE STAGE IS SET FOR FIRST WOMAN SPEAKER IN BRITISH EMPIRE TO TAKE OVER DUTIES

The choice of Nancy Hodges as BC's (and the Empire's) first female Speaker of the legislature is covered on *The Province*'s women's pages.

The Province, February 14, 1950

SHAUGHNESSY HOME ALL READY FOR ATOMIC BOMB RAID

A Page One picture and Page 2 story are devoted to what *The Sun* describes as possibly Canada's first atom-bomb shelter. It is constructed of concrete, with a plug-in for a portable Geiger counter.

Vancouver Sun, August 29, 1950

PARK ROYAL MAGIC EYE CAPTURES MYRA'S FANCY

Homemaker columnist "Myra" is thrilled at the opening of the "smartest shopping centre in Canada." Park Royal, in West Vancouver, introduces the mall phenomenon to BC.

The Province, September 1, 1950

MISSING ORDERS BLAMED FOR 20 RAIL WRECK DEATHS

A troop train carrying Korean War recruits to Fort Lewis, Washington, for training collides with a CNR passenger train at Canoe River, about 400 miles northeast of Vancouver. The death toll is later set at 21, with 15 identified as soldiers.

Vancouver Sun, November 21, 1950

MAYBE PERCY DIDN'T HAVE ORTHODOX STYLE BUT HE COULDN'T LOSE FOR WINNING

Vancouver's Percy Williams, winner of two Olympic gold medals in 1928, is named Canada's outstanding track and field athlete of the half-century.

The Province, December 27, 1950

Forecast—Clear, little change; Sunday sunny (Details on Page 2)

The Daily Colonist.

Vancouver Island's Leading Newspaper Since 1858

It should be a point of honor to leave the crippled children's beach to them alone

NO. 197—NINETY-FOURTH YEAR   VICTORIA, BRITISH COLUMBIA, SATURDAY, AUGUST 2, 1952

7 CENTS DAILY
10 CENTS SUNDAY

22 PAGES

Premier Completes Formalities

Minutes after he had been sworn in as B.C.'s new premier, Hon. W. A. C. Bennett signs the Government House note book as Lieutenant-Governor Clarence Wallace and new minister of education, Hon. Mrs. Tilly Rolston, look on. Mr. Bennett, Mrs. Rolston and nine other ministers of the Social Credit government attended the swearing-in ceremony at Government House at 9 p.m. last night.—(Colonist photo by Jim Ryan.)

New Social Credit Government Takes Over B.C. Administration

Swearing Queried By Winch

C.C.F. Leader Harold Winch has questioned the authority used to swear in the new Social Credit government.

Informed last night that a Social Credit cabinet had been sworn into office, he suggested two questions be directed to Lieutenant-Governor Clarence Wallace.

"By what authority was the government sworn in before the writs of election were returned? Vancouver-Point Grey and Vancouver Burrard have not yet been returned."

"Was his decision made by recommendation of ex-premier Byron Johnson, or who, in his estimation, had support in the House?"

Mr. Winch said he would have further comment today on the procedure.

The fact that two cabinet ministers are not members of the legislature is extraordinary," he said.

SHOULD BE RESPONSIBLE

"A cabinet minister should be responsible to the Legislature from the floor of the Legislature. The C.C.F., under any circumstances, would not appoint any cabinet minister who was not elected to the Legislature by the people."

Herbert Anscomb, Progressive Conservative party leader, showed interest in the cabinet, but declined comment.

Post Waits For Islander

Premier W. A. C. Bennett said last night he hopes Vancouver Island will be represented in the cabinet "at an early date."

"I hope that two sitting members will see their way clear to resign, in order that the appointed members of the cabinet (Vancouver lawyer Hon. Robert Bonner and accountant Hon. E. M. Gunderson) may run in by-elections," the premier said.

He did not say just how Island representation in the cabinet would be achieved. There is not an Islander among the 19 Social Credit M.L.A.'s.

HON. ROBERT W. BONNER

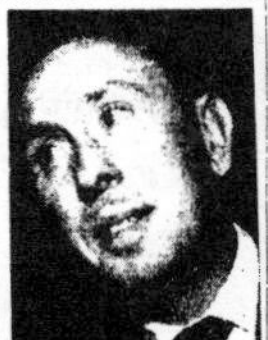

HON. EINAR M. GUNDERSON

HON. WESLEY D. BLACK

HON. P. A. GAGLARDI

HON. KENNETH KIERNAN

HON. RALPH CHETWYND

HON. LYLE WICKS

Johnson Gives Resignation; Bennett Cabinet Sworn In

BY T. A. MYERS

British Columbia's first Social Credit government took office last night.

William Andrew Cecil Bennett, 51-year-old hardware merchant from Kelowna, was sworn in as premier of B.C. in a short ceremony at Government House.

Also sworn in were 10 cabinet ministers, two of them have not been elected to the Legislature.

Immediately after the ceremony, Premier Bennett called his first cabinet meeting for 11 a.m. today.

The formation of the new government ended a day of dramatic action that broke the 50-day-long stalemate that has existed ever since the general election of June 12.

The Bennett government holds only 19 of the 48 seats in the Legislature. In the opposition are 18 C.C.F.'ers, seven Liberals, three Progressive Conservatives and one Laborite.

The narrowness of the margin between Social Credit and C.C.F. has been the chief factor in the delay. Recounts and court actions will mark the transfer of power from the defeated, 11-year-old government last headed by Premier Byron Johnson.

NEW ATTEMPT

The deadlock appeared to have been broken Thursday when a C.C.F. bid for a recount in Vancouver-Burrard—the seat which might have put the C.C.F. in power—was turned down.

But yesterday morning a new C.C.F. court action appeared likely to block the formation of a new government indefinitely.

It was 2 p.m. before Premier Johnson slipped off to Government House. He emerged at 3.10 p.m. to tell the press that he had handed in his resignation and those of his six cabinet ministers, and had recommended that Social Credit be called on to form a government.

The resignations were not immediately accepted by Lieutenant-Governor Clarence Wallace.

BENNETT CALLED

Then, at about 5 p.m., Mr. Wallace called Mr. Bennett at his Empress Hotel headquarters and asked him to form a government.

At 9 p.m. Mr. Bennett and his lieutenants were waiting in the drawing room at Government House.

The Lieutenant-Governor, who had just officially accepted the resignations of Mr. Johnson and his cabinet, walked into the room and administered the oaths to the new cabinet.

After the ceremony, Premier Bennett issued his first official statement:

"I want to make it clear that our government will not be a government of the Right or of the Left. The Social Credit government will be a middle-of-the-road government.

NO PRIVILEGE

"It will be the policy of our government to give fair treatment to all and special privileges to none. In this task I ask for the support of all the citizens of British Columbia."

The Social Credit attorney-general and finance minister are the only two ministers who have never been appointed to a B.C. cabinet without first being elected to the Legislature.

The attorney-general as predicted by The Colonist Thursday.

HON. ERIC MARTIN

HON. R. E. SOMMERS

Premier Bennett explained why he had chosen "outsiders" for these two senior cabinet posts:

"First let me make it clear that they are not 'outsiders.' They are Social Crediters.

"It was vitally important that the attorney-general be a lawyer. There was not a lawyer among our elected members. We are fortunate in securing a young and brilliant lawyer for that post.

TRAINED MAN

"As to Mr. Gunderson, for the handling of the finances of any business so large and important as British Columbia it is necessary to have an outstanding man and one well trained in financial matters. Mr. Gunderson brings a wealth of experience to his job."

Premier Bennett summed up his government's policies:

"Our main plan is to bring stability and progress to our province. I am sure our cabinet meeting today will be simply a preliminary meeting. No action will be taken.

Union Men Non-Committal

Victoria union officials were non-committal last night on receiving news that Hon. Lyle de Wicks had been sworn in as a labor minister. Some officials said they would withhold comment until the new minister in the new government.

Most frequently asked question was "Who is he—what does he do?" Premier Bennett called his first cabinet meeting today will be "simply a preliminary meeting. No action will be taken.

New Cabinet Ready for Action

A new, young, inexperienced cabinet prepared today to manage the affairs of booming B.C.

With an average age of 48 and only four of the 11 members more than 50 years of age, the untried Social Credit cabinet is probably the youngest in B.C.'s history.

Here, in brief, are sketches of the nine first-time ministers:

B.C.'s new finance minister, Hon. Einar M. Gunderson, is a man who knows something about finance.

He is married and has three children, Mrs. John Bridgham, Seattle; Derek, 23, Calgary, Alta. and Garth, 14, who attends school in Vancouver.

The man who nominated W. A. C. Bennett for leadership of the Conservative Party in the revolt against Herbert Anscomb is Hon. Robert W. Bonner, B.C.'s new attorney-general.

Hon. Robert W. Bonner is one of two outsiders named to cabinet posts by Mr. Bennett yesterday.

Member of the Vancouver firm of chartered accountants at Gunderson, Stokes, Walton & Co., city and graduated with a B.A. from U.B.C. in 1942. After the war he went back to university and graduated with the degree of LL.B.

Youngest member of the new cabinet, Mr. Bonner had an impressive record during the Second World War. He served with the

Continued on Page 10

Born in Vancouver in 1920, Mr. Bonner attended school in that Mr. Gunderson is considered one of the first of his profession in the province.

He was born in Cooperstown, North Dakota, attended high school in Canada and then went to the University of Saskatchewan.

He has held four different government posts in Alberta.

In 1936 he resigned to enter private practice and in 1942 was appointed comptroller of Marshall Wells Canadian companies. He entered the Vancouver firm of accountants in 1945.

Difference Apparent

Premier Byron Johnson and Lieutenant - Governor Clarence Wallace apparently took different views on the formation of a new British Columbia government.

The lieutenant-governor, it was said, did not want to accept the resignation until all recounts and legal actions in connection with the June 12 election had been settled.

Yesterday, apparently, Mr. Johnson decided the time had come for action.

He drove, alone, to Government House at 2 p.m. He talked with the lieutenant-governor for an hour and 10 minutes.

When he returned to his office, he announced that he had submitted his resignation and those of his cabinet. The lieutenant-governor, he said, had not accepted them.

Then he said he had no idea just when the resignations would be accepted, a new C.C.F. court action, started yesterday, might delay the acceptance for some time, he indicated.

Until the official acceptance, he said, he would continue to function as premier.

Reporters who had been working on the story gave up hope that a new government" would be formed last night. A surprise phone call from Government House summoned them to witness the swearing-in of the new cabinet at 9 p.m.

his resignation. Each time he returned to his office with the letter still in his pocket.

The lieutenant-governor, it was said, did not want to accept the resignation until all recounts and legal actions in connection with the June 12 election had been settled.

Premier's Assistant

RONALD B. WORLEY

Young former Liberal who bolted the party September last year has been given the important post of executive assistant to the new Social Credit premier, Hon. W. A. C. Bennett. Mr. Worley will replace Perry Richards, executive assistant under Premier Byron Johnson. Mr. Richards at present also holds the post of deputy minister of railways. Former executive of the B.C. Young Liberal and Victoria Liberal Associations, Mr. Worley joined the Social Credit League late last year.

New Cabinet Listed

British Columbia's new cabinet:

Premier, Hon. W. A. C. Bennett, South Okanagan.

Provincial secretary, municipal affairs, Hon. Wesley D. Black, Nelson-Creston.

Attorney-general, Hon. Robert W. Bonner, of the Vancouver firm.

Lands and forests, mines, Hon. R. E. Sommers, Rossland-Trail.

Finance, Hon. Einar Maynard Gunderson, no seat.

Public works, Rev. the Hon. P. A. Gaglardi, Kamloops.

Railways, trade and industry, fisheries, Hon. Ralph Chetwynd, Cariboo.

Labor, Hon. Lyle Wicks, Dewdney.

Health and welfare, Hon. Eric Martin, Burrard.

Education, Hon. Mrs. Tilly Rolston, Vancouver-Point Grey.

Housewife's Champion Makes History as Head of Department

BY JIM NESBITT

Tilly Jean Rolston, 65, today makes history as Canada's first woman head of a government department.

True, years ago, in B.C., Mary Ellen Smith was a cabinet minister—but without portfolio. Mrs. Rolston has one of the heaviest portfolios of government—education.

Only two women in Canadian history have broken up to on the highest councils of government—Mrs. Smith, and Mrs. Mary Irene Parlby, one-time minister without portfolio in Alberta.

For more than a decade now, Mrs. Rolston, once a very pillar of the Tories, has been a bright light in the Legislature. She knows what's on her mind, speaks it right out, bang, like that; sometimes she wishes she could hold her tongue, but when she lets it slip she shrugs, knowing words can't be taken back.

Like her new leader, Premier Bennett, she was for long a buzzing bee irritating Tory chieftain Herb Anscomb. She thought she should have been a Conservative cabinet minister in 1946. Mr. Anscomb wouldn't go for her, and she never forgot nor forgave. Today her revenge must be sweet, though she had to leave the party she loved to get where she is now—the Honorable Tilly Rolston.

The war was on, and Vancouver-born Tilly Rolston is no weak battler. She pummelled one Coalition cabinet minister after another; "the 11 boys in the ivory tower," she called them. The phrase made a hit, she used it over and over again. She particularly stirred up Conservative R. C. MacDonald. There was an uproar that Coalition supporters and Coalition called out to him: "At least we have loyalty."

That was when Mr. Anscomb banged his desk so savagely that C.C.F. leader Harold Winch chuckled: "I'm a first aid man if your wrist is broken." And Mr. Bennett shouted to Mr. MacDougall: "What do you mean by loyalty?—to principles and the people—or to the party?"

Strange, isn't it?—Messrs. MacDonald, MacDougall and Anscomb are gone; Bennett and Rolston ride high.

Mrs. Rolston is now widowed, didn't go into politics until her two daughters and a son were grown up.

"I don't believe a woman should be in public life while her children need her at home," she says. Today she's a grandmother of eight—seven grandsons. She's a world traveler, has flown to Europe, South America, Australia, the South Seas, China and Japan.

"I've enough to live on," she explains. "Why shouldn't I spend my sensual indemnity on educational travel?"

With C.C.F. Laura Jamison back in the House, there'll be some good hot rows. Grandmothers Rolston and Jamieson know how to fly at each other about women's place in life. Mrs. Jamieson once said there should be government nursery schools so mothers could park their infants and go about their business. Children, said Mrs. Jamieson, would be a lot happier if they weren't with their mothers all day, and mothers would be a lot pleasanter if children weren't hanging to their skirts all day.

Up jumped Tilly Rolston. "It's an insult," she said, "to suggest that a mother can't bring up her own children better than some parched, dried-up, starched, cultured academician."

Ever since 1946, Tilly Rolston was agin' just about everything the Coalition did. She fought the sales tax, increases in hospital insurance premiums, she scoffed at the milk board, she battled for colored margarine until she won.

She called the sales tax discriminatory legislation, retrograde, unsound, unfair, a nuisance tax.

She thundered in the House: "This sales tax may be a finance minister's dream, but it's a housewife's nightmare." She has a quick tongue and she knows how to laugh, and

often at herself—a rare virtue in women. Once, in the House, she apologized for a raspy voice, a cold, she said.

"I've got something in me room that'll fix you up, Tilly," sang out Tom Uphill.

"Thanks, Tom, I'll see you later," said Mrs. Rolston, and got along with her speech.

She said one day the legislative chamber should be cleaned and painted. Burnaby's Mr. Winch looked up to the nudes on the ceiling. Surely, he said, Mrs. Rolston wasn't suggesting painted ladies in the House.

"No," said Tilly. "Just clean ladies."

Before she showed her hand openly, as a Coalition-Conservative-Anscomb-hater, she took pot shots at the government. As long ago as 1947, C.C.F. Bert Gargrave told Premier Johnson to keep his eye on the Coalition's Tory wing. "Watch 'em pretty carefully, Mr. Premier," said Gargrave. "They're feeling their oats."

"Why shouldn't we?" snapped Mrs. Rolston, looking mad and very pretty at one and the same time, in a shapely black suit, and big corsage.

M.L.A.'s who sat in the House with her will never forget her margarine battle.

"That white, lardy stuff," she sneered. "Why should it be that awful, frightening, sickening color?" She called uncolored margarine mournful-looking. She painted a grim picture of many kitchens, with the poor, exhausted housewife unrolling margarine, putting it into a bowl, emptying the color in, whipping it and beating it, getting splashed and messy, dirty dishes piled around her, hungry children howling for their breakfast, father so discouraged at the confusion he slams the door, goes to town for coffee and a doughnut.

The legislative stories about our new woman cabinet minister are already legend. Mrs. A. R. Ritchie got into an argument, something about man vs. woman. "Do you consider yourself as good as a man?" shouted Mr. Ritchie.

Mrs. Rolston said 'yes, and sometimes better. To which Mr. Ritchie barked: "Well, it's too damn bad for you—because you ain't." Mrs. Rolston was so astonished she couldn't reply—rare for Mrs. Rolston.

On another occasion Mrs. Rolston and Conservative Don Brown argued about Garibaldi Park. Mr. Brown said Mrs. Rolston went around talking about members of Garibaldi Parks Board, sniping at them, whispering mean things behind their backs. Ha told Tilly that Mrs. Rolston to stop her busy-body tactics.

"This has been a vile, vicious, dirty, personal attack," said Mrs. Rolston, huffing with indignation. "We have reached a new low in this House."

Well, Mr. Brown was defeated, too.

Mrs. Rolston's good at a wisecrack. C.C.F. Arthur Turner said the Coalition's next election was, should be Oh Promise Me.

"Sounds kinda romantic," sighed Mrs. R., almost to herself. A smart dresser, she has been called the Clare Booth Luce of the British Columbia politics. She has plenty of bounce and umph, but she's a chilly sort.

Other M.L.A.'s may be gasping for air, but Mrs. Rolston calls for a page to get her for coat, wraps it cosily about her shoulders. Her private room in the Buildings has always looked like a hot house, though Mrs. R. is not the cold type. She likes a party, takes a drink, smokes cigarettes, says she's a good plain cook, but has served her day at stove and sink.

This, then is Canada's first real woman cabinet minister—a woman of much drive, a great deal of charm that is distinctly feminine, but a woman who has the good sense, unlike so many women, not to briskly flaunt those charms, not to laid always hurt, not to take the rough and tumble of political life too personally.

Fifty days after the bizarre election of June 12, Social Credit's emergence as the new BC government occupies the entire front page of The Colonist.

magic number is not reached, the last-place finisher in the riding is dropped and the second choices in his or her pile are then counted. This elimination and transferral continues until a winner emerges.

Despite a *Vancouver Sun* editorial touting (predictably) the Liberals and *The Province*'s warning to not "dabble in questionable experiments," the voters did what they wanted. While *The Province* was referring to the burgeoning popularity of Social Credit, the actual questionable experiment was the voting system itself. The percentage breakdown of the popular vote (CCF, 30.7; Social Credit, 27.2; Liberals, 23.4; Conservatives, 16.8) indicated the Socreds were a popular second choice. Going down to personal defeat along with a boatload of old-time politicians were Premier Boss Johnson and Tory leader Herbert Anscomb.

That left CCF leader Harold Winch, re-elected and fully expecting to become premier. After all, his party had eighteen seats, the lead in the popular vote and much experience in the legislature. Besides, that funny-looking Socred machine didn't even have a driver. True. Even though Bennett had been making leader-like announcements all spring and summer, the post was still officially vacant. The party took care of that July 15, choosing—naturally—W.A.C. Bennett.

Thus the manoeuvring began. Winch argued that the CCF deserved its chance, while Bennett pointed out that nineteen seats still added up to one more than eighteen. Lt.-Gov. Clarence Wallace, the target for all these broadsides, was more confused than stubborn. He let the hot summer drag by while he sought advice on which to base his Solomon-like decision. Boss Johnson tendered his resignation, but Wallace refused to accept it. He kept muttering about needing more time, which prompted the *Victoria Times* to predict on the fateful day that no decision would be made "at the present time." Bennett, however, prevailed late that afternoon and Wallace summoned him to Government House.

(*The Sun* had no such compunction about anointing Bennett. In its July 16 editions—fully two weeks before he was chosen by Wallace—*The Sun* called Bennett either "premier" or "premier-elect." It was either a case of uncanny foresight or one of appalling ignorance of the machinery of government.)

For Bennett, his ascension to premier was a personal triumph as well as a political one. Born in New Brunswick in 1900, he was a successful hardware merchant in Kelowna when he was elected to the BC legislature as a Conservative in 1941. Re-elected in 1946, he tried to oust Anscomb as party leader. Soundly rejected, Bennett festered on the backbench until he quit the provincial wing to run federally in 1948. He lost, and remained out of politics until returning to the legislature in the 1949 provincial election. Back in Victoria, Bennett became more and more disenchanted with the government's shortcomings. Once again he ran against Anscomb for the Tory leadership, and once again he lost. In 1951, he delivered a major speech in the House which was openly contemptuous of the Coalition in general and the hospital insurance deficit in particular, then quit to sit as an independent.

While taunts of "traitor" wafted gently through the House, Bennett started paying attention to the Social Credit movement. Blossoming in Depression-scarred Alberta under the leadership of "Bible Bill" Aberhart, it was a strange blend of economic theories, Christian values and non-partisan government. By the time Social Credit reached BC, the "funny money" and evangelical aspects were muted, but the solid theories about responsible government remained. Only weeks before the 1952 election was called, Bennett allied himself with the upstart party. The

THE DECADE IN HEADLINES
« 1951 »

VANCOUVER SOLDIER FIRST KOREAN CASUALTY

RSM James Wood is accidentally killed by a mine during a training exercise and the story gets prominent play on Page One. The actual date of the incident is not mentioned.

Vancouver Sun, January 19, 1951

THE DECADE IN HEADLINES
« 1952 »

LUMBERMAN'S ARCH OFFICIALLY DEDICATED

A new structure replaces the original Stanley Park arch erected in 1912 in downtown Vancouver to mark the Duke of Connaught's visit. The original, moved to the park in 1913, is dismantled in 1947 because of its rotting condition.

The Province, July 15, 1952

NEW SOCIAL CREDIT GOVERNMENT TAKES OVER B.C. ADMINISTRATION

With W.A.C. Bennett as premier in a minority government, Social Credit begins its domination of BC politics during the last half of the century.

The Colonist, August 1, 1952

500 MET BY 5000 HERE AS FIRST PGE TRAIN REACHES CITY

The local paper notes that the largest number ever to ride a Pacific Great Eastern Railway train is greeted by the largest crowd in the city's history. The special train (with Premier W.A.C. Bennett aboard) formally completes the rail link between Quesnel and Prince George.

Prince George Citizen, November 1, 1952

REDS BLASTED FROM VITAL KOREAN KNOB

This is the story that *The Sun* runs three days in succession on Page One as a commentary on the dullness of the Korean War news. The repetition goes virtually unnoticed.

Vancouver Sun, November 18, 19, 20, 1952

rest, as they say in history books, is history.

While Bennett and Winch were skirmishing on the lawn of Government House, other British Columbians were engaged in a more deadly charade on the other side of the Pacific. By mid-1952, the Korean War had been occupying space on the front pages for two years; in fact, two Esquimalt-based destroyers—HMCS *Athabaskan* and HMCS *Cayuga*—had each completed their second tour and entered harbour even as the votes in the June 12 election were being counted. Along with HMCS *Sioux*, they had constituted Canada's first fighting presence in the war theatre.

When the three RCN warships first sailed from Esquimalt July 5, 1950, the war was only days old. North Korea invaded South Korea Sunday, June 25, and the United Nations responded within days with a resolution directing members to "furnish such assistance to the Republic of Korea as may be necessary to repel the attack and restore international peace and security in the area." With those words, Canada was obliged to go to war and Ottawa's eyes fell immediately on the West Coast. Within a week, *Athabaskan*, *Cayuga* and *Sioux* were "in all respects ready for sea"—and for battle. The trouble was, nobody quite knew what to do with them. Gen. Douglas MacArthur, the US Army legend who was in charge of UN forces in Korea, desperately needed men, not ships.

Indeed, when the three destroyers sailed, under command of Vancouver-born Capt. Jeffry Brock aboard the *Cayuga*, the UN had not yet accepted Canada's offer of naval support. Thus the orders to Brock—and the stories in the local press—were carefully equivocal. The headline in the *Victoria Times*, "Destroyers Headed for Pearl Harbor," and the noncommittal Page One story that accompanied it reflected the confusion of the moment.

In all, the ships each completed three tours of the war zone, lasting (in the case of the *Sioux*) until 1955. At various times during Canada's five-year commitment, they were relieved by another West Coast destroyer, HMCS *Crusader*, and four Halifax-based warships. During the shooting war (a ceasefire came into effect July 27, 1953), these men-of-war became familiar with every wrinkle of Korea's coastline. Actions ranged from messy confrontations with Chinese junk fleets near the mouth of the Yalu River to support of the Inchon invasion and trainbusting along the vulnerable eastern coast of North Korea. *Athabaskan* fired the last RCN shot in anger July 25, 1953.

While the naval personnel were the first of 25,000 Canadians to see action in Korea, their land-based counterparts in the army had a rougher war. Of the 516 who died in the cause of peace, only nine were in the RCN. And, unfortunately, fifteen soldiers died even before they were fully trained. On November 21, 1950, the last of the troop trains carrying recruits to Fort Lewis, Washington, collided with a CNR passenger express near Canoe River in remote east-central BC. The recruits were among the twenty-one dead. (Several months later in Prince George, a lawyer named John Diefenbaker secured the acquittal of a young telegrapher accused of causing the wreck by sending an incomplete transmission to the westbound train.)

The federal government had dithered for several weeks before authorizing an initial expeditionary force of 5,000 volunteers. Vancouver was one of the recruiting centres, and most of the British Columbians who answered the call found themselves in the Princess Patricia's Canadian Light Infantry. They were led overseas by Col. Jim Stone, a Second World War veteran who had been running a BC resort. The 25th Canadian Infantry Brigade was commanded by John Rockingham, who was superintendant of Pacific Stage Lines in Vancouver when he got the call on August 7 from Ottawa. Rockingham was a retired brigadier with a chest full of ribbons and a no-nonsense reputation earned five years earlier.

The first elements of the PPCLI were in Korea in early December, but there was still a long stretch before any Canadian soldier saw battle. *The Sun*, desperate for a local angle from the front with a hint of action in it, overplayed on Page One the accidental death of Canada's first war casualty. He was RSM James Wood of Vancouver, and he died January 18, 1951, after a land mine exploded during a demonstration. Eventually, other BC soldiers died more dramatic deaths—often covering themselves with glory in the process—at such battle sites as Kapyong and Hill 677.

In 1952, the war news became dull and repetitive. Unlike the Second World War, when Canadian correspondents provided dramatic copy from the heart of the action, the Korean coverage was boring—at least to *The Sun*. In November, Himie Koshevoy, a newsroom executive, ordered the identical story placed on Page One three days in a row to see whether anyone would notice. Only one person did. "It wasn't the fighting that was dull. It was the coverage," Koshevoy said in a 1995 interview. "The stories kept saying the same thing, which gave me the idea to repeat one of them."

There was plenty of other news to distract the readers of *The Sun* and other BC papers. The curious election of 1952 was followed by a more predictable one in 1953, which gave the Socreds the solid majority they sought. The British Empire Games were coming to Vancouver and visitors to the Pacific National Exhibition grounds could check on the progress of Empire Stadium. After the 1954 Games, the new BC Lions of the Western Interprovincial Football Union would move in. Closer to home—in fact, right in their very living rooms—Lower Mainland families were offered on December 16, 1953, another distraction that would do more to affect their lives than all the stadia and edifices constructed during the boom years of the century.

It was local television. While many Vancouver-area and Victoria homes could already pull in fuzzy Washington State stations via ungainly antennae atop their roofs or by judiciously tinkering with "rabbit ears," the inaugural broadcast of CBUT linked BC with the rest of Canada through the CBC network. The Vancouver papers ran the story inside. *The Province* treated the event as if it were another ribbon-cutting ceremony, while *The Sun* concentrated on the quality of the reception.

Actually, it didn't take the newspapers long to fear and loathe television. Firstly, it was a much more attractive medium for many advertisers. Secondly, the mere fact the TV set was in the home, offering hours of mindless diversion, kept subscribers from actually reading their papers. Together, the two elements contributed significantly to the decline of the newspaper in general in North America and the evening paper in particular.

It is hard to imagine, in these days of extensive print coverage of television events and personalities, and weekly TV sections fat with ads among the grids and rolling logs, that the Vancouver dailies once debated whether they should run TV schedules (as they already did with radio in the classified section). There were strong voices who argued that the picture tube was a competitor and should be resisted. Some competitor. From 1953, when CBUT first offered viewers four hours of programming as an alternative to US reception, TV availability has become so

THE DECADE IN HEADLINES
« 1953 »

BUTCHART'S GARDENS FIND NEW BEAUTY

Almost 50 years after Mrs. Ralph Butchart creates a sunken garden in a limestone quarry in 1904, night lighting is installed. The world-famous gardens are on Tod Inlet, north of Victoria.

Victoria Times, June 24, 1953

DOUG HEPBURN TOPS WORLD AT STOCKHOLM, SETS WEIGHT-LIFTING RECORD WITH VICTORY

Vancouver strongman lifts 1,030¼ pounds to become world champion. The details are on the sports pages, with a short feature about his mother on Page One.

The Province, August 30, 1953

ALBERTA'S CRUDE STARTS TO FLOW TO BURNABY'S HUGE TANK FARM

The 711-mile, $97-million Trans Mountain Pipe Line is completed from Alberta to the BC coast. The line is the Lower Mainland's first direct link to a major oil-producing area.

The News-Herald, October 15, 1953

THE DECADE IN HEADLINES
« 1954 »

25,000 SEE SPECTACULAR EMPIRE GAMES OPENING

BC's spanking-new stadium is christened by the British Empire Games. A week later, on August 7, the Miracle Mile is run, with Roger Bannister defeating John Landy. It is one of the most memorable moments in BC sports history.

The Province, July 31, 1954

widespread and complex that Friday's editions of most BC daily papers have healthy circulation numbers because they carry the weekly grids of dozens of channels.

Before television, however, there was royalty. British Columbians, holding true to the predominantly European antecedents reflected in their province's name, still held a deep affection for the Royal Family. The royals seem to like BC, too; they've been coming here since the early years of the century, and there were four visits in the fifties alone.

The first was in October, 1951, when Princess Elizabeth and husband Philip slipped across the Alberta border toward the end of a Canada-wide railroad tour. It was night, it was snowing, and Jack Scott, one of *The Sun*'s finest writers, was there. In this short, evocative sentence for the paper's October 19 editions, Scott captured the magic that always seemed to surround the Royal Family on its visits:

"Out of the softly falling snow a Princess suddenly appeared before the people of Golden as if she had stepped directly from the pages of a storybook."

Scott then wrote of how Elizabeth "broke free from the bonds of red tape" to mingle with her subjects. It was a hint of the "walkabouts" that would characterize her trips around the Commonwealth when she became Queen. Philip, the Duke of Edinburgh, was back in 1954 to attend the British Empire Games in Vancouver—among other duties—before accompanying Her Highness on another royal tour in 1959. Officials estimated that more than 500,000 people saw the pair at various appearances around the Lower Mainland. During the "busiest day of the Queen's life," according to one member of her entourage, she officially opened the Deas Island (Massey) Tunnel under the Fraser River. In 1958, Princess Margaret paid a two-week visit.

The British Empire and Commonwealth Games (BEG for short) were the athletic centrepiece of the fifties. As well as providing the impetus for the construction of Empire Stadium, they were the occasion for one of the century's most sparkling moments in track and field. This was the Miracle Mile—the meeting of Roger Bannister and John Landy in the final of the men's mile competition on August 7, 1954. Both Bannister, from England, and Landy (Australia) had previously run the event in less than four minutes—the watershed clocking for that distance at the time—and Landy was a slight favourite. Bannister won, however (in 3:58.8 as the pair became the first two men to break the four-minute barrier in the same race), and the crucial moment was captured for all time by *Sun* photographer Charlie Warner. Stationed on the final turn, Warner clicked the shutter of his Speed Graphic just as Landy, who was leading, looked over his left shoulder as Bannister passed him on the right.

Warner's shot became world-famous, leading to an equally celebrated statue that enshrined the moment and the Games, and which stood outside Empire Stadium for many years. (Charlie's picture didn't make Page One of *The Sun* for two days—on the Monday following the Saturday race. For its final edition Saturday, the paper ran an eight-column shot of Bannister beating Landy at the finish line.)

BC also played a role on the global sports stage in 1953, when Vancouver's Doug Hepburn won the world weightlifting championship. Born with a club foot, Hepburn climaxed a remarkable odyssey of pain and perseverance by lifting 1,030¼ pounds—a world record—to take the heavyweight title in Stockholm.

Then in 1955, the Penticton Vs won a world hockey crown for the province. Hardnosed and tenacious, this ragtag mixture of home-grown boys and former pros was led by the Warwick brothers, each tougher than the next: Dick, Grant

Frozen in time, this famous photograph by The Sun's *Charlie Warner captures the decisive moment of the 1954 British Empire Games, when John Landy looks the wrong way as Roger Bannister passes him on the final turn.*

and Bill. They rode to the title in Dusseldorf, Germany, on the elbows and leadership of the Warwicks, defeating the hated Russians (the USSR team) 5–0 in the final game. BC went bonkers. Minutes after the game, Penticton's downtown streets were an impassable sea of delirious citizens, while a Vancouver cleric interrupted communion to intone the final score. Preceded by congratulatory telegrams from Governor General Vincent Massey and Prime Minister Louis St. Laurent, the team received on its return a welcome that rivalled 1945's victory celebrations.

To no one's surprise, the BC Lions hardly beat anybody during their formative years as a professional football team. Vancouver did host a Grey Cup, though, in 1955. Unfortunately, the first East-West championship game November 26 in Empire Stadium between Montreal Alouettes and Edmonton Eskimos was overshadowed by the rampaging of some world-class yahoos. Under the headline, "Police Avert Grey Cup Riot," *The Sun* reported that a "howling, drinking, fight-hungry mob," 100,000-strong, roamed downtown streets the Saturday night after the game. This pattern of lawless behaviour was to be repeated during subsequent Cup weekends in Vancouver.

Over on Vancouver Island, readers of the *Victoria Times* weren't paying much

THE DECADE IN HEADLINES
« 1955 »

BOARD LAUNCHES SEARCH FOR NEW CHIEF OF POLICE

Walter Mulligan is fired as Vancouver police chief amid charges of graft and corruption on the force. On February 28, 1956, a Royal Commission headed by Reginald H. Tupper finds Mulligan guilty of accepting bribes from bookmakers.

Vancouver Sun, October 24, 1955

attention to what was happening on the mainland. They were captivated by a succession of heroic, daring, plucky, exhausting and laughable attempts to swim Juan de Fuca Strait between the Island and the Olympic Peninsula.

It began in 1954, when *Times* publisher Stuart Keate offered noted long-distance swimmer Florence Chadwick $10,000 if she could swim from Victoria to Port Angeles, Washington ($7,000 if she tried and failed). Chadwick was quickly defeated by the cold water and relentless tides, but Keate's co-sponsor, a paint manufacturer, gave her the ten grand anyway, and the challenge of Juan de Fuca caught on. For a prize of $1,000, some fifty-three disparate challengers—ranging from genuine athletes to genuine kooks—attempted the thirty kilometres of chilly tide rips. The first to do it (on his fifth attempt) was Bert Thomas, a 270-pound Tacoma logger who began his swim in Port Angeles.

Keate's show-stopper, however, was Marilyn Bell, who was dubbed "Canada's Sweetheart" (yes, newspapers actually used phrases like that back then) after she became the first person to swim Lake Ontario. For a $30,000 guarantee, Bell made it on her second try across the strait as 10,000 Victorians cheered from the cliffs above her landing beach and Canada's print media sparred viciously to get exclusive coverage. The craze ended with Marilyn, but Keate was satisfied. He had promoted both his newspaper and his city around the world, and the publicity was gratifying. (That same year, 1956, saw the culmination of another of Keate's circulation-building stunts. On July 2, Chief Mungo Martin finished carving the "world's tallest totem pole" in a Victoria park. It was 127 feet, 7 inches high.)

The sports world was not immune to the tragedy that occasionally accompanies the unfolding of history. On December 9, 1956, a Trans-Canada Airlines plane carrying sixty-two passengers and crew slammed into Mt. Slesse in the Cascades near Chilliwack. Among the dead were five professional football players who had appeared in the all-star game at Empire Stadium the day before. It was the worst air disaster in BC's history. The landscape in the area is so forbidding that the location of the crash site was not determined until months later, and the remains of the victims were left on the mountain. This decision would spark a scandal almost forty years later when *Province* columnist Don Hunter revealed in 1994 and 1995 that the site had been disturbed and some looting had occurred.

The third disaster of the decade, following the Canoe River train wreck and the Mt. Slesse crash, also involved transportation. A new Second Narrows bridge across Vancouver's Burrard Inlet was under construction on June 17, 1958, when a temporary support buckled, bringing down one of the spans. A concrete pier then shifted, knocking another span into the inlet. Eighteen workers were killed. They were either crushed in the steel wreckage or drowned after being tossed into the water.

On a broader labour front, an umbrella group with a familiar name was reborn in 1956 to represent the working man. This was the BC Federation of Labour, which had been "founded" twice before in the century. The first Federation, born in May, 1910, died in 1920 when the One Big Union became the brotherhood of choice in BC (only to expire itself within a few years). On October 1, 1944, the BC Fed was reformed under the wing of the Canadian Congress of Labour. Then, on November 15, 1956, at a "unity convention" in Vancouver, the BCFL reinvented itself again by absorbing the BC Trades Union Congress and merging the trade and craft branches of the labour movement.

In Victoria, meanwhile, Premier Bennett spent the latter half of the decade

The author at a tender age. Bill Rayner, sports editor of the Trail Daily Times *at 24, poses at his desk in 1954.*

skirting political calamity. With the election of June 9, 1953, safely out of the way (twenty-eight of forty-eight seats for the Socreds), Bennett's gamble in letting his minority government fall had paid off. He started making big plans for BC's future. This included ribbons of new blacktop (making a media star of the buffoonish highways minister, Phil Gaglardi), extension of the PGE and myriad schemes to lure business and investment to the province.

THE DECADE IN HEADLINES
« 1956 »

BENNETT PROMISES HOMEOWNERS AID

No details are given until later, but *The Sun* sniffs in an editorial the next day that Premier Bennett's plan is a "political poultice rather than an economic cure."

Vancouver Sun, April 24, 1956

MARILYN'S OWN STORY OF EPIC SWIM

Marilyn Bell, conqueror of Lake Ontario and the English Channel, swims Juan de Fuca Strait. She is one of several long-distance swimmers to brave the frigid waters separating Vancouver Island and Washington State, beginning with Florence Chadwick in 1954.

Victoria Times, August 23, 1956

HELEN'S RECORD THRILLS TEAM

On the eve of the Olympic Games in Australia, Helen Stewart sets a world record of 57.6 seconds in the 100-yard freestyle at Vancouver's Crystal Pool.

The Province, October 27, 1956

UNIONS MERGER COMPLETED

Craft and industrial unions are united at the "founding" convention of the BC Federation of Labour. The BC Trades Union Congress is dissolved.

Vancouver Sun, November 15, 1956

VANCOUVER GIVES SHOUTING WELCOME TO OLYMPIC HEROES

Cheers and tooting horns greet return of the University of BC's four-oared rowing crew after winning a gold medal at the Melbourne Olympics. The university's eight-oared crew won a silver medal.

Vancouver Sun, December 15, 1956

But there was a fly in this grand pot of bubbling progress, and his name was Robert Sommers. Called "Honest Bob" by some, Sommers was one of Bennett's original cabinet ministers (from an extremely thin talent pool) in 1952. A year later, he was still in cabinet, as minister of lands and forests, despite rumours he had recurring problems with drinking and gambling. It is still conjectural why Bennett made such an error in judgment — something to do with accepting a man's word of honour, perhaps—but schoolteacher Sommers was in over his head almost from the moment he arrived in Victoria from his Rossland-Trail riding. Already in debt, he compounded it by living in a manner not supported by his combined legislative salary of $10,500. He began accepting loans and favours from H. Wilson Gray, a small-time logging operator with shadowy connections to the big boys in the industry.

Soon, whispers began circulating that forest management licences could be bought from Sommers' ministry. At the time, the FMLs were used to manage the harvesting of the province's forest resources. A licence to cut down trees meant guaranteed riches for the lucky company holding one. Finally, Gordon Gibson, the tough-talking "Bull of The Woods" and Liberal MLA, brought the whispers into the open when he told the House in 1955 that "money talks" in the issuance of the licences.

Quickly, two key players emerged: David Sturdy, a young Vancouver lawyer, and Charles Eversfield, who was Gray's bookkeeper. Egged on by the Liberal-friendly Keate of *The Times* and Don Cromie, publisher of *The Sun*, Sturdy pursued the revelations offered up by Eversfield until Bennett was forced to act. In February, 1956—a full year after Gibson's bombshell—he asked for Sommers' resignation.

In his farewell speech to the legislature, Sommers dwelt upon "the most dirty and slanted news coverage in the history of BC, conducted principally by Mr. Stuart Keate, publisher of the *Victoria Daily Times*," and claimed the charge against him "is as phoney as the man (Eversfield) who makes it." Not quite. Despite further stonewalling by the premier and Att.-Gen. Robert Bonner (and a surprise election in September, 1956, which Social Credit won handily), Sommers was charged with bribery on November 21, 1957. The knock on his front door by the RCMP came more than 1,000 days after Bonner had heard Gibson's allegations in the House. Moreover, it took another year before Sommers was convicted of conspiracy on November 1, 1958, and the specific bribery charges, involving $7,107, four days later. He was sentenced to five years in prison, as was Gray. BC Forest Products Ltd., owned by Eastern industrialist E.P. Taylor, was acquitted of conspiracy charges.

Sommers was the first minister of the Crown in the history of the Empire to serve time for bribery, but Bennett swallowed the embarrassment and sailed on with his grand vision. During the decade, neither inflation nor unemployment were a cause of concern. The bellwether resource industries luxuriated in impressive growth. Population increased from 1,165,200 to 1,629,100—almost 40 percent. However, the good times were tempered by another small embarrassment, one that stemmed from Bennett's urge to develop the north.

Into British Columbia's ken one day fluttered Axel Wenner-Gren, a wandering millionaire gadfly who was a really big thinker. The Swedish industrialist's plans to develop the Rocky Mountain Trench area of the province as part of a billion-dollar private scheme (complete with a 100-mph monorail to help pluck out nature's riches) were embraced by Bennett and revealed to a startled legislature in 1957. The immediate public storm over Wenner-Gren's shady past, his possible Nazi

TODAY: Sunny and warmer.
High 63, low 43.
TUESDAY: Sunny and warmer.
High 68, low 45.

The Vancouver Province
A Dependable Newspaper

EXTRA

59th YEAR—No. 56   PA 4211   🏵️   MONDAY, MAY 7, 1956   44 PAGES   7 CENTS

THIS STORY FOR A LIFE!

★ ★

A report from the editor

The Province publishes this extra edition tonight as part of a successful effort to save the life of a guard at Oakalla prison farm.

It climaxes an incredible sequence of events, set off when three convicted men grabbed the guard as hostage at the prison and threatened to kill him with razors if certain conditions were not met.

One of the conditions was that The Province tell the convicts' story. Warden Christie of Oakalla telephoned Bruce Larsen. The Province city editor, late this afternoon advising us of this condition.

It was clearly our public duty to do all we could to prevent the murder of the guard—all we could within our privilege in law as a newspaper.

So we geared up for this extra and Bruce Larsen rushed out to Oakalla to get the story that was to help save a life.

Our 29-year-old city editor went down into the prison cells to interview the convicts. During this interview, he persuaded the prisoners to let their hostage walk out of the cell with him.

Polio shots in 2 weeks

Greater Vancouver's postponed polio vaccination program—delayed almost a month owing to delivery tieups—is now scheduled to start May 22.

But only about 43,000 Vancouver children will receive vaccinations this month instead of the 60,000 initially scheduled.

This means that every child in B.C. from grade 1 to 9, not already vaccinated, and the pre-school age group scheduled to start school next September, will receive at least one vaccination this year.

City Health Officer Dr. Stewart Murray said the delay in starting the program, and the lack of guarantees of continued regular deliveries, would result in a modified program which will:

Give only one vaccination to each child instead of the two initially planned.

TAKE ABOUT 17,000 children those who received two shots in the 1955 Salk vaccine test, off this year's program for their "booster" shots.

"We may be able to get in the second shots. We will try to, but we've got to get the first one over with before we start thinking about the second dose," said Dr. Murray.

"ONE SHOT is not as good as two, naturally. But it will have some effect and will be better than none at all," said Assistant Provincial health officer Dr. George Elliot.

Dr. Elliot said that no vaccine will be shipped elsewhere in B.C. for second doses, until every child in the program this year has had the first shot.

The entire B.C. program covers more than 350,000 children in grades 1 to 9 and the pre-school age group, scheduled to enter school next September.

DR. ELLIOT said that with shipments of vaccine leaving Vancouver today and Tuesday morning, all of B.C. will have been covered for first vaccinations, with the exception of the north side of the Lower Fraser Valley, including Victoria, Chilliwack and Surrey areas will receive their first-dose quotas Tuesday.

VACCINE for metropolitan Vancouver and the Mission area on the north side of the Fraser will receive priority claim on all subsequent shipments until children in those areas are vaccinated.

This week's regular shipment of 30,000 cubic centimeters is expected to arrive Wednesday.

The Greater Vancouver program was originally scheduled to start April 23. It was delayed one week owing to production difficulties in Connaught Laboratories in Toronto.

BANK CHIEF ASSAILED BY BENNETT

By GORDON McCALLUM
Province Legislative Reporter

REGINA — British Columbia's Premier Bennett today called for the resignation of James Coyne, governor of the Bank of Canada, because of his new credit-restriction regulations.

"I call for a complete change in policy, if that is not forthcoming, then we should have the governor's resignation," Premier Bennett said in an interview.

It looked suspiciously like a Social Credit pre-election invasion of this about-growing province as Mr. Bennett came to the city, and for Alberta's Premier Manning was due to arrive shortly.

MR. BENNETT said he wasn't here to enter Saskatchewan's politics, but it certainly looked like it as he promptly started to talk about the problems of the Saskatchewan farmer, such as wheat and credit.

When we suggested that he might be preparing a campaign in Mr. Bennett answered "I am speaking as Premier of British Columbia."

Mr. Bennett said the Bank of Canada's higher interest rates had restricted credit "at a time when we need it."

(Continued on Next Page)
(See BENNETT)

Markets

Afternoon sales on Vancouver Stock Exchange:
400 Bethlehem Copper 1.38.
600 Cowichan Copper 2.45.
3500 Jackson Mines 40.
5000 Quatsino .02.
500 Mill City Oil 44.
500 Van Tac 1.33.
500 Advance Primer 43.
1000 Com W A R 15.
100 Inland Gas 3.40.

Someone around here took a slap at a helping hand

HAMILTON — (CP) — Talk about biting the hand that feeds you:

Police said today thieves made an unsuccessful attempt during the weekend to break into the offices of the Hamilton branch of the John Howard Society.

The society is dedicated to the rehabilitation of freed convicts.

30 STUDENTS HURT AS TRAIN DERAILED

WAUKESHA, Wis.—(AP)—At least 38 persons were injured today in the derailment of a special Milwaukee road passenger train after a collision with a gravel truck.

The 16-car train originated at Portage, Wis. and was loaded with 500 persons, most of them high school pupils en route to Milwaukee to attend the Milwaukee Braves-Brooklyn Dodgers baseball game.

Race Results

Laurel
Monday Results

FIRST RACE 6 furlongs
Ses Barned (Nunno) $11.60, $5.60.
Toge Top (Stout) $5.80, $3.40.
Provincial Shad (Chandler) $3.60.
Time 1.13. Sly-High Game, for Ray Jr. Mary Pandente, Steel Blue.

SECOND RACE 6 furlongs
Knight Hawke (Bush) $26.20, $9.40.
Sleepy Mate (Moger) $3.40.
Time 1.12. 5/5 Barnda's Pride, Royal Rocket, Come Ilare-y, Burta Temp, Pleasant Land, Scholarly Lass, Hobo Joy. and Call Col also ran.

THIRD RACE 6 furlongs
Neenon (Shuk) $6.90, $4.40, $3.40.
Advice (Dimauro) $5.40, $3.40.
Flying Portal (Morrison) $3.20.
Time 1.13. 1/5 Okefenokee, King Mowlue, Sergeant Monk, a Lure chee, The Scholar, Quatsugh. Carkadon, Piment, Special and Davis also ran.

FOURTH RACE 6 furlongs
Golden Cape (Nelson) $3.30, $5.20.
Mr. C'd (Vasile) $4.00.
Time 1.15. 3/5. Shlemo, Lasting King Ted (Culshaw) $15.50, $7.40.

FIFTH RACE 1 1/16 miles
Challenge Bud (Zanora) $2.80.
Time 1.48. 3/5. Master Piece, Blowick, Forglo, Easter Bud also ran.

SIXTH RACE 1 1/16 miles
Eagle Low (Catalano) $7.20, $5.20.
Oliver Island (Tabson) $12.60, $4.60.
Sartay (Catalano) $4.40, $2.40.
Time 1.46 4/5. Battler II, Rama Hood, Buck Cottage, Powder Flash also ran.

SEVENTH RACE 1 1/4 mile
Princes (Zabone) $6.00, $4.00, $3.00.
Warbler (Culshaw) $6.20, $3.80.
Count of Monk (Zanino) $3.60.
Time 1.45. On, In The Market, Red Yellow, Bad Pat and Stimulon also ran.

Jamaica
Monday Results

FIRST RACE 4 furlongs
Robert W. (Moger) $7.80, $7.20. $3.20.
Deep River (Atkins) $3.90, $2.40.
Hardworky (Stout) $2.40.
Time 1.13. 3/5 Justa Sister, Broom

Tanforan
Monday Results

FIRST RACE—6 furlongs
Premier Saga (Valenzuela) $8.90, $2.90, $2.20.
Full Craig (Longden) $3, $2.40.
Ah D'Ashley (Pulido) $2.20.
Time 1.13. 3/5 Methodist, Fairy Kambler, Kenzie Queen, Superstar, Golden Rush, Madera Sele also ran.

(Race Entries on Page 36)

Province city editor frees kidnapped guard

Talks convicts into releasing captive

By BRUCE LARSEN
Province City Editor

Three desperate Oakalla inmates who kept a razor at a guard's throat for almost six hours surrendered that hostage guard to this reporter at 7:25 p.m. tonight.

They gave up their prisoner—guard Ernie Loveless, 38, after gaining assurance that the attorney-general's department would study their case plus my promise that I would write this and other stories.

Prisoners Bob Tremblay, Marcel Frenette and Charlie Talbot talked to me in their hostage room — a barbering space at the end of a 90-foot corridor in the west wing of the prison.

WHILE WE TALKED, guards with rifles at the ready stand at the other end of the corridor, the closest any prison official had been to Tremblay, Frenette and the hostage for six hours. Talbot had been walking the corridor with messages.

The three prisoners kept them at bay with the threat: "Stay back—we have nothing to lose through cutting his throat. We've got 20 years and another charge waiting."

Prison officials had to believe that threat—the three and two other inmates had lost their appeals from 20-year sentences for attempted murder earlier in the day and spokesman Tremblay had said: "It makes little difference if I hang."

HE MADE MANY DEMANDS; many were jumbled, many of them inconclusive. As a desperate prisoner he suddenly had an Aladdin's Lamp but he didn't know quite how to get it working.

At 3:45 p.m. he asked for me—I had met him last year when I went to the house where he was staying and collected $97.50 for a Province camera he had damaged.

He wanted me to print everything, he said.

I told him I could write what I could within reason if he would take the razor from the guard's throat. I told him we would publish this extra in return for a man's life.

He agreed—but he wanted his wife (a tall, dark woman who visited him midway

paper could not publish of his story we would supply to the attorney-general's department.

The three prisoners had seized Loveless at 1:40 p.m. Monday when they were on the way to the barbering quarter at the end of the long corridor. No other prisoners were handy.

One grabbed a razor and held it to Loveless' throat. Another held barbering shears pointed into his back. They forced him to the floor and bound him with wire—later Tremblay asked for handcuffs to replace the wire.

Through the long ordeal in the 90-foot, several people tried to reason with Tremblay. He was the key, he were the decisions.

Senior prison officials planned the entire strategy. Warden Hugh Christie and his senior officers were at the end of the corridor throughout the six-hour session and supervised all conversations with the prisoner group.

The group had stoutly defended the innocence throughout the trial and appeal.

Tremblay, in our interview insisted that facts had been held out or not entered at their trial. His request to me was that our paper run his complete side of the story.

MY PROMISE in return was that my paper would run what seemed reasonable and what was legally our right to publish. I also promised that what our

(Turn to Page 3)
(See PRISONERS)

See The Province home edition tomorrow for further details and all the pictures of this amazing story.

THINGS ARE LOOKING UP for Steve Bilko of the Los Angeles Angels who started out this road trip with a windmilling bat and then belted out three homers in the last two games against Vancouver Mounties. His team is expecting more of the same when they play close-out game of four, at Capilano Stadium tonight.

Sentenced to three years

Girl, 16, wins new hearing

A 16-year-old Dawson Creek girl sent to the penitentiary for three years for her first offence was awarded a new trial in Court of Appeal today.

Mabel Bessie Clisby was sentenced by Magistrate C. S. Kitchen of Dawson Creek on Feb. 8, for 12 charges of cashing forged cheques totalling $1025.

Her case was appealed by F. G. Lewis and the convic tion was set aside for a new trial so that she can be tried what she told the court after either in the County Court pleading guilty could be a or at the Assizes.

M. G. Capie appeared for defence in the charges.

She has been given the the crown.

THE DECADE IN HEADLINES
« 1957 »

PROVINCE, SUN POOL RESOURCES

Pacific Press is born, ending head-to-head competition in BC's largest city. Vancouver's two dailies agree to share production and other assets, with *The Province* entering the morning field June 17.

The Province, May 30, 1957

PEACE RIVER SPAN CRASHES TO GROUND

The suspension bridge north of Dawson Creek collapses after a pier is buckled by erosion. Failure of the bridge—built in 1943 as part of the Alaska Highway—is a major blow to transportation in northern BC and The Yukon.

Prince George Citizen, October 16, 1957

FINEST LIBRARY ON CONTINENT OURS

Although the lead paragraph touts Vancouver's new library at Robson and Burrard as "the most modern ... on the continent," its opening received only a brief story inside *The Sun*'s late editions. Compared with the frenzy that will surround the library's move in 1994 to Georgia and Homer streets, the media response is muted.

Vancouver Sun, November 1, 1957

leanings and his inability to complete a project gave the Socreds pause and the mad dream of the north subsided into oblivion. (*The Province*, which occasionally swallowed the Social Credit agenda, took the whole illegitimate project at face value, deadpanning the original Wenner-Gren announcement February 12 with this streamer on Page One: "Billion-Dollar Deal For Northern BC.")

While the Rocky Mountain Trench slumbered on, another real-time development was actually being built on the other side of the province. This was the massive Kitimat-Kemano project by the Aluminum Company of Canada, 650 kilometres north of Vancouver. It involved a dam, a sixteen-kilometre tunnel through a mountain and a smelter. Unlike the Wenner-Gren splash, its genesis was innocuous, but it would become the largest single industrial development in BC's history. Starting with the original agreement between BC and Alcan in March of 1949, newspaper stories about the project usually made the inside pages.

Another inside story (at least in *The Province*) was the choice of Nancy Hodges in 1950 as the first woman Speaker of the legislature. Although this was a first for the British Empire, the paper covered the story on the women's pages. Frank Calder, the first Native MLA, also took his seat at this session.

One more first for BC was duly noted in the press but hardly treated as earth-shaking news. This was the Bennett announcement in 1956 of the homeowner's grant, which was set at $28 to help offset a portion of a family's property taxes. Despite being dismissed by *The Sun* as a "political poultice," the grant would grow to hundreds of dollars and survive tinkering by a New Democratic Party government in the nineties.

Confrontational violence makes better news than dull industrial developments or government attempts to placate voters with their own money, so the Doukhobors maintained their high profile in the press during the fifties. With the ascension of the Bennett cabinet, however, came a change in attitude. With much of their strength coming from Interior constituents, the Socreds favoured a hard line against the troublesome sect. There had been an outburst of arson in Krestova in 1950. When it resumed in 1953, retaliation against the Sons of Freedom minority was swift. On September 9, RCMP arrested 148 adults for allegedly parading in the nude. In Vancouver the next day, the usual efficient trial brought the usual sentence: three years in jail.

This time, however, there was a new twist in the war against the Douks. Their children—104 of them—were placed in an unused sanitarium at New Denver. This was an obvious attempt to remove the children from the rebellious atmosphere of the community and reeducate them. Probably, it was only partly successful. Some of the youngsters who spent time at New Denver during the six years of its existence no doubt participated in a later outburst of terrorism in the sixties.

During the fifties, Ottawa took some positive steps. In 1955, it removed the punitive penalty of three years in jail for nude parading, and in 1957 restored the franchise in federal elections. The Doukhobors also got to vote in provincial elections. This apparently failed to impress the fanatics. In 1958, a wave of bombings in the Kootenays and Okanagan spread terror through the Interior. Because the violence was at its height when Princess Margaret visited the Okanagan, 140 RCMP officers were supplied as protection.

For one organization, the struggle to keep the Freedomites law-abiding ended in 1950. This was the year the BC Provincial Police disbanded. Formed in 1858 to help patrol the colonial gold-rush camps, the force accomplished much more in its ninety-two-year history than simple policing. Especially in the remoter reaches of the province, the BCPP officer performed myriad community duties that ranged from collection of fees to making weather reports.

The end came with brutal swiftness. Although the force was aware of a legislative amendment authorizing the switch to the RCMP, it was given less than a week's notice when the time came in August, 1950. Nine senior officers were fired and most of the 500 Provincials were told they could apply for a job with the Mounties. Eleven refused; during the following two years, several more resigned. The reason for the changeover? Costs. The Coalition government saved $1.7 million a year by signing up with the federal force.

On a more individual level, another abrupt police change would be made in BC's largest city. In 1955, just as the Sommers case was gathering steam, the Vancouver press had another circulation-friendly scandal on its hands. The city's top cop, it seemed, had gone bad. With the papers pouncing on every allegation, Police Chief Walter Mulligan was finally fired in October amid charges of graft and corruption. A Royal Commission headed by lawyer Reginald H. Tupper began probing the force while George Archer, the new chief, cracked down on discipline. In February, 1956, the commission found Mulligan guilty on four charges of accepting bribes from bookmakers. Mulligan, by this time, had moved to the United States.

One of the icons of the entertainment world, Errol Flynn, chose Vancouver for his own unseemly departure. The famous actor, a bloated fifty, died of a heart attack October 14, 1959, while in the city to sell his yacht to a stock promoter. *The Province*, because of its earlier press start, got the break on the story, but Jack Wasserman, *The Sun*'s legendary saloon columnist, responded with a classic piece of Page One reportage. His perfect opening paragraph, containing all the elements necessary to nail the reader to the story, went like this: "Movie swashbuckler Errol Flynn died on the bedroom floor of a West End penthouse Wednesday while his young blonde protege desperately tried to breathe life through his pain-twisted lips." They don't write declarative sentences like that any more.

This was also the decade when transit moved from the rails to the pavement. In April, 1955, Vancouver's last streetcar made its ceremonial final run, while in February, 1958, the last interurban tram shut down. Thus ended a street-railway era that began in June, 1890 (Victoria began operating its own system in February of that year). At its peak, interurban trackage on the Lower Mainland and in the Fraser Valley totalled 373 kilometres. All that was left in 1958 was the Marpole-Steveston line. The change to rubber tires was gradual. Gasoline buses started operating in Victoria in 1944 and conversion picked up steam, so to speak, after the war. Vancouver began switching on a permanent basis in 1947. Trolley buses arrived in 1948.

At sea, BC's most dangerous hazard to navigation—Ripple Rock, in Seymour Narrows near Campbell River—was blown to bits April 5, 1958. In a delicate feat of engineering, underwater tunnels were dug to the base of the two-pronged rock and 1,375 tons of high explosive placed in dozens of drill holes. The impressive explosion, which was the biggest non-nuclear, peacetime detonation up to that time, permanently removed a hazard that had menaced West Coast shipping since the Narrows were charted in 1792. It also ended a twenty-seven-year political fight with the federal government to get the obstruction removed, prompting *The Sun* to editorialize: "Now let BC bitterness disperse with the smoke from the shattered rock."

THE DECADE IN HEADLINES
« 1958 »

MARPOLE-STEVESTON TRAM MAKES FINAL RUN OF ERA

Service ends on the remaining interurban tram line on the Lower Mainland. At one time, the network stretched from downtown Vancouver all the way to Chilliwack.

Vancouver Sun, February 28, 1958

SPAN DISASTER STILL MYSTERY

The new Second Narrows Bridge, still under construction, collapses and kills 18 workers. A few days later, a diver drowns while searching for bodies.

Vancouver Sun, June 17, 1958

MARGARET FORMALLY DECLARES SPAN OPEN

Both the city and the newspaper glow with pride over the visit by "a fairy princess." Margaret's dedication of the Okanagan Lake Bridge is part of her centennial tour of BC.

Kelowna Courier, July 19, 1958

B.C. LETS 100TH BIRTHDAY SLIP QUIETLY INTO HISTORY

Although several events mark BC's latest centennial year, there is no official recognition of August 2, 1858, the day Queen Victoria gives Royal assent to a bill establishing the Crown colony of British Columbia.

The Province, August 2, 1958

SOMMERS FACES COURT AGAIN AFTER WEEKEND IN CITY JAIL

Robert Sommers, BC's forestry minister, is convicted of conspiracy in the issuance of forest management licences. Four days later, he is convicted on specific bribery charges.

Vancouver Sun, November 1, 1958

Weather: Fog in low lying areas overnight. Sunny by noon Friday. Little change in temperature. Winds light. Low tonight 45; h[illegible] Friday 57.

FOG

The Sun

Index: Names in News, 15; Sport, 22; Finance, 28; Gardens, 38; Crossword, 39; Theatres, 51; Women, 57; Comics, 78; TV, 79; Bridge, 79.

FOUNDED 1886 VOL. LXXIV—No. 12 MUtual 4-7141 | 80 PAGES | VANCOUVER, BRITISH COLUMBIA, THURSDAY, OCT. 15, 1959 | FINAL ★★★C | PRICE 10 CENTS | BY CARRIER $2.00 Per Month

Starlet Fails to Save Errol Flynn

EXCLUSIVE PICTURE of actor Errol Flynn and protege Beverley Aadland, 17, was taken shortly before the film star's death by West Vancouver host George Caldough, of 1026 Eyremont Street. Flynn was stopping here to negotiate sale of his $100,000 luxury sailing yacht to Caldough.

Actor Dies in Vancouver Suite

By JACK WASSERMAN
Sun Staff Writer

Movie swashbuckler Errol Flynn died on the bedroom floor of a West End penthouse Wednesday while his young blonde protege desperately tried to breathe life through his pain-twisted lips.

The 50-year-old actor succumbed apparently to a heart attack, after undergoing treatment for a slipped disc in surgeon Dr. Grant Gould's apartment at 1310 Burnaby.

It was Flynn's third heart attack in recent years.

He had been taken to the apartment by his West Vancouver host, George Caldough, while en route to Vancouver airport to catch a plane to Los Angeles.

Flynn came to Vancouver last Thursday accompanied by 17-year-old starlet Beverley Aadland, to complete sale of his sailing yacht Zaca to stock promoter Caldough, of 1026 Eyremont, British Properties.

Complained of Malaria

The one-time Warner Brothers star had complained of recurring malaria attacks several times during his week-long stay and was visited by a doctor on Saturday. He remained in bed over the weekend.

He had planned to leave Vancouver at 4:30 p.m. Wednesday but complained of inability to move his legs or to sit down.

Caldough, Miss Aadland and Flynn arrived at the doctor's apartment at 3:45 p.m. and Flynn required assistance to mount the stairs to the suite.

DR. GRANT GOULD
...tried to save Flynn

He received a light injection of demerol and stood in the apartment living room for 45 minutes regaling the doctor's guests and his associates with stories about John Barrymore and W. C. Fields, both personal friends.

He then went into the bedroom and stretched out on the floor. This had been prescribed by the doctor for relief of the stiffness accompanying the disc condition.

'Something Terribly Wrong'

A few minutes later, Miss Aadland stepped into the bedroom and returned immediately to cry out in terror, "Something is terribly wrong with Errol—he's turned black."

She whisked a package of amyl nitrate capsules from her purse, broke one and attempted to force it into the actor's nostril.

Meanwhile, Dr. Gould injected adrenalin directly into the heart and Miss Aadland, following the doctor's instructions, attempted to perform mouth-to-mouth resuscitation.

Flynn had stopped breathing when she fell to her knees and pressed her lips to his in a vain attempt to re-start his breathing.

Please Turn to Page Two See: "Errol Flynn"

Financiers 'Ready' to Promote New First Narrows Bridge

WEST VANCOUVER — At least three financial houses are interested in financing a new First Narrows bridge.

"I've been approached by three financial houses," West Vancouver Reeve Stanley Collier disclosed today.

"All of them were interested in the promotion of a new bridge."

The reeve said one firm was British and two were American.

"They told me not to let this thing drop, that there was money available for such a project," the reeve said.

By "project," he was referring to a suggestion by Premier W. A. C. Bennett that if West Vancouver and the City of Vancouver would combine and build a new crossing at First Narrows, he would recommend to the Legislature that the government give the Lions Gate Bridge to the municipality and city.

The reeve observed that if the premier's suggestion included "taking the tolls off now," it would consitute a very attractive offer.

Municipal councillors, having heard second hand of Premier Bennett's suggestion through the newspapers, TV and radio, want the premier to make the offer official and in writing so they may consider it seriously.

A resolution to this effect was passed at Tuesday's council meeting.

9 RCAF Squadrons Due for Scrapheap

OTTAWA (CP)—The government is planning to scrap the RCAF's nine interceptor squadrons in Canada, it was learned authoritatively today.

The dismantling would come progressively in the next two to three years.

No formal government decision to scrap the CF-100 jet squadrons has yet been taken but informants said this action is in the government's mind and is the likely course.

It is felt here that the main menace to North America a few years from now will be long-range rockets.

A manned interceptor replacement for the subsonic CF-100 would be capable of destroying bombers only and not intercontinental missiles.

It is suggested in some quarters that the RCAF may switch its main endeavor in Canada from interceptors to counter-missiles.

The RCAF is fighting a desperate rearguard action to obtain a new interceptor to replace the CF-100, but informed sources said their chances of getting one are practically nil.

The RCAF's nine interceptor squadrons in Canada are now located in these centres: two at Bagotville, Que., two at St. Hubert, Que., two at Ottawa, two at North Bay, Ont., and one at Comox, B.C.

Field manager Charlie Metro has been granted release by Vancouver Mounties of the Pacific Coast Baseball League. (Story Page 22.)

FOUR MEN DIE IN BLAST NEAR U.S. ATOMIC LAB

LOS ALAMOS, N.M. (AP)—Something slipped in a truckload of waste explosive near Los Alamos scientific laboratory Wednesday.

Four men died in the explosion.

Spokesmen for the atomic laboratory said no radioactive materials were involved.

Not even parts of two of the bodies could be found.

Ticketed for speeding on Georgia Viaduct was New Westminster Mayor Beth Woods, on way to freeway meeting.

Mackay Voted Out As Calgary Mayor

CALGARY (UPI)—Mayor Don H. Mackay early today conceded defeat to city hall newcomer Harry Hays after a close civic election race.

DON MACKAY
...probe his downfall

The 44-year-old Mackay, outspoken chief magistrate of the city for the past 10 years, was voted out in the wake of a judicial report that Mackay "had derived improper advantages through his position."

Businessman - agriculturist Hays, 49, played the report of Judge L. S. Turcotte to the full in his campaign for office.

A civic probe that appeared to have caused Mackay's downfall followed complaints that he had borrowed city cement for construction at his summer home and failed to return it.

Former Alberta CCF leader Elmer E. Roper, 66, was elected mayor of Edmonton.

He succeeds William Hawrelak, who resigned six weeks ago after a judicial inquiry found him guilty of "gross misconduct" in connection with land transactions.

Hawrelak did not contest Wednesday's election.

Woman Says Suspects Not At Holdup

BURNABY—A Crown witness told a preliminary hearing here today two men charged with holding up a bank in Burnaby were in Surrey at the time.

Charged with holding up the Bank of Nova Scotia at 778 Edmonds Sept. 10 are Lewis Dalladonna, 29, of no fixed address; Patrick Michael Miller, 26, of 6476 Brantford, Burnaby, and Jack Dow, 28, of 14597 Sixty-ninth Ave., Newton.

Crown witness Mrs. Catherine Dow of 12118 Old Yale Road, the mother of one of the suspects, told the court that at 10:30 on the morning of the holdup she had seen Dalladonna and Miller in her car.

RED FEATHER HAS 41.3 PCT.

The Community Chest has collected $1,291,114 of its United Red Feather Appeal in Greater Vancouver, officials said today.

This is 41.3 per cent of its $3,131,542 objective. The campaign closes Oct. 31.

Murder Appeal Lost

LONDON (AP) — Appeal Court judges dismissed an appeal on behalf of Guenther Fritz Podola against his conviction for murder.

The 30-year-old photographer, who emigrated to Canada and lived for a time in Montreal, is under sentence of death for shooting a London policeman.

City, Winnipeg In Race for TV

WINNIPEG (CP)—The first of eight private television stations should be in operation next July 1 in either Winnipeg or Vancouver, Carlyle Allison, a permanent member of the board of broadcast governors, said today.

It will be a case of which city "moves the faster," said Allison.

Shah to Pay Visit

AMMAN, Jordan (UPI) — Shah Mohammed Reza Pahlevi will make an official visit to Jordan on Oct. 28 at the invitation of King Hussein, it was announced Wednesday.

BARRY MATHER ON THE ROAD

No Federal Cash For Provinces

By ALEX YOUNG
Sun Ottawa Bureau

OTTAWA — A full-scale federal-provincial fiscal conference will be held in mid-1960, Finance Minister Donald Fleming announced today.

Accidental hanging Wednesday night took life of Colin Fox, 12, of North Vancouver. (Story P. 33.)

There would be no point in holding an earlier meeting, he said, because the federal government is in no position to give the provinces any more money.

He made the promise of a meeting in a conference with provincial finance ministers, who are pressing for a larger piece of the federal government tax pie.

Fleming's announcement dashed hopes of some provincial officials — B.C.'s Premier Bennett included — for an earlier conference.

Bennett, at the luncheon adjournment, said he "knew their tight-money policies would bring about this situation where they can't help the provinces more."

The mid-1960 conference of provincial premiers and Prime Minister Diefenbaker, said Fleming, will be followed later in the year by another one.

This will enable the government to take to parliament in 1961 legislative proposals for a new federal-provincial agreement.

SOVIET ASTRONAUT. Alexei Grachev is one of Russia's three potential spacemen. Soviet magazine "Ogonek" claims "Grachev will climb into the upper layers of the atmosphere."—AP wirephoto via radio from London.

Flynn 'Old, Sick Before His Time'

Movie idol Errol Flynn was "tired, sick and old before his time" when he died Wednesday.

An autopsy this morning performed by Dr. T. R. Harmon disclosed the actor died of a heart attack.

The probe also found fatty degeneration of the liver and an infection of the lower intestine.

Officials of the coroner's office said the man's body was that of "a tired old man—old before his time, and sick."

More Pictures, Stories On Flynn on Pages 2, 3

Flynn's autopsy was third on the list of examinations done by Dr. Harmon this morning.

About 80 telephone calls were received from persons wanting to look at the actor's corpse.

But no one but officials was allowed in the room.

Meanwhile it appeared Flynn would be buried in Jamaica.

His girl friend, Beverley Aadland, said: "The body will not be taken anywhere but Jamaica except over my dead body." His secretary and representative of his wife, Pat Wymore, appeared to agree.

Plans to claim body of Errol Flynn are being made by his wife, Pat Wymore.

Missile Passes Test

WHITE SANDS MISSILE RANGE, N.M. (AP)—The U.S. Army Wednesday completed the first successful firing of the Nike-Zeus — being developed as a defence against intercontinental ballistic missiles.

Danes Cut Polio

COPENHAGEN, Denmark (Reuters) — Denmark, called the world's most vaccinated nation against polio, had only 15 cases this year, the lowest figure since the 2,600-case 1952 epidemic.

Jack Wasserman, The Sun*'s legendary saloon columnist, covers the death of movie idol Errol Flynn with a classic piece of reportage.*

In February of the following year, economic conditions forced the mothballing of one of BC's most familiar fleets, the midnight ferries between Vancouver and Victoria. For many years, the most comfortable way to travel between the two cities was to go to bed at midnight in one harbour and wake up at 7 a.m. the next day in the other. But Canadian Pacific, which didn't want to spend big bucks on a new, automobile-oriented fleet, pulled the plug. A few years later, the daytime steamships were gone, too. A *Sun* reporter rode the *Princess Elizabeth* on her last midnight run out of Vancouver and noted that the vessel carried only 120 passengers—mostly company executives and newsmen.

One newspaper not aboard to record the final run was the *Vancouver Herald*. The brash broadsheet (born in the Depression as *The News-Herald*) ceased publication June 15, 1957. Bought by Thomson Newspapers Ltd. only a few years earlier, the *Herald*'s demise conveniently left the morning field open to *The Province*, which switched from afternoon publication two days later. This was part of the formation of Pacific Press Ltd., when *The Sun* and *The Province* agreed to share production facilities and other assets.[1]

Otherwise, the decade ended on a celebratory note, sort of. The year 1958 was yet another "centennial" (we've had four of them—marking 1846, establishment of the Crown colony of Vancouver Island; 1858, establishment of the Crown colony of British Columbia; 1866 the two colonies are united; 1871, BC joins Confederation). Although there were lots of celebrations during 1958, this anniversary attracted only a token royal visit (Princess Margaret, sister to the Queen). On the actual date (August 2), *The Province* ran a brief box allowing that nothing really historic was going on that day.

Then in August, 1959, Premier Bennett declared that BC was debt-free. Despite guffaws from several quarters, he maintained that the direct public debt and the indirect "contingent liabilities" of various Crown corporations and agencies were not the same thing. Thus the direct legal debt of British Columbia was dissolved, so let's have a party! In a public-relations exercise of such schmaltz that it would raise eyebrows even in today's era of spin merchants, Da Preem threw a "bond-burning" on the waterfront of his home town, Kelowna. Something like $70 million in cancelled bonds—symbolizing the debt-free status — were piled on a barge in Lake Okanagan. After a day-long orgy of hoopla and politicking, Bennett shot a flaming arrow at the gasoline-soaked bonds.

He missed. Fortunately, a lurking RCMP officer had some ignition handy, and the fifties went out in a blaze of glory.

---

1 As a sportswriter at *The Herald* that spring, I distinctly remember a Thomson executive standing on a chair in our newsroom on West Georgia Street to deny rumours about the paper's imminent demise. He lied. We got two weeks' notice and a return railroad ticket to anywhere in Canada as severance pay.

THE DECADE IN HEADLINES
« 1959 »

FERRY NEARLY EMPTY EVEN AT FUNERAL

The last of the midnight ferries sets sail between Vancouver and Victoria. Only 120 passengers—mostly CPR executives and newsmen—are aboard the *Princess Elizabeth* when she leaves Vancouver's harbour at 12:06 a.m.

Vancouver Sun, February 28, 1959

ALL-OUT BATTLE LOOMS ON 'GET-TOUGH' LABOR BILL

Described as the "toughest labour laws in Canada," a new Trade Unions Act introduced by the Socred government sharply curtails picketing and further restricts other union activities. The legislation is roundly condemned by labour and hailed by the business community.

Vancouver Sun, March 3, 1959

MANTHA DIES ON THE GALLOWS

The last execution in BC is witnessed by *Province* columnist Jean Howarth, who reports that the spectacle of Leo Mantha being hanged sickens her. Capital punishment is abolished in Canada in 1976.

The Province, April 28, 1959

CROWDS JAM QUEEN'S PATCH

During a busy, 10-hour visit to the Lower Mainland, Queen Elizabeth officiates at the opening of the Deas Island (Massey) Tunnel under the Fraser River. The first vehicles were actually allowed through on May 23.

Vancouver Sun, July 15, 1959

ERROL FLYNN DIES IN CITY

A morning paper since mid-1957, *The Province* beats the afternoon *Sun* by several hours in reporting the swashbuckling movie idol's death in Vancouver.

The Province, October 14, 1959

THE SIXTIES:
ROUGH, TOUGH
AND LOUD

« 1960 – 1969 »

THE DECADE IN HEADLINES
« 1960 »

NEW BRIDGE OPEN AMID SUBDUED AIR

The death of 20 steelworkers during construction brings a note of retrospection to the official opening of the Second Narrows Bridge in Vancouver.

The Province, August 25, 1960

Pages ripped from a violent decade: An airliner is blown out of the sky over 100 Mile House. A baseball bat fractures a player's skull during a brawl at Vancouver's Capilano Stadium. Hysterical fans are trampled at a rock concert. The century's worst storm batters the southern coast. Terrorism paralyzes the Kootenays as the Sons of Freedom bomb, burn and disrobe in the name of God. The prime minister of Canada strikes back at an abusive demonstrator on a Vancouver street. An American president and his brother are both assassinated as BC watches in horror on that new medium, television.

For the first time since the twenties, British Columbians were not actively involved in a war somewhere. The ill-conceived US adventure in Vietnam, however, helped foster a peace movement in the province that grew as the sixties unfolded. Draft dodgers from south of the border, finding a haven in the hippie cultures of Vancouver and Victoria, kept the spirit of dissent alive: Anti-war, anti-nuclear testing, anti-establishment, anti, it seemed, everything that the grownups stood for.

Looking back, one might conclude that those uneasy times, which seemed to teeter on the very edge of anarchy, were thoroughly dominated by the voices of unreason. Not so. Although the irrational act, the loud bang and the mass protest all gained their share of Page One, this was also a decade of prosperity, stable government and balloting. Premier W.A.C. Bennett, who appeared to be turning into an election junkie during his second decade in the driver's seat, called four of them between 1960 and 1969. Despite the clouds of alienation growing on the horizon, there were few protests and no discernible violence during any of the campaigns. Bennett's majorities were all comfortable, peaking in 1969 at thirty-eight seats out of fifty-five.

In between elections, the premier kept the province moving. Although a recessionary dip that began near the end of the fifties slowed growth a trifle early in the decade, it was nothing serious. The blacktop connection, which would bind BC's communities together more efficiently than any railroad schemes of fifty years earlier, was well in hand. The maritime void left by the shrinkage of CP Steamship service and the financial difficulties of the Black Ball Line was eventually filled by a Crown entity called the BC Ferry Corp. Its birth (not to be officially registered in the legislature until June of 1976) came as the logical corollary to the govern-

★ **DEBUTANTES:** *They'll sparkle at annual Trafalgar Day Ball. Page 25*

★ **WORLD SERIES:** *Red Smith wonders: Will it ever end? Page 17*

★ **BYELECTION:** *Can outsider Douglas be beaten in socialist seat? Page 5*

WEEKEND 10¢ EDITION

Attend the church of your choice this Sunday

THE PROVINCE

FINAL

MU 3-9242

VANCOUVER, B.C., SATURDAY, OCTOBER 13, 1962

65th YEAR—No. 167

HURRICANE-FORCE STORM HITS CITY AFTER DEALING U.S. SAVAGE BLOW

Code of the sea

Russian ship, U.S. 'copter save 3 Cubans

N.Y. Herald Tribune

MIAMI—The code of the mariner prevailed over the lesser loyalties Friday when Russian seamen and United States Coast Guardsmen pitched in together and fished three Cuban refugees from the sea.

The refugees, three young men, had set out in their 15-foot sailboat for Florida ten days before, they said, from the northeast coast of Cuba.

Early Friday, before daylight, the boat began to ship water and founder. A little later the young Cubans saw the lights of a big ship approaching, and they shouted for help.

The ship was the 705-foot Russian tanker Druzhba. The Druzhba stopped and sent a radio message—in English—over the international distress frequency: "Man overboard. Man in water." The location, about 50 miles southeast of Miami, was also given.

The Coast Guard here picked up the message and dispatched an amphibian plane, a helicopter and a patrol boat from its Key West base to the scene.

The Russians meanwhile, had lowered a small motorboat and had set about looking for the source of the shouts. They found the sailboat and threw a line to it.

The young Cubans grabbed it with great relief and tied on. Then they realized they had been picked up by Russians. Out of the frying pan into the fire, but it was better than drowning.

At 7:19 a.m., just as they reached the side of the tanker, the Coast Guard helicopter hove into sight.

It made a low pass over them and the Cuban refugees jumped from their boat and swam away.

The Russians did not try to stop them. They sat in their boat and watched while Lt. Cmdr. W. C. Wallace brought his helicopter down to five feet above the swimming Cubans.

The Druzhba then went its way and the helicopter brought the Cubans to Miami and turned them over to the Immigration and Naturalization service.

The young men, one 18, the others in their 20s, were sunburned, hungry and thirsty, but they did not require hospitalization. They wolfed down coffee and doughnuts.

U.S. toll of deaths mounts

By The Canadian Press

A devastating storm slammed into the Pacific Northwest Friday night, spreading death and destruction over hundreds of miles.

Seven persons died in Oregon, six were known dead in California, one was dead in Washington State and four others were killed in an auto accident which may have resulted from the storm, and one died as a direct result of the storm in B.C.

A second B.C. death, that of 70-year-old retired fireman, Harry Young, was indirectly attributed to the blow. He died of a heart attack while repairing a damaged television aerial on the roof of his home.

FAIR CLOSED

Chartered accountant Francis Copithorne, 39, stepped on a live wire while investigating storm damage behind his Vancouver home. He was electrocuted.

Portland, Oregon's largest city, was virtually paralyzed.

In Seattle, World's Fair officials closed the exposition at 9:15 p.m. as winds up to 57 miles an hour whistled through the grounds.

Gusts up to 75 miles an hour hit Aberdeen, Longview, Tacoma and Bremerton in Washington.

Damage at Longview was reported as extensive. A reporter said hardly a tree was left standing in the city. Dozens of parked cars were damaged but few houses were hit.

TACOMA HARD HIT

Longview hospitals were operating on emergency power and called in extra nurses and doctors.

"The only light in town comes from the moon the Longview reporter said.

City Light officials at Tacoma described the storm

(Continued on next page)
(See U.S. SCENE)

Cars smashed in park

Terror among giant trees

By ORMOND TURNER

Stanley Park causeway became a scene of terror and death Friday midnight as the violent wind flung giant fir trees across the road.

Six cars were smashed by the toppling trees and firemen with chain saws tried to clear the road and extricate the injured. Two buses and 42 cars were blocked while their panic-stricken passengers huddled near their vehicles and gazed up in terror at the swaying trees.

Joseph Plag described how he watched with horror as a giant tree toppled with a roar and smashed a car in front of his. Police say one woman died and another was injured in the wrecked car.

Mr. Plag said: "In another 30 feet I would have got it too. Our cars were about to pass each other. I was going to the North Shore—the other car was heading toward Vancouver. I had to brake very sharply to avoid the falling tree."

As he spoke, trees exploded and groaned in the darkness around the stalled motorists. The causeway lights went out, flickered on again, and went out as firemen with flashlights hurried by.

During a particularly violent blow, while trees waved like matchsticks, a policeman ordered everyone to get into the buses and lay on the floor.

The motorists refused, but pressed firmly against the outside of the bus. "If I'm going to get hit, I want to see where it's coming from."

Ambulances raced into the causeway from the North Shore.

Insurance agent Geoffrey Hopkins said he leaped from his car just as the trees started to fall. His car was surrounded by wrecked cars and fallen branches.

Motorists attempting to leave the park had to run a gauntlet of swaying trees. The wind constantly shifted and people raced, then hesitated, and ran again.

2 deaths reported so far

The worst storm in many years hammered a path of death, destruction, fear and fire through Vancouver and the lower mainland early today.

One woman was killed and a number of persons injured as trees trapped passengers in 40 cars in Stanley Park.

A man was killed in a traffic crash at Clark Drive and Powell.

Traffic was stopped, houses caught fire, and winds up to 87 mph scattered debris throughout the area.

Police from afternoon and night were faced with hundreds of calls, plus reports of looting.

POLICE IN CONTROL

Mayor Alsbury talked with police officials, insisted that everything possible be done to protect lives and property. Police told him they had the situation under control. They said they called in extra police and would call more if necessary.

In Stanley Park there was a scene of near panic.

About 40 cars were trapped by falling trees, and in one of these a woman was believed killed.

People milled about in the dark, trying to get protection in automobiles from falling trees.

The hurricane force winds were accompanied by driving rain and strange flashes of white light. The weather forecaster said it was a form of lightning.

POWER FAILS

Power went out in vast sections of the city.

Telephones were dead.

All traffic was cut off through Stanley Park.

At one point there was a report that police had told everyone to get off the streets.

Emergency vehicles screamed through the streets.

Two barges broke loose from their moorings and drifted under Burrard Bridge and out to sea.

Radio stations went off the air.

The Fraser Bridge, swept up in a mass of tangled wires,

(Continued on next page)
(See STORM)

Bank cuts rate of interest

OTTAWA (CP)—A further reduction in the Bank of Canada's interest rate, to five per cent from 5½, was announced Friday by Louis Rasminsky, Bank of Canada governor.

A statement announcing the cut indicated the move was made in the light of further strengthening of Canada's foreign exchange reserves since early September — when the rate was last reduced — and "continued improvement in the bond market."

It was the second change in the rate since the central bank announced June 24 that it was pegging its rate, and set it at six per cent as part of the government's emergency program to meet the foreign exchange crisis existing at that time.

The rate—minimum charge by the central bank on its loans to chartered banks — was reduced to 5½ per cent on Sept. 7 following a large gain during August in foreign exchange reserves. Governor Rasminsky said then that conditions warranted "a moderate reduction" in the rate from "the very high level of six per cent."

The bank rate generally is seen as a leading indicator of interest rates generally across Canada, and it appeared that Friday's reduction might be a signal for easier financial conditions.

Friday's statement did not specifically spell out the central bank's reason for reducing its rate.

It's peace or death, Pope warns nations

Province News Service

VATICAN CITY — Pope John XXIII offered the nations of the world Friday an awesome choice between peace and destruction.

The 80-year-old Pontiff chose the Sistine Chapel to deliver his grave demand for world peace. He told envoys from 79 foreign governments and seven international organizations:

"All the heads of state who bear responsibility for the fate of nations must remember that they will one day have to account for their actions to God."

The Pope urged world leaders to "give ear to the anguished cry of 'peace, peace' which rises up to heaven from every part, from children and old people, individuals and communities.

64 in B.C. draw horses in sweep

At first count, 28 persons in Gerater Vancouver and 36 elsewhere in B.C. have drawn horses in the Irish Hospital Sweepstakes to be run at Newmarket, England, Wednesday.

Three of the ticket-holders could split $240,800 if the horses they've drawn come in first, second and third. Top prize is $150,500, second is $60,200 and third place wins $30,100.

Here are the lucky Greater Vancouverites:

Miss Dora Dowell, DRS 94701; horse Pagan Prayer.

A. Henderson, CEQ 80627; horse Shady Street.

Charles Vail, CCD 06198; horse Noughts and Crosses.

Peter Gloch, CDC 03087; horse Richmond.

M. R. S. Wrigglesworth, CKC 93602; horse Royal Sanction.

Foon Wong, CAL 11411; horse Tipstaff.

Those who used pseudonyms were:

Smile on Me, CEP 15077;

(Continued on next page)
(See 64 RESIDENTS)

Labor-business accord dies in pigeon-hole

OTTAWA (CP)—Labor and management agreed more than 18 months ago to work together with the federal government in tackling Canada's economic problems, reliable sources say.

The agreement was reached March 15, 1961, at an Ottawa conference of labor, management and government leaders then promptly suppressed on orders from a high level in the cabinet, the sources say.

Most of Canada's top business and union leaders attended the Ottawa meeting—at the personal invitation of Trade Minister Hees and Labor Minister Starr.

They were reported to have agreed to establish a permanent council, to be financed by all three groups, to foster continuing co-operation and consultation on economic problems among labor, management and government.

They also agreed to meet again—but never did.

They set up a high-powered steering committee to recommend a basis for organizing the permanent body — but it was never called into session.

Instead, the sources say, the government abandoned the whole project.

INDEX

On the Editorial Page:

A tree falls in Stanley Park.

Shy violet from Saskatchewan.

Chest passes quarter mark

The Community Chest Red Feather drive passed the "quarter pole" Friday as contributions totalled $758,159 — 25.3 per cent of the $2,995,000 objective.

One elderly gentleman who lives on East Georgia, several blocks east of Main, walked to the Chest headquarters at Eighth and Fir Friday to make his donation — a one-dollar bill — and then walked home again.

North Burnaby again moved into the lead in residential district canvassing Friday.

Nehru orders troops to drive out Chinese

New York Times

NEW DELHI—Prime Minister Nehru said the Indian army had been ordered to oust the Chinese Communist forces from Indian territory near the Tibetan border.

After 12 hours of severe fighting on the Tibetan border Indian and Chinese troops have ceased firing. But indications are that both sides are preparing to renew hostilities.

Officials listed Indian casualties at six killed, 11 wounded and seven missing. Chinese casualties were estimated at nearly 100 dead or wounded. Peiping has acknowledged 22 dead.

The Indians have access to the eastern sector of the border by land. The Chinese are reported airlifting all their equipment and men.

It is reported the Chinese are anxious to entrench themselves on Indian territory before the severe winter, when operations would be impossible.

New Delhi is worried about a report that the Chinese have built two airfields 50 miles north of the Tibetan frontier with India. The Chinese are reported to have stationed bombers, jet fighters, transport planes, and helicopters here.

Politicians in New Delhi fear the prospect of a large-scale war with Red China.

Correct answer still missing in puzzle quiz

A pair of scissors, newspaper clippings, the division in the window of a bus, the handle of a plate scraper and a magnifying glass were incorrect guesses in The Province-CKWX picture puzzle Friday.

The correct answer could win $389 for a Province subscriber. See puzzle on page 30.

★

DON'T TOUCH WIRES

Police warned citizens to treat every fallen wire as if it were a hot one.

A spokesman said: "Don't take chances even though most of the downed wires are harmless. Ordinary wiring into a house can be lethal under some circumstances."

Police advise any motorist who has a wire fall across his car to sit where he is. Tires will insulate him from any shock.

Hot wires at Fifth and Yukon

French customs calling Monte Carlo's bet

Province News Services

MONTE CARLO, Monaco—France threw a customs blockade around pint-sized Monaco at midnight Friday in an effort to force Prince Rainier's subjects to pay taxes to France.

The blockade was lifted after 30 minutes.

Cars were lined up for more than a quarter of a mile on either side of the Monegasque border as French customs officers swung into action on orders from President Charles de Gaulle's government.

The prince arrived here only moments before from Paris where last-ditch talks had been held between the two sides.

The scene at the border, normally so quiet it goes by unnoticed, was one of comic confusion early today. The French customs agents wearing long raincoats to protect themselves from the driving rain took up their stations at the stroke of midnight.

They brought with them red, white and black signs that read: "Stop Customs". These signs were soon put in place.

Despite the rain hundreds of curious people moved about slowing down the traffic as much as the customs agent themselves. Although the agents' questions were perfunctory, "Do you have anything to declare?" and cars were passed without search, Traffic on the main road between Nice and Monaco was soon hopelessly blocked.

Horns began blasting on the Monegasque side of the border to the rythm of the illegal and well known chant of France's Secret Army organization "Algerie Francaise." Some motorists were irked at the delay. But most were amused at the wild tangle of traffic on the road.

Almost everyone on the scene was concerned that the border check, now a perfunctory one, might evolve into a total closing of the border.

France has given Monaco a six-month warning that she would take action to seal the customs-free border unless agreement were reached. Thursday night this deadline was extended for 24 hours.

But the Monegasque delegation, although agreeing in principle to many of the French demands, refused to yield on certain points. The talks broke down at midday.

The central issue in dispute between the two countries is France's objections to the fact that French companies, or companies of any nationality, can set up headquarters in Monaco and not pay an income tax.

However, the fairyland of sun, sand and tax evasion was shattered when customs men went into action. A heavy rain fell as scores of cars lined up on either side of the border.

The French half of Monte Carlo, Beausoleil, is on the heights on the upper half of the town. Monte Carlo and, indeed, all of tiny Monaco, is dependent on France for water, gas, electricity, telephone service and all of its food.

The borderline between Monte Carlo and Beausoleil runs down the middle of a narrow street. One goal of Monaco's soccer field is in France, the other in Monaco.

Reacting quickly, the morning paper delivers the first details of the century's worst storm only hours after this remnant of Typhoon Frieda hits Vancouver.

ment's purchase of Black Ball in 1961 for $6.8 million. From a tiny beginning, the people's ferry fleet has grown into a major enterprise, regularly carrying millions of vehicles and passengers between Vancouver Island and the mainland.

Apart from randomly demolishing schools, dwellings and aircraft, explosives played another, more positive role in the sixties. This was in the construction of massive power projects. Bennett's "two-river policy" focused on the Peace and the Columbia. Hydroelectric dams of unprecedented scale and potential would not only provide the energy BC required for industrial expansion, but also deliver cheap electricity to most British Columbians.

First of all, the Socred leader indulged in a bit of muscle-flexing. On August 1, 1961, the government expropriated the BC Electric Co. It was such a startling move—one that could be expected from the socialist CCF on the opposition benches rather than the free-enterprise Socreds—that the *Vancouver Sun* published an Extra Edition to pass on the news. The premier's reasoning was that the good, old, comfortable, entrenched, monopolistic BCE was too set in its ways to climb aboard his visionary bandwagon. So the BC Hydro and Power Authority was created to shepherd Bennett's dam-building program into reality.

From the outset of negotiations, the premier had been unhappy with the impending Columbia River agreement between Canada and the United States. And although the two senior governments had signed a draft treaty January 17, 1961, he was not through haggling about the extent of BC's jurisdiction over the river. It took three years before a revised Columbia River Treaty was signed January 22, 1964. Under it, BC received—in round figures—$274 million in cash. For that money, the province was committed to build three storage dams to control the flow of the Columbia, and the Americans would keep for the next thirty years all the downstream power US plants could produce.

On September 16, Bennett, Prime Minister Lester Pearson and US President Lyndon Johnson participated in a brief, largely symbolic ceremony at the Peace Arch on the BC-Washington border. In the pouring rain, they each signed an "agreement of accord." The cash payment of $253,929,534.25 in US funds had already been made to Ottawa. In Canadian money, it worked out to $273,291,661.24, and a cheque for precisely that amount was handed to a BC government representative in Vancouver the same day as the Peace Arch photo op (some flood-control payments would be added later). Bennett had in fact already earmarked the money for investment. A week earlier, he had loaned Quebec $100 million at 5.05 percent. This was reportedly the first instance of one province borrowing money from another.

The Columbia River Treaty was so high-profile and involved such a major natural resource that it achieved international attention. Critics, operating on all eight cylinders of hindsight, claimed over the years that the price was too low. Which, as it turned out, it probably was. But in 1964, the $274 million figure was the end product of intense political negotiations, with neither side possessing any particular insight into the future. The sale of "downstream benefits" (Canada's birthright, to some detractors) also drew heat, because one country was selling a resource of vast potential to another. But, as one supporter pointed out, this valuable water "birthright" was coursing unfettered to the US anyway. As it happens, the river and its timeless flow of life-giving water shouldn't be listed among the beneficiaries of the treaty. In time, the number of dams on the Columbia and its tributaries would grow to five in BC and more than twenty in the United States, making the Colum-

THE DECADE IN HEADLINES
« 1961 »

TRAIL PROVES CANADIAN HOCKEY STILL THE BEST

With two headlines above and below 17 pictures of team members, *The Times* shouts out the news that the Smokies have won the world hockey title.

Trail Daily Times, March 12, 1961

B.C. TAKES OVER BCE, PEACE POWER

The announcement in the legislature that the Socred government will nationalize the giant BC Electric Co. utility prompts *The Sun* to publish a late-afternoon Extra Edition.

Vancouver Sun, August 1, 1961

BLACK BALL LINE TAKEN OVER BY GOVERNMENT

A cabinet order, retroactive to October 31, seals the deal for the struggling ferry company. In February, 1962, the legislature is told the cost of the takeover is $6,795,467.

Vancouver Sun, November 30, 1961

THE DECADE IN HEADLINES
« 1962 »

15 YEARS FOR PYLON BOMBERS

Nine Sons of Freedom Doukhobors get 15 years in prison for conspiracy to blow up a power pylon in the Kootenays. The loss of the tower on March 6 shuts down Cominco operations and puts 1,100 men out of work.

The Province, May 10, 1962

ROGERS PASS STAYS OPEN FOR TRAFFIC

The $40-million link between Revelstoke and Golden is declared open by BC despite ongoing construction. The 92-mile stretch completing the Trans-Canada Highway from coast to coast is "officially" opened by the federal government September 3.

Vancouver Sun, July 30, 1962

WILL CONSIDER 1963 AIR SHOW AFTER INITIAL SUCCESS

The weekly *News* reports that the crowd of 14,000 attending a "thrilling" air show at Abbotsford Airport spurs planning for a repeat event. The show has since become a hugely popular annual fixture.

Abbotsford, Sumas & Matsqui News, August 11, 1962

STORM DEATH TOLL 5

A vicious storm leaves a trail of chaos and wreckage across southwestern BC. Spawned by Typhoon Frieda, which had originated south of the Philippines a week earlier, the hurricane-force winds are described as the worst in BC history.

Vancouver Sun, October 12–13, 1962

OUR FINEST 10 MINUTES PRODUCES 2 GOLD MEDALS

Vancouver swimmer Mary Stewart wins a gold medal in the British Empire Games' 110-yard butterfly final. The same day, Prince George's Harold Mann nails a gold in the middleweight boxing class.

The Province, November 30, 1962

bia probably the most managed, diverted, constrained, electrified and fragmented stream in the world.

In contrast, our splendid Fraser, which was safely distant from the clutches of greedy American capitalists, ran relatively unhindered to tidewater. Despite a blockage of the Fraser Canyon in 1913, caused by railroad construction, it remains a prime salmon river. In the latter decades of the century, however, industrial and population encroachment on its lower reaches brought pollution to dangerously high levels. In the nineties, the Fraser was a dying river, coursing through its own coffin.

The other half of Bennett's two-river policy was the Peace. The development of this great northern stream went ahead with much less acrimony and attention. The Peace power project actually arose as a consequence of the ill-fated Wenner-Gren bubble in the fifties. Surveys then indicated the Peace River canyon was a prime source of power if a dam was built in the right place. While Bennett was still arm-wrestling the feds over the Columbia River deal, plans to shackle the Peace were well under way. On September 12, 1967, only weeks after he had dedicated the Duncan, first of the Columbia treaty dams, the premier did the same at the W.A.C. Bennett Dam on the Peace by briefly operating a machine carrying the last load of earthen fill. (Naming public projects after living politicians seems to be a thing in this province. In 1937, Premier T.D. Pattullo officiated at the opening of the Pattullo Bridge across the Fraser River at New Westminster. Later, in 1986, the Alex Fraser Bridge downstream from the Pattullo would be named after a well-known Socred cabinet minister.)

One of the necessary components of BC's headlong expansion was the working class. The Social Credit government—like others before and after it—claimed to be on the side of the ordinary stiff holding down a job. With the Socreds, though, the working man and the union man were not necessarily synonymous. Ever since the Pattullo Liberals passed the Industrial Conciliation and Arbitration Act in 1937, organized labour had made serious strides. For the first time, legislation gave workers the right to organize, bargain collectively and seek arbitration of disputes. There were later versions passed into law, but the basic thrust remained: The working class now had some clout. By 1966, the BC Federation of Labour claimed an affiliated membership of 125,000.

This growing strength of the labour movement prompted Bennett's cabinet into efforts to curb its influence. In the fifties, restrictive provisions were placed on strike actions, secondary boycotts and picketing. Then in 1961, labour's obvious affection for the CCF (and its successor that year, the New Democratic Party) led to Bill 42, which prohibited unions from contributing to the NDP through their dues.[1] It could be argued that these unabashedly political amendments to the Labour Relations Act, which were passed March 27, achieved a result exactly opposite that which was intended, cementing forever the embrace of the New Democrats by Big Labour. In the nineties, this marriage would become so strong that naked favouritism by the NDP government of the time added significantly to the cost of public works in the province (and, not incidentally, helped re-elect the party). The rationale by the Bennett apologists in 1961 was that many unionists resented having part of their dues go to the support of socialists.

One of the unions arrayed against Social Credit was the IWA, the biggest in the province. The International Woodworkers of America, whose membership would approach 50,000 later in the century, was almost as ubiquitous in the sixties as the trees the union loggers cut down. As an entity in BC (and a branch of a larger, international union), the IWA had been around since 1937. After it purged itself of Communist leanings in the forties, the woodworkers on the coast and in the interior gritted their way through a number of strikes and near-strikes as they sought decent hours, better pay and safer working conditions.

With progressive union-management settlements, the coast locals edged ahead of the Interior in pay and benefits. This led to the big strike of southern interior workers in 1967. They wanted wage parity as well as a common expiry date for their contracts. Management demurred. The strike lasted 219 days, from October 4, 1967, to May 11, 1968, before the union accepted the company negotiators' offer of an expiry date close to that on the coast, and an hourly wage rate within 14 cents of parity. It was the longest walkout in forest history.

Midway through the decade, technological change began insinuating its way into the delicate labour-management relationship. This complex issue, called "automation" in the sixties, would lead to many bitter battles over job security, severance requirements and retraining. Unions would be pitted against other unions in desperate skirmishes to hold on to job jurisdiction. By the end of the century, use of computers would revolutionize the workplace. In 1965, however, it was one union, the Oil, Chemical and Atomic Workers, against the major oil companies. They went on strike over an unresolved automation agreement and the BC Fed stepped in. It called for a forty-eight-hour general strike that November in support, forcing Bennett and his cabinet to come up with a solution. The government smoothed matters over by "suggesting" a formula that gave employees more protection while establishing a joint labour-management committee to study the issue. Tech change, however, was in BC to stay.

Another innovation, which affected everyone in the province and not just the workers, was universal medical care. This important component of Canada's "social safety net" (as it would be called in the nineties) arrived in British Columbia in 1968. It was the most important link in a string of medicare initiatives going back to the thirties.

In 1936, a Pattullo government attempt to establish a form of health insurance foundered on the rock of overwhelming opposition from BC's doctors. There the matter rested until the private Medical Services Association was formed in 1940. This was a group plan for employees that involved fees paid through their employers. In 1954, BC Medical Services Incorporated was born to offer coverage to those not eligible for MSA. Although the indigent were already taken care of through a social-assistance fund, a bill passed March 19, 1965, provided government assistance to low-income persons paying monthly premiums. The BC Medical Plan was separate from hospital insurance, which the Bennett cabinet had rescued following its disastrous implementation in 1949.

Immigration among the provinces and their various health plans necessitated a trans-Canada scheme to make coverage portable to some extent. However, the hodge-podge of private, semi-private, voluntary and public plans across the country was becoming so unwieldy that a comprehensive national package was needed.

Under federal legislation passed in December of 1966, Ottawa committed itself to pay approximately half the costs of provincially organized and operated medicare plans. A bill was introduced in the legislature March 13, 1967, establishing an "umbrella" authority that would bring nonprofit voluntary plans into the national system. On July 1, 1968, the effective date of the federal plan, British Columbia

THE DECADE IN HEADLINES
« 1963 »

A UNIVERSITY IS BORN AMID QUIET REJOICING

After half a century of precarious existence, Victoria College becomes a full-fledged university on a new campus at Gordon Head.

Victoria Times, July 2, 1963

KENNEDY SHOT DEAD

Basing its huge headline on a three-paragraph bulletin, *The Sun* hits the street with its second Extra Edition of the day. (The first said, "Kennedy Shot Down".) These are the last Extras ever published by the then-afternoon paper.

Vancouver Sun, November 22, 1963

OH NUTS!

Eight days after it stopped the presses to report Kennedy's assassination, *The Sun* is caught up in Grey Cup fever. A special edition of its 5-Star Final is available downtown minutes after the BC Lions lose at Empire Stadium in their first Canadian professional football final.

Vancouver Sun, November 30, 1963

THE DECADE IN HEADLINES
« 1964 »

TIDAL WAVE HITS ALBERNIS — MILL DOWN, DAMAGE RUNS INTO MILLIONS

A series of ocean waves generated by the earthquake that devastates Anchorage, Alaska, causes havoc in Port Alberni and the Alberni Valley.

Nanaimo Free Press, March 28, 1964

LANGLEY: 16 MINUTES

Opening of the Port Mann Bridge and freeway establishes a four-lane link from Vancouver's city limits to deep in the upper Fraser Valley. *The Columbian* timed a trip from Langley to a Burnaby interchange. Some stretches of the new highway are posted for a 70-mph speed limit.

The Columbian, June 12, 1964

AQUARIUM LANDS KILLER WHALE

The newspaper describes in dispassionate detail how a killer whale is harpooned and dragged across Georgia Strait so that Vancouver Aquarium curator Murray Newman can study it. The world's first captive killer whale dies after 86 days. Its capture is the start of the controversial program to pen up marine mammals.

The Province, July 16, 1964

CINDERELLA KIDS GRAB GOLD AND JEROME BAGS A BRONZE

University of BC coxless pair George Hungerford and Roger Jackson win a gold medal in rowing at the Tokyo Olympics. It is Canada's first Olympic gold since 1956. In the 100-metre track final, Richmond's Harry Jerome finishes third.

The Province, October 15, 1964

NEVER A DOUBT!

The BC Lions defeat the Hamilton Tiger-Cats, 34-24, in Toronto to win their first Grey Cup football championship.

Vancouver Sun, November 28, 1964

and Saskatchewan were the first two provinces to climb aboard.

Meanwhile, a few blemishes had surfaced on Premier Bennett's facade of jovial imperturbability. One was the "Dear Hal" letter, apparently signed by the premier himself. The recipient was Hal Dornan, a former Vancouver newspaper reporter who had moved on to become an assistant to Prime Minister Pearson. The letter wanted Dornan to help obtain landed-immigrant status for Harry Stonehill, a shady American wheeler-dealer who had been involved in some suspect shenanigans in the Philippines.

It turned out that the missive was composed by Al Williamson, a high-profile public-relations hotshot who was closely connected to Bennett and the Socreds. Williamson's unauthorized use of the premier's name and office (the reasons for which never being adequately explained) brought criminal charges of fraud and uttering. He was sentenced June 10, 1965, to six months in prison. Bennett denied any involvement, and the signature on the letter was judged to be a crude forgery.

Along with Bennett and the PM, several other prominent names popped up during Williamson's trial. One was Einar Gunderson, a failed Socred politician who had given up trying to get re-elected. An old pal of the premier, he was allowed to hang around, and was given several cushy directorships on public and government bodies. Gunderson was also the party's bagman, a role that he admitted to *The Sun* while Williamson was being tried. As controller of the "BC Free Enterprise Education Fund," Gunderson was responsible for topping off the Socreds' campaign coffers. This secret, double life in politics and public affairs incurred the wrath of opposition politicians. "Gunderson and the backroom boys must go," Opposition leader Robert Strachan thundered to *The Sun*. In the patronage-rich atmosphere of the nineties, a party bagman taking deep draughts off the public teat would scarcely raise an eyebrow, but in the sixties, the revelation was deemed to be shocking.

A more serious matter for Bennett was the fall of BC's hyper highways minister, Phil Gaglardi. The combative Gaglardi was in a loud scrap with the Opposition over alleged patronage and misuse of highways department resources when it was revealed that his daughter-in-law had flown to Dallas on a government Lear jet. Gaglardi resigned March 21, 1968, not because of the unauthorized use of the jet, but because he had fudged when Bennett had asked him point-blank about who was aboard. As with the Robert Sommers scandal, another colleague had proved to be lacking in honesty when dealing with his premier. Bennett did let Gaglardi back into the cabinet (as welfare minister, of all things), but his high-rolling days were over.

Two court proceedings early in the decade underscored the commitment of the Crown toward containing the Doukhobor problem. In Nelson, a guilty verdict resulted in lengthy prison terms; in New Westminster, a blanket dismissal frustrated attempts to jail Sons of Freedom leaders for conspiracy.

The Doukhobor violence that marked the waning years of the fifties intensified as the sixties got underway. In 1961, the number of incidents of bombing and arson passed the one-hundred mark. That number more than doubled in 1962, with the destruction March 6 of a transmission tower near Riondel on Kootenay Lake, the worst of the bombings. The loss of power to this mining area threw 1,100 people out of work for weeks. Because of the commitment by the Freedomites to full-scale terrorism, the RCMP established a Special D Section ("D" for Depredations, not Doukhobors) in 1961, whose mandate was to combat the violence.

Soon the D Squad started making arrests, and in Nelson on March 21, 1962, Mr. Justice J.G. Ruttan sentenced twenty terrorists to prison terms ranging from three to ten years. Justice Ruttan called the guilty men "resolutely and depressingly insane."

While the Nelson trial unfolded, planning was in its final stages for a new prison at the head of the Fraser Valley. Realizing that arson-prone Doukhobors would be the primary occupants, the authorities made sure Agassiz Mountain Prison was as fireproof as possible. The first of a hundred-plus convicted zealots moved into Agassiz in July. Even more were expected later that summer, but a judicial decision in New Westminster went in favour of the accused this time instead of the Crown.

One of the D Squad's targets was the Fraternal Council, the shadowy leadership that directed the Freedomites' depredations. After painstaking detective work, enough evidence was collected to indicate a conspiracy had existed for several years to commit acts of violence. The Crown decided to lay four separate conspiracy charges against seventy leaders and their supporters. After a number of weeks hearing evidence and rebuttals, Magistrate William Evans ruled August 7 at a preliminary hearing that the Crown had not established conspiracy.

The Doukhobors' attention then focused on their brethren in Agassiz Prison. In September, several began "marching" (mostly they rode in vehicles) from their Kootenay enclaves toward Agassiz. Eventually, they numbered more than 1,000, and camped near the prison from September 30 until January of 1963. Then many of them moved to Victory Square in downtown Vancouver, where they hung out for several more weeks. The square was overlooked by the editorial offices of *The Province* and was only a short block away from the Sun Tower, but both newspapers resolutely ignored the squatters. They knew the Doukhobors had publicity on their minds more than any sort of "justice" for their convicted brothers and sisters. Eventually, they drifted back to their makeshift communities in the Kootenays.

Just as the Doukhobor trekkers of 1962 were settling down in their encampments near Agassiz and Hope, they got a dousing from Frieda. In early October, a dangerous low-pressure system christened Typhoon Frieda when she formed in the Western Pacific had been downgraded to a bad storm by the time she slammed ashore in northern California. This angry remnant then headed north, raking the coast with long fingernails of destruction.

She barrelled into Victoria with hurricane-force winds shortly before midnight, October 12, registering gusts of 90 mph (145 km/h in metric-speak). The winds plucked a forty-two-ton Martin Mars water bomber from its lashings at Patricia Bay airport and deposited it 300 yards away. Power was knocked out to the Gulf Islands and several areas of southern Vancouver Island. Dozens of trees were toppled and windows blown away. Early the next day, the storm hit Vancouver, the Lower Mainland and the Fraser Valley. In Vancouver, wind gusts were clocked at 87 mph. Stanley Park became a disaster zone. As *The Province* described it, there was "terror among the giant trees" when the wind toppled them on to stranded cars. Other motorists and pedestrians reckless enough to be outside had to avoid live power wires on some streets. Other sections of the city were without electricity. Bridges were virtually impassable. Barges and other shipping were ripped from their moorings.

Heading up the Valley, the storm lost intensity, and rain was the main ingredient as it shook itself out over the coastal mountains. Seven deaths were attributed to the storm, and damage estimates exceeded $10 million. A *Sun* editorial praising

THE DECADE IN HEADLINES
« 1965 »

NO TRACE OF TWO SLIDE VICTIMS

The weekly *Standard* reports four days after the slide severing the Hope-Princeton Highway that searchers have virtually given up hope of finding two missing persons.

Hope Standard, January 9, 1965

B.C. ENJOYS BANNER DAY WITH CHAMPAGNE, MUSIC

The new Maple Leaf flag becomes official, and BC responds positively. "Long may it wave," editorializes *The Sun.*

Vancouver Sun, February 15, 1965

FIRST BODIES DUG FROM SLIDE

An avalanche buries the mining camp at Granduc, near the BC-Alaska border 800 miles northwest of Vancouver. Although one survivor is found after 72 hours, the slide claims 26 lives.

Vancouver Sun, February 18, 1965

B.C. MAY INSURE HEALTH OF SOME

During debate on the medical grants bill, Premier Bennett hints that his government may enter the health insurance field if private coverage is inadequate. The bill passes third reading.

The Colonist, March 19, 1965

BURNABY'S CROWN JEWEL, SIMON FRASER U OPENS

The province's new university is described by the local paper as the municipality's premier showplace and "a space-aged system of higher education."

Burnaby Examiner, September 9, 1965

THE DECADE IN HEADLINES
« 1966 »

DREAD LINGERS ON AT OCEAN FALLS

The morning paper puts a classic "follow" headline on its story two days after a landslide kills seven in the coastal community.

The Province, January 3, 1966

PORT EXPANSION DEAL OKAYED

The National Harbours Board and the CPR end their long dispute over control of Vancouver's waterfront. The pact, splitting the foreshore into east-west segments, ushers in a 30-year period of expansion along Burrard Inlet.

Vancouver Sun, June 10, 1966

TRUMPETS HERALD SWIMMERS BRINGING HOME HARDWARE

West Vancouver's Elaine Tanner returns after winning four gold medals at the British Empire Games in Jamaica. Her harvest of pool victories is unprecedented in Games competition.

Vancouver Sun, August 16, 1966

BANK OF B.C. NOW OFFICIAL

Two years after it was introduced, the federal bill establishing the Bank of British Columbia becomes law. The BC government originally proposed to own 25 percent of the bank's shares, but an amendment removes this condition.

Victoria Times, December 14, 1966

the aid and comfort provided by selfless neighbours called this spawn of Frieda an "ill wind." As the storm of the century, indeed it was.

In the middle of the afternoon on July 8, 1965, the sky exploded just west of 100 Mile House. But this disaster was man-made: Canadian Pacific Airlines Flight 21 blew up while en route from Vancouver to Prince George. It fell 5,000 metres (about 16,000 feet) straight down to the ground in two pieces and all 52 persons aboard were killed. The smoke-blackened trees surrounding the main fuselage were "like a ceremonial guard of honour over the dead, wearing their black as a sign of mourning," wrote a *Sun* reporter at the scene.

There is no doubt a blast of some sort ended Flight 21. A witness reported seeing a puff of white smoke before the tail separated from the aircraft. There was a noise like the crack of dynamite. Even before RCMP investigators found physical clues indicating an explosion in a rear lavatory, the newspapers were leaning heavily on that angle. A piece of what was believed to be a detonator, along with traces of acid and chemicals consistent with the composition of gunpowder, indicated a bomb of some sort was aboard the DC-6B.

Among those passengers whose pasts were given close scrutiny by the Mounties was a gambler who unaccountably bought $125,000 worth of flight insurance minutes before takeoff. Another was an explosives expert once charged with murder. A third scenario tried to make a murder victim out of a senior auditor involved in an Ontario financial scandal, but police discounted it. In the end, a coroner's jury returned a verdict of "unnatural and accidental deaths." Coroner Glen McDonald, who was as opinionated and outspoken as the usual public servant is bland and cautious, disagreed. He didn't think the deaths were "accidental." But no charges were ever laid, and the final chapter of the Flight 21 tragedy still remains to be written.

The decade was not without more positive sports moments. In the water, another one of those diminutive female dynamos from BC, Mary Stewart, won a gold medal in the 110-yard butterfly at the British Empire Games in Perth, Australia. She also set world records at 110 yards and 100 metres. "Vancouver's Swimming Sweetheart," Stewart also pranced about Empire Stadium for several years as the BC Lions' mascot. At the 1966 BEG in Jamaica, West Vancouver's Elaine Tanner ("Mighty Mouse") won an unprecedented four gold and three silver medals in swimming.

"Not much bigger than a deep breath" (in the words of *Sun* sportswriter Denny Boyd), Tanner was named Canada's athlete of the year, then went to the Pan-American Games in Winnipeg in 1967, where she added more golds and silvers to her hardware collection. A year later, on August 1, 1968, Ocean Falls' Ralph Hutton swam to a world record in the 400-metre freestyle, after taking a silver medal at the 1964 Tokyo Olympics. On the water, the coxless pair from the University of British Columbia, George Hungerford and Roger Jackson, rowed to a gold medal at those same Olympics. On the snow, skier Nancy Greene, from Rossland, nailed a gold and a silver at the Grenoble Winter Olympics later in 1968. The medals, which followed Nancy's World Cup title in 1967, solidified her ranking as one of the best woman skiers on the planet.

Demonstrations, sit-ins, hysterics, scuffles and rude confrontations are neither amateur nor professional sport forms. Nevertheless, they were all part of the sixties' spectator package, too, as free love, flower power, long, lank hair (on both sexes), lost causes, rock music, drugs and dropouts were much in evidence. The

GREY CUP SPECIAL

The Sunday Sun

FOUNDED 1886 VOL. LXXVIII—No. 31 MUtual 4-7141 1?? PAGES VANCOUVER, BRITISH COLUMBIA, SATURDAY, NOV. 30, 1963 PRICE 14 CENTS

OH NUTS!

WRENCHED FROM our grasp at Empire Stadium this afternoon, this ancient piece of hardware will go back to Hamilton with the Tiger-Cats, who defeated our Lions—but wait till next year!

GREY CUP SPECIAL HAS FULL COVERAGE

Full coverage of the Grey Cup festivities is carried in today's Grey Cup Special.

Football fans will find other pictures and stories of today's action and pre-game hijinks on Pages 2, 3, 7, 22 and 29.

100,000 Throng Parade Route

Ships' Sirens Join Send-Off For Grey Cup Color Spectacular

A crowd of more than 100,000 lined sunny Vancouver streets today to watch the big, colorful Grey Cup parade swing through downtown.

It was a gay procession of floats, bands, clowns, horsemen and marchers that brought cheers from the watchers.

From the roar of a starting gun at 9 a.m. and the screams of ships' sirens in Vancouver harbor, it was noise, color and spectacle all the way.

The parade entries ranged from large, intricate floats to a last-minute entry of four Northwest Territory fans who carried a banner and marched to the music of a saxaphone.

There were dozens of pretty girls who waved and blew kisses to the crowd.

GOOD HUMOR

Good humor abounded in the parade that was the brassy kick-off to Canada's biggest football day of the year.

Toronto's entry made fun of the misfortunes of its football club this season.

Victoria poked fun at itself and the little-bit-of-old-England routine with a float bearing

Parade Pictures on Page 22

tea-drinking big game hunters making a safari from their Vancouver Island home—"The heart of the Empire."

And it was a parade that demonstrated the solidarity of the West, in a football final that is.

The Calgary School Patrol band tootled the B.C. Lions song and other club entries wished Lions the best of luck.

There were no major hitches following the kick-off from Georgia and Thurlow.

One thousand balloons were released and floated skywards as the parade went on cross-Canada television networks.

It tooks the more-than-125 entries about an hour and a half to pass any given point.

Crowds were thick at the saluting base in front of the court house. Lieutenant-Governor George Pearkes took the salute, flanked by Mayor Bill Rathie and Premier W. A. C. Bennett.

Streamers floated from hotel windows and there was a ticker-tape shower from the Devonshire and Georgia hotels.

Police said there were more than 100,000 on the streets and the windows of all buildings were packed. Youngsters climbed up poles and vantage points to get a good look.

WILLIE FLEMING
. . . taken to hospital

ANGELO MOSCA
. . . heavy tackle

Fleming Taken to Hospital

B.C. Lions' all-star halfback Willie Fleming went to hospital after today's Grey Cup game for treatment to head and neck injuries.

Late in the first quarter Fleming was run out of bounds and crushed in a jarring tackle by Hamilton's 260-pound line man Angelo Mosco. Sun football writer Denny Boyd reportetd the tackle was made beyond the sidelines.

Fleming was badly shaken up and staggered as he was helped off the field.

He spent the rest of the first half on the bench, holding an ice pack to the back of his head.

He took off his uniform at halftime.

Index

Nesbitt, 8; Franck, 14; Theatres, 14; Churches, 16; TV, 18; Sport, 21; Finance, 2?; Names in the News, 28; Women's, 30; Comics, 35; Bridge, 35; Gardens, 38; Crosswords, 40.

PLANE CRASH ON PAGE 12

Details of the Trans-Canada Air Lines DC-8 crash near Montreal Friday night, in which 118 died, will be found on Page 12.

Press Thanked

WASHINGTON (AP) — The family and aides of the late President Kennedy have conveyed their appreciation for the dignified manner in which they covered the death of the president.

Ticats Win Grey Cup

Hamilton Tiger-Cats won their third Grey Cup championship today by defeating the British Columbia Lions in the Canadian professional football final at Empire Stadium.

The score was Hamilton 21, B.C. Lions 10.

A crowd of 36,465 saw the game at the Stadium while millions more watched on television. Lions represented the Western Conference for the first time in their 10-year history, while Hamilton, the Eastern champion, was making its seventh appearance in the past 11 years during which it won the cup twice—in 1953 and 1957.

Hamilton Grabs Lead

The hard-hitting Tiger-Cats, playing it rough and tough from the opening whistle, completely dominated the first half and went to the dressing room with a 14-3 lead.

Hamilton threatened early in the first quarter when defensive ace Gene Ceppetelli pounced on Neil Beaumont's blocked punt on the B.C. 12-yard line. Quarterback Bernie Faloney went for seven yards on a keeper play over the left side of the Lions' line and fullback Art Baker tried over right guard but was stopped a yard short of a first down. Hamilton came out running on a third-and-one situation but Baker stopped for no gain by Lions' Tom Brown and Dick Fouts. The Lions took over on their own three.

Early in the second quarter, Faloney, passing with uncanny accuracy, brought the Ticats all the way from their own 22 to their major in just 10 plays. Faloney completed three passes in the series, including a final four-yard toss to halfback Willie Bethea, who was all alone in the right corner, for the major. Don Sutherin's convert made it 7-0, Hamilton.

After the kickoff, Lions quarterback Joe Kapp got the Lions rolling and they went from their own 19 before the attack bogged down on the Hamilton 22. Peter Kempf came into the game and booted a 29-yard field goal to cut Hamilton's lead to 7-3.

The five-minute warning whistle had just gone when Faloney picked holes in the B.C. defence and Hamilton scored its second major.

Starting from the mid-field stripe, Faloney found halfback Garney Henley open on the left side and the fleet Ticat went 40 yards to the B.C. 15. Faloney, dropping straight back, hit end Hal Patterson and Hamilton had a first down on the Lions' one. Fullback Baker crashed over the right side and Sutherin's convert made it 14-3.

Fleming Knocked Out

B.C. suffered a tremendous loss in the first half when halfback Willie Fleming, who was named to every all-star team in the country, was knocked out of the game by burly Angelo Mosca, the Hamilton tackle who was named top lineman in the Eastern Conference.

Fleming, on a pitch left, had been tackled on the 55-yard line when Mosca drove into him as he went down. Fleming was helped off the field and was not in the st[?]ing backfield when the second half started.

The Ticats stormed right back after receiving the second-half kickoff and went 70 yards for another major. The payoff pass was Faloney to Hal Patterson, who got in behind B.C. safety Steve Shafer. Sutherin's convert made it 21-3.

Kapp got the Lions rolling and they looked as if they were going to go all the way when the attack bogged down on the Hamilton 23. Gambling on third down, Kapp passed into the end zone but defensive half Ralph Goldston knocked down a pass intended fo rend Jerry Janes and the Ticats took over on their own 23.

B.C. got another offensive going late in the third quarter but Don Sutherin intercepted a Kapp pass intended for Janes and the Ticats took over on their own 45. The quarter ended with punter Joe Zuger kicking to Shafer on the B.C. one.

After the Lions were forced to punt in the fourth quarter, the Ticats started another march from their own 40. Sticking to the ground, the Ticats moved to the B.C. 40 and then Faloney connected on a pass to end Davie Viti that gave Hamilton a first down on the B.C. 27.

After a two-yard loss and an incomplete pass, Sutherin tried a field goal from the B.C. 37. But it was blocked and the Lions took over on their own 35.

Lions Try Shotgun

Kapp, dropping back into the shotgun formation for the first time, passed 17 yards to Jerry Janes and the Lions had a first down on the B.C. 52.

Sticking to the shotgun, fullback Nub Beamer took a direct snap and went for a first down. Then Kapp passed complete to end Pat Claridge for another first down on the Hamilton 32.

Beamer then picked up five yards and Kapp rolled left and ran eight yards for the first down to the Ticat 17. After a three-yard gain by Shafer, Kapp tried for a major score on a pass to Claridge in the end zone. But the Lions were called for offensive interference and the Ticats were awarded the ball.

With time running out on the clock, Faloney swept right end for a first down to the Hamilton 35. The five-minute warning whistle sounded and Faloney, the only man to quarterback both an Eastern and Western team to the Grey Cup championship, stayed on the ground to use up precious time.

With 3:24 left, the Lions started their final offensive and Kapp, by sheer desperation, took them to a touchdown in six plays.

End Greg Findlay, in on offence for the first time, caught two passes that brought the ball to the Ticat five and then Kapp tossed deep into the end zone to Mack Burton who made a diving catch for the touchdown. Peter Kempf's convert was good and final score was 21-10, Hamilton.

Iraqi Defects Using Airplane

MOSCOW (AP) — A 34-year-old Iraqui army lieutenant has defected to the Soviet Union in an Iraqui plane, Tass has reported.

The Soviet news agency identified the defector as Zuher Abdel Wahid El-Selim and said he crossed the state frontier of the U.S.S.R. in a plane and touched down at Nakhichevan airport.

CROWD IN HIGH SPIRITS

Even the Sun Was Beaming

By TOM ARDIES

Bright sunshine beamed down today as the B.C. Lions marched into Empire Stadium in their first bid after 10 long years of despair for the Grey Cup.

It was perfect football weather—blue skies, a nip in the air, and hardly a trace of wind.

Every seat in the stadium was filled as the Lions and the Hamilton Tiger-Cats opened their classic battle for the battered old cup emblematic of football supremacy in Canada.

More than 1,000 fans were already waiting in line when the gates swung open at 11:30 a.m.—an hour and a half before the 1 p.m. kickoff.

The high-spirited, gaily bedecked rooters trooped in like a mad legion.

They were laughing, shouting, singing songs, ringing bells, and blowing horns.

They wore every possible kind of get-up, from parkas to mink and had them set off by every possible kind of topper, from cowboy hats to straw boaters.

Among the early arrivals were Lieut.-Gov. George Pearkes, Premier W. A. C. Bennett, and Mayor Bill Rathie, who drove up in a cavalcade of long black cars under motorcycle escort.

Highlight of pre-game ceremonies was the presentation of a sports car to Miss Grey Cup—Dalene Henderson, 19, who was Miss Edmonton Eskimo.

Following the introductions, two youths paraded in front of the crowd with a huge banner reading: "Leos will tear those meeces to pieces."

Sydney Halter, commissioner of the Canadian Football League and Harry McBrien, co-ordinator of Grey Cup planning, inspected the field two hours before game time and pronounced it in top condition.

Just before the game there was one minute of silence to mark the assassination of U.S. President John Kennedy and the deaths of 118 people Friday night in a Trans-Canada Air-lines crash near Montreal.

RACING NEWS ON PAGE 9

RACING

GOLDEN GATE RESULTS

FIRST RACE—Six furlongs:
Armed Escort (Volzke) $18.20 $11.00, $6.40.
Hasty Abbey (Hunt) $18.70, $9.00.
Happy Camp (Heath) $5.40.
Time 1:11 3/5.
Sir Agent, Trunion, Solid Nap, Gracious Moon, Capt. Coco, Read It, Little Maverick, Prince Pepi, Sle La Vie, also ran.

SECOND RACE—Six furlongs:
Swirling Abbey (F. Alvarez) $3.80, $3.40, $3.20.
Orbital (P. Porter) $4.40, $3.80.
Know The Facts (D. Hall) $4.40.
Time—1.11-5.
Spacer, Prince Curragh, King Ara, Miss Zeus, Gliding Wings, Popocatepetl, Way Dark, Steel Ayress, Pay Load also ran.
Daily Double—Armed Escort to Swirling Abbey paid $47.60.

Eight days after stopping the presses to report an assassination, The Sun *succumbs to Grey Cup fever.*

THE DECADE IN HEADLINES
« 1967 »

WHO USED ALL THE HOT WATER?

The first Nanaimo to Vancouver bathtub race almost degenerates into chilly chaos. The finish line—Fishermen's Cove in West Vancouver—is later switched to English Bay.

Vancouver Sun, July 30, 1967

DAM NAMED AFTER PREMIER BENNETT

Completion of the huge Peace River power project is marked by ceremony and assurances that the earth-filled dam "will never leak."

Peace River Block News, September 12, 1967

TWO CIVIC HEADS PEEK INTO FUTURE

On the day that Kamloops and North Kamloops amalgamate to form a city of 22,000, *The Sentinel* looks at what lies ahead.

Kamloops Sentinel, November 4, 1967

protest generation was mostly a teenage phenomenon, but one night in 1964, the pre-teens helped make the headlines.

The British group that revolutionized popular music—the Beatles—came to Vancouver August 22 to help open the annual PNE fair. On the trampled grass of Empire Stadium, the Fab Four provoked a riotous melee of frightening proportions. On hand was *Province* columnist Ormond Turner, who said the screaming mass of 20,261 children caught up in Beatlemania was a horror to watch.

"A solid wall of hysterical children, 100 deep, stretched across the stadium field behind steel barriers in front of the Beatles' stage—sobbing, flailing at policemen and themselves, crushing smaller children against the barriers, and screaming," he wrote. "... From thousands of throats came an avalanche of animal-like screams as the thousands of youngsters surged forward." According to a psychologist at the time, becoming hysterical over rock 'n' roll is normal. It is a safety valve for children taught by society to repress emotion.

Maybe. And perhaps invasion of private property is yet another way to blow off some of the steam of immaturity. On October 24, 1968, a scruffy American nihilist named Jerry Rubin incited some 1,000 UBC students and freeloaders to invade the university's Faculty Club. Rubin, head of the Youth International Party, suggested to his impressionable audience that the Yippie gospel of personal freedom meant occupation of some place that was out of bounds. So off they went to take over the private club. Also involved were members of the radical Students for a Democratic Society, who demanded that all the seats of "authoritarianism" on campus be open to everyone. The sit-in lasted for twenty hours, during which time there was minor looting, rock music, group discussions and marijuana smoking.

The press was not impressed. Bob Hunter, *The Sun*'s "alternative" columnist, who had been hired by publisher Stu Keate to present the views of the counter-culture, called the occupation "a perfect absurdist's gambit. It accomplished nothing, it liberated no-one, it had at bottom, no organizational goal." A *Province* editorialist sneered that "snake-oil vendor" Rubin was a "showman-seditionist whose arguments about university structure have no validity here."

Nevertheless, the happening at the Faculty Club—and another occupation in November at Simon Fraser University—were symptomatic of the problems facing Canadian universities during the decade. By the mid-sixties, the first wave of confused, tightly-wound baby boomers dumped their alienation on to the cloistered halls of higher learning. British Columbia was no exception: UBC by 1964 was soon admitting reasonably affluent, privileged, comfortable high-school graduates who accepted the perks of growing up in the buoyant Socred economy as their due. When Simon Fraser opened September 9, 1965, initial enrollment of 2,207 at this "Cecil B. DeMille movie set" (as one reporter put it) atop Burnaby Mountain exceeded expectations. Within a year, Chancellor Gordon Shrum's administration was begging Victoria for more money to fund expansion.

On both campuses, as well as at the University of Victoria, the status quo of being part of an elitist hierarchy was not enough for many of these boomers. They had decided, on their way up the educational ladder, that much of what their parents and role models fed them was basically bunkum. The stress of the Cold War with the USSR had exposed many of the myths of the Western style of democracy, and with that exposure came disillusionment. Idealism, activism and rebellion followed as surely as sheep follow a bellwether.

There were many causes to pursue, from minor administrative reform at the universities to the grander dream of making the Atomic Age disappear. At Canadian campuses, the peace movement held sway as the New Left sought and failed to keep nuclear warheads out of the country. (Although the great bulk of BC college students were not involved with protests, and many activists were not members of the New Left, the label has been uniformly slapped on the "peaceniks" of that decade. As opposed to the Old Left, which was ideological, the New Left was moralistic.) Atop Burnaby Mountain, the movement seemed to be more vocal than out at Point Grey. Perhaps the academic radicalism in SFU's professorial ranks had something to do with the volume level.

Just as it took an itinerant demagogue like Rubin to excite UBC's grumblers into immoderate action, their counterparts at SFU were undoubtedly swayed by the march on the Faculty Club. On November 20, 1968, they pulled a sit-in of their own at the university's administration building. Close to 200 activists invaded the premises to protest administrative and financing policies. Police arrested 114 after an occupation of almost four days, and 105 were charged with committing mischief.

The politics of protest took to the streets the following August when Prime Minister Pierre Trudeau came to Vancouver for a fundraising dinner. Outside the Seaforth Armory, where the Liberal party faithful were gathered, demonstrators protesting the Vietnam war confronted the PM. There were curses, shouts, the waving of placards and some flying fists. One long-haired rowdy took a swing at Trudeau, who slapped the hand down and on to the brim of the startled protester's hat. Trudeau also ripped up an offending placard and took a banana peel in the back of the neck. *The Sun* dismissed the demonstration as "trendy," and suggested that "A small, hooting, hollering, swearing, throwing, smashing, burning minority uses a cause, any cause, as a device to intimidate and humiliate, to frighten and coerce—not just an engaging man called Pierre Trudeau but the responsible majority of Canadians of whom he is a symbol."

In Victoria, it wasn't so much the protesters as the unwelcome guests that had many citizens fretting. The issue was a downtown piece of real estate called Centennial Square. Approved by the voters in December, 1962, the project was undertaken to mark Victoria's incorporation in 1862 and at the same time revitalize a portion of its historic old town. At a long remove from the office towers, apartment buildings and snooty hotels that surround the Legislative Buildings, this part of the city is in a more earthy neighbourhood.

Hard by Chinatown and the more unsavory bits of Victoria, Centennial Square attracted the unwashed and transient almost from the day the rubble was cleared from the site. Even before the final element was completed in October, 1965, the papers were running stories about the hordes of hippies hanging about. *The Colonist* reported on September 10, 1964, that city council had simultaneously voted to keep the square's public washrooms open longer and to restrict loitering to two areas of the complex. In August of 1969, merchants in the area were complaining that "long-haired, unwashed, unattractive people" were hurting business.

On October 1 of that year, the student activists on the mainland were at it again. Some 4,000 of them—mostly from UBC—gathered at the Peace Arch border crossing to protest US nuclear testing in Alaska. However, this was a peaceful demonstration, with placards, pamphlets and speeches the only action during the one-hour happening. Also, there was virtually nobody around but the media to witness the rally: US border agents had diverted northbound traffic to another

THE DECADE IN HEADLINES
« 1968 »

COLISEUM ITSELF STAR OF EVENING
Vancouver's sparkling new Pacific Coliseum opens at the PNE—without an NHL franchise. The "big league" hockey team arrives a year later and stays for 25 seasons. First event at the Coliseum—virtually abandoned in 1994—is the Ice Capades.

The Province, January 8, 1968

'NAVY' TO BE BURIED AT SEA
With HMCS *Naden* and the dockyard complex in suburban Esquimalt a big part of its constituency, *The Times* concentrates on how unification of Canada's armed forces affects the RCN.

Victoria Times, February 1, 1968

HUGE JET CRASHES HERE, KILLING 2
A CPA airliner landing in foggy conditions at Vancouver International Airport slams into an airport building, narrowly missing the crowded main terminal. The afternoon *Sun* has five stories and 13 pictures about the crash in its Home Edition that day.

Vancouver Sun, February 7, 1968

NANCY STRIKES GOLD
Onlookers chant "Nancy, Nancy, Nancy" as BC skier Nancy Greene wins the women's giant slalom gold medal at the Grenoble Winter Olympics. Earlier, she wins a silver in the slalom.

The Province, February 15, 1968

THOUSANDS SEE PREMIER OPEN HERITAGE COURT
The new Provincial Museum in Victoria, a centennial project, is hailed by Premier Bennett as a symbol of "cooperative federalism."

Victoria Times, August 16, 1968

EXTRA　　　The Sun　　　**EXTRA**

VOL. LXXVIII—No. 41　MUtual 4-7141　74 PAGES　VANCOUVER, BRITISH COLUMBIA, FRIDAY, NOV. 22, 1963　★★★V　PRICE 10 CENTS　$2.50 Per Month

KENNEDY
SHOT DOWN

Separatism Threat Clear

Canada Now Facing Its Biggest Crisis

By BRUCE HUTCHISON
First of a Series

QUEBEC CITY — No English-speaking Canadian can guess the depth, the nature or the threat of so-called Quebec separatism until he sees it here at first hand.

Separatism is not, of course, a single or coherent thing. It is many different and incoherent things, most of them misjudged outside Quebec.

But the meaning of all these things, as they fuse in practical politics, is perfectly clear—Canada now faces the largest crisis of its history.

Deaf Mutes' Dialogue

If the crisis is to be resolved short of national disruption, each side in the present racial dialogue between deaf mutes must quickly grasp the intentions—and more than that, the emotions—of the other.

The time left to us is short. We have wasted years already in evading, denying and totally misconstruing the separate problems and the interdependent interests of the two Canadian races. Now we must come to grips with these issues at the worst imaginable moment when all our energies are required to solve our non-racial economic problems.

Nov. 25 will be a decisive milestone on the long, joint march of two peoples that began on the Plains of Abraham in 1759.

BRUCE HUTCHISON
...studies Quebec

Awful Truth of Duality

Next week's federal-provincial conference can settle anything finally but it will begin to show whether any settlement is within our reach.

Meanwhile the English-speaking visitor to Quebec feels, like a physical blow, the awful truth of Canada's duality. Then he slowly senses the opposite forces warring within the French Canadian spirit and threatening to split the nation.

Dimly, and very late, we AngloSaxons have started to oppose, as the Anglo-Saxon surmise the mixture of genius and folly, of selfishness and idealism, of good will and mastice, of logic and perversity that makes contemporary Quebec.

Bridge Between Solitudes

Our supreme need today is easy to state, hard to fulfill. The moderate, sensible elements of the two races—the vast majority on each side — must join to subdue the extremists, who are minorities but make noise and trouble out of all proportion to their numbers.

This is Prime Minister Lester Pearson's task, undoubtedly the most difficult and dubious ever undertaken by a prime minister since Sir John A. Macdonald built the nation.

Pearson has to mobilize the moderates and build a bridge between the two solitudes. His success or failure will make or break him and his government.

This, claims the outspoken minister, would be a lot more effective than establishing a province-wide automobile inspection system.

Motor vehicles superintendent George Lindsay said recently that study is being given to a mobile auto inspection program that might be introduced next year.

Since Quebec Premier Jean Lesage came to office and launched a quiet French Cana

Please Turn to Page Two See: "Canada's"

PRESIDENT KENNEDY . . . shot

Phil Would Padlock Pubs Rather Than Test Vehicles

Sun Victoria Bureau

VICTORIA—If safety experts want to cut the B.C. traffic accident toll they should padlock the pubs, according to Highways Minister Phil Gaglardi.

On Thursday, the B.C. Parliament-Teacher Federation asked the provincial cabinet to order establishment of vehicle testing stations and legislation requiring annual inspection of all vehicles.

"I'm opposed to that," said Gaglardi.

"We know that only around one per cent of accidents are caused by faulty vehicles, compared with 70 or 80 per cent where it is the driver and drinking," he said.

"Before we spend hundreds of thousands of dollars on inspection to eliminate one per cent of the accidents, I'd sooner close down all the beer parlors and bars to solve the 80 per cent."

Minus Signs In Early Trade

Minus signs predominated in quiet early trading on Vancouver stock market today.

Endako took a 10-cent loss at $4.10 and Grandue was off five cents at $4. Cowichan dropped one cent to $1.01. Western Mines was unchanged at $3.80.

'SPIES' SEE
NATO GAMES

'SPIES' SEE NATO GAMES

HALIFAX, N.S. (UPI)—Commodore Robert P. Welland, the senior Canadian navy officer afloat, says Russian trawlers spied on recent NATO exercises between Scotland and Iceland.

Welland said the trawlers were there solely to acquire information and not to admire the anti-submarine exercises being conducted in poor weather to test equipment.

Slaying Confessed, Say Police

NEW WESTMINSTER (Staff)—A statement in which a man admitted he murdered a young Mission City girl was read Thursday to an Assize Court jury.

The statement was read by Staff Sgt. E. D. Anderson, in charge of Kimberley RCMP detachment, at the trial of Kenneth Lloyd Meeker, 30.

Meeker is charged with capital murder in the death of Alice Mathers, 12, who disappeared while walking home on June 9. Her body was found in a gravel pit 14 miles east of Mission City on June 24.

Anderson said he took the statement from Meeker at Kimberley police office on July 3.

Admission of the statement as evidence was the subject of two days of legal argument in the absence of the jury. The judge ruled it admissible.

IN BATHING SUIT

In the statement, Meeker said he had travelled in his small European car through the interior of the province last spring.

On June 9, the statement said, Meeker left Vancouver and at Mission stopped to pick up a little girl dressed in a bathing suit and green sweater.

She refused to get in the car and he grabbed her and drove about 20 miles to a gravel pit, the statement said. Meeker said in the statement that at the gravel pit he took the girl's clothes off and molested her.

STARTED TO SCREAM

She started to scream, the statement said, and he strangled her, with his hands "at first."

Fearing she was not dead, the statement said, he took a rope from the car and put it around her neck until her face turned blue. He said he took her body to the bush nearby, put her bathing suit back on and threw her sweater over her.

The statement said he then drove 200 miles to a park site, the name of which he did not know, and stayed two days.

Questioned by Staff-Sgt.

Please Turn to Page Two See: "Trial"

Sped to Hospital

DALLAS (UPI) — President Kennedy was cut down by an assassin's bullets as he toured downtown Dallas in an open automobile today.

Texas Gov. John B. Connally, riding with him, was also struck.

Reporters about five car-lengths behind the president heard what sounded like three burst of gunfire.

Secret service agents in a follow-up car quickly unlimbered their automatic rifles.

The president, his limp body cradled in the arms of his wife, was rushed to Parkland Hospital.

The governor also was taken to Parkland.

Representative Albert Thomas of Texas said he was informed both men were alive but that Kennedy was in very critical condition.

He was rushed to an emergency room in the hospital.

The corridors of the hospital erupted in pandemonium.

The incident occurred just east of a triple underpass facing a park in downtown Dallas.

The bubble top of the president's car was down.

The agents drew their pistols, but the damage was done.

The president was slumped over in the back seat of the car face down. Connally lay on the floor of the rear seat.

It was impossible to tell at once where Kennedy was hit, but bullet wounds in Connally's chest were plainly visible, indicating the gunfire might possibly have come from an automatic weapon.

There were three loud bursts.

If Kennedy is dead or dies, Vice-President Lyndon B. Johnson would take over as president. Ironically, Johnson is from Texas.

Dallas motorcycle officers escorting the president quickly leaped from their bikes and raced up a grassy hill.

At the top of the hill, a man and woman appeared huddled on the ground.

In the turmoil, it was impossible to determine at once whether the secret service and Dallas police returned the gunfire that struck down Kennedy and Connally.

It was also difficult to determine immediately whether Mrs. Kennedy and Mrs. Connally were injured.

Both women were in the car.

Both women were crouched down over the inert forms of their husbands as the big car raced toward the hospital.

Mrs. Kennedy was on her knees on the floor of the rear seat with her head toward the president.

Vice-president Johnson was in a car behind Kennedy's.

The president had flown to Dallas and was on his way to deliver a luncheon speech.

Next president of the United States if President Kennedy dies will be Vice-President Lyndon Johnson.

Two Escape Blazing Rig

LYTTON (Staff)—Two men escaped when fire broke out in their tractor-trailer rig on the Trans-Canada Highway nine miles north of here.

James Stepp of Renton, Wash., said he was driving the heavy rig up a hill when a sheet of flame broke out in the front part of the cab.

He stopped the truck and woke up Ward Allen, of Seattle, who was sleeping in a compartment behind him, then leaped to the ground.

Allen followed but broke a bone in his left foot when he hit the ground.

In the first of two Extra Editions that day, Vancouver's afternoon paper reports the shocking news from Dallas.

crossing. Meanwhile, 300 young people protesting the N-tests paraded outside the Patricia Bay airport north of Victoria as a flight from Seattle arrived. The passengers hardly noticed.

As the sixties expired to the sound of marching feet, Premier Bennett squared off with a new champion of the left and blew him away. Thomas Berger, a prominent young labour lawyer, succeeded Robert Strachan as leader of the NDP in April, 1969; in August of that year, Bennett presided over another of his clockwork elections. This time, the experts opined, the Socreds were in trouble, even though a government redistribution bill in 1966 (written by Gerry and Mander, said Strachan at the time) favoured the party's rural candidates. Berger was young and responsible, while Bennett was old and over the hill, they said. But the premier was also as familiar and comfortable as an old shoe, and British Columbians were used to slipping on their Social Credit administration each morning. The relieved Socreds took thirty-eight seats out of fifty-five, close to the highest total of the seven elections they had won.

The illusion of W.A.C. Bennett's infallibility was never higher than after that election. It seemed the Old Man could never do wrong. But the protests and demonstrations that pockmarked this decade would take uglier and more significant forms in the next. One of the casualties would be Wacky himself.

---

1   Each legislative session, bills are introduced in numerical order, to be debated and (usually) passed into law. Newspapers use these numbers (Bill 42, Bill 33, for example) as a shorthand form for the actual Act, which may have a long and complex title. A bill does not become law until it receives royal assent.

THE DECADE IN HEADLINES
« 1969 »

FIRST WAVE SWAMPS GUARDS AT HILLSIDE'S H-HOUR

A huge, $10-million shopping centre opens in Victoria and 30,000 people show up. *The Times* marks the occasion with a 24-page supplement the day before.

Victoria Times, February 12, 1969

POSTMEN START 5-DAY WEEK

The end of Saturday mail delivery in Canada is noted by *The Times* in a Page 2 story about new post office hours.

Victoria Times, February 15, 1969

TRUDEAU HITS BACK AT PAINTED HIPPIES

In Vancouver for a fundraising dinner, Prime Minister Pierre Elliott Trudeau is mobbed by demonstrators. He rips up a sign and shoves one protester's hat over his forehead. *The Sun*'s headline pulls no punches about labelling the demonstrators in a year that saw several anti-war incidents.

Vancouver Sun, August 8, 1969

BENNETT NETS EASY SEVENTH WIN

After his Social Credit party takes 38 of 55 seats, the premier tells *The Colonist* that "the people of British Columbia have stopped the socialists right in their tracks."

The Colonist, August 27, 1969

PRAYER OPENS TERMINAL

Vancouver International Airport's new terminal is officially opened by federal Transport Minister Paul Hellyer, who quotes a Biblical passage.

The Province, October 25, 1969

THE SEVENTIES: A WHIFF OF SOCIALISM

« 1970 – 1979 »

On a raw, blustery January day in 1971, 2,000 demonstrators milled about on the lawn in front of the Legislative Buildings. It was an orchestrated display by union members and young roughnecks timed to disrupt the opening session of the legislature. With the BC Federation of Labour paying the shot, busloads of pot-smoking rowdies from the mainland joined the legitimate unemployed aboard government ferries. They were responding to a notice in the *Georgia Straight*, a counter-culture newspaper, offering a free trip to anyone willing to join a BC Fed march of the "jobless" on Victoria.

British Columbia had never seen anything like it. Proudly displaying obscenities and rude gestures as part of their credentials, the protesters jeered the MLAs and their frightened guests. They broke through the House's security and invaded the public galleries. Catcalls and curses drowned out the reading of the Throne Speech. Some windows and glass doors were smashed and a number of brawls broke out. Remarkably, no one was seriously injured. The government, sorely shaken by the near-anarchy, cited the "unholy wedlock" between the New Democratic Party and the Federation.

Rising inflation, unemployment and Social Credit's stiff-necked attitude toward unions also contributed to the January 21 confrontation. The good feeling surrounding the government's comfortable election victory barely eighteen months earlier had apparently dissipated. Smiling bravely through a stiff upper lip, Premier W.A.C. Bennett carried on as if the business of running BC had not been compromised. With 1972 a probable election year within his normal three-year window, Bennett took his entire cabinet on a hokey ramble around the province. The tour, in the spring of '72, was a big mistake. While it gave the cabinet lots of chances to dispense grants and favours to the locals, it also generated protests and demonstrations. Instead of bringing government to the people (and massaging the voter), the tour proved to be an unprecedented target of opportunity for any dissent, organized or not.

The protests reached their ugly climax outside the Royal Towers Hotel in New Westminster June 8, 1972. When the cabinet arrived, a mob of 500 was waiting. The jeering, cursing, flailing unionists hammered on cars carrying some of the cabinet ministers and physically attacked others. Altogether, eight ministers re-

THE DECADE IN HEADLINES
« 1970 »

BOLT FROM BLUE: SEX'S FRESH START

Vancouver MLA Agnes Kripps draws laughter and embarrassment with her plan to replace "that nasty little three-letter word S-E-X" with BOLT — Biology On Life Today. "You certainly had us all bolt upright in our chairs," calls out fellow Socred Herb Capozzi.

The Colonist, February 19, 1970

CITY ROLLS OUT RED CARPET FOR QUEEN AND PRINCESS

The Queen and Princess Anne (along with Prince Philip, who flew in later in the evening) spend less than a day in Vancouver en route to the Antipodes. *The Sun* and *The Province* weren't publishing, so the brief visit is reported by *The Express*, a newspaper produced by unionists during the Pacific Press dispute.

Vancouver Express, March 2, 1970

B.C. ENTERS SUPERPORT ERA

The 50-acre Roberts Bank coal-loading facility, dredged from the sea next to the Tsawwassen ferry terminal, opens for business.

The Province, June 15, 1970

THE DECADE IN HEADLINES
« 1971 »

PM SECRETLY WEDS W. VAN GIRL HERE

Despite extreme secrecy, *The Province* breaks the news to an astonished Canada that Pierre Elliott Trudeau has married Margaret Sinclair, who is 29 years younger.

The Province, March 4, 1971

13 REPORTED DEAD IN SHIP FIRE

The Norwegian cruise ship *Meteor* catches fire near Hornby Island in Georgia Strait. Despite a concerted rescue effort, the final death toll is 32.

Vancouver Sun, May 22, 1971

FISCHER SCORES 6-0 SWEEP IN WORLD CHESS MATCH

Bobby Fischer, described as the best grandmaster in the history of the game, begins his march toward a world title by humiliating the Soviet Union's Mark Taimanov in a qualifying match played at the University of BC.

Vancouver Sun, June 2, 1971

WEST WINS CAMPAIGN TO BLOCK FRENCH

At the end of a three-day constitutional conference, the so-called Victoria Charter exempts the three Western provinces from choosing English or French in their legislatures. The whole agreement is later vetoed by Premier Robert Bourassa of Quebec.

Vancouver Sun, June 16, 1971

CRUX SENTENCED TO SEVEN YEARS

A.G. Duncan Crux, head of the Commonwealth Trust group is jailed for fraud. The Commonwealth collapse in 1968 led to an official inquiry and opposition charges of a government bailout.

Vancouver Sun, July 4, 1971

ported various bruises, lumps and at least one broken bone. The premier and the press called it a black day for labour. "Cut it out," said *The Sun*, which was upset at both the union leadership for its hypocrisy and the RCMP for posing as newsmen. Bennett put the blame squarely on the shoulders of NDP leader Dave Barrett, calling the "anarchy" in the Royal City another result of NDP-labour collusion. Barrett sued him for libel and slander, but quietly dropped the action after the 1972 election.

William Andrew Cecil was getting pretty tired. He would, after all, observe his seventy-second birthday seven days after the election. The spark, the control, the easy affability were being replaced by a certain degree of testiness. Barrett, the young, energetic, bouncing Opposition leader, seemed to be a refreshing change from a premier beginning to display grumpy feet of clay. Even as he promised great new things and prosperity, Wacky and his advisers were moodily contemplating as few as seventeen Socred seats.

The actual results were even more troubling. On August 30, the New Democrats swept up thirty-eight of fifty-five seats. Social Credit was reduced to a rump of ten elected MLAs. The twenty-year ride was over and the socialist hordes that Bennett had often described as being at the gates of British Columbia were now inside the counting house.

More than a few words have been written about the Social Credit defeat of 1972. Among the reasons advanced is the one ascribing the NDP victory to some sort of avenging socialist paraclete interceding on behalf of the people. Actually, the election result was rather a fluke. The weary ennui of just enough of the populace translated itself into the required amount of votes to unseat the government. What most of the voters wanted to do was bring Bennett and his gang down a peg. They ended up throwing the Socreds out with the bathwater. That the citizenry trashcanned the left-wing interlopers in the very next election and returned to Social Credit for another fifteen years tends to bear out the "Oops!" scenario.

After twenty years, the Socred machine of 1972 exhibited the unhealthy patina of age. The cabinet wasn't a strong one. Bennett the one-man band played virtually all the instruments himself. He had to. With the exception of Robert Bonner as attorney-general and a couple of other ministers over the years, cabinet material was unremarkable. (Few of them are, no matter what party. The sharpest of minds seldom answer the siren call of politics.)

Bennett's two decades of governments were parsimonious and tightly administered. Bureaucracy and patronage were kept to a minimum as the old-fashioned values of the fifties persisted through the sixties. As his own finance minister, Bennett's budgets always seemed to be balanced. Surpluses popped up from nowhere, because Bennett cunningly underestimated revenues and overestimated expeditures, making the voter feel good about economic performance. His governments built roads, dams, bridges and ferries. He dreamed of greater grandeur for himself and his beloved province, but was practical and political enough to play to the little man. It worked for twenty years.

The Sun never did climb aboard the Bennett express. "During 20 years under Social Credit, this province's physical face was scarred permanently by the actions of a government intent on pursuing economic growth in the cowboy tradition of the frontier," it growled in a 1975 editorial.

"Great river valleys—the Columbia and the Peace—were turned into wasted areas, pools of muddy water stored to generate the electricity to supply power lines ripped for long, loping miles across the wilderness." *The Sun* said a vote for either the NDP or the Socreds in the 1975 election was "a choice between cowboys." In railing against the perceived rape of pristine BC, the paper was joining the tentative chorus of environmental concern that was beginning to be heard in the seventies. Before then, there were virtually no questions raised about the price of progress.

With the distressing events of 1972 still over the horizon, and the memory of the January debacle conveniently suppressed, Premier Bennett was grinning in anticipation at the banner year of 1971 that lay ahead. The Throne Speech so rudely upstaged by the union-subsidized louts spoke of "faith, courage and optimism" as the province entered its centennial year. Yes, we were about to celebrate yet another centennial. As already chronicled in these pages, BC has had four of them. But 1971—the hundredth anniversary of the year we joined Confederation—was the big one.

Naturally, the Queen came, along with her husband and daughter. It was a whirlwind visit of ten days in early May, but in that short span Her Royal Highness did the grand tour: 8,793.7 miles and twenty-four communities. At every stop, British Columbia wrapped its arms around the radiant monarch and gave her a great big hug. Elizabeth was the star attraction, but a few other unscheduled events, such as a surprise wedding, a marine disaster and another riot, would help make 1971 newsier than your normal year.

Futility first, however. In June, Premier Bennett played host to a constitutional conference in Victoria. Although hammering out an amending formula to appease Quebec was not among Bennett's top priorities (he had thrown the 1969 conference into disarray with a proposal to rearrange Canada into five regions), the Victoria talks were important as part of the centennial agenda. There were also high hopes that the agreement, which would become known as the Victoria Charter, would settle once and for all Quebec's status. Prime Minister Trudeau, champion of both bilingualism and (in Bennett's words) "hyphenated Canadians," was sure Quebec would go along this time. It didn't. Premier Robert Bourassa refused to commit himself in Victoria's legislative chamber, and flatly rejected the deal soon after returning to Quebec. Thus the Victoria Charter was the first in a string of high-profile constitutional disasters that would include Meech Lake and Charlottetown.

After the premiers and their advisers departed, BC got down to some serious celebrating. Trudeau and fourteen of his federal ministers held a ten-minute, ceremonial cabinet meeting in Victoria on Dominion Day, July 1. There were speeches, fireworks, parades and a big party July 20 in Vancouver's Empire Stadium, where a Confederation Pageant marked our hundredth birthday. The day before, *The Sun* had published a special, sixty-eight-page centennial edition that was an overwhelming success. It was sold out in hours and the demand necessitated an extended press run. (Eminent author and journalist Peter C. Newman, in a note to publisher Stu Keate, called the edition "the best single issue of any Canadian newspaper I have ever seen.") *The Province* produced a seventy-two-page edition, while other papers also marked the occasion with special sections.

The wedding of the year—and perhaps the decade—took place March 4 in St. Stephen's Roman Catholic Church, North Vancouver. The bride was Margaret Sinclair, twenty-two, daughter of Liberal stalwart Jimmy Sinclair. The groom was Pierre Elliott Trudeau, fifty-one, prime minister of Canada and the most eligible bachelor in international politics. The ceremony was a well-kept secret, witnessed only by a dozen others. Along with the rest of Canada, the local press was caught

THE DECADE IN HEADLINES
« 1972 »

'BCR' OPPOSED BY BARRETT

Legislation changing the name of the PGE to British Columbia Railway receives third reading despite opposition by NDP leader Dave Barrett.

Vancouver Sun, February 28, 1972

HOWARD HUGHES ARRIVES HERE

The reclusive, eccentric billionaire holes up on the 20th floor of the Bayshore Inn for several days. Despite the best efforts of the media, he is never spotted, although his presence at the hotel is confirmed. Unknown to *Sun* reporters (or anyone else), publisher Stuart Keate interviews Hughes secretly by telephone – a fact not made public until the recluse's death in 1976.

Vancouver Sun, March 14, 1972

MINISTERS HIT, JOSTLED BY ANGRY PROTESTERS

Premier W.A.C. Bennett and his cabinet are greeted by union demonstrators when they arrive for a meeting in a New Westminster hotel. The protesters are upset at the government's handling of labour issues.

The Columbian, June 7, 1972

BARRETT BOUNCES BENNETT

The NDP wins 38 of 55 legislative seats to end the W.A.C. Bennett era in BC. *The Times* calls the Socred defeat "brutal" and "stunning."

Victoria Times, August 30, 1972

WEATHER
Mo... cloudy today, with
a few ...now flurries. Canada's ...igh-low Thursday:
Abbotsford 41, Inuvik 42
below.

PM SECRETLY WEDS
W. VAN. GIRL HERE

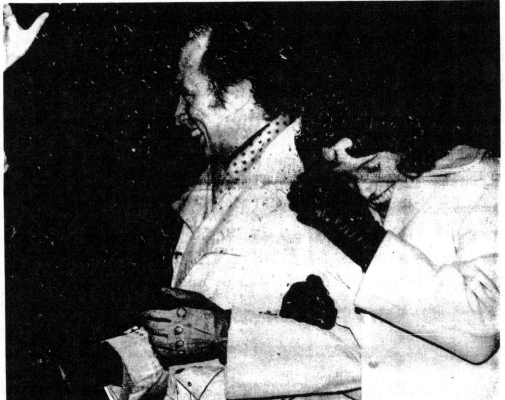

Mr. and Mrs. Pierre Elliott Trudeau leave the home of Mrs. Trudeau's parents in West Vancouver in a shower of rice Thursday night. Mrs. Trudeau is the former Margaret Sinclair. — *Bill Cunningham photo*

22-year-old Margaret Sinclair the bride

Prime Minister Pierre Elliott Trudeau was married Thursday night to 22-year-old Margaret Sinclair in North Vancouver.

His bride, described by a friend of the family as "magnificent," is the daughter of James Sinclair of West Vancouver, a former Liberal cabinet minister.

Sinclair said his daughter and the 51-year-old prime minister had been engaged for about six months.

But the word was kept so secret that only one of the bride's four sisters, the bridesmaid, knew of the wedding until the last minute — the others thought they were dressing up for "a family portrait."

Rev. John Swinkels, the Roman Catholic priest who performed the ceremony, and the wedding photographer had been told that Margaret Sinclair was marrying a "Pierre Mercier."

And Trudeau arrived in Vancouver on a government aircraft Thursday afternoon accompanied by an announcement that he was "going skiing" in the Vancouver area for a couple of days.

The new Mrs. Trudeau is five feet, six inches tall and has dark red hair. She met Trudeau three years ago.

The so-called "playboy prime minister" and "most eligible bachelor in Canada" was late at the church.

Scheduled to be there at 5 p.m., he didn't appear until 6:30, delayed by bad weather in the East.

Only immediate family attended the ceremony at St. Stephen's Roman Catholic church, a modernistic structure on East Twenty-fourth in the Lynn Valley district.

Margaret's four sisters, Betsy, 19; Rosalind, 24; Janet, 25, and Heather (Mrs. Tom Walker), 28, were there along with Mr. and Mrs. Sinclair and Margaret's grandmother, Mrs. Rose Bernard of Roberts Creek.

Rosalind was bridesmaid. Charles Trudeau, the PM's brother, was best man. Other relatives of Trudeau were kept from the wedding by bad weather in Montreal.

After a wedding reception at the Capilano Golf and Country Club (Canada's new First Lady made the cake) and a stop at the Sinclair home, the Trudeaus were reported to have gone to the Whistler Mountain area where the Sinclairs have a condominium. There was no confirmation.

Family members said the Trudeaus would be back in Ottawa on Tuesday.

Doreen Robson, sister of Mrs. Sinclair, said Margaret was an Anglican but recently became a Catholic.

A friend of the Sinclair family said Trudeau and his bride first met on holiday in Tahiti in 1968.

The friend described Margaret Sinclair as a beautiful and "magnificent" woman.

"She is especially attuned to things, she has shown remarkable maturity since she met Trudeau.

"She is the type of person who could take two pots and provide a gourmet meal for an impromptu party. She is a home-maker, everything a woman could be."

He said some observers in Ottawa has speculated for some time that the two would marry.

"But Trudeau always insisted any of his dates not publicize their association with him. Margaret did not let him down."

He said Miss Sinclair had been the only serious

See Page 1A — 22-YEAR-OLD

Barrett expelled from House -- Page 29

Taken by surprise by Prime Minister Trudeau's secret wedding in North Vancouver, The Province *does manage to get an engaging picture of the happy couple.*

by surprise. It was aware that the prime minister was in town to "go skiing," and only twigged to the real reason in time to get pictures of the happy couple leaving their wedding reception.

As the centennial celebrations neared, another unscheduled news event claimed Page One. Off Hornby Island in Georgia Strait on May 22, the Norwegian cruise ship *Meteor* caught fire. The blaze, in the forward part of the ship, killed thirty-two of the ninety-one crewmen aboard. None of the sixty-seven passengers died.

And on August 7, the Gastown Riot in Vancouver led to outcries about police brutality. The trouble began when some 1,200 demonstrators protesting a crackdown on the use of marijuana were confronted by the cops. During the melee, which lasted for three hours, riot-equipped police (and some on horseback) waded into the young crowd, their truncheons swinging, and manhandled many of them. There were seventy-nine arrests and thirty-eight charges laid. More than a dozen people were injured. Mayor Tom Campbell garnered headlines by promising a probe of police conduct, but only one officer was eventually disciplined.

Two other maritime incidents early in the decade reminded British Columbians that the sea on their doorstep lent itself to tragedy as well as some forms of protest. On August 3, 1970, the BC government ferry *Queen of Victoria* was rammed by the Russian freighter *Sergey Yesenin* at the south end of Active Pass. Three passengers aboard the ferry died. There were no injuries on the freighter ("Reds Safe," said a headline deck in *The Province*).

The narrow, twisting pass between Galiano and Mayne islands is a marine superhighway for ferries travelling from Tsawwassen on the mainland and Swartz Bay on Vancouver Island. As the Bennett government dramatically increased its people's fleet (the *Queen of Victoria* was one of the new "stretch" ferries), traffic became more intense. It remains so to this day, because Active Pass, despite its tidal action, close quarters and hundreds of sportfishing boats getting in the way, is the quickest route.

The pass is seldom used by merchant ships (even before they reached the huge dimensions of later in the century), which take Boundary Pass to the south. The *Sergey Yesenin*, however, at 523 feet was not overly long; she headed into the pass without warning just as the ferry was leaving it. Despite automatic assumptions that the Russians were at fault (and some talk of impounding the freighter), a subsequent inquiry laid most of the blame on the handling of the *Queen of Victoria*.

On September 15, 1971, the Don't Make A Wave Committee set sail from Vancouver in a small boat bound for Amchitka, Alaska. Its purpose was to protest US nuclear testing in the Aleutian Islands. Among the twelve persons aboard were Bob Hunter, a *Sun* columnist, and Ben Metcalfe, a former *Province* staffer and CBC freelancer. They were all unshaven, unkempt and uninhibited. Pictures taken during that era depict the crew as decidedly unsavory. Thanks to the media background of Hunter and Metcalfe, there was plenty of publicity when the boat sailed. That it never did reach the Aleutians was news not so widely disseminated.

Of more significance is the fact the DMAWC changed its name to Greenpeace. As the century reaches its end, Greenpeace claims to be the largest environmental organization on earth, with membership in 1996 of 2.9 million in 158 countries. In the course of its history to date, it has proven to be as adept at harvesting headlines and television clips as campaigning to save the whales, halting nuclear testing and protecting the globe from environmental harm.

When the Social Credit cabinet held its final meeting in September of 1972,

THE DECADE IN HEADLINES
« 1973 »

INDIANS SEE VICTORY IN JUDGMENT

Despite a Supreme Court of Canada decision dismissing their claim for aboriginal land rights, BC's Nishga Natives are gratified that the vote was only 4-3. In later years, Native land-claim negotiations become a controversial process.

The Province, January 31, 1973

QUEEN KAREN COMES HOME TO A DAY OF CHEERS

North Vancouver's Karen Magnussen has "a day to remember" after returning as world figure skating champion. She won the title March 1 in Bratislava.

Vancouver Sun, April 3, 1973

BACK TO VINEYARDS AND REAL PEOPLE

W.A.C. Bennett ends a 32-year political career by resigning his seat. The former premier, 72, tells *The Colonist* he will devote his retirement years to the cause of "the private enterprise system."

The Colonist, June 5, 1973

INDIRA UNDAUNTED BY PICKETS

India's Prime Minister Indira Gandhi makes a quick visit to Vancouver and Victoria during her eight-day tour of Canada. In a speech in Vancouver, she says dissent is a "part of democratic life."

The Province, June 23, 1973

'I'M MY OWN MAN' – BENNETT

On the first ballot at the party's Vancouver convention, Bill Bennett is chosen Social Credit leader. He replaces W.A.C. Bennett, who resigned June 5.

Vancouver Sun, November 24, 1973

THE DECADE IN HEADLINES
« 1974 »

BARRETT LENDS AN EAR AT ICBC

On the day the NDP government's Autoplan goes into effect, Premier Dave Barrett touts the "unique and fantastic accomplishment" of the Insurance Corporation of BC.

The Province, March 1, 1974

TRANSIT ACT GIVES GOV'T HEFTY CLOUT

The NDP introduces the Transit Services Act, which provides for operation of bus, rail and other passenger systems. Eventually, BC Transit takes over the bus routes of BC Hydro in major communities.

The Province, March 13, 1974

WRONG TIME OF YEAR

The newspaper is not convinced the new BC Day holiday is a good idea. Instead of the first Monday in August, an editorial says, "It is a pity the legislators did not instead pick a day in that long, dreary period between New Year's Day and Easter...."

The Colonist, August 6, 1974

FINAL PARTY FOR CITY TO WRAP UP 100TH YEAR

The Island centre marks its first 100 years with a presentation of an illuminated scroll. Nanaimo received its charter December 24, 1874.

Nanaimo Free Press, December 24, 1974

before handing the province over to the New Democrats, BC's finances were in reasonably good shape. Bennett reported to the press that current reserves were $574.8 million and the fixed, paid-for assets totalled $1.42 billion. He couldn't help noting that BC had a net debt of $224.5 million and assets of only $188.7 million when he took office in 1952. *The Sun* summed up his economic wizardry by calling it "a hard act to follow."

Within a month, the economic picture began to change. Premier Dave Barrett, sworn in on September 15, called a special session of the legislature for mid-October. It lasted less than two weeks, but Barrett and his cabinet used the time to start spending money. In eleven days, the NDP passed thirteen pieces of legislation, including a bill guaranteeing $200 a month to the elderly and handicapped (while hoping Ottawa would pick up half the tab).

Barrett, who was forty when he became premier, had a career background as a social worker. Son of a Jewish fruit peddler, he grew up in East Vancouver and became a CCF MLA in 1960. In 1970, when Tom Berger quit, Barrett became the NDP leader. None of this prepared him for the challenge of taking over the till of such a huge, multifaceted, billion-dollar enterprise as the government of British Columbia. Nevertheless, Barrett decided to imitate his predecessor and retain the finance minister's portfolio for himself. Oh, dear.

When the Barrett government shuffled back to the opposition benches after the 1975 election, the province's books were somewhat more chaotic than they were three years earlier. Just as the world entered an economic downturn, Barrett tried to be a mini-W.A.C. and blithely started spending. The budget ballooned to $3.2 billion—three times more than Bennett's last budget in 1972.

Barrett doubled his own salary as premier (as well as those of the other MLAs), increased the civil service by 28 percent and raised public-sector salaries by 56 percent. Executive and other administrative costs of government more than doubled, from $37.6 million in 1972–73 to $80 million in 1974–75. Spending by the ministries was careless and uncoordinated. Human resources, for instance, overspent by $100 million in 1974.

The government tried to do so much so quickly that one had to suspect they knew they were a one-term wonder. Legislative sittings consumed much of each year, instead of the spring sessions favoured by the previous administration. Public acts registered in the statute books for 1973 totalled 162. Over the three-year period, the number of bills exceeded 400. (The legislature became such a complex beat that *The Sun* assigned as many as ten persons to it during the 1974 spring session. It was unprecedented legislative coverage.)

Among the bills hustled into law were several controversial ones. Among them: The Land Commission Act, which sought to dictate the disposition of all the property (including private) in the province; the Mineral Royalties Act, which imposed taxes and royalties so onerous that activity in that major resource industry virtually came to a halt; the Insurance Corporation of BC, which delivered a body blow to private insurers of automobiles; the Public Service Labour Relations Act, which granted full bargaining powers to government employees.

The one that got Barrett and his cabinet in real trouble, however, was Bill 146 in October of 1975. That summer, four major labour disputes had dragged on for weeks. Some 50,000 workers in the forest and propane industries, Lower Mainland supermarkets and the BC Railway were involved. The Collective Bargaining Continuation Act ordered everyone back on the job for a 90-day "cooling-off" period.

The NDP's erstwhile buddy, the BC Federation of Labour, went ballistic. It condemned the bill roundly and vowed to fight "in every way possible" the back-to-work order. Without stressing the point too much, an easy conclusion is that more than a few of those 50,000 betrayed unionists voted against the New Democrats later in 1975.

Barrett did institute some legislative reform, such as Hansard, which is a daily written record of everything said in the House, and a question period. (Opposition leader Bennett asked the very first oral question March 5, 1973. It was ruled out of order by Gordon Dowding, one of the most partisan Speakers in BC's legislative history.)

Premier David Barrett may be best remembered, however, for loudly and publicly cursing a female newspaper columnist March 12, 1974. That afternoon, Marjorie Nichols of *The Sun* and her bureau chief encountered Barrett in a corridor of the legislature. The premier, who was being regularly skewered by Nichols' deft prose, screamed an obscenity at her over and over again. "F— you! F— you! F— you!" he shrieked before storming off.

Meanwhile, as Barrett and the socialists were having their thirty-nine-month taste of power, there was a change of Bennetts on the political scene. William Andrew Cecil resigned June 5, 1973, as MLA for the South Okanagan. On September 7, William Richards won the seat for Social Credit in a by-election. W.R. (Bill) Bennett was W.A.C.'s third child and second son. He was born April 14, 1932, and grew up to become an Okanagan businessman with his brother, R.J. While Mother and Father were on a world cruise, recuperating from the trauma of electoral rejection, young Bill had decided to enter politics. His by-election victory and his elevation to the Socred leadership at a November convention put him in the House as Opposition leader. In that raucous neighbourhood at the corner of Government and Belleville streets, the new Bennett was raw, untested fodder. As such, he was routinely cut to pieces by the experienced Barrett.

But while learning on the job, Bennett quietly let his father and Socred eminence Grace McCarthy rejuvenate the party's constituency. Unlike Dad, the younger Bennett was somewhat stilted in his relationship with the press. He did realize, however, that the newspapers weren't about to give an Opposition politician the same amount of ink they would the government. Especially one as juicily newsworthy as the NDP. So, as legislative bureau chief for BC's most dominant paper, *The Sun*, the author had little trouble arranging an interview with Bennett in the spring of 1974. During that chat in his office (some of which was off the record), he accurately predicted that not only would the NDP lose the next election, but that Barrett would lose his own seat. The Socreds' grassroots recovery had become that strong, he said.

Which is exactly what happened. Barrett's economic excesses, speculation about an imminent, unheard-of deficit in the provincial treasury (revealed later to be $40 million), the perceived wrath of Big Labour over Bill 146 and general voter dissatisfaction with their socialist fling all contributed. During the campaign, *The Sun* reminded its readers that the government went $59 million in the hole in the 1973–74 fiscal year alone. On December 11, 1975, the NDP sank to eighteen seats, while Social Credit formed the government with thirty-five. Bill Bennett would become premier of British Columbia, replacing a failed leader who was out of the legislature entirely. As Bennett had predicted, Barrett lost his seat in Coquitlam —by nineteen votes. (He was returned to the House in a 1976 by-election. Bob

THE DECADE IN HEADLINES
« 1975 »

THIS SUMMER, 25 CELSIUS MEANS BIKINIS

Canada's agonizing conversion to the metric system does away with Fahrenheit as the measurement of temperature. More shocks are to come, including—exactly one year later—the expression of barometric pressure in kilopascals, whatever they are.
The Province, April 1, 1975

EVERYBODY BACK TO WORK

The NDP government enacts sweeping back-to-work legislation designed to end major labour disputes in the forestry, pulp, food and propane industries. Some 50,000 workers are affected by the various shutdowns. The move is "a political master stroke" by Premier Barrett, *The Times* says in an editorial.
Victoria Times, October 7, 1975

BARRETT GETS A PERSONAL BOOT

BC's first flirtation with socialism ends abruptly after three years. Suffering rejection along with his NDP government is Premier Barrett, who loses his own seat to a Social Credit candidate.
Vancouver Sun, December 11, 1975

THE DECADE IN HEADLINES
« 1976 »

IN TRIUMF, PIERRE'S LOST ...

While admitting he didn't quite understand how UBC's new particle accelerator works, Prime Minister Trudeau officially opens the facility. In reluctantly promising enough federal funds to barely get TRIUMF running, he foreshadows the money problems that will dog the accelerator in subsequent years.

Vancouver Sun, February 9, 1976

PRIORITIES FOR HABITAT ASSURE CONFERENCE SPLIT

Deep political schisms between the Third World and the West mar the idealistic and controversial United Nations Conference on Human Settlements.

The Province, May 31, 1976

1 MILLION JOIN IN DAY OF PROTEST

An estimated 7,000 unionized workers protest in downtown Vancouver against federal wage and price controls. Although the protest is termed the biggest labour demonstration the city has seen, one observer notes that workers elsewhere in Canada are not nearly as militant as in BC.

The Province, October 14, 1976

Williams, a former cabinet minister and one of the most powerful men in the NDP, resigned as MLA for the safe seat of Vancouver East to make room for the ex-premier.)

As well as voting goodbye to Dave Barrett and his New Democrats in 1975, British Columbia waved a reluctant farewell to a name that had been around quite a bit longer: Fahrenheit. On April 1 (the significance of changes taking place on April Fools' Day has not been lost on students of irony), the Celsius system of recording temperatures was instituted across Canada. No longer could anyone officially enjoy a sunny day of 75°. From now on, that would be expressed as 24°. Newspapers told readers to subtract 32 from any Fahrenheit temperature they might bump into, then multiply the remainder by 5/9ths to get Celsius. If you wanted to convert to F out of C, reverse that procedure. Sure.

The country had been struggling its way through metric conversion since 1971, when Ottawa set up a commission to plan and coordinate the switch from the old Imperial inch and pound measures. In doing so, Canada had succumbed to growing pressure to join the rest of the world (almost) in embracing a system based on the French unit of linear measurement. There was every expectation that the United States would follow suit, but as any traveller south of the border at the end of the nineties knew, it didn't.

Nevertheless, by 1983 BC and the rest of the provinces were more or less metrified. This included energy, speed, weather data, linear equivalents, mass and volume. Recalibration of equipment was a major task (hey, someone had to change all those gas pumps to litres). For BC, which concentrates on exports—especially in forest products—the changeover was particularly vexing. Right into the nineties, shipments of lumber could be expressed in either cubic metres or board feet, depending on the customer. Also, some habits die hard. More than twenty-five years after Canadians started hearing about these strange new terms, houses and condominiums are still sold by the square foot, personal weight is still reckoned in pounds and most supermarkets feature the old-fashioned Imperial price structure over metric.[1]

In 1976, Vancouver suspended its struggle with metric nomenclature and welcomed the world. The event was the United Nations Conference on Human Settlements. Its short name was Habitat and it was held over a twelve-day period in May and June at two sites. The stuffy main sessions were held downtown at the Queen Elizabeth Theatre, while Habitat Forum at Jericho Beach hosted a non-governmental program. Under the inspired goading of producer Al Clapp, a "pushy idea man," more than 150 volunteers had recycled an abandoned seaplane base at Jericho into a centre for discussions, workshops and lectures.

Mother Teresa came to Habitat. So did Margaret Mead, Buckminster Fuller, Pierre Trudeau, Kurt Waldheim and Imelda Marcos (who was greeted by jeering demonstrators).

However, more than False Creek separated the two sites. In fact, the gulf between Jericho Beach's touchy-feely people-in and the dry speeches at the plenary session was almost as wide as that between the Third World and the developed nations. While the idealism and symbolism of this new concept of global togetherness filled the city with pride, Habitat was essentially a failure. The high aims of the conference—eradication of slums, clean water for the planet, a permanent UN agency for human settlement—were subverted by the pro-Palestinian agenda of the undeveloped nations. In its closing hours, the conference could not agree on a

Declaration of Principles. The main stumbling block was a passage equating Zionism with racism. Because of this anti-Israel rhetoric, the West rejected the declaration. The gulf between the Third World and developed nations doomed all attempts at a consensus. As *The Province* observed, "a mob of Arab, African, Asian and Latin-American countries and their bedfellows" thwarted the goals of Habitat.

Bennett the Younger was not Bennett the Elder. Although a wealthy businessman, he was not the measure of his father as a keeper of the political purse strings (nor was Barrett, obviously), so when Bill Bennett took over as premier on December 22, 1975, he began using all the tools of the modern executive—expert advice, planning, coordination, committees, staff input and consultants. Already, Bennett had revived an unofficial version of the old Coalition and ensured that a right-left focus had returned to BC politics by luring three Liberal personages into the Social Credit fold. The defection of Garde Gardom, Pat McGeer and Allan Williams (all would become cabinet ministers) buried Liberal fortunes in the same graveyard as the long-dead Conservatives.

As the second Bennett to become premier, Bill eased gingerly into his new role. After the shouting and breakneck pace of the Barrett years, his stewardship appeared to be colourless but stable. There were a few bumps along the way, however, to keep things interesting. Scandals surrounding young women and the fraudulent conversion of airline tickets brought resignations in the cabinet.

Then in June of 1978, the affair of "Gracie's Finger" had the opposition howling. As part of the redrawing of the electoral map (which added two seats to the legislature), Grace McCarthy's Vancouver-Little Mountain riding somehow sprouted a digit-shaped appendage that just happened to be chock-full of Social Credit voters. The NDP alleged interference and corruption, but of course nothing came of it.

Bennett got back on track with the voters in late December of that year by taking on big, bad Canadian Pacific. The Eastern-based transportation and resources behemoth had the temerity to seek acquisition of British Columbia's own MacMillan Bloedel Ltd. "BC is not for sale," thundered Bennett, while threatening all sorts of strategems to block the takeover. Despite "expert" opinion that Bennett was bluffing, Canadian Pacific folded its hand.

In the summer of 1977, a bill had been introduced establishing the BC Resources Investment Corporation. A noble experiment in people's capitalism, BCRIC became the repository for several resource-industry assets acquired by the previous government to the tune of $151.5 million. Then, while BC was still buzzing over his defence of MacBlo, Bennett on January 11, 1979, offered everyone in the province "a piece of the rock"—five free shares in BCRIC. They were worth a book value of $6 each, and anyone wishing to invest their own money in BC could purchase up to 5,000 more.

An awful lot of people took the plunge. The government raised $487 million through the share offering, as well as invaluable voter goodwill in the election held May 10 of that year. As it was, Bennett the Younger just squeaked through to his first victory as premier, taking thirty-one seats to the NDP's twenty-six in the new, fifty-seven-seat legislature. (Eventually, the BCRIC would hang heavily around the Socred government's neck. A rash investment policy and unwise decisions sank the corporation into a morass of red ink from which it would never recover. BCRIC eventually became something called the Westar Group, and all the little $6 investors lost virtually everything).

THE DECADE IN HEADLINES
« 1977 »

SEA BUS READY FOR MAIDEN VOYAGE

A special supplement of *The Citizen* prior to the event heralds the new ferry link across Burrard Inlet between Vancouver and North Vancouver.

North Shore Citizen, June 17, 1977

SOCREDS GIVE B.C. RESIDENTS CHANCE TO INVEST IN RESOURCES

Legislation is introduced establishing a corporation which will take over several companies acquired by the previous NDP government. Known as BCRIC, it will later offer shares to the public.

Vancouver Sun, August 23, 1977

PREMIER OFFICIALLY DEDICATES MICA DAM

With his father looking on, Premier Bill Bennett dedicates the last of the Columbia treaty dams. Then-premier W.A.C. Bennett launched the huge Columbia power program in the sixties.

Revelstoke Review, October 13, 1977

ARCTIC SOLO A 'DUET'

As Arctic sailor Willy de Roos gets a hero's welcome in Vancouver, news stories cast doubt on his "solo" claim by reporting he has had help during parts of his Northwest passage.

The Province, October 18, 1977

THE DECADE IN HEADLINES
« 1978 »

CRASH KILLS 41

On the Monday following the Saturday crash of a Pacific Western Airlines Boeing 737 at Cranbrook airport, the *Townsman* devotes Page One and three inside pages to the tragedy.

Cranbrook Townsman, February 11, 1978

« 1979 »

BENNETT DEAD, LEGEND LIVES ON

The death of BC's longest-serving premier dominates the pages of his home-town paper until the funeral four days later.

Kelowna Courier, February 23, 1979

The 1979 election campaign was a messy one for the Socreds. Apart from the head-to-head clash of two opposing wills (Bennett and Barrett never really liked each other), which gave the voters a clear choice of leadership styles, the Social Credit campaign was sloppy and ineffective. The "Dirty Tricks" scandal—phoney letters written to the media—and persistent reports of cash freely changing hands were two manifestations of party ineptness. (Most of this took place in a curious sort of silence. BC's two biggest newspapers, *The Sun* and *The Province*, were shuttered by a labour dispute, depriving many thousands of voters of any coherent coverage of the election.)

That his party had almost piddled away a fifteen-seat majority was a point not lost on the premier. While skating gingerly around a four-seat margin (one of his thirty-one MLAs had to be Speaker), Bennett initiated a restructuring of the Social Credit organization. No longer would the folksy populist approach of W.A.C. suffice. The party, like the government, would become modernized.

Among the least coveted assignments in journalism is the preparation of obituaries. When world or local figures become famous (or infamous), their obits are written beforehand by the newspaper staff or news services (which call them sketches), and stored in readiness for the fatal moment. As soon as the newsmaker departs this world, the papers run his or her obituary. These contain the relevant biographical material pertaining to the subject and can become quite long. As the occasion dictates, they are updated and retopped and slapped into the paper to accompany the report of the death.

In the late seventies, two major obituaries were retrieved from their resting places. The first was for Harvey Reginald MacMillan, who died February 9, 1976, at the age of ninety. H.R. was the first chief forester of BC in 1912, who went on to found MacMillan Bloedel. He served his country behind the scenes in both world wars and became a noted philanthropist after retiring in the sixties. H.R. was the century's dominant force in BC's primary industry.

Three years later, on February 23, 1979, William Andrew Cecil Bennett died in his sleep, aged seventy-eight. The former premier had been ill for some time. In 1952, Bennett had picked up a rootless, languid BC by the scruff of the neck and given it a good shake. He believed in private initiative, free enterprise and strong government. The province that was so well endowed with natural resources was shoved precipitously into the future. Those resources, and Bennett's exuberant tilling of them, helped fuel one of the great expansionary economies in modern North American history. W.A.C. Bennett was the longest-serving and most dynamic of the province's premiers. In the words of *The Colonist*, he made waves and BC rode the crest. With the seventies coming to an end and the Old Man gone, the crest had subsided into a fretful ripple.

---

1 This book wavers between Imperial and metric terms. The author believes many readers are still more comfortable with the old than with the new. Besides, translating US and/or historic Imperial measurements is cheating.

THE EIGHTIES:
THE MARK
OF ZALM

« 1980 – 1989 »

LAST 6 PRISONERS LEAVE SILENT PEN

As *The Sun* reporter puts it, "only a sixpack" of prisoners remain as the BC Penitentiary in New Westminster closes for good. Opened September 28, 1878, and holding as many as 760 inmates at one time, the pen is to be replaced by a "correctional facilities" system.

Vancouver Sun, February 15, 1980

A NEW CHAPTER AT THE LIBRARY

Opening of Victoria's Central Library on Broughton Street is covered by a picture and a caption on an inside page.

The Colonist, May 2, 1980

As the penultimate decade of the twentieth century unfolded, British Columbians were transfixed by the courage of a young, one-legged man from Port Coquitlam. His name was Terry Fox, and on April 12, 1980, he began running across Canada. With Newfoundland his starting point, Fox planned a Marathon of Hope to raise money for cancer research.

Terry didn't make it. The cancer that had cost him his right leg had spread through his body and he was forced to abandon the run (it was more of a hop-step) on a highway near Thunder Bay, Ontario, on September 2. Fox was only eighteen when a malignant tumour was found in his leg, forcing an amputation above the knee. During his stay in hospital, he was so moved by the suffering of other cancer patients that he conceived his cross-country run.

Terry Fox died June 28, 1981, at the age of twenty-two. In a Page One editorial, *The Sun* said that not only was it important to remember Terry, but also "that we do not forget to finish what he started." We didn't, because the Fox legacy lives on. There are memorials to his courage on the Trans-Canada Highway near Thunder Bay and outside BC Place in Vancouver. (In the beginning, Fox's quest got little attention. Stories about the early days of the run were hard to find in the BC press. It wasn't until the Toronto print and electronic media "discovered" Terry when he reached Ontario that the Marathon of Hope became a national story. His final, faltering strides outside Thunder Bay were given saturation coverage.)

On May 29, 1985, Steve Fonyo, another one-legged runner, finished what Terry couldn't by dipping his artificial limb in Juan de Fuca Strait near Victoria's Beacon Hill Park. The Marathon of Hope became an annual event, with hundreds of thousands participating in runs around the world. By 1997, more than $180 million had been raised.

Pomp, pageantry and pride. That's how one reporter described an event in 1983 at Vancouver's brand-new BC Place Stadium. The Queen and her consort, Prince Philip, had dropped in for yet another visit. This time they came by sea, sailing into Victoria's Inner Harbour on March 8 aboard the Royal yacht *Britannia* for a fast-paced, three-day dash-about. And once again she was greeted by large and enthusiastic crowds. At the stadium, Elizabeth invited the world to come to the Expo 86 fair three years hence.

Olson was paid to locate bodies

▼ COLOR

BEST COPY AVAILABLE

The provincial government paid $100,000 to confessed murderer Clifford Olson for information on where he hid seven of the bodies of the 11 young people he murdered, prosecutor John Hall said today.

The money went to "someone associated" with Olson, he said.

In an interview Hall said the payment was a joint decision of everyone involved with the investigations, including the RCMP and the federal and provincial attorneys-general.

Asked why the money was paid, Hall said that people should understand it was a difficult case, and there were grave doubts that Olson was the murderer.

"It really was far from conclusive (before the money was paid)," Hall said.

However, he said, the payment "is still under police investigation," and he refused to comment on a report that $90,000 of the money has disappeared.

Insp. Larry Proke, one of the senior RCMP officers involved in the case, told The Vancouver Sun today that he will meet B.C. Attorney-General Allan Williams in Vancouver later today to discuss the reward.

He said a statement or a press conference may be held after this meeting. He refused to comment further.

In answer to questions from reporters, Hall said Olson was present with police at several locations where bodies were discovered, and he nodded his agreement that Olson had led police to the locations.

Asked if Olson was paid $10,000 per body to locate his victims, Hall said: "I don't want to go into too many details."

Asked if police are trying to get the money back, Hall said: "Police are working on that and I don't want to comment."

Other officials in the RCMP, the attorney-general's ministry and the federal solicitor-general's department refused to discuss the payoff even after Olson pleaded guilty today in B.C. Supreme Court.

But numerous sources associated with the case have confirmed details of how Olson was paid. All asked not to be identified.

The reason for the payoff was to ease the strain on the victims' families so they would not spend the rest of their lives wondering whether their children were alive, one source said.

Another said the payoff was to ensure "a good Christian burial" (of the bodies, once they were located.)

The Sun has learned that the money was paid to locate the bodies after Olson had already admitted the murders to police.

Sources said the money was routed to a bank account set up for Joan Olson, wife of the 42-year-old construction worker, and their infant son, Clifford Jr.

The story about the payoff was widespread in the Lower Mainland for many weeks. The Sun first heard it from police sources and from an anonymous telephone call following Olson's arrest last Aug. 13.

Later, Sun reporters heard it from sources in the Crown prosecutor's office, from a witness in the case, from a source in Riverview psychiatric hospital, and even from a prisoner inside the Kent maximum security prison.

Solicitor-General Robert Kaplan's executive assistant Stephen LeDrew did not return phone calls referring to the matter.

Supt. John Bentham, head of RCMP information in Ottawa, said the commissioner of the RCMP will "not address himself to that question because it's a provincial matter. If you ask Supt. (Bruce) Northorp you will get a direct answer."

Northorp, formerly a spokesman for the RCMP in B.C., said that as a matter of policy he would never comment. He has retired from the force.

Supt. Lyman Henschel said today: "I am not prepared to comment on that story. I hope to have a meeting with the attorney-general, after which there "Payment' A2

The Vancouver Sun

THURSDAY, JANUARY 14, 1982   VANCOUVER, BRITISH COLUMBIA   ★★★★   **25 CENTS**

Olson given life for 11 murders

By MOIRA FARROW
LARRY STILL
and JACK BROOKS

Child killer Clifford Olson pleaded guilty today to the murders of 11 Lower Mainland youngsters and was sentenced to life in prison with a strong recommendation that he never be paroled.

Mr. Justice Harry McKay said in sentencing the 42-year-old unemployed construction worker:

"I do not have the words to adequately describe the enormity of your crimes and the heartbreak and anguish you have brought to so many people.

"No punishment a civilized country could give you could come close to being adequate."

In sentencing Olson to consecutive terms of life imprisonment on each of the charges, "without eligibility for parole for 25 years," the judge added:

"I would normally not presume to express my views to the National Parole Board which is a separate function. But in this case my considered opinion is that you should never be granted parole for the remainder of your days. It would foolhardy to let you at large."

In a dramatic ending to his trial, Olson stood in the dock of B.C. Supreme Court and 11 times spoke the word "guilty."

The change of plea to guilty on the murders of 10 youngsters aged 9 to 18, expected since Wednesday's surprise adjournment, was made in a court packed with spectators.

In addition Olson pleaded guilty to a last-minute addition to the murder charges against him, that of Sandra Lynn Wolfsteiner, 16, of Langley, who disappeared May 19.

Prosecutor John Hall later outlined the bare essentials of the crown's case, namely that Olson:

● Took Christine Ann Weller to Richmond on Nov. 17, 1980, and there caused her unlawful death. The killing was planned and deliberate. The cause of death was multiple stab wounds.

● Took Daryn Todd Johnsrude to Deroche on April 21, 1981, and there caused his unlawful death. The killing was planned and deliberate. The cause of death was skull fractures.

● Took Ada Anita Court to Agassiz on June 21, 1981, and there caused her unlawful death. The killing was planned and deliberate. The cause of death was strangulation.

● Took Simon Patrick Partington to Richmond on July 2, 1981, and there caused his unlawful death. The killing was planned and deliberate. The cause of death was strangulation.

● Took Raymond Lawrence King to Agassiz on July 23, 1981, and there caused his unlawful death. The killing was planned and deliberate. The cause of death was skull fractures.

● Took Terri Lynn Carson to Agassiz on July 27, 1981, and there caused her unlawful death. The killing was planned and deliberate. The cause of death was strangulation.

● Took Louise M. Chartrand to Whistler on July 30, 1981, and there caused her unlawful death. The killing was planned and deliberate. The cause of death was skull fractures.

● Took Sigrun Charlotte Arnd to Richmond on July 25, 1981, and there caused her unlawful death. The killing was planned and deliberate. The cause of death was skull fractures.

● Took Judy Elizabeth Kozma to Agassiz on July 9, 1981, and there caused her unlawful death. The killing was planned and deliberate. The cause of death was multiple stab wounds.

● Took Colleen Daignault to Surrey on April 16, 1981, and there caused her unlawful death. The killing was planned and deliberate. The cause of death was skull fractures.

Hall later told reporters that there was evidence of sexual assault in some of the cases, but it was impossible to determine in others. He denied reports that there was evidence Olson had tortured any of his victims.

Olson entered the court this morning wearing the same cocky expression he has worn since the case started Monday. But three times, as he pleaded guilty to charges of murdering the 10 children, he took a white handkerchief from the jacket pocket of his grey suit and wiped his eyes.

He was wearing the same grey suit and carrying the same tan briefcase that he has had each day.

He flung one arm over the back of the bench in the prisoner's box and gazed

"No punishment" A2

CLIFFORD ROBERT OLSON ... he said "guilty" 11 times in court today — UPI photo

Killer held in custody four times before final arrest for murder

By RICK OUSTON

Police in B.C. had Clifford Olson in custody four times last year — twice on sexual assault charges — before they finally arrested him for his string of 11 murders.

As well, there is considerable evidence that Olson had committed other sexual attacks during his long criminal career, and was on two occasions charged with serious offences — but again, police failed to identify him as a chronic sexual offender.

Their records showed he had never been convicted.

A Vancouver Sun investigation uncovered the tragic details of six sex crimes involving Olson, starting with two that occurred during the string of 11 murders:

● Jan. 1, 1981: (Christine Weller had disappeared Nov. 19, 1980 and her body was found Christmas Day). Olson picked up a 16-year-old female hitchhiker on Scott Road, Surrey. He drove her to Squamish, where he raped her in a hotel room and sodomized her on the way back.

The girl pressed charges and Olson was arrested at his home Jan. 8, charged with rape, buggery, indecent assault and possession of a gun. He was sent to Oakalla.

Before the case came to trial, it was learned that the girl was a former prostitute. That fact, coupled with her poor memory of the night of the attack, prompted the crown to drop the sex charges.

Olson appeared in Squamish provincial court Aug. 8 on the gun allegation.

Because the sex charges had been dropped, he was released on bail until the trial could resume. He was represented by lawyer Bob Shantz.

● July 7, 1981: Olson enticed a 16-year-old Burnaby girl named Sarah into his car in front of a Burnaby pinball arcade with the promise of a window-washing job which would pay $10 an hour.

He told her he was a real estate man. He drove her to Surrey, offered her some alcohol, which she accepted, and told her to get into the back seat.

He fondled her and tried to remove her jeans; she resisted.

The man who had already murdered at least six children by this time returned Sarah to the arcade.

The owner of the arcade was suspicious of Olson's behavior and notified police. Police interviewed him and gave the information to Crown counsel.

Olson appeared in court July 22, charged with indecent assault. He was ordered to stand trial in November.

There were other arrests, both during and before the murders. They go back to the early 1970s and stretch across the country.

But because there were no convictions, for a variety of reasons, Olson's name did not come to detectives' minds as a man who would be capable of murdering children.

In jailhouse talk, he wasn't on the "skin list."

But his record also includes:

● May 26, 1981: Olson was driving in the Agassiz area, accompanied by a 15-year-old Coquitlam girl who has never been publicly identified.

Police arrested him, after he was involved in an accident, on charges of drunk driving and contributing to juvenile delinquency.

Then they let him go. Olson appeared in Chilliwack provincial court June 22; pleaded not guilty — again represented by Shantz — and a trial date was set for Dec. 11.

● April 27, 1981: Surrey RCMP arrested Olson and charged him with shoplifting at a Surrey hardware store. They took him to the police station, charged him, and let him go.

● February, 1980: A month after

"Olson" A11

Classified 732-2211   Circulation 732-2371
FOUNDED 1886 ● VOL. 96 ● No. 81   88 PAGES

The Sun's special report on mass murderer Clifford Olson wins a National Newspaper Award for the paper.

The following year, Pope John Paul mesmerized thousands of the faithful during a nineteen-hour stay. The pope conducted two masses—at Abbotsford Airport and BC Place—on September 18 and 19, 1984. The airport ceremony attracted an estimated 200,000 worshippers as the organizers prayed for good weather and got it. The crowd was reported to be the largest ever gathered for a single purpose in the province. In his homily at the end of the Abbotsford mass, His Holiness described British Columbia as "a land of splendour without diminishment." (The pontiff also met briefly with twelve winners of a newspaper promotion. *The Sun*, not with the greatest of taste, had conducted a Meet The Pope contest.)

With all this positive evidence of hope, renewal and pluck, the eighties appeared to be shaping up as one decade with a happy face on it. Besides the aforementioned news tidbits, Expo 86 lay over the horizon, as did SkyTrain, a Commonwealth conference and a determined wheelchair athlete named Rick Hansen. Ah, but there be monsters ahead, also. One of them (according to the Opposition and the unions involved) was Premier Bill Bennett. Another was Clifford Robert Olson.

Olson was a mass murderer who killed eleven Lower Mainland youngsters in the early years of the decade. On January 14, 1982, he pleaded guilty in Vancouver to the brutal slayings and received eleven consecutive life sentences. "I do not have the words to adequately describe the enormity of your crimes and the heartbreak and anguish you have brought to so many people," BC Supreme Court Justice Harry McKay told Olson, forty-two. "No punishment a civilized country could give you could come close to being adequate."

The Sun won a National Newspaper Award for its "Olson File" coverage of the case. A team of reporters dug deeply into the life and crimes of Olson well before he came to trial. Their detailed findings were assembled into a special package that awaited only the final disposition of the charges before being printed. Among the facts revealed on January 14 was the sensational disclosure that the provincial government had paid Olson $100,000 to tell police where he had hidden seven of the eleven bodies.

The day William Richards Bennett turned into a political monster was July 7, 1983. That afternoon, the Social Credit leader and his finance minister, Hugh Curtis, delivered a series of body blows that left the legislature, the press, the unions and the public reeling. To begin with, Curtis presented his budget—the first for the government since its re-election May 5. As usual, the press gallery was given Curtis' speech and supporting material early in the morning. (This is the "lockup," at which reporters can digest the financial implications and prepare their stories, but cannot release them until the minister begins his speech after lunch.)

They noted the sales tax would be increased, and that it would now apply to restaurant meals over $7. The civil service would be reduced and its wages remain frozen. The budget deficit for the coming fiscal year would be a record $1.6 billion, despite the restraint and various tax increases. It was a somewhat meatier budget than usual. However, the real substance was contained in the deluge of tough legislation that followed Curtis' speech.

In all, twenty-six bills were dropped in the laps of the MLAs. "Bedlam" was one reporter's description of the House that afternoon. In one sweeping fusillade, Bennett's restraint barrage eliminated the human rights branch and rent controls, dissolved a number of commissions and boards, gutted regional districts and tinkered with pension plans. This ticking package of government proscriptions was ominous enough, but the flashpoint was legislation dealing with public servants.

THE DECADE IN HEADLINES
« 1981 »

THOUSANDS JOIN ANTI-NUKE RALLIES

Vancouver's first Peace March draws an estimated 3,500 people on its route from Kitsilano Beach across the Burrard Bridge to downtown. In later years, the march attracts crowds reaching an estimated 100,000 before petering out in 1995, when organizers call it quits.

The Province, April 25, 1981

HE DIED QUIETLY AS DAWN BROKE

The death from cancer of Terry Fox dominates Page One the following morning. The one-legged BC marathoner had captured the hearts of all Canada with his courage.

The Province, June 28, 1981

2 COLOR

The Province

Vancouver, B.C.
Monday, September 10, 1984
25 cents

(50 cents minimum
outside Lower Mainland)

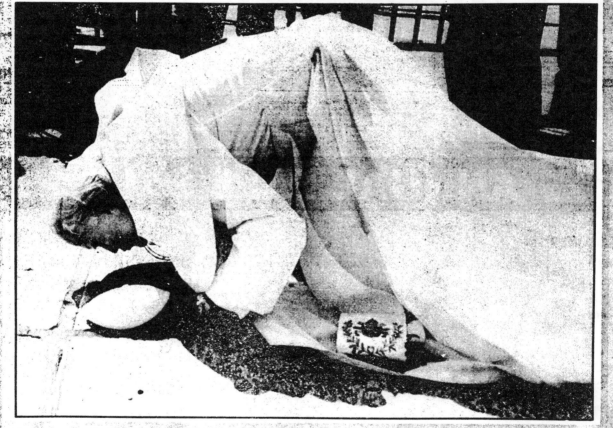

WELCOME!

POPE JOHN PAUL II KNEELS TO KISS THE GROUND UPON HIS ARRIVAL AT QUEBEC CITY YESTERDAY.

B.C.'s teen stowaway still making waves Page 4

Protesters blockade Tranquille airlift Page 5

The Province, *now a tabloid, uses a familiar pose by Pope John Paul in advance of his visit to BC.*

The Public Service Labour Relations Act (Bill 2) and the Public Sector Restraint Act (Bill 3) contained provisions severely restricting collective bargaining and eliminating tenure for civil servants. Another bill provided for wage rollbacks. As the shock wave dissipated, outrage became the dominant emotion in some quarters. The widespread furore had eerie echoes of 1934, when Duff Pattullo's Special Powers Act "made the capital's flesh creep." Like Pattullo, Bennett was employing extreme measures in order to keep the province from going down the toilet.

In about the same amount of time it took to light Bennett's provocative fuse, the BC Government Employees' Union and the BC Federation of Labour rumbled into action. The voices of protest coalesced into the movement called Operation Solidarity. As the summer waxed and waned and debate droned on in the legislature, Operation Solidarity took to the streets. Eventually, the BCGEU would hit the bricks.

The R-word had emerged from the closet on February 18, 1982, when Bennett announced a policy of restraint. Spending would match revenue and public-sector wage increases would be curtailed. A two-year program of strict controls went into effect immediately. The premier knew that the twin burdens of a deepening recession and escalating inflation would be too much for the government to shoulder unless it came to grips with the changing economy. This was at a time when 17-percent pay increases were tolerated and all unions, both public and private, looked forward to slurping up more of the gravy. Throughout the remainder of 1982, there were hospital layoffs, education cuts and hiring freezes.

The long-awaited campaign leading up to the election of May 5, 1983, was one opportunity for Bennett to get the voters onside. So, along with touting such job-friendly projects as BC Place (Canada's first covered stadium), the Coquihalla Highway, a light rapid transit system for the Lower Mainland, Expo 86 and the northeast coal development at Tumbler Ridge, he emphasized restraint and "initiative." It was a tough sell to a largely uncomprehending electorate. Fortunately for the Socreds, the NDP's Dave Barrett promised to borrow millions of dollars for a job-creation scheme. The voters had seen that before, during the 1972-75 NDP reign: the taxpayers' credit being shovelled off the back of a truck. No, thanks. On May 5, Social Credit won thirty-five seats, while the New Democrats dropped to twenty-two.

Which brings us to the summer of Solidarity. On July 23, the coalition of unionists and social democrats lured an estimated 20,000 people (rally organizers claimed 35,000) to an anti-government demonstration outside BC Place. Four days later, 25,000 more congregated in front of the Legislative Buildings to sing, chant, wave placards and listen to more fiery speeches. It was described as the largest demonstration in the capital's history. In an editorial, the *Victoria Times-Colonist* observed that the rally was "an alarm bell," which merited thoughtful response from Bennett. Meanwhile, government workers were occupying the buildings of the Tranquille institution at Kamloops, reacting to a cabinet decision to close the complex and disperse its physically and mentally challenged wards.

Operation Solidarity reached a plateau with a mass shout-in at Vancouver's Empire Stadium on August 10. There were 40,000 present, including a significant number of unionists. As one newspaper noted, books, beer and buses were scarce that day because so many transit, liquor store and library employees were at the stadium instead of working. Art Kube, the BC Federation of Labour president and a key organizer of Solidarity, told the crowd to join in "a common bond of peaceful

THE DECADE IN HEADLINES
« 1982 »

KILLER WAS PAID TO LOCATE BODIES
The paper wins a National Newspaper Award for its "Olson File" revelations about serial killer Clifford Olson, who pleads guilty to 11 murders.

Vancouver Sun, January 14, 1982

ISLANDERS WIN THIRD CUP
New York disposes of the Canucks in four straight games in Vancouver's first Stanley Cup final since 1915. This is the year of "Towel Power," sparked by Canuck coach Roger Neilson's waving of a white towel at a referee.

The Province, May 16, 1982

JEROME LEAVES LASTING LEGACY
Sprinter Harry Jerome, the fastest BC runner since Percy Williams, dies of cancer, aged 42. Jerome once tied the world record in the 100-yard dash, and won various medals at Olympic, Commonwealth and Pan-American games.

Vancouver Sun, December 7, 1982

THE DECADE IN HEADLINES
« 1983 »

ROYAL FEVER BREAKS OUT IN VICTORIA

Queen Elizabeth sails into Victoria's Inner Harbour for yet another visit. She will also return in 1987.

The Province, March 8, 1983

OPENING DAY, AND ALREADY THE STADIUM LOSES MONEY

The official opening of BC Place in Vancouver is greeted by pessimism in *The Province,* which notes that the 60,000-seat showpiece of the Social Credit government is far from sold out for its premiere.

The Province, June 19, 1983

BARRETT DRAGGED FROM THE HOUSE

The removal of the Opposition leader during debate on the government"s restraint measures is the first time in the history of the legislature that an MLA has been forcibly evicted.

Victoria Times-Colonist, October 6, 1983

protest, one that is destined to grow and grow until the government listens to us and acts upon our demands."

As far as Bennett was concerned, the rally was irrelevant and not indicative of public opinion. Just a bunch of sore losers "demonstrating against the results of the last election," he sniffed. Bennett, who happened to be in Toronto that day at a premiers' conference, pointed out that 100,000 people in BC's private sector lost their jobs during the recessionary year of 1982, without any protests. "They didn't have tenure, they had no security, nobody held rallies for them," he said. Bennett showed no signs of wavering when he returned to Victoria.

There wasn't much more Operation Solidarity could do, barring a self-defeating wave of illegal strikes. The BCGEU, still negotiating with the government, would be free to walk out at midnight, October 31, when its contract expired. Until then, sound, fury and TV clips were all the Fed and its coalition had going for it. On September 16, protesters occupied the government's cabinet offices in Vancouver, and on October 15, another impressive march paralyzed parts of downtown for a few hours. Some 50,000 (police estimate) to 65,000 (Solidarity estimate) paraded past the Hotel Vancouver, where the Social Credit party was having its annual convention.

But there were indications the general public wasn't buying the Solidarity option. Meanwhile, Bennett tightened the screws. He ordered round-the-clock sittings in the House so that the major restraint bills could become law before October 31. This legislation by exhaustion (not a new tactic by any means in BC politics) culminated in Opposition leader Barrett being hauled from his chair and dragged out the doors of the legislative chamber on his back. It was 4:35 a.m. on October 6—not exactly a defining moment for democracy.

Barrett's ejection by the acting Speaker, John Parks, kept the Opposition leader out of the House until the spring session of 1984. More immediately, the NDP's desperate delaying tactics (mostly frivolous amendments) failed to keep Bill 3 from grinding its inexorable way into law. Finally, after more than twenty hours of unseemly wrangling, continual ringing of the division bells (calling the members to vote) and several invocations of closure (a rarely used measure to shut off debate), Bill 3 passed its last major hurdle on October 12, 1983.

Bill 3 was the Public Sector Restraint Act, which gave the government wideranging powers to arbitrarily dismiss employees without regard to seniority. Nine days later, Bennett adjourned the legislature for a "cooling-off period" without further action on Bill 2, the other contentious piece of legislation gutting the BCGEU contract. Then everybody stood around and waited for the government employees to go on strike.

Which they did, one minute past midnight on November 1. Within a matter of days, the 35,000 BCGEU members were joined by BC Teachers Federation pickets and the Canadian Union of Public Employees. In no time at all, 80,000 workers had walked out in the public sector, and Operation Solidarity started muttering about a general strike.

All this talk of shutting down BC—both publicly and privately—got the attention of Jack Munro, who as president of the International Woodworkers of America and vice-president of the BC Federation of Labour was one of the most powerful union bosses in the province. Munro, spewing profanity from every pore, was ticked off at the prospect of his IWA hitting the picket lines to fight someone else's battle over the social consequences of restraint. He decided to take a direct part in the confrontation between Bennett and Solidarity, which led to the famous (or infamous, depending on your spin) Kelowna Accord.

On Sunday evening, November 13, three men ended up in the living room of Bill Bennett's home in Kelowna—the premier, Munro and Norman Spector, the government's chief negotiator. That afternoon, Spector had reached a tentative deal with the BCGEU. Now the three of them had to put Operation Solidarity to rest. After four hours, Bennett and Munro emerged to announce that the crisis was over. The 80,000 workers were told by their unions to return to work. Newspaper analysts picking through the entrails of the accord decided that both sides won something. Bennett agreed to scrap Bill 2 and exempt the BCGEU from some of Bill 3's provisions. But the remainder of the July legislative package remained virtually in place. (Some of these bills, such as the Human Rights and Rentalsman acts, were deferred until the spring session in 1984.)

The Sun put it best in an editorial November 14: "Each side also has something to think about. The government gets a second chance at 'fairness' and a program that is supposed to be 'lean' without being 'mean.' The labour movement must be aware of the risks of repeating a threat to confound the democratic process through widespread political strikes."

In the ensuing weeks, some of the groups making up Solidarity wondered exactly what they had gained from the long months of marching and shouting. Many called the settlement a sellout and ostracized Munro for not wringing more concrete concessions out of Bennett. But Solidarity had long since started fraying, and Munro and others knew the strikes had shifted public opinion toward the government's side. "It wasn't a sellout," Munro wrote later in his book, *Union Jack.* "By this time there was nothing to sell out. The whole thing was down the tube."

Trade union schisms aside, calm was more or less restored. Barrett, who had been virtually shut out of any meaningful part in the restraint dialogue, quit as both MLA and NDP leader and became a radio talk-show host (a not uncommon career move for former politicians; they must love to yap, no matter the medium). He was replaced by a nonentity named Bob Skelly, who fought and lost one election, then faded from sight.

Because of his status as a loser, Dave Barrett's departure from the legislative scene in 1984 was not unexpected. What the found-ins who prowled Victoria's political corridors didn't count on, however, was Bill Bennett's own resignation two years later. Bennett, his Tough Guy image only slightly leavened by the compromises of the Kelowna Accord, was a winner. He had never lost an election, and his control over the party, the House and the voters' perceptions appeared to have survived the assault by Operation Solidarity. That he had decided to step down even as Expo 86 and the other big-ticket items on his agenda were paying off was a shock even to party insiders.

In the words of *Province* reporter Glen Schaefer in a retrospective story on the fair, "Expo 86 wrapped itself around the north shore of False Creek like a brightly coloured scarf adorning Vancouver's neck." It ran for five months during that benign summer and lured a resounding 22,111,118 people through the gates—far above the rosiest of projections. Getting to opening day on May 2, however, was something of a cliff-hanger.

Expo 86 was announced by Bennett (as Transpo 86) in 1980, after the busy, busy, busy Grace McCarthy had planted the seed in 1978. At lunch in London with diplomat Patrick Reid, who was vice-president of the International Bureau of Ex-

THE DECADE IN HEADLINES
« 1984 »

ZHAO LASHES U.S., SOVIETS
Chinese Premier Zhao Ziyang goes on TV in Vancouver to blame the two superpowers for escalating the arms race. Zhao has paused in BC on the way home from a 17-day North American tour.
The Province, January 23, 1984

JAILED COUPLE TRADED PUNK ROCK FOR TERROR
Juliet Belmas is sentenced to 20 years in prison, and her boyfriend, Gerry Hannah, to 10 years, for their involvement in the "Squamish Five" reign of anarchy and terrorism in BC and Ontario. *The Sun,* which was shut down by a labour dispute when the pair was sentenced in BC Supreme Court at New Westminster, catches up to the story on May 24.
Vancouver Sun, May 18, 1984

AIN'T WE GOT FUNG!
Vancouver's Lori Fung wins an unexpected gold medal in rhythmic gymnastics at the Los Angeles Olympics. The men's eight-oared shell, predominantly crewed by BC rowers, also wins a gold in a close race with the Americans.
The Province, August 11, 1984

THRILLER UNDER THE DOME
Entertainer Michael Jackson's concerts at BC Place are described in *The Province* as the biggest rock event in BC history. More than 100,000 tickets are sold for Jackson's three weekend shows.
The Province, November 16–18, 1984

THE DECADE IN HEADLINES
« 1985 »

FISHERMEN FUMING

In an eight-paragraph story on an inside page, *The Province* condenses the controversial and far-reaching Pacific Salmon Treaty into a complaint by sports fishermen that the signing of the pact by Canada and the US ruined their day.

The Province, January 28, 1985

VANCOUVER KEY POINT IN AIR CRASH

The BC Sikh connection is quickly established in the wake of the Air-India disaster over the Atlantic. The death toll of 329 is attributed to a terrorist bomb.

Vancouver Sun, June 23, 1985

positions, she floated the proposition that Vancouver needed a world-class fair to help celebrate its centenary. So be it. An undeveloped strip of land along False Creek was acquired from Canadian Pacific Ltd. for $60 million and construction began under the direction of super-rich, super-efficient industrialist Jimmy Pattison.

So did the controversy. After finally persuading Ottawa to build a convention and cruise-ship centre as its contribution, Bennett took on Big Labour. The construction unions had demanded that all nonunion contractors be banned from the site. Nope, said the premier; the government's policy was for union and nonunion workers to toil side by side. The unions threatened to shut the site down, spurring Bennett into an overhaul of the provincial labour code in May of 1984. Secondary picketing was made illegal, along with other union sins. Expo was declared a "special economic development project," making it exempt from the usual strictures attached to union contracts (and stifling protests and demonstrations).

While Expo was being built, so was the Coquihalla Highway. In fact, they were a twosome, because Bennett dearly wished that the freeway between Hope and Merritt be in place so it could become one of the jewels of Expo's transportation theme. When he realized this first stage of the new link with the Interior was far behind schedule, Bennett ordered accelerated construction. Estimates of the extra expense of overtime and related costs ran from $40 million to $160 million. A 1987 inquiry into the fast-tracking accepted the $40 million figure, while noting that haphazard Socred bookkeeping muddled things nicely. Two weeks after Expo's opening, the extra millions were buried deep behind the premier's smile as he rode triumphantly along the virgin stretch of blacktop in an open convertible.

To help meet the construction cost, Bennett also announced that users would pay a toll—the first in BC for more than twenty years. The new highway had a lot of collecting to do before BC would break even: The Hope-Merritt section bottomed out at $414,718,454, while the later extensions to Kamloops and Peachland added almost $500 million more.

Another transportation link that cost millions of dollars ($854 million plus interest for the first phase, to be more or less exact) was SkyTrain. This rapid transit line starts as a subway in Vancouver's downtown core, then runs along an elevated corridor all the way to the corner of the King George and Fraser highways in Surrey. The initial stage, through Burnaby to downtown New Westminster, accepted its first paying customers January 3, 1986. Despite critics and opposition politicians who claimed SkyTrain was doomed because of bad design, wrong technology and prohibitive expense, the computer-operated system was an instant hit. As far as people living within reasonable distance of a SkyTrain station are concerned, every dollar spent on it is golden. Instead of stewing in traffic (and ingesting sundry pollutants), riders are whisked from, say, New Westminster to downtown theatres, shopping or their jobs in less than half an hour.

SkyTrain has also generated billions of dollars in development. The showpiece is Metrotown in Burnaby, which opened its first phase September 25, 1986. Once a dispirited stretch of Kingsway, the Metrotown shopping district that has mushroomed out from the SkyTrain station is a growing community of malls, services and commercial and residential towers. New Westminster's once-neglected riverfront was transformed into a vibrant collection of high- and low-rise condominiums. Developers elbowed each other out of the way in order to build more housing near SkyTrain's Vancouver stations. The four Surrey stops, opened in stages in the nineties, were catalysts for several more major commercial undertakings.

Shiny new blacktop and a shiny new transit link both went well with Expo, which debuted in the rain May 2, 1986, but glittered with promise and excitement. Prince Charles and Diana, Princess of Wales, opened the Canadian pavilion at Canada Place on the harbour while the paying customers thronged to the False Creek grounds. Despite the weather (which improved dramatically within days), the labour tension surrounding the construction and some gloomy predictions that hardly anybody would come, opening day was a solid success. Here's how *The Sun* put it:

"It had a prince and a princess, a prime minister and three premiers. It had head-spinning rides, fireworks and traffic jams. It had umbrellas, aerobatic jet planes, marching bands, magicians and 107,000 clicks on the turnstiles. It even had a 60,000-strong standing ovation for chairman Jim Pattison at BC Place Stadium. Expo had it all on opening day."

Boosterism and glowing coverage aside, Expo was a signal event in Vancouver's history. Overnight visitors to BC that year spent $5.5 billion. Since then, billions more have been invested in Vancouver by Expo tourists who liked what they saw and returned to spend some more of their money. Grace McCarthy, who wanted so badly back in 1978 to have a "world-class" label affixed to Vancouver, got her wish. The city is now among the upper tier of desirable destinations on the globe. It's a prime cruise-ship port. Investment, especially by Asians, has transformed downtown. The Expo land, sold to Hong Kong developer Li Ka-shing in 1988 for $320 million, was designated Concord Pacific Place, a still-building complex that will eventually boast 12.5 million square feet of residential, office and retail space and be home to 15,000 people.

The city's attitude has changed, too. Despite the snide "left coast" slurs of Eastern columnists, Vancouver's laid-back attitude has given way to a new awareness of the future and its place in history. Overpriced designer coffee houses, traffic gridlock and the uptight manifestations of corporate culture are the dubious signs of the big time, replacing the peace marches, pot smoking, Robsonstrasse ambience and eccentric personalities of the past.

Barely a week after his triumphant joyride along the Coquihalla, Bill Bennett announced he was stepping down as premier and MLA. "I'm retiring from public life" was his simple statement to the press. Always an aloof, inward man to those who didn't know him, the premier had little more to say. Some insist Bennett was pushed, or that he realized the party couldn't win another election while he was at the helm. Perhaps. More simply, it was just time for a change. As it was, his departure brought some predictable responses. The reaction from union leaders could be summed up in three words: "It's about time."

Bennett resigned August 6, 1986. The same day, Wilhelmus Nicholaas Theodore Maria Vander Zalm, more popularly known as Bill, took over as leader of the Social Credit party and (unelected) premier. Bill Vander Zalm was born in Noordwykerhout, Holland, May 29, 1934. His parents were in the bulb-growing business and young Bill got into flowers himself after the family emigrated to BC in 1947. He first dangled his feet into politics as a Surrey alderman and mayor.

Originally a Liberal, Vander Zalm switched to Social Credit in May of 1974. Elected an MLA in 1975, he became a cabinet minister under Bennett, but took a "sabbatical" in 1983 by not seeking re-election. While the heavy hand of restraint had much of the province grumbling, Vander Zalm wrote gardening columns for *The Sun* and started development of a Richmond theme park called Fantasy Gar-

THE DECADE IN HEADLINES
« 1986 »

SKYTRAIN HAS RIDERS SMILING
The opening of the rapid transit line between downtown Vancouver and New Westminster is an instant hit.

The Province, January 3, 1986

TRUE GRIT CRAFTED OUR CITY
On Vancouver's 100th birthday, *The Province* pays tribute to those who built the city. Civic celebrations include a giant cake, a 100-gun salute, a children's parade and a rock concert in Stanley Park.

The Province, April 6, 1986

CAVALCADE OPENS TOLL HIGHWAY
Opening of the Coquihalla link to the Okanagan gets inside treatment from *The Sun* the day after Premier Bill Bennett opens the new route. Because of deadline restrictions, the "evening" paper has only a sketchy story in one May 16 edition.

Vancouver Sun, May 16, 1986

BENNETT'S SHOCK: OUT BY SUMMER
Premier Bill Bennett surprises most of the province by announcing he is stepping down.

Times-Colonist, May 22, 1986

THEY'VE DONE IT ONCE AGAIN! SOCREDS WIN 49 TO NDP'S 20
Under a headline hinting at its surprise, the paper attributes Social Credit's re-election to the charisma of new Premier Bill Vander Zalm and the benefits of redistribution.

Times-Colonist, October 22, 1986

HONGKONG BANK WINS THE BATTLE FOR BANK OF B.C.
The Vancouver tabloid breaks the news that the failed financial institution has been sold to the Hongkong Bank of Canada. The provincial bank was a proud achievement of Premier W.A.C. Bennett in 1966.

The Province, November 26, 1986

THE DECADE IN HEADLINES
« 1987 »

HI RICK!

Wheelchair athlete Rick Hansen trundles home to a hero's welcome in Vancouver after a 26-month, globe-girdling odyssey to raise money for spinal cord research.

The Province, May 22, 1987

LEADERS TIGHTEN SANCTIONS SCREW WITHOUT BRITAIN

A divisive Commonwealth conference in Vancouver votes to intensify economic sanctions against South Africa. The six-day meeting of 1,000 delegates was brightened by the fleeting presence of the Queen.

Vancouver Sun, October 16, 1987

NOSEDIVE

With a succinct Page One banner and an inside spread, the paper details the October stock market crash. In percentage terms of stock values lost — 22.6 — it was the worst drop in history.

The Province, October 19, 1987

den World. In time, Fantasy Gardens would become a favourite journalistic synonym for the Vander Zalm government—and ultimately lead to his downfall.

In August of 1986, there was little fantasy surrounding the new administration. Upon becoming premier, Vander Zalm allowed that the job was "a piece of cake," but he still had some tough decisions to make. One of the biggest was the timing of an election. The Zalm, realizing that his new regime must be approved by the voters, chose October 22. That this was only nine days after the close of a wildly successful Expo on October 13 couldn't hurt. Besides the anticipated euphoria of a post-Expo electorate, the Socreds had a couple of other things going for them: Redistribution, which added twelve seats to the House (most of them in staunch Social Credit country), and Bob Skelly, the leader of the NDP. In contrast to a perpetually smiling, confident, quotable Bill Vander Zalm, Skelly came across as a nervous, bumbling amateur. It was, literally, no contest. The Socreds won forty-seven of sixty-nine seats.

Behind Vander Zalm's 1,000-watt teeth lay the soul of a relentless salesman whose deep religious background coloured his political thoughts. Among the moral issues he cared deeply about were AIDS and abortion. But the voters didn't really need any preaching from a politician. Leadership was preferred over sermons. The province was cautiously feeling its way out of the recession and wanted strong direction from its government. What it got was another attack on organized labour and the Peter Toigo affair.

The budget in the spring of 1987 raised some taxes, but modified a number of the provisions of Bennett's restraint package. Then the premier decided to tidy up BC's labour code. A new bill, the Industrial Relations Reform Act, swept away the Labour Relations Board, replacing it with an Industrial Relations Council and a new administrative framework. Although the new act was more complex and radical than onerous, Big Labour puffed itself up and shut down the province, including its major newspapers, June 1 with a twenty-four-hour general strike (and caused a dilemma for unionized reporters, who couldn't cover this big story if they joined the 300,000 strikers. Some walked out, some didn't). Another act challenged the control of the BC Teachers Federation over education, so that militant organization went into a snit and organized its own one-day walkout. In deference to the uproar, some amendments were included before the bills passed, and a few of the controversial sections were withheld from proclamation (which meant they could become law in the future as the cabinet saw fit).

Businessman Peter Toigo was an old friend and supporter of the premier. When the Expo parcel went on the market, he wanted a piece of the action. This led to some curious manipulations in Vander Zalm's office before the land was sold to Li Ka-shing in 1988. Allegations of impropriety from within Vander Zalm's own cabinet helped fuel a secret RCMP investigation into his relationship with Toigo concerning Fantasy Gardens. Although the Mounties eventually concluded there was no evidence of a financial benefit conferred on the premier by his friend, the episode provoked strong reactions in Vander Zalm's caucus.

Attorney-general Brian Smith and Grace McCarthy, who was economic development minister, both resigned. Much of their disillusionment had to do with David Poole, Vander Zalm's arrogant principal secretary. Many people both in government and out felt Poole meddled far too much in matters that were none of his business. Finally, Poole also quit (carting away a sweetheart severance package that caused another rumpus). Despite winning a vote of confidence at a party convention in Penticton that October, Premier Vander Zalm limped through the final year of the decade at the helm of a dispirited and divided party. Everyone knew an election had to be called by 1991, and there were more than a few who feared it.

Two international events also claimed their share of headlines in the latter half of the eighties. On June 23, 1985, a bomb exploded in the cargo compartment of an Air-India jet off the coast of Ireland. All 329 aboard the flight from Toronto and Montreal to Bombay and New Delhi died. The same day, luggage being transferred from a CP Air flight from Vancouver to another Air-India jet exploded at Tokyo's Narita airport. Two baggage handlers were killed. It was later determined that the Air-India bomb had been checked aboard a CPA flight originating in Vancouver, then transferred to the Bombay aircraft in Toronto.

Most of the Canadians killed off Ireland were of Indian descent, and the New Delhi government laid the blame for the mass murders on Sikh terrorists. Inderjit Singh Reyat, a former resident of Duncan on Vancouver Island, was later convicted of manslaughter in the Japan incident at a trial in Vancouver. No one has yet been convicted in the primary Air-India case.

Closer to home, a tanker called the *Exxon Valdez* ran on to Bligh Reef in Alaska's Prince William Sound on March 24, 1989. Approximately 37,000 metric tonnes of North Slope crude oil fouled 1,750 kilometres of coastline. Thousands of birds and mammals were killed. The frantic cleanup efforts cost $2.5 billion.

The spill and the negligence that caused it sent a sharp tremor of apprehension through BC's environmental and political community. It could happen here, was the universal cry in the press. (Juan de Fuca Strait has evolved into the busiest waterway in North America; in the mid-nineties, there were 700 tanker trips through the Strait each year.) Premier Vander Zalm flew to Alaska, as did reporters for BC newspapers. While the premier and state officials conferred about a regional environmental task force, the papers ran stories about a drunken tanker captain.

The Province, in an editorial, observed that "villains abound" in the *Exxon Valdez* tragedy and said the moral was that "governments cannot rely on the commercial interests to assess and minimize risks, prevent accidents and take sufficient responsibility for cleanups." A decade after the spill, controversy surrounded various claims that the Sound had recovered. According to some experts, the shoreline may look clean and oil-free, but the flora and fauna will never be the same.

Cross-border dickering about the future of two major resources also had considerable impact on British Columbians in the eighties. Fish and wood are two of the province's most job-intensive and revenue-generating products. During this decade, they came under heavy pressure from the United States.

The Pacific Salmon Treaty, signed by Canada and the US January 28, 1985, provided for an equitable division of the total allowable catch and set down conservation measures. It was supposed to be a lasting deal, but attempts to keep the treaty alive foundered as fishermen from Washington and Oregon lobbied for a greater share of the catch and began ignoring any pretenses of conservation. As the decade ended, tension between the competing BC and American fleets remained high. The situation worsened in the nineties, with Canada catching fewer fish and the US significantly more.

Another source of unrelenting pressure is softwood lumber. The chronic historical protectionism of America is exemplified by the high-profile whinging of special-interest lobbyists, and US politicians tremble at their approach. There are many targets, and one of them is BC's forest production. Canadian lumber can

THE DECADE IN HEADLINES
« 1988 »

LITTLE FANFARE AS PM, REAGAN SIGN TRADE PACT

Canada's Brian Mulroney and the US president sign the Free Trade Agreement between the two countries. *The Sun* accurately predicts that the deal will split the nation.

Vancouver Sun, January 2, 1988

THE DECADE IN HEADLINES
« 1989 »

LONGEST RAILWAY TUNNEL IN NORTH AMERICA OPENS

CP Rail's Mt. Macdonald tunnel in the Selkirk Range realigns the main line and reduces the grade in the Rogers Pass area. At 14.6 kilometres, the tunnel is billed as the longest on the continent.

Vancouver Sun, May 4, 1989

CASE NOT CLOSED

Former premier Bill Bennett is cleared of insider trading charges in a Vancouver court. Bennett, his brother Russell and lumber baron Herb Doman had been charged after the Bennetts made $2.1 million by selling Doman company shares an hour before trading was halted. As the headline suggests, the principals are to face more charges in the nineties.

The Province, May 12, 1989

reach US markets at a much lower price than American lumber, so this has provoked many attempts at intervention.

In the eighties, the lobbyists claimed BC's stumpage system of pricing and allocating its timber harvest was an unfair subsidy, and demanded a duty on our softwood exports. Canada, which had fought and won a similar battle in 1983, backed down in 1986. In the midst of countervail proceedings at the US Commerce Department, Washington and Ottawa reached a memorandum of understanding just before midnight December 30, 1986. Under the agreement, Canada would collect an export charge of 15 percent on lumber heading south, which would be replaced by increases in provincial royalties and stumpage charges. This deal got the beast off our backs for a few years. Like the salmon issue, however, the softwood lumber dispute would intensify in the nineties.

In 1988, Tory Prime Minister Brian Mulroney fought and won a federal election on the issue of free trade with the US (an interesting departure from the mood of seventy-seven years earlier, when "no truck or trade with the Yankees" won an election for the Conservatives). The FTA between the two countries was signed January 2, 1988. As far as the forest sector was concerned, this agreement was supposed to provide a dispute-settlement mechanism to reduce the threat of American countervailing action. Because US trade-remedy practices are constantly influenced by political pressures, this so-called "mechanism" would grind very slowly in subsequent years.

Depending on whose plate you shared, the FTA would either boost employment in BC by thousands of jobs, or shred it, open up the US market, or erode our cultural integrity and social programs, and so on. True, tariffs have slowly fallen over the several years since the agreement was signed, but BC's consumers are still "protected" from the much lower dairy and poultry prices across the line in Washington state. (One of the expected victims of free trade was the BC wine industry. Instead of folding under the onslaught of cheaper US imports, however, Okanagan vineyards have hung on and even begun to flourish. Statistics released in the mid-nineties showed production of grapes had almost doubled to more than 6,000 tonnes, sales of wine had more than doubled to almost 1.7 million litres, and the quality of the product is gaining international respect.) As one analysis suggests, the FTA is more a "managed" trade deal than a free one. Also, the later emergence of the North American Free Trade Agreement, which includes Mexico, has clouded any future impact of the original accord.

But enough of politics, monsters, disasters and international wrangling. It's time for another hero. On May 22, 1987, the Man in Motion, Rick Hansen, propelled his wheelchair into Vancouver's Oakridge Shopping Centre to complete a 24,901.55-mile odyssey around the world. It began more than two years earlier on March 21, 1985, when Hansen, who was rendered paraplegic in a 1973 truck crash, wheeled himself away from that same mall. The boy from Williams Lake, only fifteen years old when he lost the use of his legs, was twenty-seven and a world-class athlete that March day. His Man in Motion tour was partly inspired by the courage of Terry Fox and the Marathon of Hope. Rick's goal was to raise funds for spinal-cord research and other rehabilitation programs.

British Columbia and the world embraced Rick and his lean, mean wheelchair. He met Pope John Paul, wheeled across Red Square in Moscow and along the Great Wall of China as thousands responded to his message of hope and inspiration. The day after he returned to Oakridge, 50,000 people honoured Hansen at

BC Place. "He inherited the mantle of those other British Columbians, Terry Fox and Steve Fonyo, and graced it with a spirit that enlarges all our lives, as their one-legged runs across Canada did before him," wrote a *Province* editorialist. Hansen's global appeal has raised millions of dollars for research.

THE NINETIES:
OF LIES
AND MEN

« 1990 – 1997 »

THE DECADE IN HEADLINES
« 1991 »

NDP SWEEPS OUT SOCREDS

Michael Harcourt's socialists brush aside Premier Rita Johnston's Socreds in an election that sees the Liberal party become the official Opposition.

Times-Colonist, October 17, 1991

"Lying bastards!"

Deep in the heart of Burnaby-Edmonds, which is an NDP riding, a coffee drinker at McDonald's offers his opinion of the current provincial government. It is October, 1996, and the full duplicity of Premier Glen Clark and his New Democrats has become public knowledge. Most every weekday, the elderly gentleman quoted above and his cronies gather to sip their brew and discuss current affairs. They don't think much of politicians—especially the ones in power in British Columbia for most of the nineties.

Scandals, resignations, malfeasance and incompetence dominated the headlines. Before the decade was half over, the province had been governed by four separate premiers—the most in such a short span since the chaotic years at the beginning of the century. Two of the premiers were forced to step down because their administrations were tainted by wrongdoing. Another was accused of "relentlessly lying" about the state of BC's finances before, during and after an election.

The first premier to walk the plank was Bill Vander Zalm. When we last encountered The Zalm and his riven, scandal-prone Social Credit caucus in the eighties, they were nervously contemplating an election that they had scant chance of winning. In 1991, any lingering hopes were dashed by Vander Zalm's involvement in a real-estate deal. The premier's use of his public office to expedite the sale in 1990 of Fantasy Gardens World Inc., a family business, broke several conflict-of-interest guidelines laid down by Vander Zalm himself.

During the night of August 3-4, Bill and wife Lillian had reached a deal with Taiwanese billionare Tan Yu in a suite at Vancouver's Westin Bayshore Hotel. Press coverage of Vander Zalm's final hours left the reader with one compelling image: The premier of British Columbia stuffing an envelope containing $20,000 in US hundred-dollar bills into the pocket of his jacket after Yu had agreed to buy.

This revelation was contained in a report by conflict-of-interest commissioner Ted Hughes. He was asked by Vander Zalm to examine the $16-million sale after persistent newspaper stories cast doubt on the premier's insistence that it was strictly a private matter. Hughes' report was devastating. Released publicly April 2, 1991, it indicated that Vander Zalm's conduct was evasive, contradictory and devoid of certain ethical considerations.

WEDNESDAY **Times** 🏛️ **Colonist**

April 3, 1991 ★   Victoria, British Columbia, 133rd year, No. 111   50 cents. Carrier home delivery: $2.70 per week.

ZALM QUITS AFTER REPORT, JOHNSTON NAMED PREMIER

▪ VANDER ZALM said he had anticipated a more favora...l report.

John McKay photo

> 'The premier's problem stems not just from his inability to draw a line between his private and public life, but in his apparently sincere belief that no conflict existed so long as the public wasn't aware of what was going on.
>
> '... Further, the premier stated that charges of conflict arose only when the media became aware and publicized what was going on.
>
> 'With due respect to the premier, it was what went on that was wrong — not the media's discovering and publicizing of those events.'
> — The Honorable E.N. Hughes, QC

Swearing-in caps day of upheaval

By Les Leyne/ Legislature staff

Bill Vander Zalm resigned as premier Tuesday amid searing condemnation of his personal business dealings by acting conflict of interest commissioner Ted Hughes.

Four hours after stepping down in disgrace at 2:20 p.m. following public release of Hughes's report on the sale of Fantasy Garden World Inc., Vander Zalm was replaced by deputy premier Rita Johnston, sworn in at Government House as B.C.'s 29th premier.

Cabinet ministers and key bureaucrats applauded as Lt.-Gov. David Lam administered the oaths of office to Canada's first woman premier in a hurriedly arranged ceremony.

The event capped a day of unprecedented upheaval in B.C. politics with highlights including:

● Statements in the 119-page Hughes report that Vander Zalm breached several of his own guidelines by mixing personal business with official duties.

● Serious questioning in the report of Vander Zalm's testimony at the review that he as premier requested.

● Vander Zalm's resignation — for the second time in five days — three hours after reading the full report, this time, effective immediately.

● A quick huddle by the Social Credit caucus, which was bitterly preparing to oust Vander Zalm in a showdown after the Hughes report, to vote Johnston in as a replacement.

● The Socred party board met Tuesday night to set a date and location for a leadership convention

▪ HARCOURT

— with Johnston not ruled out of the running. With no decision by 9 p.m., the board adjourned its deliberations until today.

The Hughes report, delivered to the premier and Opposition Leader Mike Harcourt about 11 a.m., concluded that Vander Zalm was the main negotiator for the sale of Fantasy Gardens in Richmond to Taiwanese billionaire Tan Yu.

He said Vander Zalm breached three of his first four guidelines against conflicts of interest.

☐ Related stories/A6, A7, A8

"The premier's problem stems not just from his inability to draw a line between his private and public life, but in his apparently sincere belief that no conflict existed so long as the public wasn't aware of what was going on."

Hughes also rejected Vander

Zalm's long-standing complaints that the media were unfairly keeping up coverage of the Fantasy Gardens sale.

"With due respect to the premier, it was what went on that was wrong, not the media's discovering and publicizing of those events."

Hughes also rapped Vander Zalm's testimony at two separate interviews he had with the conflict of interest commissioner.

Vander Zalm did not mention the $20,000 he got from Tan Yu during

detailed questioning by Hughes investigators. When he did, Hughes said his explanation of events "borders on the incredible."

In his brief resignation speech, Vander Zalm expressed disappointment with the report's findings which he said he was "encouraged" to believe would be "favorable" on the basis of submissions made by his lawyers to Hughes.

Vander Zalm did not comment on

ZALM QUITS A2

▪ NEW PREMIER Rita Johnston says report was truly damning.

Alex Barta photo

Last bit of fantasy: He knew days ago

It ended, not inappropriately, in a flight of fantasy.

Having had the opportunity to read the Hughes report, a grim-faced Premier Vander Zalm said, "I must now reconsider my decision of last Friday to remain as premier until a successor is chosen."

And, voice raspy with strain: "Yesterday, in meetings with my lawyers, I was encouraged by the strength of their submissions to Mr. Hughes and believed the findings would be favorable."

If the words were designed to elicit sympathy from a massed press corps, they failed.

The report ...s ...hered to watch the final act of a ...perate man had also read the Hughes report, and obviously with far greater grasp and memory than Premier Vander Zalm.

It stated in the final paragraph of the introductory chapter: "Following the final interviews, I prepared tentative findings of fact. By agreement, they were communicated to counsel for the Premier and Mrs. Vander Zalm. The majority were

JIM HUME Talk politics

transmitted on Wednesday evening, March 27, 1991, with the remainder being transmitted late the following afternoon..."

The premier's lawyers, then, had been in possession of Hughes' findings for two days before the premier announced his intention to call for a leadership convention but to continue in power until that event could be staged.

And they had been in possession of the tentative findings of fact for five days before yesterday. It is difficult to believe that they had failed to

JIM HUME A2

Premier abused office 'three different ways'

By Bruce Skeaff
Legislature staff

Premier Vander Zalm abused his office with conflict of interest three different ways as he played the "primary and dominant role" in the Fantasy Gardens sale in September, former deputy attorney general Ted Hughes revealed in a damning report Tuesday.

Vander Zalm believed he was doing nothing wrong so long as no one found out, Hughes said.

"Perhaps more fundamentally, the premier's problem stems not just from his inability to draw a line between his private and public life, but in his apparently sincere belief that no conflict existed, so long as the public wasn't aware of what was going on," Hughes wrote.

"Further, the premier stated that charges of conflict arose only when

the media became aware and publicized what was going on.

"... It was what went on that was wrong, not the media's discovering and publicizing of those events," wrote Hughes, who found Vander Zalm "less than forthcoming" with him during examination under oath.

Commissioned by Vander Zalm Feb. 14, supposedly to prove he was never in conflict of interest, Hughes's report did exactly the opposite, painting a picture of a man whose behavior was seriously out of line for the province's highest public office.

Hughes found:

● Vander Zalm did not ensure his ability to exercise his duties and responsibilities objectively was unaffected, or even apparently unaffected, either by his own or familial financial interests.

● Vander Zalm was involved in the

day-to-day activities of Fantasy Gardens in a way conflicting with his public duties.

● Vander Zalm used information obtained as premier, which was unavailable to the general public, for personal gain.

Vander Zalm committed the first two breaches of the 1987 conflict guidelines he wrote himself "by providing the proposed purchasers of Fantasy Gardens World prior to the completion of the sale of the property with special privileges and the 'red carpet' treatment which appeared, at least, to be affected by his and his family's financial interests."

He also breached the guidelines in accepting $20,000 in cash from Tan Yu in conjunction with the sale.

And he committed the third breach when he, acting as premier, phoned William Hopper, chief executive offi-

▪ HUGHES: found breaches

cer of Petro-Canada, to discuss selling to Tan Yu the Petro-Can land adjacent to Fantasy Gardens.

Hughes found Vander Zalm wrote Elwood Veitch, international business minister, on April 5, 1990, asking him to meet with his Vancouver real estate agent, Faye Leung, to discuss

DAMNING REPORT A2

WEATHER
Rain, windy/A2

SERVICE CALLS

Circulation and delivery
7:00 a.m.-5:30 p.m. Mon.-Fri.
7:00 a.m.-4:00 p.m. Sat.
382-2255

Classified advertising
8:00 a.m.-5:30 p.m. Mon.-Fri.
8:00 a.m.-4:00 p.m. Sat.
386-2121

General inquiries
8:00 a.m.-5:00 p.m. Mon.-Fri.
380-5211

Weekends, holidays and weekdays after 5:00 p.m. only.
(Connects all phones after 5:00 p.m. and on weekends.)
News desk   **380-5335**
Sports desk   **380-5344**

GST shockwaves

☐ Major banks cut their prime rate to 10.75% amid devastating economic news that the GST sent shockwaves through the economy in January. Story/C11

Chiefs file title appeal

The Canadian Press

VANCOUVER — The hereditary chiefs of the Gitksan-Wet'suwet'en said Tuesday they have filed their appeal of B.C. Chief Justice Allan McEachern's controversial March 8 land claims decision.

The chiefs' lawyers filed papers in the B.C. Court of Appeal on Tuesday but whether the case would be sent directly to the Supreme Court of Canada was not yet kno~n.

In their lawsuit, t.e chiefs asked for a declaration from the courts that they still hold aboriginal title to their 57,000-square-kilometre traditional territories in northwest British Columbia.

McEachern found their title — and all aboriginal land rights in the province — had been extinguished before the westernmost province entered Confederation in 1871.

Federal Justice Minister Kim Campbell has not ruled out a direct referral of the case to Canada's highest court.

Afghans fire Scuds at rebel-held city

Reuter

ISLAMABAD — Afghan government forces retaliated for the humiliating loss to rebels of the garrison city of Khost by launching four Scud missiles at the city, killing at least 10 people, news sources said Tuesday.

More than 30 people were wounded in the attack Monday night, including some government soldiers and militiamen captured in Khost, 25 kilometres from the Pakistan border.

It was the first military response by the Soviet-supported government in Kabul since heavy bombing Sunday night, rebel information minister Najibullah Lafraie said in Peshawar, a Pakistani border city.

Khost, under siege for most of the 12-year civil war between western-backed mujahedeen guerrillas and the Moscow-backed Kabul government, capitulated to rebels Sunday, the rebel sources said.

Pakistan appealed to the United

Nations on Tuesday to restrain Kabul from firing Scud missiles and to stop aerial bombing of Khost.

The mujahedeen took Khost after a 16-hour assault launched Sunday from four sides of the town, nestled in the Hindu Kush mountains, Afghanistan's ambassador to India Ahmad Sarwar said.

Afghan President Najibullah implicitly acknowledged the fall of Khost Monday night when he said on television and radio that Tuesday would be

a national day of mourning for those who died.

He repeated charges that Pakistani artillery and armor took part in the assault on the garrison, but Pakistan denied the allegations.

The day of mourning was observed throughout Afghanistan Tuesday, official Kabul radio said. The radio cancelled its normal programs for the day and broadcast only verses from the Koran, the sacred book of Muslims.

As heads roll in the scandal-prone nineties, Bill Vander Zalm is the first premier to lose his job.

"The premier's problem stems not just from his inability to draw the line between private and public life, but in his apparently sincere belief that no conflict existed so long as the public wasn't aware of what was going on," Hughes wrote. "... With due respect to the premier, it was what went on that was wrong—not the media's discovering and publicizing of those events."

Vancouver Sun political columnist Vaughn Palmer was even blunter. Premier Vander Zalm "lied about who owned his property," Palmer wrote. "He lied about the sale. He lied by omission to his cabinet colleagues and the lieutenant-governor ... keeping them in the dark about his dealings, even as he involved them with the buyer of his property. He lied to Mr. Hughes, under oath. And he lied to the people of BC ... when he declared in a televised press conference that he was stepping down without knowing the contents of the Hughes report, when in fact the tentative findings had been transmitted to him two days before."

Vander Zalm resigned the day the Hughes report hit the fan. Four hours later, Rita Johnston, deputy premier and the MLA for Surrey-Newton, was sworn in as his replacement. Canada's first woman premier, she would also serve one of the shortest terms in the province's history. Fewer than eight months later, on October 17, 1991, Mike Harcourt and his New Democrats came into power. Johnston's caretaker government was unceremoniously discarded by an electorate fed up with the peccadilloes of the Social Credit party. The socialists had promised an open, honest and caring administration—apparently the exact opposite of the Socreds—and the weary voters bought it.

As usual, they were in for a rude surprise. Dogged by scandals even more unpalatable than Vander Zalm's personal trespasses, Premier Harcourt would himself resign after only four years and seven months at the helm. For the NDP, however, those Harcourt years were only a prelude to a political pastiche of deception and ineptitude that grew more tangled as the decade deepened. But for now, enough of politics. The nineties had other things to offer, including sports spectaculars, confrontations and scientific honours.

In the eighties, Vancouver was the focus of international attention with Expo 86. That interest shifted to Victoria in 1994, when it hosted the Commonwealth Games, August 18–28. The Victoria event was not as dramatic as the 1954 British Empire Games in Vancouver, but it had its moments. The Queen came. So did Barbra Streisand, a popular American singer (who sailed into the Inner Harbour "on one of the biggest yachts ever seen in local waters," then went on a shopping spree).

Despite negative coverage that concentrated on reports of chaotic organization before and during the venture, the Games opened on time and were deemed a success. They drew some 70,000 visitors, and tourism revenues for the Victoria area climbed to $810 million in 1994 from $750 million in 1993. In 1995, international visits showed a healthy increase, just as they did in Vancouver after Expo. On the playing venues, BC athletes helped Canada win 40 gold, 42 silver and 46 bronze medals for a second-place finish behind Australia in the hardware stakes.

On the larger stage of the Olympics, BC rowers whipped the world at the Barcelona Games in 1992. The flood of gold medals began August 1 when the coxless fours—three of them from BC—finished first. They were followed by Vancouver's Kathleen Heddle and Vancouver-born Marnie McBean (who had moved to Ontario) with a gold in the coxless pairs. Heddle was also among five BC rowers in the eights with cox crew that won yet another gold. In the men's coxed eights race, six

THE DECADE IN HEADLINES
« 1992 »

VANDER ZALM 'FOOLISH,' NOT GUILTY

The former premier is acquitted of criminal breach of trust in respect to the sale of Fantasy Gardens.

Times-Colonist, June 25, 1992

THE DECADE IN HEADLINES
« 1994 »

SAWICKI GIVES IN TO PRESSURE

Burnaby MLA Joan Sawicki resigns as
Speaker of the legislature after only two years
in the chair. Members on both sides of the
House had quietly criticized her performance.
She is replaced by Emory Barnes after a
secret ballot.

Burnaby Now, March 21, 1994

RIOT TRASHES MUCH OF DOWNTOWN

Elimination of the Canucks from the Stanley
Cup final provokes a rampage along Robson
Street by a riotous crowd. *The Sun* replates
hurriedly to include pictures and stories of the
violence.

Vancouver Sun, June 14, 1994

WORLD'S TALLEST TOTEM POLE REACHES FOR THE SKY

Erected for the Commonwealth Games in
Victoria, it tops out at 55 metres and surpasses
the 52.7-metre pole raised June 6, 1973, in
Alert Bay.

Times-Colonist, August 4, 1994

QUEEN OPENS 'JOYFUL' GAMES

It's a dazzling display, says the hometown
paper as Victoria hosts the Commonwealth
Games. However, many press reports dwelled
on "organizational and logiscal nightmares"
behind the glitter.

Times-Colonist, August 18, 1994

more BC rowers were aboard as Canada finished first in one of the closest Olympic rowing finishes ever.

At the 1996 Olympics in Atlanta, Canada didn't make nearly as big a splash as in 1992. Heddle and McBean did take another gold in the double sculls event, but this was the only bright spot. For Vancouver's Heddle, her three Olympic gold medals are the most ever earned by a Canadian athlete.

In marketing news, Canada (but not the consumer) won a major victory under the North American Free Trade Agreement. A dispute panel ruled in July, 1996, against a US challenge of Canada's high tariffs on dairy and poultry products. This meant British Columbians, held captive by a marketing system that ensured artificially high prices, would continue to pay roughly twice as much for these products as their neighbours in Washington State.

Early in the decade, one of BC's grand old mercantile names bit the dust. Woodward's, which began life as a small retail outlet on Main Street in Vancouver before the turn of the century, went belly-up in 1993. Its department stores—including the landmark building at Hastings and Abbott, which opened November 2, 1903 — were either absorbed into the Zeller's chain or sold. Alas, the Woodward family descendants (and the managers they hired) could not sustain the vision and drive of the founders.

Another family empire to falter was the Griffiths' franchises in sports and broadcasting. Frank Griffiths, Sr., who established Western International Communications Ltd. (CKNW and a clutch of other radio and TV stations) and Northwest Sports Enterprises (Vancouver Canucks), died April 7, 1994, aged seventy-seven. His sons, Frank, Jr. and Arthur, took command of the family businesses. Again, alas. The challenge of running a complex communications conglomerate proved too much for young Frank. He was fired in September, 1996, and the family uneasily shared control with Edmonton investors. Meanwhile, young Arthur plunged ahead with GM Place in downtown Vancouver as the new home of the Canucks and the NBA's Vancouver Grizzlies. Overextended, Arthur and the family had to sell successive chunks of their holdings to partner John McCaw, a Seattle billionaire. By November, 1996, the Griffiths' twenty-two-year investment in sports was over.

Out at the University of BC, a singular world honour brightened the front pages in 1993. On October 13, professor Michael Smith won the Nobel Prize for chemistry. The award—for Smith's breakthrough techniques in reprogramming genetic codes — elevated UBC to the front ranks of molecular biology.

While Smith and his team of researchers were tracking the wily gene, a less enlightening episode was unfolding across campus in the political science department. Beginning in June, 1992, charges of "profound racism and sexism" escalated into a gender war. Aggravated by a biased report from a feminist lawyer hired to investigate, this turbid stew of politically correct thinking, predatory white males and seething feminist commandos did little more than polarize this self-centred academic community.

Womanhood's fight for equal status with males has, of course, been going on for a long time. They have won both small and large victories—in the courts and elsewhere—but it wasn't until the rise of radical feminism in the latter decades of the century that the struggle assumed "politically correct" intensity. Much innocent language, such as chairman, actress and stewardess was deemed sexist. Concerns over sexual harassment, turned many business offices into tense arenas, where the male-female relationship had to conform to a new reality. Even a benign pat on the

6/49

$2.5 MILLION

THE Province

50 cents
75¢ minimum
outside
Lower Mainland

Mostly sunny
Page C16

GRIT LANDSLIDE

Chretien's Liberals wipe out Tories

KIM WHO?

VOTE '93	% of vote	Elected	Leading	Total
Liberal	41.6	178	0	178
Reform	18.2	52	0	52
PC	16.1	2	0	2
Bloc	13.9	54	0	54
NDP	6.1	8	0	8
148 of 295 seats needed for majority				

FULL ELECTION COVERAGE INSIDE

REFORM RULES THE WEST

Adding insult to injury, the cheeky tabloid rudely kisses off Kim Campbell after her brief stint as prime minister.

THE DECADE IN HEADLINES
« 1995 »

A NEW BATTLE BEGINS

The twice-weekly *Progress* chronicles the shock felt by the community after Ottawa announces that CFB Chilliwack will be closed as a cost-cutting measure.

Chilliwack Progress, February 27, 1995

$167-MILLION FEDERAL RESCUE PACKAGE HAILED AS TRIUMF FOR B.C.

After a decade of uncertainty, new funding is announced for the UBC particle physics laboratory. Unfortunately, the bailout involved the loss of 50 jobs—news that was not made public until August.

Vancouver Sun, June 14, 1995

CIVILIAN CLASSES BEGIN AT ROYAL ROADS

The military college, closed down as part of federal cutbacks, reopens as Royal Roads University, an extension of the University of Victoria.

Goldstream News Gazette, September 6, 1995

ROCKER SETS NEW ARENA OPENING

Bryan Adams, a local musician, stages the first show in Vancouver's GM Place. A crowd of 18,000 attends.

The Province, September 19, 1995

CASTRO SEES NO QUICK END TO BLOCKADE

During a brief stop in Vancouver while en route home from Japan, the Cuban dictator calls Americans "scorpions, vipers and snakes," and expects US sanctions of his regime to continue indefinitely.

Vancouver Sun, December 15, 1995

shoulder of a co-worker could be viewed as incorrect behaviour.

Nevertheless, real women inched painfully toward the equality they deserved. In the nineties, it was not unusual to find female names occupying the executive levels of the press, industry, politics and public service. In BC, two of these names became (briefly) household words. The first was Kim Campbell, a Conservative Vancouver MP and former Social Credit MLA. In 1993, she was a member of Brian Mulroney's federal cabinet when he resigned as prime minister after a torrent of derision and abuse from disaffected Canadians. At a party convention on June 13, she was chosen to replace him as PM—the first female to hold that post in our history. Within months, the forty-five-year-old Campbell was enmeshed in a hopeless election campaign. Although Mulroney was gone, voters saw the scarlet letter "M" emblazoned on Campbell's breast.[1] She lost the election to Jean Chretien's Liberals so resoundingly that the Conservatives returned only two MPs in the entire country. Campbell, who lost her own seat in Vancouver Centre, was appointed Canada's consul general in Los Angeles in 1996.

Rita Johnston became premier of BC a few weeks short of her fifty-sixth birthday. Born Rita Margaret Leichert in Melville, Saskatchewan, April 22, 1935, she came to the coast in 1941, and married George Johnston at the age of sixteen. The Johnston and Vander Zalm names were politically linked almost from the beginning of her public career. Rita served with Bill on Surrey council, and followed him into the provincial field by becoming an MLA in 1983. A staunch supporter of the premier before and after his disgrace, Johnston had little opportunity during the summer of 1991 to either repair or further tarnish the Social Credit image. When the inevitable election occurred in October, the NDP took fifty-one of seventy-five seats, while the rejuvenated Liberals (under leader Gordon Wilson, who subsequently quit to form his own party) captured seventeen. After almost forty years as the dominant BC political force, the Socreds sank with scarcely a whimper—electing only seven MLAs. Johnston lost her own seat and dropped out of politics.

Like Johnston and Vander Zalm before him, Michael Franklin Harcourt tinkered with municipal politics before graduating into the big leagues of the provincial legislature. He was born in Edmonton on January 6, 1943. The family moved to BC, and Mike grew up comfortably in Vancouver's Kerrisdale district. Immersed in the political climate of UBC in the sixties, he became a storefront lawyer and social activist. After two decades as a Vancouver alderman and mayor, Harcourt became an MLA in 1986. He was chosen NDP leader in 1987, following Bob Skelly's resignation.

Harcourt's 1991 election victory was achieved in part by NDP promises to introduce higher standards to government. The following May, however, *The Sun* broke the news that the Nanaimo Commonwealth Holding Society, an organization with strong links to the party, had apparently stolen millions of dollars in bingo money raised by charities. While police and others began lengthy investigations into allegations of corruption and kickbacks, a few NDP appointees and cabinet ministers were getting into trouble of their own. Almost before the echoes of Harcourt's swearing-in ceremony had died away, the New Democrats went out of their way to renege on one of their most solemn campaign promises—that the NDP would "put an end to secret deals and special favours for political friends."

In fact, the crush of failed NDP candidates, party hacks, left-wing academics and privileged insiders getting cushy jobs with the government became so overwhelming that the cabinet had to make a special patronage appointment of a patronage coordinator to handle all the patronage appointments. ("Oink, Oink," went a *Sun* headline in June, 1992, over a story detailing the NDP's pork-barrel largesse during its first eight months in power.)

Inevitably, arrogance, infighting over priorities and just plain dumbness led to unscheduled—and embarrassing—departures of more than one appointee. Joining them was the occasional cabinet minister forced to resign. One was kicked all the way out of the party after sexual harassment charges were made by several women. Another, Environment Minister Moe Sihota, had to quit in May, 1995, after the Law Society of BC found him guilty of professional misconduct for wrongly borrowing money from a client's funds. Although Sihota was banned from practising law for eighteen months, Harcourt reinstated him after only fifteen weeks. (There would be another "Moe Moment" in 1996, when Sihota was turfed from cabinet a second time for becoming too closely involved with a friend's application for a limousine licence.)

Aware that twelve ministers resigned during Vander Zalm's single term for transgressions ranging from the premier's Fantasy sins to unguarded telephone conversations, veteran observers started wondering whether the New Democrats would outdo the Socreds on the sleaze meter. Meanwhile, the NCHS scandal wouldn't go away. In April, 1994, the RCMP alleged that four societies in Nanaimo—all politically linked to the NDP and the complex NCHS apparatus—had breached the Criminal Code twenty-seven times. That summer, the four societies all pleaded guilty and were ordered to pay fines or restitution totalling $150,000. Still insisting there was no official connection to the criminal activity in Nanaimo, the government consented to a forensic audit of the NCHS books.

Like Ted Hughes and his report on Bill Vander Zalm, auditor Ron Parks' disclosures were crushing. Finally released on Friday, the 13th of October, 1995, after being kept secret for four months, the Parks report declared that the NDP and the Nanaimo Commonwealth organization collaborated on diverting charity funds for political purposes. He described NCHS as a "bank" from which the party drew funds to finance its activities. Furthermore, the NDP tried to cover up its involvement by secretly returning $60,000 to the society in 1993.

The Parks report was part of a one-two punch to the NDP's midsection that week. The day before, after raids that included NDP headquarters in Burnaby, the Mounties linked longtime party stalwart Dave Stupich to a sum of money that totalled $936,758. Then in March of 1996, they alleged bribery, breach of trust and criminal conspiracy involving former premier Dave Barrett and another NDP eminence, Bob Williams. In question was the 1976 deal that saw Williams resign his seat so that Barrett could return to the legislature in a by-election. When Williams resigned, he was immediately awarded an $80,000 consulting fee by NCHS.

By this time, Harcourt no longer mattered. Linked to his inability to bury the bingo scandal was the public perception of him as a benign bungler. His painful performance at the Charlottetown constitutional conference in August, 1992, when he agreed to a Commons redistribution plan that left BC badly underrepresented, cemented his reputation as "Premier Bonehead." With the opinion polls showing a dismal 23 percent of the voters favouring the NDP, Harcourt suddenly announced his resignation November 15, 1995. The following February, heir-apparent Glen Clark was chosen party leader and premier.

Along with politics (from which it seemed inseparable much of the time), the Native issue was another persistent story of the nineties. During the century's long

THE DECADE IN HEADLINES
« 1996 »

LAST OF SOCREDS DECIDES NOT TO RUN FOR REELECTION
Cliff Serwa, the remaining Social Credit MLA, leaves politics. Of the seven Socreds elected in 1991, four jumped to the Reform party and the other two quit.
Vancouver Sun, January 9, 1996

PROVINCE PROBE HALTS 'MADNESS'
The newspaper's award-winning series on mental illness forces the government to halt bed closures at Riverview Hospital. *The Province*'s investigation reveals fatal flaws in the plan to switch to community-based mental health care.
The Province, February 21, 1996

HYDRO DEAL ROCKS CLARK'S FIRST DAY
The BC Hydro insider scandal, sprung by the Liberal opposition, mars Glen Clark's swearing-in as premier.
Vancouver Sun, February 22, 1996

SOCIAL, MEDICAL NET'S BEEN RESTRUNG
The federal government downloads the cost of health, welfare and post-secondary education on the provinces via a new funding scheme and transfer of responsibilities.
The Province, April 1, 1996

FROM JOY TO GRIEF
A Vernon family preparing for a wedding is slain by a spurned husband. The death toll of nine makes it BC's worst mass murder.
The Province, April 5, 1996

THURSDAY
NOVEMBER 16, 1995

TIMES  COLONIST

VICTORIA, BRITISH COLUMBIA

70 CENTS

137TH YEAR · NO. 330 ★ ★ ★

DEAR READER

THE NHL SEASON is well into its second month and readers will find our weekly TIMES COLONIST/Circuit City Hockey Draft Sweepstakes report in today's newspaper. We will report every Thursday until the NHL season is completed. All weekly winners may pick up their prizes at the TIMES COLONIST, 2621 Douglas St., during regular office hours.

John Crerar,
ci......tion marketing manager

FASTREAD

A quick look at the day's headlines, and other highlights of life interest

Pension blues

Canadians may have to pay twice as much into the Canada Pension Plan in the years ahead to keep the ailing retirement fund afloat · **A3**

We're guilty, too

Quebec Premier Jacques Parizeau's referendum-night declaration was a racist and divisive bullet. But let's not ignore a fact: We handed him the bullet. Comment · **A5**

Take heart

A study suggests a drug that lowers cholesterol could dramatically reduce the risk of first-time heart attacks in otherwise healthy people · **A7**

Stockpiling drugs

Seniors are stockpiling prescription drugs in anticipation of the provincial government's controversial reference-based pricing strategy · **B1**

Political penmanship

Former B.C. premier Dave Barrett doesn't tell all in his memoirs, which is no surprise. But it's the scribe Dave chose to not tell all to which caused surprises at the TIMES COLONIST. Jim Gibson · **B2**

Writing for kids

Nature calls for author Jan Thornhill who's in town this week as part of Canadian Children's Book Week · **C1**

Cloudy, periods of rain. High 15 Detailed forecast, **E7**

FAST FORWARD

File this one under everything you wanted to know about building but were afraid to ask: Blueprints, Hammers and Saws, the Royal B.C. Museum's current showcase exhibit offers insights into architecture and interior design and features examples of work from 20 local designers. And right next door B.C.'s oldest house — Helmcken House — features a display from the Canadiana Costume Museum and audiotaped tours.

FAST FIND

HARCOURT RESIGNATION

Why I quit

> " The task can best be carried on by a new leader who will be free of the baggage I've been harnessed with as I have undertaken to clean up some of the problems of the past
>
> *Premier Harcourt, announcing his departure*

By Les Leyne/ Times Colonist staff

Premier Harcourt stunned B.C. on Wednesday by giving his resignation notice, acknowledging his scandal-smeared New Democratic Party can't win an election with him in charge.

The NDP's provincial council meets this weekend to set a leadership convention, perhaps in February, after which Harcourt will resign. He will serve out his term as a Vancouver-Mount Pleasant MLA, but won't run again.

The move caps weeks of unrest in the government and the party. A crisis was triggered by revelations of the party's tangled involvement with a corrupt Nanaimo society that acted as the NDP's financial arm.

Although Harcourt was not implicated in the improprieties stretching back 20 years, critics ripped his handling of the affair. He was widely condemned for his failure to find out about recent attempts to cover up the society's dealings, and for his refusal to pin the blame on anyone for keeping him in the dark.

One cabinet minister, Joan Smallwood, was fired two weeks ago after criticizing him. Backbenchers were grumbling openly about the disastrous effect the scandal was having on the party, which must go to an election within a year.

Harcourt's resignation announcement was a low-key affair, given with 15 minutes notice and no time for questions.

He said: "I look back over the last nine years I have been leader with a sense of pride, accomplishment. …

"I consider it essential, though, that the work of this

HARCOURT · **A8**

RAY SMITH/TIMES COLONIST

SURPRISE ANNOUNCEMENT Harcourt tells a news conference he's stepping down

▶ **Why premier's exit lifts NDP**
Editorial, **A4**

▶ **Our top 10 list of possible leadership candidates/ A8**

▶ **Blencoe's view: NDP hijacked by feminists/ A9**

SPACE FLIGHT

Family knows no bounds

An Esquimalt grandmother is in Cape Canaveral. Her son-in-law is riding the shuttle Atlantis. Hello up there, Chris!

By Norman Gidney
Times Colonist staff

Esquimalt grandmother Gwen Walter is flying high this week, even though she's earthbound in Florida.

She's in Cape Canaveral, where son-in-law Chris Hadfield took off Sunday in the space shuttle Atlantis.

Daughter Helene is married to the 36-year-old Canadian Forces fighter pilot, whom she met in high school in Ontario at age 15.

Gwen moved west 10 years ago and is grandma to their three children, who were off at Disneyworld on Wednesday.

"They've actually just opened the hatch. This a big occasion for Chris," she said, watching her son-in-law on television give the Russian cosmonauts several carnations and pose for photos.

Seeing the shuttle take off early Sunday morning,

SPACE · **A2**

A WEEKEND PLANNER

Accepting blame for the New Democratic Party's sins, Mike Harcourt bows out.

march into history, the overwhelming bulk of news coverage concerned only the white folks. The descendants of the province's first inhabitants were left struggling in the dust of progress. In 1871, the terms of union with Canada made no mention of aboriginal title, and as far as succeeding generations of British Columbia governments were concerned, Ottawa was responsible for all matters pertaining to the Natives.

Under the paternalistic neglect of the reserve system, which fostered poverty, resentment and abuse (including sexual), the aborigines were routinely mistreated and their complaints ignored. As in the cases of Victoria and Fort George in 1910 and 1913, tribes were removed from their traditional land to make way for civilization. Others had their tribal allotments reduced. The potlatch, a ceremonial time of feasting and celebration, was outlawed until 1951. One amendment to the federal Indian Act in 1927 made it illegal for Natives to raise money to advance claims.

Although the Natives persisted in seeking ownership of their land, there was little progress until 1973, when the Supreme Court of Canada rejected, on a technicality, a Nishga claim that they still enjoyed aboriginal title. The closeness of the vote prompted the federal government of Pierre Trudeau to modify its position on Native rights. However, in a landmark decision in March, 1991, BC Chief Justice Allan McEachern dealt the Natives a further setback by ruling they didn't have exclusive title to the land they had occupied for centuries. In rejecting their claim to 57,000 square kilometres, McEachern also ruled that the Gitskan and Wet'suwet'en had no right to govern themselves. On June 25, 1993, a special panel of BC Appeal Court judges varied McEachern's decision by deciding the two tribes did indeed have unextinguished, nonexclusive aboriginal rights, but that these did not extend to ownership, property rights or self-government.

In due course, the question of aboriginal lands moved from the courthouse to the bargaining chamber, spawning more controversy. Sixteen months after the BC Treaty Commission began the process, *The Sun* reported, on April 1, 1995, that the Natives had claimed 111 percent of the province's land mass. In its first annual report, released September 1, 1994, the commission criticized the secrecy surrounding the treaty talks. The papers began running leaks of "interim-measures agreements" between the NDP and various bands that, without the benefit of due process or public input, ceded control of various chunks of real estate to the Natives. Ernie Fedoruk, outdoors columnist for the *Victoria Times-Colonist*, alarmed everyone by revealing on August 11, 1994, that one of these agreements gave total control of the recreational fishery in the Queen Charlotte Islands to the Haida.

The uproar forced Harcourt to rescind the deal, and helped bring more openness to the negotiation process (while prompting some Native leaders to complain that they weren't consulted about the decision to invite public scrutiny). Finally, the long, torturous road of accommodation between whites and aboriginals reached a milestone of sorts on February 15, 1996, when Ottawa, BC and the Nisga'a (formerly spelled Nishga) initialled an agreement in principle giving the Nisga'a 1,930 square kilometres of land in the Nass Valley, plus $190 million in cash. When and if it is formally ratified (there are some concerns about the commercial fishing, and non Native access to the area), it will be the province's first comprehensive aboriginal land-claim settlement.

Treaty optimism notwithstanding, the increased frustration of some Natives at their shut-ended existence led to more than one instance of anarchy. In many areas of the province, rail and highway traffic was occasionally blocked by militants pro-

THE DECADE IN HEADLINES
« 1996 cont'd »

FROM JOY TO GRIEF
A Vernon family preparing for a wedding is slain by a spurned husband. The death toll of nine makes it BC's worst mass murder.
The Province, April 5, 1996

MAIDEN FLIGHT GETS WET WELCOME
The first aircraft arriving at Vancouver Airport's new international terminal is greeted by fire trucks' spray. The $260-million terminal is to be followed by a new control tower and runway.
The Province, May 1, 1996

ASTRONAUT CARRIES STUDENTS' MEMENTOES
Robert Thirsk rides into space aboard the *Columbia* shuttle. BC's first astronaut, Thirsk carries mementoes from Surrey's Hjorth Road elementary school, which he attended in 1963.
Vancouver Sun, June 20, 1996

DELEGATES SEEK END TO GLOBAL PANDEMIC
An international conference on AIDS attracts 14,137 delegates and is billed as the biggest ever held in Vancouver. Despite the headline, *The Sun*'s story does not spell out the nature of the "pandemic."
Vancouver Sun, July 7, 1996

'DECEIT, GREED, CONSPIRACY'
Former premier Bill Bennett, brother Russell and lumber baron Herb Doman are found guilty of insider trading by the BC Securities Commission. The case involves trades the Bennetts made in Doman stock just before the value of the shares plunged. The trio were acquitted of criminal charges in May, 1989.
The Province, August 29, 1996

THE DECADE IN HEADLINES
« 1996 cont'd »

BISHOP GETS JAIL TERM FOR RAPE OF INDIAN TEEN

Roman Catholic Bishop Hubert Patrick O'Connor is guilty of raping a Native girl in Williams Lake in the sixties. Although O'Connor is the highest ranking Catholic in the world to be convicted, several priests have been found guilty of sex crimes.

Vancouver Sun, September 13, 1996

STUPICH STOLE $1 MILLION: COPS

The most evocative headline of the entire NCHS charity bingo saga distills the issue down to one name, one sum of money and a blunt action verb.

The Province, October 12, 1996

DIAL 250 FOR B.C.

Our second telephone area code is activated. The Lower Mainland and the Fraser Valley keep the familiar 604 (in place since 1961), while the rest of BC switches at 12:01 a.m.

The Province, October 19, 1996

UNIVERSITY NAMES WOMAN NEW PRESIDENT

Martha Piper of Edmonton is chosen to replace David Strangway as head of UBC. The appointment is controversial because the ad campaign seeking applications favours females and minorities over white males.

The Province, November 19, 1996

FEMINIST PIONEER DEAD AT 87

Dorothy Livesay, activist and one of Canada's most influential poets, dies in a Victoria nursing home. Because of a major snowstorm the same weekend, the *Times Colonist* (which has dropped the hyphen in its name) doesn't report her death until January 2, 1997.

Times Colonist, December 29, 1996

testing everything from land-claim inertia to logging and fishery practices. During the summer of 1995, an occupation of private ranchland at Gustafsen Lake near 100 Mile House by armed Native squatters escalated into a full-scale confrontation with the RCMP.

The rebel group, which had been using the site for a sundance ceremony, claimed it was sacred and refused to leave when issued an eviction notice June 13. The situation worsened when shots were allegedly fired at police. Eventually, the stand-off became the RCMP's biggest and costliest operation ever (some 400 officers involved; a bill of $5.5 million). There was at least one apparent shootout, explosions and the deployment of high-powered military equipment. The month-long confrontation ended peacefully September 17 when the renegades surrendered. Charges were laid against fourteen Natives and four non Natives, and some convictions obtained several months later.

During most of the nineties, three loaded phrases resonated throughout the woods: Clayoquot Sound, the Forest Practices Code and Forest Renewal BC. In April of 1994, FRBC was established "to renew BC's forests and safeguard thousands of forest-dependent jobs." Funded by a drastic rise in stumpage charges—the levy on felled trees—FRBC is designed as a partnership of forest companies, unions and environmentalists. The money raised through the stumpage increase is supposed to be invested in jobs and forest regeneration.

Forest Renewal BC was followed June 15, 1995, by the Forest Practices Code, which is a process-driven set of intricate guidelines controlling every conceivable aspect of the logging industry. Although something was needed to protect the province's primary resource from further plunder, the code is a nightmare of red tape. Adhering to its myriad rules and regulations (before some promised amendments in 1997) had made BC's logging costs among the highest in the world. Some smaller operators just gave up, throwing people out of work. The bigger ones, such as Repap BC, MacMillan Bloedel and Fletcher Challenge Canada, either sought bankruptcy protection or restructured to the extent that more jobs were lost. This unemployment—despite a promise by Harcourt that not one logger would be out of work because of the code—had a widening impact on communities whose service and other industries rely on a stable workforce.

One of MacBlo's cost-saving decisions was to walk away from Clayoquot Sound in 1997. Earlier in the decade, Clayoquot, which is on the west coast of Vancouver Island, was one of the province's great environmental battlegrounds. The "tree-huggers" made the front pages in the spring of 1993, when an anti-logging rally at the legislature escalated into a rumble. Later in the year, protesters began blocking roads near Tofino so that the loggers couldn't get to the trees. MacMillan Bloedel got an injunction and police started hauling the lawbreakers away. (Among those charged was MP Svend Robinson, who later did a stretch in jail. It was the second such conviction for the publicity-hungry federal politician.)

On July 6, 1995, the Harcourt government bowed to the protesters and announced new guidelines for cutting in Clayoquot Sound. Rhetoric aside, the policy actually led to the virtual shutdown of all logging in the area. In a letter to employees December 30, 1996, announcing its decision to suspend operations, MacBlo cited costs and the lack of available timber. Stoney-faced environmentalists applauded the forest giant's decision while ignoring the loss of jobs that went with it.

Meanwhile, Forest Renewal BC was in trouble. Dogged by reports of unconscionable operating expenses, the fund also had to survive a raid by the cash-hungry

NDP cabinet in 1996. Amid cries in the press of "betrayal" and "double-cross," the FRBC board agreed on September 12 to return up to $500 million of its "surplus" to general revenue each year should Premier Clark reach for it. This type of windfall was sorely needed, for the freshly minted Clark government of 1996-97 was in parlous financial straits.

The gentle people of British Columbia awoke the morning of May 29, 1996, to wonder what they had wrought. The day before, May 28, was the occasion of the 36th general election in the province's history, and it was a puzzlement: 661,929 voters—41.82 percent of those who cast ballots—had chosen Liberal party candidates, compared with 642,395 (39.45 percent) who had plumped for the NDP. Yet the NDP, under its new premier, had taken 39 of 75 seats. For the New Democrats, this quirk of the electoral system was sweet revenge. Twice before the socialists had outpolled the opposition, but failed to form the government. This time, the shoe was on the left foot: NDP, 39; Liberals, 33; Others, 3. (The Socreds attracted only 6,276 votes.)

If it weren't for subsequent revelations, the campaign might have faded into relative obscurity. Clark shovelled money at the voters with blinding speed, trumpeted his party's miracle budget that even showed a surplus and waited for the right-wing vote to split. It did. Liberal leader Gordon Campbell (yet another ex-Vancouver mayor playing with the big boys) could do little more than sling mud, mumble out a murky economic platform and appeal to other parties to hop aboard his bandwagon. It was probably the worst election performance since that of the NDP's Skelly in 1986. Campbell blew a big lead in the opinion polls—built on the Nanaimo Commonwealth and other scandals—and watched morosely election night as the upstart Reform party siphoned off 146,734 anti-NDP votes.

Glen David Clark was sworn in as premier on February 22, 1996. Born in Nanaimo November 22, 1957, he became a dedicated unionist after leaving UBC. Following his election in 1986 as MLA for Vancouver-Kingsway, Clark became one of the Opposition "pit bulls" that savaged the government (and, according to reliable insiders, also his own boss, Mike Harcourt. Contributing heavily to Harcourt's decision to quit was the backstabbing in his own cabinet and a thumbs-down from the BC Federation of Labour). Clark easily gained the party leadership February 18 at a Vancouver convention.

On the eve of his swearing-in a few days later, the Liberals sprang the BC Hydro scandal on the unsuspecting government. In this one, NDP and Hydro insiders were linked to a private investment deal involving the Cayman Islands and a thermal power plant in Pakistan. Although the news made Clark "look like a stunned deer caught in the headlights," as a *Province* editorialist put it, he quickly fired Hydro's two top executives, and moved on to his bundle of pre-election campaign goodies.

Which, it turned out, contained some lies. Now, all politicians tell a few whoppers now and then. Along with the broken promises and failed programs embedded in the detritus of provincial and federal politics are always a goodly number of falsehoods. Comes with the job. The premier's first departures from the truth came in April, 1996, when the budget speech claimed a surplus for the 1995 fiscal year, plus another for the year ahead, when in fact the finance ministry's own staff had warned that revenues were overstated by $800 million.

Nobody outside Clark's inner circle knew this at the time—least of all the voter. The real facts started emerging within four months of the election, when opposi-

THE DECADE IN HEADLINES
« 1997 »

REGULATIONS CITED IN DRASTIC EARNINGS DROP

The paper quotes MacMillan Bloedel's 1996 financial statement, which estimates the Forest Practices Code added $80 million to logging costs.

Vancouver Sun, February 13, 1997

PORT SAILS TO RECORD

Port of Vancouver, busiest in Canada, sets another record with 72 million tonnes handled in 1996. Gains were registered in container traffic, coal and total foreign tonnage. The cruise ship industry set another record with 701,500 revenue passengers.

The Province, February 18, 1997

SMOOTH START AT DELTAPORT TERMINAL

The first ship arrives at the new Roberts Bank terminal, which doubles Vancouver's container-handling capacity.

Vancouver Sun, June 8, 1997

FOREST CODE GETS MAJOR OVERHAUL

The NDP government announces sweeping changes to the Forest Practices Code, designed to make it more palatable to the industry.

Vancouver Sun, June 9, 1997

CLARK BACKS DOWN ON CHANGES TO LABOR CODE

Controversial amendments giving more power to unions—especially in the construction sector—are shelved by Premier Clark after a storm of protest from BC businesses.

Vancouver Sun, July 16, 1997

tion politicians and the press obtained explosive treasury board documents confirming the lie. The evidence from the ministry clearly showed a budget deficit while Clark and Finance Minister Andrew Petter were touting a surplus.

Petter did admit in July that the 1995-96 budget would indeed show a deficit. In December, the shortage was pegged at $369 million, with the province going deeper into the red each succeeding month. Accused of relentlessly lying, Clark went on television in October in an attempt to explain why the government's rosy revenue forecasts were so out of line with reality. He couldn't. That same month, the premier maintained that the budget lies weren't lies at all, but simply "variances." Still in denial, he seemed to be insisting that the lying was some sort of unavoidable statistical aberration.

The sickly pallor of the province's finances wasn't helped by some rash decisions based on ideology rather than common sense. To placate the greenie faction, Harcourt's government created Tatshenshini-Alsek wilderness park in northwestern BC during June, 1993. In doing so, it cancelled the Windy Craggy copper-gold mining project. Sued by the owner of the mine, the government agreed on August 18, 1995, to fork over $166 million in compensation and investment funding.

In March of 1994, the New Democrats announced a really good deal for their buddies in the labour movement. Glen Clark—then employment minister—revealed that the $1-billion Island Highway project from Victoria to Campbell River would be built by union workers exclusively. Not only must every contractor agree to employ unionists, they must pay what the government called a "fair wage." An accountant analyzing the labour costs estimated that the closed-shop provision jacked up the wage bill by $73 million. Along with sweetheart contracts for BC teachers, health workers and other civil servants, the highway arrangement cemented the NDP's reputation as union-huggers.

A second precipitate decision—to halt the Kemano Completion Project by Alcan Aluminum—in January, 1995, is still awaiting a final bill. Alcan had poured more than $500 million into the project, which would allow it to expand its hydroelectric generating capacity, when the cabinet stepped in because of concerns over the salmon run on the Nechako River. After months of haggling, Clark agreed August 5, 1997, to provide an estimated $750 million worth of subsidized power as long-term compensation.

Then there was the great Columbia River Treaty fiasco. Premier Harcourt announced with great fanfare September 8, 1994, that, as a follow-up to the original treaty in the sixties, an agreement with US-based Bonneville Power Administration meant BC was richer by a cool $250 million. Despite evidence that this latest piece of paper was not legally binding, the $250-million "payment" promptly became part of the 1995 budget. When Bonneville backed out May 15, 1995, Harcourt, Clark (who brokered the deal) and the budget all had egg on their faces. (When the parties did reach a binding agreement—announced December 3, 1996—BC accepted hydro power instead of cash.)

Meanwhile, the government, boaters and fishermen ground their teeth in frustration as remote bureaucrats and politicians started replacing BC's manned lighthouses with automated stations. Despite pleas that the keepers being laid off were needed to help save lives along the province's storm-prone coast, the Canadian Coast Guard (with headquarters in Ottawa, safely removed from a Force 10 gale) cited budget savings of millions of dollars. Machines are cheaper than people. While the controversy raged, so did the worst storm to hit the coast in thirty-four years—in October of 1996. At least six of the machines failed during that stretch of bad weather.

(Just two months later, Old Man Winter dealt another stinging blow to the southwest coast. The worst snowstorm in Victoria's history dumped 67 centimetres [26.13 inches] during a 24-hour period ending December 29. It surpassed the 23-inch snowfall of February 3, 1916, and paralyzed the capital. The *Times Colonist*, its circulation severely curtailed, published a special section early in 1997 containing storm news its readership missed. In Vancouver, only 34 centimetres fell. Although *The Sun* and some of the other media insisted on calling this snowfall the storm of the century, the Vancouver precipitation was well below the record of 17½ inches on January 21, 1935.)

As the new automated lighthouses blinked out, one by one, BC's maritime outrage was cresting in another sector. This was over the Mifflin Plan. In an effort to save the troubled salmon industry, federal Fisheries Minister Fred Mifflin announced in March, 1996, a controversial fleet-reduction scheme that involved an $80-million buy-back of commercial licences and a new policy forcing fishermen to buy separate licences for each area they fish and for each type of gear they use. This "stacking" drew heat from various groups, who argued that the policy would favour large, urban-based corporations which could afford the licences.

Mifflin's aim was to reduce the fleet by 50 percent. The plan also placed greater emphasis on conservation. Despite the controversy, many agreed that the sorry state of the fishery—brought about by poor management, inadequate forecasting, massive overfishing and token attempts at conservation—demanded some sort of bold initiative. Complicating the quarrel over who got what catch was the Aboriginal Fishing Strategy, a poorly regulated project that allowed Natives to catch salmon outside the commercial fishery.

Every time the voter picked up the daily paper, it seemed, there was an inquiry going on. One of them was conducted by Judge Thomas Gove into the social services ministry after five-year-old Matthew Vaudreuil was killed by his mother despite numerous warnings by social workers that he should be taken from her. Gove called for fundamental reforms to BC's child-protection system. In his report, released November 29, 1995, he savaged the chaotic, dysfunctional department and made 118 recommendations for drastic change. The poor social-work practices, he said, were "... a direct result of poor ministry management, ineffective quality-assurance measures, inadequate funding and lax standards ..." After persistent press reports about further abuses, Clark established a Ministry for Children and Families on September 23, 1996.

To paraphrase Charles Dickens, this was the worst of centuries and the best of centuries. These past hundred years have been saturated with violence. Two global conflicts and numerous lesser wars have claimed the attention—and the lives—of British Columbians. Except for minimal involvement in the Gulf War against Iraq, however, the armed forces stationed in the province in the early nineties were more concerned with cutbacks than overseas duty. For the general populace, the focus for the waning years of the century was also ingrown.

Like the violence, racism refused to go away. The obvious bigotry prevalent in the early 1900s had long since been replaced by more subtle forms. In urban areas, one of these was the furore over "monster homes." These ugly monuments to bad architecture disrupted neighbourhoods and ruined many a view. The perception was that they were occupied by extended immigrant families, which was not the

A tense moment on Hastings Street in Vancouver is captured by Province *photographer Jon Murray. The picture earned Murray a National Newspaper Award in 1994.*

Canadian way of life. Official insistence on multiculturalism at the expense of traditional white values also exacerbated the problem.

Statistics indicated the racial concerns of the Anglo-European population had some basis in fact. A 1996 study concluded that, for the first time, English was a minority language in Vancouver. In Richmond, more than 50 percent of students couldn't speak it. Surrey, which became the second-largest city in the province during the nineties, was generally regarded as a patchwork of ethnic enclaves. Affluent Asians also caused resentment by their increased visibility and the economic control they wielded over downtown Vancouver. During the years leading to July 1, 1997, when the British colony of Hong Kong was returned to Chinese control, the press concentrated on stories about the effect this could have on BC and its residents.

(The discrimination was not one-sided. In 1996, the Chinese-language daily *Ming Pao* published an informal poll in which 57 percent of respondents indicated they had discriminated against a person of another race. It also quoted community leaders as suggesting Chinese immigrants should reconsider potentially annoying personal habits, not flaunt their wealth and respect traffic rules and lineups at store counters.)

Politics also managed to hold our attention for these one hundred years. And the view from the voter's booth wasn't any better at the end of the century than at the beginning. While the early years had bickering MLAs, revolving premiers and a meddling lieutenant-governor, the nineties still had the discord but with an added dollop of partisanship. The erratic despocracy of Glen Clark recalled the toughness of a Duff Pattullo without the populist touch of W.A.C. Bennett. The distaste in Victoria for Tom Gunton, Clark's top deputy, rivalled that felt in the eighties for Premier Vander Zalm's principal secretary, David Poole.

Local governments, left to twist in the wind by Pattullo's government during the Depression, were again blindsided in the nineties. In the interest of unloading costs, the deficit-shackled NDP cabinet slashed its grants to municipalities by 28 percent in 1996. The sweeping cuts, totalling $113 million, left the cities and towns to fend for themselves in providing services once financed by Victoria.

Meanwhile, our friendly neighbourhood bully, the United States, kept leaning on BC. After fourteen years of acrimony, Canada and the US reached yet another softwood lumber agreement on April 1, 1996, that would cap exports. For BC, this meant a quota that was 69 percent of the total volume, which meant in turn a decrease of up to 20 percent for some producers. The Americans also played hardball on the sea. Ignoring Canada's concerns over depletion of stock, Alaskan fishermen kept hauling in salmon during the decade with little or no control. While lucrative salmon runs were closed to BC boats and the fleet was undergoing a traumatic reduction in numbers, our US counterparts were demanding more concessions.

But enough of conflict, confrontation and crisis—even though this is the raw material for crackling good newspaper yarns. The century had good stuff, too.

When BC demanded a rail link rather than a wagon road as a term of union with Canada, nobody dreamed that the railroad would eventually dwindle in importance and be surpassed by other modes of transportation even more boggling. The automobile, just a curiousity in 1900, was a necessity a hundred years later. Movement of people and goods throughout the province would be at a virtual standstill without highways and the internal-combustion engine. The airplane— little more than a dream in the first decade—is now almost as indispensable. Jet aircraft can traverse Canada's considerable girth in the time it once took a stage to reach the Fraser Valley from tidewater. Satellites circle our planet, aiding navigation, beaming sitcoms down to our TV sets and bringing immediacy and precision to our communications. Men have walked on the moon.

The computer has transformed our thought processes. Every industry, including the press, is as dependent on the microchip as a newborn babe is on her mother's milk. It has gobbled up jobs and spit out increased profits. Personal computers are competing with television as home-entertainment options (and further eroding the time devoted to reading the paper). Something called the Internet—a world-wide computer network connected by telephone lines—blossomed in the nineties to provide more distraction. Unregulated, disorganized and open to abuse, the Internet attracted every cyber hustler in the known universe. Judgment is still reserved on whether this communications web becomes more than a pacifier for the need-a-life crowd. For the 90 percent of the adult population not enthralled by "surfing," it joined fax machines, junk mail and cell phones as one of the irritations of the nineties.

Speaking of crowds, British Columbia keeps attracting people year after year. The population, which was 178,657 in 1901, reached 3,282,061 in 1991. Five years later, it had swelled to 3,724,500. By 1996, there were 1.6 million people in the Lower Mainland alone. A projected growth rate of 13 percent would put that number around 2 million by the start of the twenty-first century.

The immigration surge has masked job growth, leaving unemployment levels at a consistently high level. Nevertheless, governments and businesses pumped about $19 billion into the BC economy in 1997. Our bread-and-butter industries seemed able to survive the exigencies of ideology and foreign pressure. Forestry firms, despite the devout wishes of the environmentalists, would continue, somehow, to cut down trees. The mining sector, as ill-treated by the NDP as the lumber industry, was showing some strength as the decade neared its end.

Alert readers may note by now that some events described in this chapter are more current than ancient. That is because the decade was still on the cusp of history when this narrative was being completed. It is, indeed, almost over. And, after a century of unpredictable twists and turns, explosive growth and dizzying technological advances, British Columbia remains true to itself. In 1942, Bruce Hutchison wrote in *The Unknown Country* that the province is so unlike the Prairies or the East that "crossing the Rockies, you are in a new country, as if you had crossed a national frontier. Everyone feels it, even the stranger feels the change of outlook, tempo and attitude."

No longer Lotusland (a phrase attributed to Hutchison), but still distinct enough to treat other provinces—and Ottawa—with a wary condescension, this blessed blend of climate and geography follows its own drummer along the march of time. May the next century be as exciting and newsworthy as the twentieth.

---

1   In a delicious example of black political comedy, "Lyin' Brian" Mulroney, the most vilified man in Canada when public opinion forced him to resign, sued the federal government in 1996 for slandering his reputation by linking him to a bribery investigation. After newspaper cartoonists had a field day with images of Mulroney emerging from a sewer, Ottawa took the safe route and settled out of court.

CONFESSIONS OF A CANDY BUTCHER

Back in aught-54, when I was a candy butcher on the Kettle Valley Line, newspapers were among my steadiest sellers. As the CPR train felt its way through the Cascades, the Selkirks and the Rockies between Vancouver and Lethbridge, I would ricochet through the cars and peddle my wares. "Candy butcher" is railroad argot for news agent. Along with coffee, sandwiches, candy bars and magazines, I would offer the latest editions of the local rags.

Among them was the *Trail Daily Times*. Now, working on the railroad was a mildly interesting gig, but not a lifetime career. So when I spotted a former Navy buddy's byline on the sports page of *The Times*, I quit the candy butcher business and went to Trail to get drunk with my ol' pal, Gerry Gray. I woke up the next morning in the spare bedroom of the paper's editor. It seems he had hired me as a reporter during the drinking session of the evening before. Well, I could spell, I used to enjoy composition in high school and I could type, so why not? My first assignment was to scalp a court story in the *Nelson News*, which was the morning daily of the Kootenays. A "scalp" is a rehash of another paper's story without checking the facts or attempting to improve the content in any way. In those days, it was an accepted part of small-town newspapering; I suspect it still is. Anyway, despite the hangover and rusty typing skills, I managed to produce something that actually got in the paper. Out of those boozy be-

ginnings in early 1954 emerged a career that kept me gainfully employed in journalism on a daily basis until 1988, and part-time since then.

In the fifties, reporters and editors used cranky manual typewriters to prepare their stories. National and foreign news was provided by slow-speed Canadian Press and British United Press teletypes. In the back shop, as we called it, compositors set the stories and ads on linotypes, which cast words and sentences from molten lead. My introduction to newspaper design came from one of those *Times* compositors. His advice about page makeup kindled a lifelong interest in typography. Nowadays, the typecasting machines and all the other necessities of the old-fashioned composing room are long gone. They have been replaced by "cold type," which is a photographic process, and computers. At the end of the nineties, pages could be designed and reproduced from a personal computer in the newsroom and not need human intervention until the plate was made for the press. Payroll-wise, this is neat stuff so far as the proprietors are concerned. Design-wise, it ain't so good, because many of the people laying out today's papers don't know a kern from a ligature or a quoin from a hellbox.

Before I begin my rant about the state of journalism in the nineties, however, we should pause and discuss some history. For, just as British Columbia has grown and matured in the twentieth century, so has the press.

BC was little more than a collection of trading posts and mining camps when newspapers began to appear. *The Victoria Gazette* takes the honour as the first publication to serve the pioneers in this new outpost of the Empire. It was founded June 25, 1858, by three Americans and survived until October of 1859. By that time, there were other vehicles of opinion, news and advertising eager to attract subscribers. They were produced in back rooms, rude structures and even tents.

The British Colonist had its genesis in a cold, leaky shack on Victoria's waterfront on December 11, 1858, and appeared three times a week. It survives to this day as part of the daily *Victoria Times Colonist*. The *Times* arrived June 9, 1884 (using the *Colonist*'s press), following in the footsteps of the *Daily Chronicle* (1860s) and *Daily Standard* (1870s). New Westminster's *British Columbian* was born as a weekly February 13, 1861. Until 1983, when it was allowed to expire by an apathetic family owner, *The Columbian* called itself BC's oldest daily newspaper. For a while in 1866, the *British Columbia Tribune* was available in Yale. It was one of many that came and went with the swiftness of a played-out gold claim. There were *The Enderby Edenograph*, *The Scorpion*, *The Moodyville Tickler*, *The Donald Truth*, *The Canterbury Outcrop*, *The Hope Steamboat Nugget*, *The Mainland Guardian*, *The Vancouver Ozonogram*, among others.

The New Denver Ledge arrived in January, 1865. On June 1, the *Cariboo Sentinel* started publishing in Barkerville. *The Inland Sentinel*, established at Emory Creek May 28, 1880, became the daily *Kamloops Sentinel*. In Nanaimo, *The Free Press* started as a semi-weekly in 1874 and became a daily in 1888. It's still going.

From 1890 to 1910, the explosion of immigrants which followed the arrival of the railroad in 1885 helped feed a vibrant press. Extensive mining activity in the Kootenays lured many an itinerant editor to the camps. *The Nelson Miner* became the *Nelson Daily News* in 1902. Kimberley, Armstrong, Fernie, Trail Creek and Similkameen also got papers to read and argue with.

First paper in the Okanagan Valley was the *Vernon News*. Founded in May of 1891, it lasted more than a hundred years before the Thomson chain shut it down.

The *Kelowna Clarion* (1904) became the *Kelowna Daily Courier*. In the Fraser Valley, the *Chilliwack Progress* was born in April, 1891. Ten years earlier, the *Cumberland News* had surfaced. It eventually became the *Comox District Free Press*. The *Prince George Citizen*, founded May 17, 1916, became a daily in 1957 and was bought by Southam Inc. in 1969.

Vancouver's first weekly was *The Herald*, which began January 12, 1886. It was a promising venture, but the great fire of June 13, 1886, destroyed *The Herald*'s office in the heart of town. Surviving was the *Daily Advertiser*, which had been born May 8, and *The News*, which followed on June 1. *The News* struggled, though, and Francis Carter-Cotton of the *Advertiser* combined it with his newspaper on May 14, 1887, to form the *News-Advertiser*. *The Daily World* started providing competition on September 29, 1888. Later, a weekly called *The Province* began publishing in Victoria on March 3, 1894. Four years later, on March 26, 1898, it crossed to the mainland and morphed into the *Vancouver Daily Province*.

With the early newspapers came the characters. One of the first was Amor de Cosmos, who started the *British Colonist* "for amusement during the winter of 1858-59." His vitriolic pen attacked the "toadyism, consaguinity and incompetency" associated with the dominant Hudson's Bay Company. De Cosmos' assessment of the colonial legislature: "Of all the unmitigated muffs that were ever collected together perhaps our assembly is the most perfect, indeed." He became a politician himself, championed union with Canada and served as BC's second premier.

Another firebrand was John Robson. As publisher of the *British Columbian*, Robson attacked Governor James Douglas for his "high-handed and oppressive mandates," and once accused him of misappropriating funds "he had screwed out of" the public. Judge Matthew Begbie was so angered by Robson's imputations of bribery that he jailed him briefly in 1862 for contempt of court. Robson also didn't think much of de Cosmos, calling his arguments "vaporings," and remarking that "it is somewhat amusing to witness with what self-complacency *The Colonist* blows his own trumpet...." Robson also became a premier of the province.

IMAGES OF HISTORY • 151

One of the most colourful of the journeymen eccentrics was R.T. Lowery. His *Ozonogram* was so vulgar that the sensitive citizens of 1890s Vancouver hounded Lowery out of town. He started papers in several Kootenay communities, including the *Lardeau Claim*, whose last issue was printed on brown wrapping paper with the inscription "Busted by Gosh." One of his papers, the *Nelson Claim*, was refused postal privileges due to its "blasphemous and ribald character."

"For ten years I ran 'the leading excitement' in New Denver, and then moved on to prospect in other fields," Lowery once wrote in a memoir. "It was a mistake, probably, but each man's life assays high in mistakes."

John Houston was another of the pioneer editors. He was pugnacious and outspoken, wandering the same Kootenay hills and valleys as Lowery. His attempt to publish the *Empire*, which criticized the Grand Trunk Pacific in the company town of Prince Rupert, resulted in many trips to the railroad's jail in 1907.

With newspapers growing along with their communities, there was a need for an organization to help solve common problems. In 1916, the BC Division of the Canadian Press Association was formed (with daily as well as weekly members). The BC Weekly Newspapers Association came along in 1922. In 1928, it reported the total circulation of its membership at 50,000 copies. The present-day BC and Yukon Community Newspapers Association is a direct descendant of that group. In 1997, it had 105 members with a circulation exceeding 1.75 million.

When the twentieth century dawned, Vancouver was fast becoming a newspaper town, and the newsrooms were populated with characters as colourful as those in the Interior. *The Province*, *The World* and *The News-Advertiser* were duking it out for circulation and advertising. In 1901, J.C. McLagan, one of the founders of *The World*, died, and his wife, Sara Ann, took over. She was reportedly the first female owner and publisher of a daily newspaper in Canada. Until she sold it in 1905 for the handsome sum of $65,000, Sara Ann ran *The World*—to the extent of proofreading each paper before it went to press.

The World was purchased by Louis D. Taylor and partners. "L.D.," who was born in Michigan, went on to become one of the city's grandest characters. He served as mayor many times; when defeated in a 1928 election, public-spirited citizens raised $5,000 to send him on a trip around the world. Taylor was also blatantly anti-Asian, a stance not uncommon among public figures in those early decades.

Under Taylor's spirited guidance, *The World* went after *The Province*, whose circulation of 8,000 was roughly double that of its evening rival. Scurrilous rumours about who really owned what paper prompted R.J. Nichols, the brilliant editor of *The Province*, to pen a blunt and bitter editorial attacking his adversary. The result was a libel suit, won by *The Province* when the jury decided Nichols' statements weren't slanderous. Meanwhile, watching this unseemly catfight was a weekly called the *Saturday Sunset*. In July, 1907, it had the last word:

"Now that the cruel libel suit is over and both *The Province* and *The World* claim victory, I trust that those two eminent journals will forget their spat and settle down to the business of giving the public all the news and of illuminating the atmosphere of British Columbia with trenchant editorial utterances of which each is so capable."

Five years later, the owners of the *Sunset*—John P. McConnell and Richard S. Ford—were in the daily newspaper business themselves. On February 12, 1912, a new entity called the *Vancouver Sun* acquired the physical assets of *Saturday Sunset* and started publishing. Ford became managing director and McConnell, managing editor. *The Sun* was the political brainchild of a group of Vancouver Liberals anxious to counter the Conservative viewpoint of *The News-Advertiser*. One of the prime investors was John W. Stewart (of Foley, Welch and Stewart, the eminent railroad contractors, and Bloedel, Stewart and Welch, one of BC's biggest logging outfits—*that* Stewart).

An editorial in the inaugural issue made no bones about *The Sun*'s affiliation. "The necessity for a paper to consistently advocate the principles of Liberalism had been making itself felt for some time," it said. The morning paper wasn't kidding, either. Prior to the 1916 provincial election, *The Sun* managed to prominently display pictures of Liberal candidates throughout its pages. The governing Conservatives remained anonymous. (By the way, the Liberals won the election.)

Over in Victoria, there was little love lost between *The Colonist* and *The Times*. Although they published at different ends of the day, the true-blue Tory *Colonist* and the Liberalish *Times* took turns excoriating each other and their respective political leanings. In September, 1912, when a scandal broke over the 1910 purchase of the Songhees reserve in downtown Victoria, *The Times* became gleefully apoplectic. It seems Sam Matson, editor of *The Colonist*, had accepted a $75,000 fee from Richard McBride's cabinet for helping settle the sale. In a February 15, 1913, editorial, *The Times* called McBride's explanation of the deal "mysterious and oracular," and noted: "But after the sweet incenses of adulation and all the other smothering influences have passed away we are left face to face with the ugly fact that a cold $75,000, a fortune even in these days, a king's ransom in the olden times, was paid over by a Tory premier to a Tory journalist for helping to cajole, bluff, or buy a few poor Indians to sell their reserve."

Back in Vancouver, it was becoming pretty obvious that the city couldn't support four dailies. In 1917, both morning papers, *The Sun* and *The News-Advertiser*, were financially anemic as the wartime economy dragged on. John Stewart, who had put lots of bucks into *The Sun*, had gone off to the front. His construction company, which was supposed to be building the Pacific Great Eastern, was also in difficulty with the government over nonperformance. Enter Robert J. Cromie, Stewart's longtime private secretary. Placed in charge of *The Sun*, he managed to swing a deal September 1, 1917, that not only put the paper in his hands, but merged it with *The News-Advertiser*.

Meanwhile, L.D. Taylor's *World* was being pummelled by *The Province* on the evening battlefield. Taylor had gone further in debt by building "the British Empire''s tallest building" at the corner of Beatty and Pender streets to house *The World*. He lost both the paper and the building (*The Sun* eventually moved there July 23, 1937). In 1921, Charles E. Campbell acquired *The World* from Taylor's successors for $250,000, and sold it to Cromie on March 11, 1924, for $475,000. *The World* died and was replaced by an evening *Sun*, which published both morning and afternoon until 1926. At that time, the *Vancouver Daily Star*, which started June 2, 1924, as yet another afternoon paper, switched to morning publication on February 1, 1926. Cromie dumped his morning edition and took over *The Star*'s evening circulation. *The Sun* and *The Province* were now head-to-head in the afternoon field, a confrontation that would last until June, 1957. On September 1, 1928, *The Province*'s circulation was 82,000, compared with 72,000 for *The Sun*.

The Star died February 12, 1932, after its unions refused to accept a 15 percent wage cut. It was replaced as the city's third daily April 24, 1933, by *The News-Herald*, which would survive for twenty-four years. (Altered perspectives: *The Star* in 1924 vowed that it was "unalterably opposed to further invasion of British Columbia by Orientals and will advocate the elimination of Asiatics from all those industries dealing with the natural resources of the province." *The News-Herald* declared it would "uphold decency and attack corruption and … work for the advancement of Vancouver as the metropolis of the Pacific Coast.")

Those of us compelled to pick at the bones of dead newspapers wish somehow that every one that ever was could somehow have survived. This is patently unworkable, of course—there'd be maybe fifteen dailies in Vancouver alone right now if none of them had ceased publication in the past hundred years. But a failed newspaper is not a furniture store going out of business or a bankrupt sawmill. A newspaper has a voice. It was once alive. A heartbeat nourished by passion, dedication and curiosity made it special. And although the bottom line often intruded and the product was occasionally compromised by uncaring and inattentive management, each one was different and special.

Yes, and deserving to be noted even if its tenure was so brief as to be hardly noticeable. *The News-Advertiser*, *The World*, *The Star* and *The News-Herald* survived long enough to make the history books. But such daily efforts as *The Telegram*, *The Evening Times*, *The Evening Journal*, *The News* and (in 1964-65) the *Vancouver Times* lasted barely long enough to get the hellboxes warm. No matter. Newspaper heaven, where all deadlines are met and all stories are exclusive, welcomes them along with the more noteworthy that have fallen by the wayside: *Edmonton Bulletin, Calgary Albertan, Winnipeg Tribune, Toronto Telegram, Ottawa Journal, Montreal Star* and *Montreal Herald*—and such as the *Vernon News* and other small-town dailies forced to silence their presses.

Most of the brethren died quietly, but some went out with a snarl. Staffers at *The Telegram* were so incensed at John Bassett folding their scrappy daily in 1971 (and peddling its circulation list to the *Toronto Star* for $10 million) that they started the *Toronto Sun*, now one of the biggest success stories in Canadian journalism. When the tiny but proud New Westminster *Columbian* died November 15, 1983, managing editor Neil Graham wrote a blistering Page One indictment of publisher Rikk Taylor's lack of courage.

Back to the living. As *The Sun* chased *The Province* throughout the thirties, it began assembling a stable of fine writers and editors. They included Hal Straight, Cliff McKay, Andy Lytle and Bob Bouchette (a popular columnist who committed suicide by swimming out into English Bay). *The Province* countered with such top talent as Roy Brown, Torchy Anderson—probably the best reporter in the city at the time—Stu Keate, Bob Elson, Alan Jessup and columnist James Butterfield.

Some of the stuff the reporters wrote was delightfully colourful and pejorative. Here are the opening paragraphs of *The Sun*'s line story on March 29, 1932: "William Bagley, an underworld rat turned cobra, was hunted by the police of two nations today while Detective David Maxwell, the 47-year-old Burnaby police officer whom he shot down on Hastings Street, near Clark Drive, at 11 p.m. Saturday, lies near death in Vancouver General Hospital.

"Bank robber, safecracker, bandit, jail-breaker and cocaine-sniffer, Bagley emerged with startling suddenness from the obscurity that has shrouded his movements since his escape with four other criminals (all recaptured), from Oakalla Prison Farm on January 3."

The story went on for several hundred words without making any attempt to assume Bagley's innocence until proven guilty in a court of law. In the nineties, this type of rip-roaring police reporting would have civil-rights lawyers keeling over in a dead faint (not to

mention drawing sniffs of disdain from our present breed of deadly serious, sober, straitlaced, over-educated journalists).

In Victoria, Benny Nicholas ran *The Times* for many years until he dropped dead in his office in 1936. A large man, humorous, gregarious and one of the best editors in Canada, Nicholas was "Mr. Victoria" to many people. Two reporters who went on to distinguished careers elsewhere were Peter Inglis and Peter Stursberg. A *Times* alumnus who became larger than life was Bruce Hutchison. Whether writing a column for *The Times* or *The Sun*, or covering the legislature for either paper (and *The Province*), Hutchison was one of my profession's greatest ornaments. I remember meeting him in *The Times*' newsroom in the mid-fifties. I was in awe of the man who could write such books as *The Incredible Canadian*. Hutchison is certainly BC's greatest journalist.

For part of the thirties, *The Sun*'s Page One masthead included the motto "Only Vancouver Newspaper Owned, Controlled and Operated by Vancouver Men." Lest one get the impression that the newspaper game in BC was strictly a male preserve, let's switch gender for a few moments. I've already mentioned Sara Ann McLagan's contribution to *The World*; in August, 1914, Alice H. Berry was listed as managing director by that paper. Nancy Hodges, BC's first female Speaker of the House, was society editor of the *Victoria Times* for many years. Dorothy Taylor, daughter of J.D. Taylor, was a crusading editor and part-owner of *The Columbian* in the forties and fifties. (She was fired in May, 1954, in a dispute with other shareholders over acquiring a Canadian Press franchise for the paper.)

Margaret (Ma) Murray took over the *Bridge River-Lilloet News* in 1934, and for several decades was one of BC's most colourful and outspoken journalists ("That's for damshur"). Evelyn Caldwell, who as Penny Wise at *The Sun* was Canada's first consumer columnist, started at *The Star* in 1928. *The Sun* also featured Mamie Maloney and Doris Milligan in the thirties. Later came Simma Holt, Pat Carney (who went on to become a senator) and Marjorie Nichols. Moira Farrow, who died in 1997, was one of the finest reporters to ever grace a desk at that paper. Over at *The Province*, columnist Jean

Howarth covered BC's last execution in 1959. In the mid-nineties, both *The Province* and the *Victoria Times Colonist* had female managing editors.

The good life ended for *The Province* on June 6, 1946, when the International Typographical Union went on strike. After a bitter shutdown that lasted until July 22, it resumed publishing only to discover that *The Sun* had firmly entrenched itself during its rival's absence. From then onward, *The Province* was No. 2 in Vancouver. Under publisher Don Cromie (son of Robert J.) and managing editor Straight, *The Sun* in the forties honed its reputation as the liveliest, most readable newspaper in Canada. Such 1947 stunts as sending reporter Pierre Berton to "Headless Valley" in the Yukon to investigate tales of a mysterious oasis containing a lost gold mine, skeletons with their heads missing and primitive cave dwellers boosted circulation if not credibility. Berton milked the yarn for all it was worth (although he and his crew "were on the ground for maybe 20 minutes," according to a cynic in *The Sun*'s newsroom at the time).

The Sun's dominance also became apparent in advertising lineage. It boasted it had Canada's largest want-ad section, and for a number of years was among North American leaders in evening-paper classified lines sold. But this position began eroding in the seventies and accelerated in the eighties, helped by frequent labour shutdowns, some marketing blunders and the emergence of publications dedicated to want ads. In the nineties, *The Sun*'s classified was a sickly remnant of a once-healthy section. Its weakness was not helped by the practice (begun in the eighties to save production costs) of spreading the classified through every section of the paper.[1]

Into the fifties, there were still vestiges of "The Front Page" in the *Sun-Province* relationship. Even though *The Province* was perceived as the more serious of the two, it fought just as hard for the scoop or the better picture. Tales are told about *Sun* and *Province* photographers employing dirty tricks and even coming to blows in order to get the exclusive shot. There were as many as seven editions each day. That was big-time newspapering.

When I started at *The Sun* in the fifties, liquor bot-tles were still common in desk drawers and jammed behind the toilet tank in the men's washroom. Most weekday mornings, when the nearby liquor store opened, somebody would be assigned to pick up the day's requirement of "mickeys." We did our after-shift drinking at the Lotus beer parlour, just across Pender Street from the Sun Tower. I'd listen to rewrite chief Gar MacPherson and other old-timers tell about crime reporters packing a gun while covering their beat. Vancouver coroner Glen McDonald often joined us for long sessions of repartee and argument. After a certain stage in the proceedings, he'd almost invariably threaten us with duty on a coroner's jury the next time a particularly gruesome death occurred.

Tom Ardies and John Kirkwood were two of the aces in *The Sun* newsroom. Jack Scott was one of the top columnists in Canada, while the elegance of Dick Beddoes' prose and attire was beyond comparison. Jack Wasserman was the peerless saloon columnist of this or any other town. He knew everybody and heard everything. Although he had his quirks (one of them being a lousy poker player, a weakness we in the sports department in those days exploited fully), he was a damn good reporter. The opening paragraph of his story describing the death of Errol Flynn in 1959 is a classic.

The Province had Bruce Larsen, a boy-wonder city editor who won a National Newspaper Award for his scoop on a hostage-taking at Oakalla Prison. (Bruce moved to *The Sun*, helped me conquer my drinking habits and wound up as editor-in-chief before he died at much too young an age.) Ben Metcalfe, Paddy Sherman and columnist Eric Nicol were among other luminaries. The editor was Ross Munro, the noted war correspondent. *The Province* had its wackos, too. One such was Hughie Watson, as outrageous a character as any who ever sat down before a typewriter. When one of his drunken misdeeds led to a ban on his byline, he crafted a story so that the initial letters of each paragraph spelled out, BY HUGH WATSON.

The newspaper empire of Southam and Sons, which began in Hamilton in 1877, reached the West Coast in 1923, when the family bought *The Province*. Thus the Southam League (as it called itself in 1928) stretched across the country and prospered until 1946, when the

ITU strike spread havoc throughout the chain.

In 1957, the strain of competing each evening for an increasingly distracted readership began to tell on both Vancouver papers. The independent *Sun* and the corporate Southam Company looked at each other over a gulf of rising costs, and both blinked. The result was Pacific Press Ltd., which was announced May 30, 1957. Under the deal, the papers pooled mechanical production resources and other assets, with the editorial operations remaining separate. Southam paid the Cromie family a $3.85-million "equalization payment" and Sun Publishing Co. became half-owner of the new company (see Appendix E for details of the financial arrangements). *The Sun* remained in the afternoon field and *The Province* switched to mornings. In December, 1965, both papers moved from their elderly digs in the Victory Square area to a modern building at 2250 Granville Street.

(*The Province*'s first a.m. edition was Monday, June 17, 1957. Two days earlier, Thomson Newspapers' *Vancouver Herald* obligingly ceased publication, leaving the morning field unoccupied.)

For many years, Pacific Press was one of the most poorly managed companies in the business. Primitive labour relations, mechanical problems and plain dumb decision-making contributed to a poisonous atmosphere that only started to clear up in the latter half of the nineties. In July, 1997, the editorial and other departments moved back downtown to the foot of Granville Street. Modern web offset presses were installed in a new satellite building on 88th Avenue in Surrey. Finally, the two papers had some decent printing equipment to go with the computerized front end. (This new Surrey plant was the second one in that suburb; the first, built in 1989, didn't work very well. Mention the word "Flexo" in the executive warrens at PacPress and you'll get either a nervous giggle or a groan.)

Before *The Sun* and *The Province* had carved up the Vancouver market (with a sly wink of acquiescence from the Thomsons, who abandoned their metropolitan foothold with unseemly haste), equally momentous changes had taken place in Victoria. In 1949, Max Bell, an Alberta millionaire, bought *The Times* from the Spencer family for $750,000 and installed Keate as publisher

on July 1, 1950. That year, Bell paid the Matsons $1 million for *The Colonist*. Victoria Press Ltd. was formed and the papers moved to a new building at 2631 Douglas Street in 1951. Mechanical departments were shared and the editorial functions kept separate—an arrangement emulated later in Vancouver. In 1964, Bell's FP Publications Ltd. bought Sun Publishing's share of Pacific Press. (Bell's right-hand man was Richard S. Malone, who led the strikebreakers into the *Winnipeg Free Press* during the 1946 ITU strike.)

Thomson blew back into the picture in a big way on January 11, 1980, when it scooped up the eight-paper FP group for $164.7 million. Seven months later, it did a deal with Southam, unloading *The Sun* on August 27 and closing the *Ottawa Journal*. In turn, Southam shuttered the *Winnipeg Tribune*. This left Thomson alone in Winnipeg with the *Free Press*, and in Victoria, while Southam had exclusivity in Ottawa and Vancouver. Thomson then merged *The Times* and *The Colonist*, with the first joint paper appearing September 2. Four years later, it dropped the evening edition and the *Times-Colonist* was strictly a morning publication. The hyphen in the double-barrelled name was removed in late 1994.

At *The Sun*, Stu Keate, who became publisher when Cromie relinquished the reins in 1964, retired on the eve of a strike-lockout that ran from November 1, 1978, to June 29, 1979—the longest in the history of union-hostile Pacific Press. After Keate, who was one of Canada's premier journalists for many years, came a succession of feckless publishers, vice-presidents and other executives who couldn't stop the paper's slide from the mid-eighties onward. *The Province*, always sickly, arrested its decline by going to a tabloid format August 2, 1983. It was a breezy success for a while, managing to close the circulation gap somewhat. But the tab's shallowness started to wear thin in the nineties, and it joined *The Sun* in trying to hold on to its readers.

On September 16, 1991, *The Sun* also moved to morning circulation, abandoning the afternoons it had ruled for so long (in 1982, although still technically an "evening" paper, it became morning in everything but name by establishing an overnight shift to handle general news. Thus stories delivered to doorsteps the following evening were often twenty-four hours old). Becoming a morning broadsheet didn't seem to help, though. Its six-day circulation average, which once exceeded 260,000, had dwindled to the neighbourhood of 200,000 in 1997. *The Province*, as low as 125,000 before its format change, was struggling to hold 160,000.

Meanwhile, another media ogre, Conrad Black of Hollinger Inc., added more fuel to the volatile situation at Specific Stress. Black, an international press baron with holdings ranging from Jerusalem to London to Chicago, gained control of floundering Southam in 1996. While the opinionated, controversial Black (and his equally abrasive lieutenant, David Radler) spread alarm and despair through the bunker at 2250 Granville, he appeared to give Don Babick, publisher of the two papers, a vote of confidence by also appointing him the new president of Southam in August. The acquisition of Southam's thirty-two dailies, coupled with Thomson's divestiture of many of it properties, made Hollinger the major force in both Canada's and BC's daily field. (Thomson still had a presence here, notably at the *Times Colonist*, which, incidentally, began calling itself the TC and appeared to be brighter and more readable than formerly).

Another Black, David (no relation), became dominant among community newspapers in 1997. His Black Press Ltd., based in Victoria, purchased sixteen Lower Mainland publications with a combined circulation of 500,000. The deal effectively doubled the size of the chain to approximately eighty papers in BC, Alberta and Washington.

With the discipline of hot metal replaced by the freedom of cold type and computerized doodling, newspage packaging in general has gone downhill. For much of the eighties and nineties, *The Sun*'s layout was chaotic, betraying the typographical illiteracy of its design group. It seemed nobody could keep their crayons between the lines. This dog's breakfast began to improve with the appointment of a new editor and managing editor. At *The Province*, basic tabloid makeup obtained, with the occasional exception. In 1996, the paper's Take A Break section started looking pretty ugly. Too much clutter and the use of a typeface that resembled a childish scrawl severely limited the readability of the pages.

The tabloid had other problems. Its sports section, while overloaded with gingerbread, did not reflect the amount of money and resources spent on it. When Jim Taylor, its top columnist, left in 1995, *The Province* frantically hired four electronic babblers to write in his place. Awful. Flawed as they were, however, the paper's sports pages were marginally better than *The Sun*'s. Near the end of the nineties, it was still exploring the concept of sports coverage in a morning broadsheet.

Would you sell a newspaper to this man? Controversial press baron Conrad Black indulges the cameraman's little joke while visiting one of his properties.

In his novel *The Plague Dogs*, Richard Adams digressed to poke a little fun at Fleet Street. Reporter Digby Driver seldom varied from a theme that went something like this: "Windermere bank executive Geoffrey Westcott and his landlady, Mrs. Rose Green ... got a terrifying shock yesterday." I am reminded of this parody of hack journalism every time I read a *Province* story about terrified moms, homeless kittens, missing celebrity dogs or clever T-shirts. Apparently the paper believes its core readership swallows this sort of stuff. In the mid-nineties, a veteran entertainment writer fended off suggestions that perhaps she was too old for *The Province*'s post-pubescent audience. In truth, new newsroom management was apparently trying to bring more depth to the coverage, but in 1997 they had a long way to go. The editorial pages, for instance, suffered from an overdose of laconism, plus a collection of forgettable, part-time columnists.

The Sun, on the other hand, doted on depth. Even with its constantly shrinking newshole, it suffered from a lack of editing. Ever since winning a national award for the Olson File package in 1982, the paper figured any story that couldn't be wrapped up in a phone call deserved to be a twelve-part special project. Stir in sloppy editing, weak headlines and the aforementioned ignorance of design principles, and you had a recipe for ennui on the part of the subscriber. *The Sun* does have good writers. But for a journal that once stabled such topnotch columnists as Bob Bouchette, Bruce Hutchison, Jack Scott, Jack Wasserman, Dick Beddoes, Barry Mather, Allan Fotheringham, Paul St. Pierre, Marjorie Nichols and Denny Boyd, it only had Vaughn Palmer writing on a daily basis. His was a lonely voice of excellence among the clutter of canned Eastern columnists (which included Conrad Black's wife), part-time ranters, obscure Opinion Page book reviewers and even more obscure "media analysts."[2]

Then there were the Language Police. In 1991, the "women's task force" at *The Sun* gave birth to a committee to develop nonsexist language. After wrestling with the insoluble problem of how to recast the naval phrase "man-of-war," the committee produced some guidelines the following year. These included many hints about avoiding gender-specific terms, but only

two are consistently apparent to the faithful reader. These are "chair" in place of chairman or chairwoman, and "fisher" in place of fisherman. The LP attempted to replace actress with "female actor," but this solecism had apparently been abandoned late in the decade.

As 1996 turned into 1997, a memo on the notice boards at Pacific Press informed everyone that the composing room was now part of the advertising department. To old-timers such as myself, this change in procedure illustrated more forcibly than anything else the impact that technological change has had on newspapers. At one time, the comps room—domain of the ITU—was the crowded, noisy, bustling production hub of any newspaper. Linotype machines chattered to each other, page forms rumbled recklessly toward stereo (where they were shaped into matrices prior to being cast into plates for the press), and the whoosh of the pneumatic tube system signalled more copy arriving from editorial.

But then came perforated tape, which was fed into automatic linecasters, displacing union operators. Finally, the computer and the video display terminal arrived as photocomposition of the pages replaced hot metal. Beginning in 1977, the ITU at Victoria Press and Pacific Press sought control over these terminals, which they claimed were typesetting devices. "Capturing the original keystroke" was a popular phrase in the industry in those years. But the typographers lost virtually every jurisdictional battle over VDT input and computerized handling of copy.

By the nineties, it was possible to paginate—assemble a newspage from a computer screen—at remote locations inside and outside the building. For a while, compositors were needed to paste up this cold type, but ultimately entire editions written, edited, typecast and controlled by other departments could be made virtually press-ready without backshop massaging. The raison d'etre of this proud craft union dwindled to nothingness. Victims of the hellbent twentieth century, the printers and their composing room joined the buggy whip, silent pictures and the upright Underwood as artifacts on the shelf of history.

As an ol' candy butcher who stumbled into this newspaper dodge without benefit of formal preparation, I'm not sure about the whippersnappers putting out today's papers. They don't do things my way. Nor should they, despite occasional mild criticism from this corner. The press of today bears little resemblance to that of the fifties and sixties, when rapid-fire editions brought real meaning to deadlines. And the BC newspaper scene in mid-century was quite removed from the atmosphere of 1900.

But the mechanics of writing a news story have changed little. The simple, declarative sentence is still the best way to capture a slice of history. Editors still prune copy and headlines still proclaim the news. A disaster is a disaster, whether it's an explosion in one of Robert Dunsmuir's coal mines or the crash of a modern airliner. Politicians are viewed with the same suspicion as at the turn of the century.

British Columbia is no longer a stripling, wondering whether joining the Canadian family was really the right thing to do. It has grown up and changed and survived. So has the press. And, despite what I perceive to be pimples on the face of progress, the newspaper is still unequalled as the chronicler of events, large and small. As the new century reveals itself page by page, the papers will be there as usual, making sure yesterday's news is tomorrow's history.

---

1 One Saturday in April of 1990, the entire Book Review section disappeared. It was replaced by three classified pages because "bumping" the paper to make room for the extra want ads was forbidden. On Page One, *The Sun* blandly blamed "production problems" for the missing section.

2 I've often wondered how one qualifies as a media analyst. Are there night-school courses? Is newspaper experience helpful — like perhaps six months as gardening correspondent for the Spuzzum Retraction-Pessimist? Or is it just who you know?

LIST OF ILLUSTRATIONS

(Copyright for *The World* and the *News-Advertiser* is held by the *Vancouver Sun*, and the *Times* and *Colonist* by the *Victoria Times-Colonist*)

APPENDIX A
Premiers of British Columbia

John Foster McCreight	November 13, 1871 – December 20, 1872
Amor de Cosmos (William Alexander Smith)	December 23, 1872 – February 9, 1874
George Anthony Boomer Walkem	February 11, 1874 – January 27, 1876
Andrew Charles Elliott	February 1, 1876 – June 25, 1878
George Anthony Boomer Walkem	June 25, 1878 – June 6, 1882
Robert Beaven	June 13, 1882 – January 29, 1883
William Smithe	January 29, 1883 – March 28, 1887
Alexander Edmund Batson Davie	May 15, 1887 – August 1, 1889
John Robson	August 2, 1889 – June 29, 1892
Theodore Davie	July 2, 1892 – March 2, 1895
John Herbert Turner	March 4, 1895 – August 8, 1898
Charles Augustus Semlin	August 15, 1898 – February 27, 1900
Joseph Martin	February 28, 1900 – June 14, 1900
James Dunsmuir	June 15, 1900 – November 21, 1902
Edward Gawler Prior	November 21, 1902 – June 1, 1903
Sir Richard McBride	June 1, 1903 – December 15, 1915
William John Bowser	December 15, 1915 – November 23, 1916
Harlan Carey Brewster	November 23, 1916 – March 1, 1918
John Oliver	March 6, 1918 – August 17, 1927
John Duncan MacLean	August 20, 1927 – August 20, 1928
Simon Fraser Tolmie	August 21, 1928 – November 15, 1933
Thomas Dufferin Pattullo	November 15, 1933 – December 9, 1941
John Hart	December 9, 1941 – December 29, 1947
Byron Ingemar Johnson	December 29, 1947 – August 1, 1952
William Andrew Cecil Bennett	August 1, 1952 – September 15, 1972
David Barrett	Sept. 15, 1972 – December 22, 1975
William Richards Bennett	December 22, 1975 – August 6, 1986
Wilhelmus Nicholaas Theodore Maria Vander Zalm	August 6, 1986 – April 2, 1991
Rita Margaret Johnston	April 2, 1991 – November 5, 1991
Michael Franklin Harcourt	November 5, 1991 – February 22, 1996
Glen David Clark	February 22, 1996 –

Lieutenant-Governors
of British Columbia

Joseph W. Trutch	1871 – 1876
Albert N. Richards	1876 – 1881
Clement F. Cornwall	1881 – 1887
Hugh Nelson	1887 – 1892
Edgar Dewdney	1892 – 1897
Thomas R. McInnes	1897 – 1900
Sir Henri Joly de Lotbiniere	1900 – 1906
James Dunsmuir	1906 – 1909
Thomas W. Paterson	1909 – 1914
Frank Barnard	1914 – 1919
Edward G. Prior	1919 – 1920
Walter C. Nichol	1920 – 1926
R. Randolph Bruce	1926 – 1931
J.W. Fordham Johnson	1931 – 1936
Eric W. Hamber	1936 – 1941
W.C. Woodward	1941 – 1946
Charles A. Banks	1946 – 1950
Clarence Wallace	1950 – 1955
Frank M. Ross	1955 – 1960
George R. Pearkes VC	1960 – 1968
John R. Nicholson	1968 – 1973
Walter S. Owen	1973 – 1978
Henry P. Bell-Irving	1978 – 1983
Robert G. Rogers	1983 – 1988
David S. Lam	1988 – 1995
Garde Gardom	April 21, 1995 –

APPENDIX B
Election Results by Parties,
1903 – 1996

	Cons.	Lib.	CCF/NDP	SC	Others	Total
1903	27,913	22,715				60,120
(October 3)	46.43%	37.78%				
	22 Seats	17			3	42
1907	30,871	23,481				63,205
(February 2)	48.7%	37.15%				
	26 Seats	13			3	42
1909	53,074	33,675				101,415
(November 25)	52.33%	33.21%				
	38 Seats	2			2	42
1912	50,423	21,433				84,529
(March 28)	59.65%	25.37%				
	39 Seats	—			3	42
1916	72,842	89,892				179,774
(September 14)	40.52%	50%				
	9 Seats	36			2	47
1920	110,475	134,167				354,088
(December 1)	31.2%	37.89%				
	15 Seats	25			7	47
1924	101,765	108,323				345,068
(June 20)	29.45%	31.34%				
	17 Seats	23			8	48

	Cons.	Lib.	CCF/NDP	SC	Others	Total
1928 (July 18)	192,867 53.3% 35 Seats	144,872 40.04% 12			1	361,814 48
1933 (November 2)		159,131 41.7% 34 Seats	120,185 31.53% 7		6	381,223 47
1937 (June 1)	119,521 28.6% 8 Seats	156,074 37.34% 31	119,400 28.57% 7		2	417,929 48
1941 (October 21)	140,282 30.91% 12 Seats	149,525 32.94% 21	151,440 33.36% 14		1	453,893 48
1945 Coalition: (October 25)		261,147 55.83% 37 Seats	175,960 37.62% 10		1	467,747 48
1949 Coalition: (June 15)		428,773 61.35% 39 Seats	245,284 35.1% 7	8,464 1.21% —	2	698,823 48
1952* (June 12)	65,285 9.66% 4 Seats	170,674 25.26% 6	231,756 34.3% 18	203,932 30.18% 19	1	675,654 48
1953* (June 9)	7,326 1.11% 1 Seat	154,090 23.36% 4	194,414 29.48% 14	300,372 45.54% 28	1	659,563 48
1956 (September 19)	25,373 3.11% —	177,922 21.77% 2 Seats	231,511 28.32% 10	374,711 45.84% 39	1	817,397 52
1960 (September 12)	66,943 6.72% —	208,249 20.9% 4 Seats	326,094 32.73% 16	386,886 38.83% 32		996,404 52
1963 (September 30)	109,090 11.27% —	193,363 19.98% 5 Seats	269,004** 27.8% 14	395,079 40.83% 33		967,675 52
1966 (September 12)	1,409 0.18% —	152,155 20.24% 6 Seats	252,753 33.62% 16	342,751 45.59% 33		751,876 55

	Cons.	Lib.	CCF/NDP	SC	Others	Total
1969 (August 27)	1,087 0.11% —	186,235 19.03% 5 Seats	331,813 33.92% 12	457,777 46.79% 38		978,356 55
1972 (August 30)	143,450 12.67% 2 Seats	185,640 16.4% 5	448,260 39.59% 38	352,776 31.16% 10		1,132,172 55
1975 (December 11)	49,796 3.86% 1 Seat	93,379 7.24% 1	505,396 39.16% 18	635,482 49.25% 35		1,290,451 55
1979 (May 10)	71,078 5.06% —	6,662 0.47% —	646,188 45.99% 26 Seats	677,607 48.23% 31		1,405,077 57
1983 (May 5)	19,131 1.16% —	44,442 2.69% —	741,354 44.94% 22 Seats	820,807 49.76% 35		1,649,533 57
1986 (October 22)	14,074 0.73% —	130,505 6.74% —	824,544 42.6% 22 Seats	954,516 49.32% 47		1,935,453 69
1991 (October 17)	**Ref.** 2,673 0.18% —	486,208 33.25% 17 Seats	595,391 40.7% 51	351,660 24.05% 7		1,462,467 75
	(Conservatives received 426 votes)					
1996 (May 28)	**Ref.** 146,734 9.27% 2 Seats	661,929 41.82% 33	624,395 39.45% 39	**PDA** 90,797 5.73% 1		1,582,704 75
	(Social Credit received 6,276 votes and Conservatives, 1,002)					

* The 1952 and 1953 elections employed the alternative ballot method. The results in this appendix reflect the final count. The preliminary figures varied widely.

** This is the first election contested by the NDP.

Legend: CCF: Co-operative Commonwealth Federation; Cons: Conservative and Progressive Conservative; Lib: Liberal; NDP: New Democratic Party; PDA: Progressive Democratic Alliance; Ref: Reform Party of B.C.; SC: Social Credit.

APPENDIX C
Population of British Columbia

1901	178,657
1911	392,480
1921	524,582
1931	694,263
1941	817,800
1951	1,165,210
1961	1,629,100
1971	2,184,600
1981	2,744,467
1991	3,282,061
1996	3,724,500

APPENDIX D
The Victoria Cross

The Empire's highest award for valour has been bestowed on thirteen servicemen who were either born or spent a substantial portion of their lives in British Columbia.

The Great War

Name and Rank	Hometown Connection	Action and Date
Lieut. (RNVR) Rowland Bourke	Crescent Bay	Ostend, May 9/10, 1918
Lieut. Gordon Flowerdew	Walhachin	Bois de Moreuil, March 30, 1918
Sgt.-Major. Robert Hanna	Vancouver	Lens, August 21, 1917
Capt. John MacGregor	Powell River	Cambrai, September 29/October 3, 1918
Pvt. Michael O'Rourke	Vancouver	Hill 60, August 15/17, 1917
Lt.-Col. Cyrus Peck	Cassiar	Cagnicourt, September 2, 1918
Pvt. Walter Rayfield	Victoria	Arras, September 2/4, 1918
Pvt. (Piper) James Richardson	Vancouver/Chilliwack	Regina Trench, October 8, 1916

Second World War

Lieut. (RCNVR) Robert Gray*	Trail/Nelson	Onagawa Bay, August 9, 1945
Maj. Charles Hoey	Duncan	Arakan, February 16, 1944
Maj. John Mahony	New Westminster	Melfa River, May 24, 1944
Lt.-Col. Charles Merritt	Vancouver	Dieppe, August 19, 1942
Pvt. Ernest Smith	New Westminster	Savio River, October 21/22, 1944

*Gray's gallant, fatal air attack on an enemy warship in the Pacific five days before Japan's surrender made him the war's last hero.

(On October 28, 1929, a 78-year-old Vancouver woman named Mrs. Samuel G. Ball told *The Sun* she had been awarded the Victoria Cross in the South African War—but that the decoration was unofficial and was presented to her by the "Princess of Wales." There is no record of a British Army nurse called Sister Frances de la Roucque {Mrs. Ball's unmarried name] being gazetted for valour.)

APPENDIX E
Pacific Press Agreement

On May 30, 1957, *The Vancouver Sun* and *The Province* reached an agreement to pool their mechanical production resources and other assets in a new publishing company called Pacific Press Limited. Here are the financial details of that agreement, as reported in *The Province*:

"Pacific Press Limited has been formed with an authorized capital of 1,600,000 shares of $1 par value. Pacific Press creates an issue of $7,700,000 principal amount of 5½ per cent 20-year redeemable debentures.

"*The Sun* takes over 800,000 shares of Pacific Press at par and all the debentures. *The Sun* then sells all of its assets to Pacific Press for $8,500,000.

"Province Newspapers Ltd. has been formed with an authorized capital of 10,000 shares of $1 par value. Southam will take up all of these shares at par.

"Southam will sell to Province Newspapers Ltd. the assets used in the publication of *The Vancouver Province* for $800,000, which will be payable as to $10,000 in cash and as to the balance by a promissory note.

"Southam will then sell to Pacific Press Ltd. the shares and the note of Province Newspapers for the par value of the shares and the face amount of the note. Southam will then take up 800,000 shares of Pacific Press Ltd. at par.

"*The Sun* will sell to Southam for $3,850,000 one-half the principal amount of the outstanding debentures of Pacific Press Limited.

"When these steps have been completed *The Sun* and Southam will each own half the shares and half the outstanding debentures of Pacific Press Ltd."

Stuart Keate, publisher of *The Sun* from 1964 to 1978, describes Pacific Press accounting practices, circa 1969–1970:

"*The Sun* by this time was showing a before-tax profit of approximately $12 million. But it was an illusory figure. Under Pacific Press accounting, this amount had first to be reduced by the $1 million loss on operations of the morning paper. The $11 million remaining was sliced in half by corporation taxes and other charges. This left a net of $5.5 million to be divided, under the Sun-Southam agreement, equally between the two shareholders — a bizarre arrangement which thus left *The Sun* with a bottom line of $2.25 million on its gross profit of $12 million and *The Province* with exactly the same reward on a loss of $1 million."

– *Excerpted from* Paper Boy, *by Stuart Keate, 1980*

SELECTED BIBLIOGRAPHY

Although the main thrust of this history was derived from newspaper accounts, additional details and insights were provided by other published works. Among them were:

Barrett, Dave and Miller, William. *Barrett*. Douglas & McIntyre Ltd., 1995.

Beeching, William C. *Canadian Volunteers—Spain 1936-39*. Canadian Plains Research Center, 1989.

Berton, Pierre. *Starting Out: 1920-1947*. McClelland & Stewart, 1987.

Blake, Don. *B.C. Trivia*. Lone Pine Publishing, 1992.

Christensen, Bev. *Prince George: Rivers, Railways and Timber*. Windsor Publications Ltd., 1989.

Cowles, Virginia. *The Kaiser*. Collins Publishers, 1963.

Creswicke, Louis. *South Africa and The Transvaal War, Vols. 2, 3 & 4*. T.C. & E.C. Jack, 1900.

Cruise, David and Griffiths, Alison. *Fleecing The Lamb—The Inside Story of The Vancouver Stock Exchange*. Douglas & McIntyre Ltd., 1987.

Davis, Chuck and Mooney, Shirley. *Vancouver: An Illustrated Chronology*. Windsor Publications Ltd., 1986.

Dheensaw, Cleve. *The Commonwealth Games*. Orca Book Publishers, 1994.

Dugan, Mark and Boessenecker, John. *The Grey Fox*. University of Oklahoma Press, 1992.

Garr, Allen. *Tough Guy*. Key Porter Books Ltd., 1985.

Gordon, J.F. *British Columbia Railway*. Footprint Publishing Co. Ltd., 1995.

Granatstein, J.L. and Morton, Desmond. *A Nation Forged In Fire*. Lester & Orpen Dennys Ltd., 1989.

Gray, James H. *The Roar of The Twenties*. Macmillan of Canada, 1975.

Green, Lewis. *The Boundary Hunters*. UBC Press, 1982.

Gregson, Harry. *A History of Victoria 1842-1970*. Victoria Observer Publishing Co., 1970.

Hansen, Rick and Taylor, Jim. *Rick Hansen, Man in Motion*. Douglas & McIntyre Ltd., 1987.

Harris, Lorraine. *British Columbia's Own Railroad*. Hancock House Publishers Ltd., 1982.

Henry, Tom. *The Good Company—An Affectionate History of the Union Steamships*. Harbour Publishing, 1994.

Holt, Simma. *Terror in The Name of God*. McClelland & Stewart, 1964.

Hyatt, A.M.J. *General Sir Arthur Currie*. University of Toronto Press, 1987.

Jackman, S.W. *Portraits of The Premiers*. Gray's Publishing Ltd., 1969.

Keate, Stuart. *Paper Boy*. Clarke, Irwin & Co. Ltd., 1980.

Kelly, Brian and Francis, Daniel. *Transit in British Columbia—The First Hundred Years*. Harbour Publishing, 1990.

Kluckner, Michael. *Victoria The Way It Was*. Whitecap Books Ltd., 1986.

Leonard, Frank. *A Thousand Blunders*. UBC Press, 1996.

Levitt, Cyril. *Children of Privilege*. University of Toronto Press, 1984.

McDonald, Robert and Ward, W.P. (editors). *British Columbia: Historical Readings*. Douglas & McIntyre Ltd., 1981.

MacIsaac, Ron, Clark, Don and Lillard, Charles. *The Brother XII*. Porcepic Books, 1989.

McKinlay, William Laird. *Karluk*. Weidenfeld & Nicolson, 1976.

Macpherson, Ken and Burgess, John. *The Ships of Canada's Naval Forces 1910-1981*. Collins Publishers, 1981.

Mason, Gary and Baldrey, Keith. *Fantasyland—Inside The Reign of Bill Vander Zalm*. McGraw-Hill Ryerson, 1989.

Mayse, Susan. *Ginger—The Life and Death of Albert Goodwin*. Harbour Publishing, 1990.

Melady, John. *Korea: Canada's Forgotten War*. Macmillan of Canada, 1983.

Mitchell, David. *W.A.C. Bennett and The Rise of British Columbia*. Douglas & McIntyre Ltd., 1983.

————. *Succession—The Political Reshaping of British Columbia*. Douglas & McIntyre Ltd., 1987.

Morton, James. *In The Sea of Sterile Mountains*. J.J. Douglas Ltd., 1974.

Munro, Jack and O'Hara, Jane. *Union Jack*. Douglas & McIntyre Ltd., 1988.

Newsome, Eric. *Pass The Bottle*. Orca Book Publishers, 1995.

Regehr, T.D. *The Canadian Northern Railway*. Macmillan of Canada, 1976.

Roy, Patricia E. (editor). *A History of British Columbia—Selected Readings*. Copp Clark Pitman Ltd., 1989.

Shillington, C. Howard. *The Road to Medicare in Canada*. Del Graphics Publishing Dept., 1972.

Stonier-Newman, Lynn. *Policing a Pioneer Province*. Harbour Publishing, 1991.

Stursberg, Peter. *Extra! When The Papers Had The Only News*. Provincial Archives of British Columbia, 1982.

Taylor, G.W. *Timber*. J.J. Douglas Ltd., 1975.

————. *Mining*. Hancock House Publishers Ltd., 1978.

_____. *Builders of British Columbia*. Morriss Publishing Ltd., 1982.

_____. *The Automobile Saga of British Columbia*. Morriss Publishing Ltd., 1984.

_____. *The Railway Contractors*. Morriss Publishing Ltd., 1988.

Tucker, G.N. *The Naval Service of Canada, Vol. 1*. Ministry of National Defence, 1952.

Turner, Robert D. *The Pacific Princesses*. Sono Nis Press, 1977.

_____. *West of The Great Divide*. Sono Nis Press, 1987.

Waiser, Bill. *Park Prisoners*. Fifth House Ltd., 1995.

Wilson, Irving and Frances (editors). *A History: British Columbia Weekly Newspapers*. B.C. Weekly Newspaper Association, 1972.

Woodcock, George and Avakumovic, Ivan. *The Doukhobors*. Oxford University Press, 1968.

Woodcock, George. *British Columbia*. Douglas & McIntyre Ltd., 1990.

Also consulted were the B.C. Historical Quarterly, Vancouver Sun Centennial Edition (1971), encyclopediae, provincial and federal government documents, studies, papers and reports, private collections, university archives and the author's own memory.

LIST OF
NEWSPAPERS

Abbotsford, Sumas & Matsqui News
Bridge River-Lillooet News
British Colonist
British Columbia Tribune
British Columbian
Burnaby Broadcast
Burnaby Examiner
Burnaby Now
Calgary Albertan
Canterbury Outcrop
Chilliwack Progress
Chronicle
Colonist
Columbian
Comox District Free Press
Courtenay-Comox Argus
Cranbrook Townsman
Cumberland News
Daily Advertiser
Daily News
Donald Truth
Edmonton Bulletin
Enderby Edenograph
Evening Journal
Evening Times
Fort George Herald
Georgia Straight
Hope Standard

Hope Steamboat Nugget
Inland Sentinel
Kamloops Sentinel
Kelowna Clarion
Kelowna Courier
Lardeau Claim
Mainland Guardian
Ming Pao
Montreal Herald
Montreal Star
Moodyville Tickler
Nanaimo Free Press
Nelson Claim
Nelson Miner
Nelson News
News-Advertiser
News-Herald
North Shore Citizen
Omineca Miner
Ottawa Journal
Peace River Block News
Prince George Citizen
Province
Prince Rupert Empire
Prince Rupert News
Revelstoke Mail-Herald
Revelstoke Review
Saturday Sunset

Scorpion
Standard
Telegram
Times-Colonist
Toronto Star
Toronto Sun
Toronto Telegram
Trail News
Trail Times
Vancouver Express
Vancouver Herald
Vancouver Ozonogram
Vancouver Star
Vancouver Sun
Vancouver Times
Vernon News
Victoria Gazette
Victoria Times
Winnipeg Free Press
Winnipeg Tribune
World